VALUES, LIFESTYLES, AND PSYCHOGRAPHICS

ADVERTISING AND CONSUMER PSYCHOLOGY

A series sponsored by the Society for Consumer Psychology

AAKER/BIEL (1993)	• Brand Equity & Advertising: Advertising's Role in Building Strong Brands
CLARK/BROCK/STEWART/ (1994)	• Attention, Attitude, and Affect in Response to Advertising
ENGLIS (1994)	• Global and Multi-National Advertising
KAHLE/CHIAGOURIS (1997)	• Values, Lifestyles, and Psychographics
MITCHELL (1993)	• Advertising Exposure, Memory, and Choice
THORSON/MOORE (1996)	• Integrated Communication: Synergy of Persuasive Voices
WELLS (1997)	• Measuring Advertising Effectiveness

VALUES, LIFESTYLES, AND PSYCHOGRAPHICS

Edited by

LYNN R. KAHLE
University of Oregon

LARRY CHIAGOURIS
Brand Marketing Services

LEA LAWRENCE ERLBAUM ASSOCIATES, PUBLISHERS
1997 Mahwah, New Jersey

Lawrence Erlbaum Associates, Inc., Publishers
10 Industrial Avenue
Mahwah, New Jersey 07430

Cover design by Kathryn Houghtaling

Library of Congress Cataloging-in-Publication Data

Values, lifestyles, and psychographics / edited by Lynn R. Kahle, Larry Chiagouris.
p. cm.
Includes bibliographical references and index.
ISBN 0-8058-1496-5 (cl : alk. paper).
1. Advertising—Evaluation. 2. Psychographics. I. Kahle, Lynn R. II. Chiagouris, Larry.
HF5821.V334 1997
659.1'042—dc21 96-50053
CIP

Books published by Lawrence Erlbaum Associates are printed on acid-free paper, and their bindings are chosen for strength and durability.

Printed in the United States of America
10 9 8 7 6 5 4 3 2 1

Contents

Preface

Values, lifestyles, and psychographics represent the softer side of science. Even researchers used to tolerance for ambiguity, such as advertising researchers, have moments of affection for and moments of frustration with this type of research. Nevertheless, the past decade has witnessed considerable progress both conceptually and methodologically in this research. Its persistence continues to befuddle doomsayers. Many advertising researchers have continued to develop ways to incorporate value, lifestyle, and psychographic information into their models, even as others have abandoned it in frustration. Consumer researchers have continued to probe areas in which it proves particularly interesting, such as cross-national research and trend research. Many authors persist in their convictions that individuals differ in important ways above and beyond demographics and that understanding these differences matters greatly in advertising. Many scholars continue to echo Milton Rokeach's (1973) view:

> The concept of values, more than any other, is the core concept across all the social sciences. It is the main dependent variable in the study of culture, society, and personality, and it is the main independent variable in the study of attitudes and behavior. It is difficult for me to conceive of any problem social scientists might be interested in that would not deeply involve human values. (p. ix)

The concepts of *values, lifestyles,* and *psychographics* overlap. *Values* are enduring beliefs "that a specific mode of conduct or end-state is personally or socially preferable to an opposite or converse mode of conduct or end-state of existence" (Rokeach, 1973, p. 5). One author of a chapter from this book defines *lifestyle* as an exhibited "set of shared values of tastes" (Solomon, 1994, p. 621), thus making clear the overlap between values and lifestyles. Another author from this book defines *lifestyle* more conventionally as "the manner in which people conduct their lives, including their activities, interests, and opinions" (Peter & Olson, 1994, p. 463). Given the evidence of a sequence of influence from values to attitudes to behaviors (Homer & Kahle, 1988), even this second definition shows the strong conceptual overlap between values and lifestyles. Solomon defines *psychographics* as the use of psychological, sociological, and anthropological factors to construct market segments (p. 623), whereas Peter and Olson restrict their definition to the more narrow concept of "dividing markets into segments on the basis of consumer lifestyles, attitudes, and interests" (p. 465). Yet another text explicitly defines *psychographics* and *lifestyles* as nearly interchangeable: "In fact, psychographics and lifestyle are frequently used interchangeably. Psychographic research attempts to place consumers on psychological—as opposed to purely demographic—dimensions" (Hawkins, Best, & Coney, 1995, p. 328). They describe the other dimensions as values, attitudes, activities, interests, demographics, media patterns, and usage rates. Thus, we again see how intertwined the concepts of values, lifestyles, and pscyhographics are.

In a sense the utility of the broader concepts of values, lifestyles, and psychographics is at the core of the utility of the field of consumer behavior to the fields of advertising and marketing. Only to the extent that consumer behavior has something worthwhile to contribute to business activities such as marketing and advertising can its inclusion in business curriculum and business research be justified. If values, lifestyles, and psychographics are fundamental constructs of consumer behavior, then their utility overlaps considerably with the utility of the entire field of consumer behavior. One example of the extension of this work into the broader area of buyer behavior is the application of business to business marketing. Market segmentation and personal sales techniques are increasingly relying on an understanding of the psychographics of the purchase decision makers in business-to-business settings. Marketing communication has been shown to be more effective when end-user psychographic profiles are understood and reflected in the content of the message (Chiagouris, 1991).

As with many professions, some researchers in the area of values, lifestyles, and psychographics are better than others. Many of the executives and research directors most frustrated with this type of research have encountered some of the weaker practitioners. When used skillfully, however, these methods without a doubt provide an added advantage to practitioners who understand their scope and range of utility.

This volume showcases papers presented at the annual Advertising and Consumer Psychology conference, sponsored by the Society for Consumer Behavior, the Marketing Science Institute, and Backer Spielvogel Bates, Inc., who also hosted the conference at their agency in the Chrysler Building in New York City. The contributors include most of the important active scholars in the world who have an interest in the general area of psychographics, values, and lifestyles in advertising. The mix of authors is remarkably interdisciplinary and international. The combinations of practitioner and academic backgrounds augmented the quality of dialogue at the conference and the quality of the chapters finally included in this book.

The volume is divided into four nonorthogonal sections. Each chapter is placed into one section, although several chapters could fit into more than one section quite conveniently.

The first section deals with theoretical and conceptual issues in this research. Reynolds, Westberg, and Olson extend their well-known work in means-end theory from product advertising to issue and image advertising. Englis and Solomon illustrate how lifestyle imagery is generated and modified by advertising, marketing, and media gatekeepers. Murry, Lastovicka, and Austin build their case that by examining the relations between lifestyle traits and consumption beliefs, one can begin to understand why beliefs are held and better understand how traits influence consumption behavior. This understanding can illuminate communication strategy. Prensky and Wright-Isak discuss the importance of communities in transmitting values. They provide evidence that "virtual" communities of mass-media consumers receive and enact values differently today from communities of the past. Fennell argues that an advertiser must understand the scope of an individual brand in the user's individual and population world. She presents a model of a behavioral episode representing an occasion for action and illustrating the value relevance for advertising. Kahle, Homer, O'Brien, and Boush test Maslow's hierarchy and find it inadequate to explain the phenomena of their research.

The second section presents chapters devoted to improving methodology. Shrum and McCarty describe their research program and make a number of recommendations for improving our understanding of the relation between values and consumer behavior, including improved measurement, improved attention to individual differences, and greater sensitivity to the relations among variables. S. Grunert and Askegaard address the semantic ambiguity inherent in the abstractness of value constructs and how they are usually presented. They propose the use of pictorial stimuli and explore the consequences of their suggestions. Wansink describes the technique of "customer profiling," which can help segment a market through a modified laddering technique. Valette-Florence proposes using a structural equations model for categorical variables for analyzing means-end hierarchies. He also illustrates his proposals empirically. Gould finds that use of psychographics remains problematic for research directors at large advertising agencies. O'Connor describes why and how attitudinal segmentation is important, and she illustrates its usage.

The final two sections illustrate how value, lifestyle, and psychographic research has been used to understanding differences among people. The first emphasizes differences among people at different times, commonly called trend research. The second emphasizes differences among people across national boundaries.

Several chapters describe what and how we know about trends. Cafferata, Horn, and Wells describe how gender roles have changed over the past 30 years, based on the DDB Needham Life Style Study. Chiagouris and Mitchell use GLOBAL SCAN data to describe how materialism has changed, which is also a topic of interest for the other editor (Kahle, 1995). MacEvoy describes how change leaders use new media and why that is important for advertisers and marketers to understand. His thinking undoubtedly has been influenced by his work with VALS. Muller focuses on the trends in values and lifestyle among baby boomers as they enter middle age. Lepisto describes the Adult Longitudinal Panel and how it can help us understand consumers across the life span.

International research deals with a variety of topics. K. Grunert, Brunsø, and Bisp discuss the issues in measurement of food-related lifestyle cross-culturally. Weber and Dubois discuss managing brand equity in the European luxury market with three specific tools. Zins uses EUROSTYLES to explore ecologically oriented tourism in Austria. Rose suggests that two basic dimensions consistently emerge in cross-cultural research: stability versus change and self versus others. He argues for the utility but the need for progress in the use of values in international advertising.

Collectively, these chapters illustrate how practical state-of-the-art research in values, lifestyles, and psychographics can be. Thoughtful consideration of values, lifestyles, and psychographics as they are manifested in quality research can improve advertising and marketing practice and help the business community deliver products and services more in line with consumers' needs.

REFERENCES

Chiagouris, L. G. (1991). *The personal dynamics of the decision maker.* Unpublished doctoral dissertation. The City University of New York, Baruch Graduate School of Business.

Hawkins, D. I., Best, R. J., & Coney, K. A. (1995). *Consumer behavior: Implications for marketing strategy* (Sixth ed.). Chicago: Irwin.

Homer, P. M., & Kahle, L. R. (1988). A structural equation test of the value-attitude-behavior hierarchy. *Journal of Personality and Social Psychology, 54*, 638–646.

Kahle, L. R. (1995). Role-relaxed consumers: A trend of the nineties. *Journal of Advertising Research, 35*, 66–71.

Peter, J. P., & Olson, J. C. (1994). *Understanding consumer behavior.* Burr Ridge, IL: Irwin.

Rokeach M. J. (1973). *The nature of human values.* New York: The Free Press.

Solomon, M. R. (1994). *Consumer behavior: Buying, having, being* (Second ed.). Boston: Allyn & Bacon.

THEORETICAL AND CONCEPTUAL PERSPECTIVES

Chapter **1**

A Strategic Framework for Developing and Assessing Political, Social Issue, and Corporate Image Advertising

Thomas J. Reynolds
Richmont Partners

Steven J. Westberg
Wirthlin Worldwide

Jerry C. Olson
Penn State University

Means-end theory provides an understanding of the basis of consumers' purchase and consumption decisions (Gutman & Reynolds, 1979). Means-end research has focused on measuring the personal or subjective relationships between products (defined by attributes) and consumers (defined by values). This product/consumer relationship is the key for understanding how products derive personal relevance and is useful in developing effective positioning and advertising strategies. Means-end theory includes laddering (Olson & Reynolds, 1983) and MECCAS (Reynolds & Gutman, 1984). Laddering is an interview methodology used to uncover consumers' means-end chains, and MECCAS is a model for translating means-end data into the components of advertising strategy. Most means-end research has focused on the strategic assessment of consumer goods advertising (Gutman & Reynolds, 1987). Still unexamined, however, is how nonproduct advertising, including ads used for political campaigns, social issues, and corporate image, taps into the decision making process. We provide a conceptual framework, extended from MECCAS, for understanding these diverse types of advertising communications as well as specify how to measure their strategic delivery or effectiveness.

OVERVIEW OF MEANS-END THEORY AND LADDERING

To develop effective positioning strategies, marketers need to understand what consumers think about when they make product choice decisions. Several academic studies have addressed this research issue. Fishbein

(1967) proposed a model in which a person's attitude toward an object depends on the individual's beliefs about the different attributes of the object, weighted by their importance. Lehmann (1971); Bass, Pessemier, and Lehmann (1972); and Bass and Talarzyk (1972) found support for this attribute-based model in different applications. Holbrook (1978) elaborated the concept of attributes by distinguishing between "logical, objectively verifiable descriptions of tangible product features" and the "emotional, subjective impressions of intangible aspects of the product." Myers and Shocker (1981) differentiated between product attributes and product benefits. Still another perspective focused on the role of personal values as a determinant of attitude and ultimately product choice (Homer & Kahle, 1988; Rokeach, 1973; Vinson, Scott, & Lamont, 1977). However, all these approaches lack the critical understanding of why product attributes are important to people.

Means-end theory (Gutman, 1982; Gutman & Reynolds, 1979), based on personal values, explains the relationships between attributes, benefits (positive consequences of the attributes), and personal values (desired personal states of the person who buys and uses the product). These three levels of a means-end chain provide a complete perceptual connection between a product and a consumer. In the means-end perspective, the product is defined by a collection of attributes, both concrete and abstract. These product-specific attributes yield consequences when consumers use the product. Consequences are important based on their ability to satisfy the personally motivating values and goals of the consumer. How strongly a specific consequence leads to the satisfaction of these values directly determines the relative importance or salience of the associated attribute. A means-end chain, then, is a sequence of attributes, consequences, and values that provides a perceptual link between a product and a consumer. Because values determine the relative importance of the consequences and therefore the importance of the attributes, means-end chains help us understand the consumer's decision making process.

Means-end theory recognizes that product-related meanings exist at different levels of abstraction. The product is defined by attributes, which are the most concrete, tangible meanings while the person is defined by personal values, which are the most abstract, least tangible meanings. The elements at each level can be further subdivided based on degree of abstraction (see Fig. 1.1). Concrete attributes can be objectively measured or evaluated such as size, weight, color, and ingredients. Abstract attributes are more subjective or personal descriptors such as taste, smell, and appearance.

Likewise, consequences are categorized as functional and psychosocial. Functional consequences are physical such as *Gives Me Energy* and *More Leg Room,* while the psycho-social consequences involve psychological or sociological benefits such as mood affects, feelings, social interactions, and ego

Means-End Chain Model

	Level of Abstraction	Example	Explanation
VALUES	TERMINAL VALUES	Accomplishment	Preferred end states, very abstract consequences of product use.
	INSTRUMENTAL VALUES	Can perform better	Preferred modes of conduct, abstract consequences of product use.
CONSEQUENCES	PSYCHO-SOCIAL CONSEQUENCES	Able to get rid of tension	Psychological (How do I feel?) and social (How do others feel about me?) consequences of product use.
	FUNCTIONAL CONSEQUENCES	Better support	Does the product do what it is supposed to do? Does it function properly?
ATTRIBUTES	ABSTRACT ATTRIBUTES	Snug fit	Abstract representation standing for several more concrete attributes. Subjective, not directly measurable. Can't perceive directly through the senses.
	CONCRETE ATTRIBUTES	Lacing pattern	Cognitive representation of physical characteristics of the product. Can be directly perceived.

FIG. 1.1. Means-end chain model. Adapted from Peter and Olson (1987), *Consumer Behavior*. New York: Irwin, p. 120.

builders. Values can be classified as instrumental (a mode of behavior that can lead to higher level values, e.g., *Accomplishment*) or terminal (an end state of existence such as *Self-Esteem*). Product attributes, functional and psychosocial consequences, and personal values also represent the strategic elements of positioning and communication strategy.

Laddering (Olson & Reynolds, 1983; Reynolds & Gutman, 1988) is the interviewing and analysis methodology that uncovers and summarizes individuals' means-end chains that are associated with the reasons for choice between products. Laddering involves asking a series questions with the form: "Why is that important to you?" For example, for light beer, an individual might choose Miller Lite over Bud Light because "it has fewer calories." Fewer calories are important to the person because it means the beer "doesn't fill me up so much," a functional consequence of fewer calories. This outcome leads to the psychosocial consequence of "I can drink more with my friends." In turn, drinking more with friends is important because it helps the person feel "more a part of the group," which is the motivating personal value or goal that drives the decision. This means-end chain, which links "fewer calories" to "part of the group," represents the consumer's reason for product differentiation and choice.

An initial product distinction (e.g., fewer calories) can be elicited using one of several techniques (Reynolds & Gutman, 1988), including triadic sorting, preference-consumption differences, or differences by occasion.

Each of these techniques requires the respondent to choose a brand from a competitive set and the primary reasons for that choice. Inasmuch as people may have multiple reasons for choice in different consumption occasions, each respondent typically can provide between 4 and 8 unique means-end chains (or ladders) for a given brand.

Means-end chains for a market segment can be summarized in a Consumer Decision Map (CDM), which is a graphical representation of the most frequent elements at each level of abstraction and the major pathways of connection between the elements (Olson & Reynolds, 1983; Reynolds & Gutman, 1988). As such, the CDM is a managerial tool to help translate the consumer's decision-making criteria into marketing strategy. CDM construction requires a series of steps: (a) means-end chains elicited from laddering are analyzed for content, (b) all mentioned ideas are collapsed into an inclusive set of meaning codes, (c) an implication matrix is constructed that contains the frequencies of all direct and indirect associations between the coded elements, and (d) the most frequently mentioned connections between codes are selected to build the map.

In general, 80% to 90% of all consumers' ladders for a category can be represented by the elements and connections on the map. Therefore, the CDM can be thought of as a perceptual playing field of the category for determining and evaluating positioning strategy because it reveals the meanings of the reasons for product choice. Of course, the goal of the positioning strategy will determine the competitive sets or the occasions from which the choice distinctions are elicited. For example, if the primary strategic issue is brand versus brand competition within a category, the competitive set might be limited to in-kind category competitors and the occasions might include only the most frequent prototypical occasions of consumption. If the strategic issue is one of category growth, the competitive set might include functional competitors and the occasions might be nontypical.

Once the CDM has been developed, strategic positioning options can be discussed. A positioning strategy is defined as the specification of strategic elements (product attributes, functional consequences, psychosocial consequences, and personal values) that will be the perceptual connection between the product and the consumer. Ideally, a positioning strategy will include elements that give consumers motivating reasons to choose the brand. As such, strategy development based on a Consumer Decision Map can follow one of four routes (Gengler & Reynolds, 1995):

1. The first is discovering a significant, yet untapped consumer perceptual orientation that is not currently associated with any products or brands in the map. This requires looking where the elements and the connections do not yet exist.

2. The second option involves establishing perceptual "ownership" of a pathway by creating a stronger link between elements that currently are only weakly associated.

3. The third option involves developing new meanings by connecting two unrelated ideas.

4. The fourth option involves creating new meaning by adding a new element to the CDM and associating it with higher and/or lower level elements.

In sum, the CDM offers a framework to help marketers think about current positionings and to develop "what if" scenarios that may become the specified positioning strategy. It is important to note that the CDM does not contain all the information that will lead to an effective positioning. Other knowledge about the marketplace will be used by managers in choosing a strategy.

Once a positioning is decided, a company should have some methodology to ensure that their advertising communications convey the intended message to the target audience. The MECCAS (Means-End Conceptualization of the Components of Advertising Strategy) model outlined next translates the means-end chains in the CDM into the components of an ad strategy (Olson & Reynolds, 1983; Reynolds & Gutman, 1984).

The MECCAS model consists of four levels: Message Elements, Consumer Benefit, Leverage Point, and Driving Force. Message Elements are the specific attributes or features of the product that are communicated in the advertising. Consumer Benefit corresponds to functional consequences, defined as the major positive consequences of consumption that are communicated in the ad. The Leverage Point equates to psychosocial consequences. A primary purpose of the Leverage Point in an advertising strategy is to activate or tap into personal values. Thus, the Leverage Point is not restricted to psychosocial consequences; any concept, idea, or visual image in the ad that causes the viewer to think about or associate a value with the lower level elements can act as a leverage point. Finally, the Driving Force is the end level, value orientation of the communication strategy.

Connections between adjacent levels in the MECCAS model are called bridges. There are three key bridges. The Product Bridge connects the Message Elements (attributes) to the Consumer Benefit (functional consequences). The Personal Relevance Bridge connects the Consumer Benefit to the Leverage Point (psychosocial consequences). The Value Bridge connects the Leverage Point to the Driving Force (personal value or goal). Bridges are critically important aspects of advertising strategy because they represent associations between different, possibly unrelated strategic elements. For example, Miller Lite's launch strategy included a product attribute of *fewer calories*, which led to a functional consequence of *less filling*.

The association that *fewer calories* leads to *less filling* had to be communicated explicitly because most people did not automatically associate the two ideas. Likewise, *less filling* had to be associated with the psychosocial consequence of *socialize*. An effective communication, then, is one that accomplishes the marketing strategy by communicating each level and forming strong associations between the elements, producing a self-relevant chain of connections between the product and important personal values and goals.

The MECCAS model provides the theoretical framework for strata™, an interview and analysis software system designed to determine the effectiveness of an ad execution in communication of a positioning strategy (Reynolds & Rochon, 1991). In a strata interview, respondents view an ad and evaluate each key strategic element based on how clearly that element was communicated by the ad. The elements are shown to respondents as statements, although code words are used in the summary charts to represent these statements. For example, the statement "this product has a sparkling, bubbly taste" represents the coded element *carbonation*. Statements are based on the consumers' verbatim remarks from the laddering interviews, which helps ensure that the assessment is measuring ideas in the consumers' language rather than the language of the marketing professional. The elements included in the strata assessment should correspond to elements in the positioning strategy, but other elements can be included as well. This can be particularly useful in the absence of a predetermined strategy when management needs a general understanding of what the ad is communicating.

Communication strength scores are reported on a zero to 100 scale, where a 60 represents a good score because it means that, on average across the sample, all respondents felt the element was clearly communicated in the ad. The strength of connections between elements at adjacent levels are also assessed in terms of consumers' perceptions. Linkage strength scores are reported on a zero to nine scale, where a five represents a fairly strong connection. Additional measures for product and brand affect are taken, using a zero to 100 scale. Generally, a product affect score of 45 or above is considered a good score. Product affect is important because it suggests how well the ad is selling the product. Interestingly, an analysis of 87 ads in one category yielded a simple Pearson correlation of 0.76 between the product affect score and the sum of the three largest connections at each bridge that creates a continuous linkage between the message elements to the driving force. This suggests that means-end connections have a strong relationship with product affect.

So far, most means-end research has focused on methodological issues (Reynolds & Gutman, 1988; Valette-Florence & Rapacchi, 1991), application to positioning strategy (Gutman & Reynolds, 1987; Reynolds & Craddock, 1988; Reynolds, Gutman, & Fiedler, 1985), and the strategic assessment of advertising (Gengler & Reynolds, in press; Reynolds & Gengler, 1991; Reynolds & Trivedi, 1989). All these applications focus on identifying the means-end linkages between a product and the consumer or on using means-end knowledge to develop product advertising strategy.

This chapter extends means-end applications beyond product–consumer relationships to three new types of relationships. We examine the personally relevant relationships between: political candidates and voters; social issues and voters or other influential decision makers; and companies and their important stakeholder groups. As with products, the key for positioning strategy is to establish the perceptual connections that create personal relevance. Personal relevance can be achieved for politicians and social issues using a means-end framework quite similar to products, with only minor changes in terminology for the different levels of the model. For example, product attributes are renamed "issue attributes" for social issue research. Otherwise, the basic model remains the same.

Achieving personal relevance for companies, however, requires additional modifications to the means-end model. The key difference concerns the psychosocial consequences that connect personal values to the more concrete and tangible elements at the lower levels of abstraction. The psychosocial consequences that are relevant for companies and their images are different from those for products, politicians, and social issues. Before we discuss companies, though, we first show how means-end research applies to developing and assessing advertising strategies for political candidates and social issues.

POLITICAL ADVERTISING

The means-end approach to developing positioning strategy and assessing advertising can be useful when applied to products, but it is not limited to them. As this next analysis shows, the same techniques can be applied to a political election campaign as was done with Reagan–Bush 1984 (Fiedler & Bahner, 1985).

In August 1984, polls showed Ronald Reagan ahead of the Democratic candidate Walter Mondale, but by only a slim margin. Reagan's reelection committee realized that something had to be done during the next 2½ months to increase this lead and ensure an election day victory. Laddering interviews with likely voters revealed that the key voting distinctions between Reagan and Mondale were primarily related to issues but also included voter beliefs about the candidates' personal traits. Importantly, the laddering data also revealed which candidate was viewed more positively on each of the voting criteria. From these ladders, a Consumer Decision

Map was constructed and then used to develop an ad campaign strategy. Ultimately, the Reagan reelection committee wanted perceptual ownership of the value level, personally motivating elements on the CDM, thereby removing the driving force for voters to choose Mondale.

The target group of the ad campaign was swing voters. As with products, some people can be considered hard-core loyal . . . their beliefs are firmly in place and are unlikely to change because of a short-lived advertising campaign. Therefore, advertising directed at these voters would be, at best, inefficient. Swing voters, the people in the middle who are undecided or have a weak preference for a candidate, are generally more receptive to messages in the advertising. This was the target group for the Reagan–Bush ads.

The Consumer Decision Map for voters shown in Fig. 1.2 is similar to a map for products. The levels of abstraction are the same, although the labels are different to better describe the voter's decision criteria. For example, product attributes are called candidate attributes, and include elements such as *Reduce Poverty, Fair Taxes,* and *Foreign Policy.* The circles and squares on the map represent perceptual ownership of an element on the map. Circled elements were concepts that voters believed were closely associated with Mondale while the boxed concepts were closely

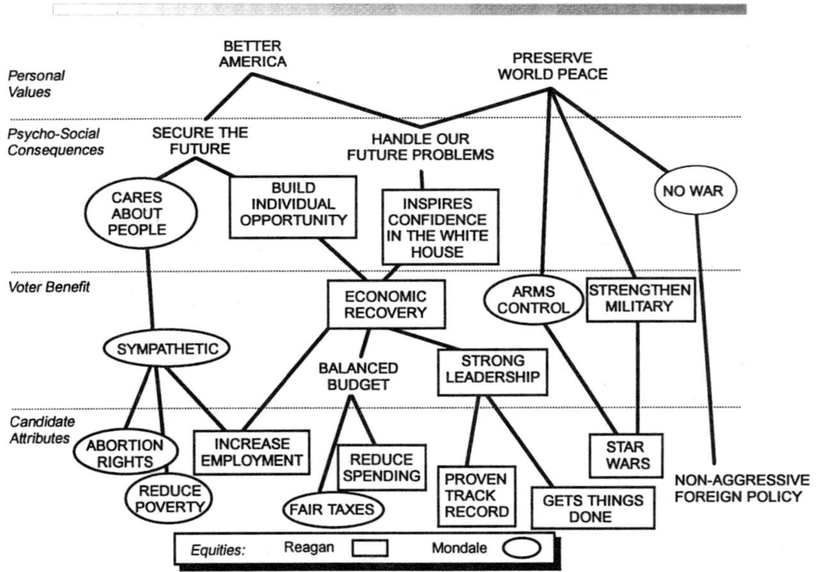

FIG. 1.2. Hierarchical value map: Reagan–Bush (August, 1984). Adapted from Fiedler and Bahner (1985).

associated with Reagan. The elements without circles or boxes were "up for grabs." Importantly, neither candidate had perceptual ownership of the top level value elements. Based on this depiction of the voters' criteria for voting decisions, positioning strategies could be developed.

Political battles in the United States are unlike product battles in a couple of key ways. First, only two or three major contenders will remain beyond the primary elections. This is unlike product markets where many competitors may operate and strategic positioning is usually defined as a single pathway from the product to the person. Second, a political battle is all or nothing. Therefore, a niche strategy is seldom desirable. Candidates would most likely strive to dominate the perceptual playing field and to achieve complete ownership of every node on the map. At the very least, candidates would want to control the upper level elements to block their opponents from achieving personal relevance with voters.

In the Reagan–Bush 1984 case, Reagan's team identified several complementary strategic directions to follow. From these, a series of ads were developed to communicate these desired positionings. One of these strategies was based on some of Reagan's key strengths at the lower levels—*Proven Track Record* and *Gets Things Done* led to *Strong Leadership*. The strategy created a new linkage with *Strengthen Military*, which then tapped into what had been a weakness . . . *No War*. *No War* then led to the value level element *World Peace*. By preempting Mondale from leveraging his strength on *Arms Control* into *World Peace*, Reagan could achieve ownership of this crucial upper level element. Additionally, *No War* could be used as a link to *Secure the Future* and *Handle Our Future Problems* as well.

The ad developed to communicate this strategic direction was called "Kids":

> Reagan's voice is heard while brief scenes of kids are shown. The kids are between three and six years old and of various racial backgrounds. The first scene is a kid standing on a porch. Then we see a kid getting a haircut in a barber shop.
>
> *Reagan (voice-over):* "We've faced two world wars, a war in Korea, then Vietnam."
>
> Scene of two kids fishing followed by a scene of kids in a fire truck. The kids look happy and content.
>
> *Reagan:* "And I know this. I want our children never to have to face another."
>
> Scene of a kid making bubbles followed by a scene of kids eating apples.
>
> *Reagan:* "A president's most important job is to secure peace, not just now but for the lifetimes of our children."
>
> Scene of a kid running with a big dog, apparently his best friend.

Reagan: "But it takes a strong America to build a peace that lasts."

Kids blowing bubbles, then kids in the rain.

Reagan: "And I believe with all my heart that working together we have made America stronger and prouder and more secure today."

Several close-ups of kids smiling.

Reagan: "And now we can work for a lasting peace for our children and their children to come."

Kid standing on a big white porch waving, while an American flag gently flaps with the breeze next to him.

Reagan: "Peace is the highest aspiration of the American people. Today America is prepared for peace."

The next scene is of Reagan speaking to an audience:

Reagan: "We will negotiate for it. Sacrifice for it. We will not surrender for it now or ever."

Text on screen: President Reagan . . . Leadership that's working.

"Kids" was assessed using strata; the results are shown in Fig. 1.3. As the scores indicate, "Kids" communicates the intended strategy quite well, particularly at the Voter Benefit and Leverage Point levels. *Strong Leader* (61) is clearly communicated with *Strengthen Military* (55) and *No War* (52) only slightly less so. Through executional techniques such as including children and Reagan's speech at the end, the elements at all the levels are communicated well and connections between levels range from moderate to very strong. Although not particularly entertaining (Ad Affect score of 44), "Kids" appears persuasive as shown by the Candidate Affect score of 48, since a score of 45 is generally considered adequate.

"Kids" and other ads strategically aimed at different pathways on the map were aired in the weeks before the election. By November 1984, Reagan's reelection campaign had produced the desired result. Reagan had captured all the value level elements and achieved either complete ownership or shared ownership of all the elements at the psychosocial level. Mondale retained sole ownership of the lower left side elements of the CDM (*Abortion Rights, Reduce Poverty, Fair Taxes,* and *Sympathetic*), but had been blocked from attaining personal relevance with voters because these elements did not connect to values for Mondale. Essentially, voters could say, "Yes, Mondale is sympathetic, but so what. It doesn't mean anything to me." Consistent with the state of the CDM on election day, Reagan beat Mondale in a landslide victory.

The Reagan–Bush 1984 example demonstrates how a means-end approach can provide clear guidance to the development of political posi-

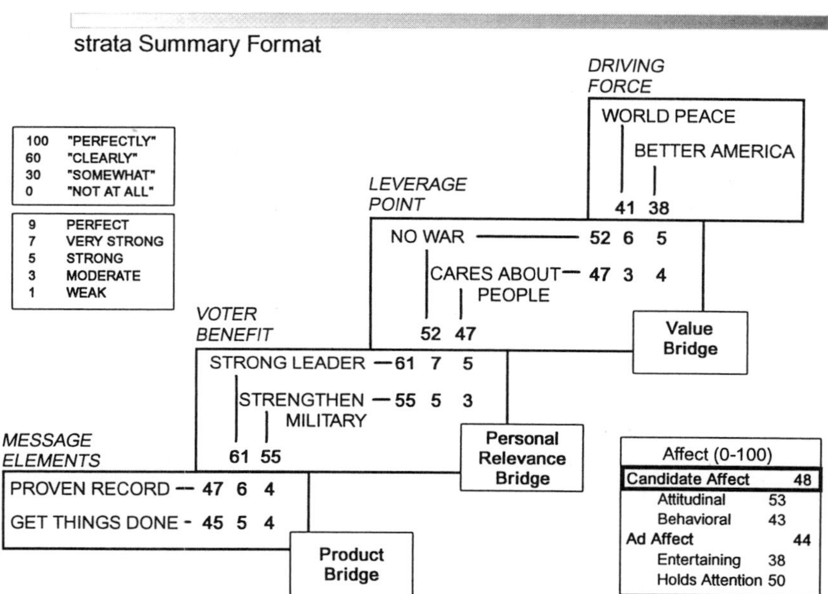

FIG. 1.3. Assessment of advertising: "Kids."

tioning and advertising strategy. For politicians, issues and personality characteristics represent the attributes and initial points of distinction between candidates, but associations between candidates and the higher level elements important to voters ultimately determine who wins the election.

SOCIAL ISSUE ADVERTISING

In this next example, we examine the application of means-end research and the strata model to social issue advertising concerning AIDS education. AIDS education is undoubtedly worthwhile and certainly everyone wants to avoid getting AIDS. But the primary target of education, teenagers who are at considerable risk from unsafe sex and drug use, are faced with many, often conflicting choices. The key positioning research issue for aids education was how to best minimize the barriers to adopting less risky behaviors such as abstinence, getting to know your partner, and using condoms. Also, any advertisement would have to promote the positive aspects of education to young people in a way that didn't turn them off. Based on means-end research, a CDM was developed (see Fig. 1.4) that described the choice criteria used to decide about low risk behaviors. The CDM

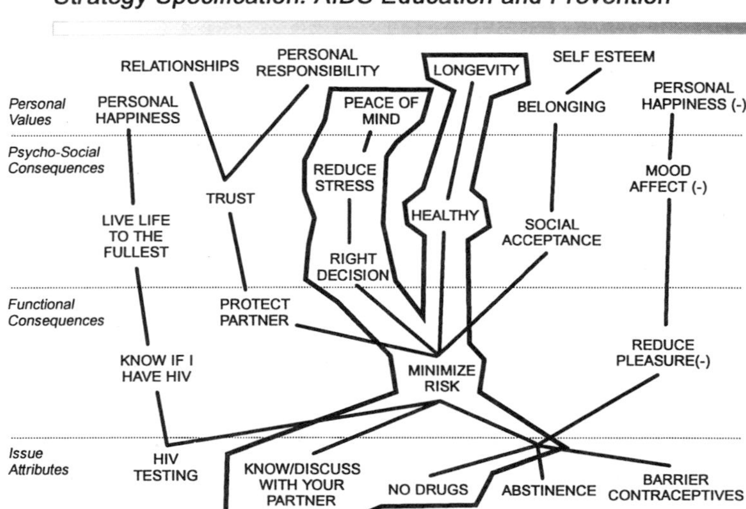

FIG. 1.4. Strategy specification: AIDS education and prevention.

outlines a strategic positioning option with two complementary pathways that have *Minimize Risk* in common.

Because social issues frequently include only two sides or ideologies, perceptual ownership of the entire map might be an achievable strategic goal, much like a political contest. Unlike politics, however, social issue debates are not necessarily all or nothing. Incremental gains may be considered worthwhile and are more likely the norm than an exception. For instance, reaching just one person through AIDS education might save a life. Therefore, a niche or single path strategy might be used if resources are limited, or multiple strategic directions can be pursued if ample funds are available. It should be recognized that social issue advertising is subject to counterargument since the practice of "selling" beliefs cuts against the grain of individualism and freedom in America.

The strategic positioning in the AIDS education example contains a primary and a secondary path. Both paths are grounded in the *Know/Discuss With Your Partner* and *No Drugs* at the Issue Attributes level. These lead to a key Functional Consequence of *Minimize Risk*. The primary route then leads to *Right Decision* and *Reduce Stress* at the Psychosocial level, and finally taps into the Personal Value of *Peace of Mind*. Importantly, this strategy has potential to turn AIDS education (represented by *Know/Discuss With Your Partner* and *No Drugs*) into a positive way for young people to reduce some of the tremendous stress that they frequently feel (and minimize counterargument). The secondary strategy leads from *Minimize Risk* to *Healthy* at the Psychosocial level and then connects to the person with the value *Longevity*. Because these strategies are complementary and the secondary one is so obvious that it only needs to be implied, both can be included in a single ad. This is the case with the ad "Campus" described here:

> A young woman of about eighteen is on a college campus that could be almost anywhere in the U.S. The first scene is a close-up of the woman looking thoughtful. Then she is walking around campus carrying a book bag, obviously between classes. Her voice is heard.
>
> *Woman's voice-over:* "HIV and AIDS, man, I'm tired of hearing about it."
>
> The screen cuts away from the young woman and shows the statement "HIV is the virus that causes AIDS." Then cuts back to the woman.
>
> *Woman's voice-over:* "Like I really have to worry about it. I don't do drugs and I wouldn't sleep with anybody I didn't know. There's no way I could get HIV."
>
> But obviously she is very worried about it. She tries to study but can't concentrate on her book. She slams the book shut.
>
> *Woman's voice-over:* "I swear, if I see one more thing about HIV I think I'm going to die!"
>
> The screen cuts to the statement "People who have HIV never thought they'd get it either" and then another statement "America responds to AIDS." A male voice is heard.
>
> *Male voice-over:* "You could be putting yourself at risk. Call 1-800-324-AIDS."
>
> A final screen shows the mentioned telephone number.

In the strata evaluation scores for "Campus" (Fig. 1.5), the primary strategy concerns the elements on top at the two higher levels while the elements on the bottom are relevant for the second strategy. As the scores indicate, "Campus" communicates the primary strategy very well at all levels, but it communicates the secondary strategy less effectively. *Minimize Risk* (73) and *Reduce Stress* (68) are communicated strongly. *Peace of Mind* (60) also scores well. Connections between these elements are very strong (8 and 6). For the secondary strategy, the *Healthy* and *Longevity* concepts are communicated "somewhat" with scores of 47 and 37, respectively. Connections within the secondary strategy are moderate to strong (4 and 5).

Connections between elements of the primary and secondary strategies (for example, *Healthy* connected to *Peace of Mind*) are moderate (2 and 3), which suggests that these strategies complement each other and can work together in the same execution. Importantly, Issue Affect (68) is very high, and the ad scores well in Holds Attention (65). Apparently, "Campus" communicates a motivating message about AIDS education.

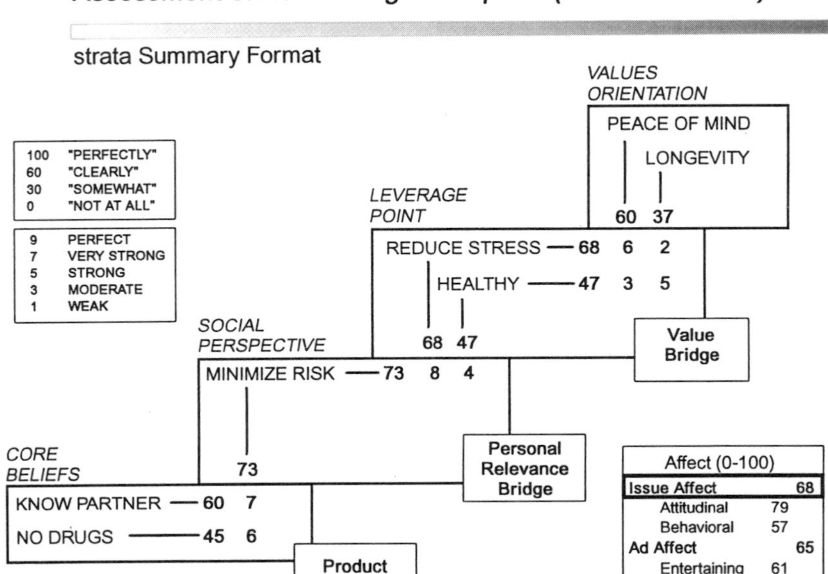

FIG. 1.5. Assessment of advertising: "Campus" (AIDS education).

As with the political example, successful social issue positioning relies on overcoming perceptual barriers at the attribute level by demonstrating positive outcomes for key attributes. "Campus" effectively linked the attributes that lead to *Minimize Risk* to the Leverage Point of *Reduce Stress.*

CORPORATE ADVERTISING AND DIMENSIONS OF LEADERSHIP

We have shown that political and social issue advertising fit within the means-end and MECCAS frameworks with little modification. The MECCAS model details four aspects of advertising strategy that correspond to the levels of abstraction in the Means-end model: Message Elements, Consumer Benefit, Leverage Point, and Driving Force. By definition, the Leverage Point is how the advertising execution taps into or activates the motivating personal values that are the Driving Force of the ad strategy. Psychosocial consequences can accomplish this, but the Leverage Point need not be limited to the psychosocial consequences of means-end theory. For corporate advertising, the Leverage Point can be dimensions of leadership because corporations act as potential leaders in society.

Corporations can be considered societal leaders because they fit key leadership-role criteria: People believe that companies influence the overall performance of society beyond just product or service offerings, and companies often serve as role models for society in philanthropic and environmental areas. Moreover, some consumer decision making is similar to voting . . . a consumer may choose a product over a competitive product because he or she knows that their purchase will help keep a strong leader in power, directly or indirectly providing benefit to society.

An important benefit of being a leader is the ability to hold the attention of followers, who tend to be responsive to what the leader does and says (Hollander, 1978). Thus, corporate leaders are ideally positioned to communicate, and should have an easier time cutting through the clutter than nonleaders. Also, a strong leader image can partially insulate a company from adverse events. For example, a strong leader image could result in fewer lawsuits and less government regulation.

Using factor analysis, we have identified seven dimensions that people use to evaluate companies with respect to leadership. These dimensions include (a) trustworthy . . . reliable and honest, worthy of trust, (b) popular . . . well-known, with a good reputation, (c) caring . . . socially responsible, cares about people, (d) efficacious . . . powerful and successful, gets things done, (e) innovative . . . new ideas and technologies, creative, (f) traditional . . . positive heritage, with long standing traditions, and (g) practical . . . and efficient, doesn't waste resources. Each dimension contains two to three subdimensions.

Further research using the laddering technique with the leadership dimensions helped identify the meanings of these dimensions with the means-end levels of abstraction. This led to the development of a dual model for understanding both the corporate and product perceptions or meanings in people's heads (Fig. 1.6). The product side of the model is the same as before . . . product attributes lead to functional consequences to psychosocial consequences to personal values. On the company side, the lowest or most concrete level is company attributes, defined as the concrete and physical assets of the company. Examples of company attributes include employees, management, technical expertise, products/services, and financial resources. At the next level of abstraction are corporate behavioral consequences, corresponding to functional consequences. These are the specific actions, activities, and behaviors of the company that can be observed or communicated such as "brings the community together," "provides drug education to children," "promotes efficient use of energy," and "doesn't pollute the water supply."

The seven leadership dimensions occupy the next level up in abstraction for the company side of the model. Personal values are the same as in the

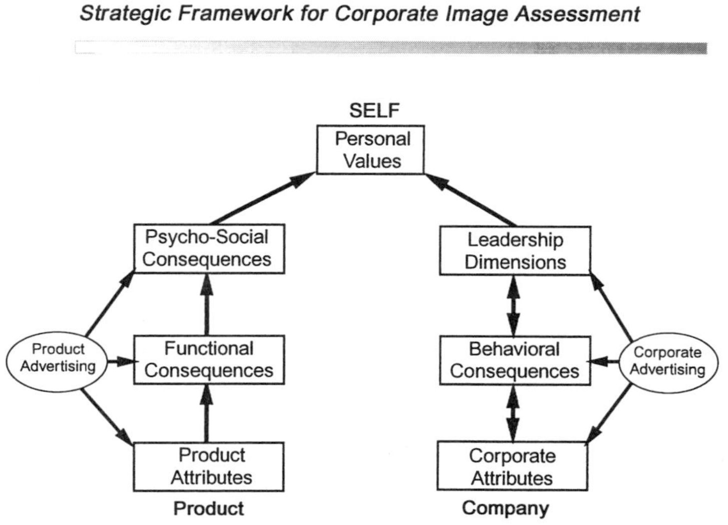

Strategic Framework for Corporate Image Assessment

FIG. 1.6. Strategic framework for corporate image assessment.

product based model, although the relative importance of these is likely to be different in the company context than in the product frame of reference. For example, *Social Responsibility* may be more important for companies than products.

In summary, the levels of abstraction are approximately the same for the corporate and product sides of the model, although some important differences exist. Products are most readily thought about by consumers at the product attribute and functional consequence levels. In other words, the most salient associations people have for products are elements at these lower levels of the means-end chain. Therefore, the directionality of the means-end chains can be thought of as going from the bottom up, at least from a consumer's perspective.

Companies, however, are most readily identified or described by people at the leadership dimension and behavioral consequence levels—further up in abstraction than for products. Because of this, the directionality of the means-end chains is not necessarily upwards and linear, from concrete to abstract, as with the product side. For understanding and assessing advertising, this linear relationship between the elements is useful for both sides of the model. But within people's heads, the associations for companies may be more circular, going from abstract to concrete and back to abstract again. Therefore, effective corporate image advertising is likely to place greater emphasis at the higher, more abstract leverage point level.

UNDERSTANDING CORPORATE IMAGE ADVERTISING

Advertising by companies can be classified into one of three categories: (a) primarily about a product (product-based), (b) primarily about a company (company-based), and (c) about both product and company. Company-based advertising doesn't include any direct information about a product; rather, it focuses only on a company message. For example, McDonald's advertises their employment of handicapped persons. Nothing about the McDonald's eating experience is ever mentioned or shown, nor can much be inferred from the ad about the consequences of eating at McDonald's.

Knowing the intended target is important for evaluating the effectiveness of company-based advertising. Unlike product-based communications that speak almost exclusively to the consumer/customer, company-based communications are aimed at strategic audience stakeholder groups including investors, lenders, vendors, government (IRS, regulators, legislators), media (newspapers, trade journals, analysts), and employees as well as industrial or business-to-business customers and end-user consumers. Many benefits may accrue from company-based communications that build perceptions of corporate leadership—customers buy more products, employees work harder or more effectively, and investors buy more stock.

The relative importance of these stakeholder groups is a function of the company's position in its life cycle as well as current business conditions. For example, during the start-up phase of a company, investors are an important audience. Employee and vendor relations then become significant as operations increase in preparation to launching the product or service. When the product or service goes to market, business customers or end-user consumers become important targets of communication.

Once the audience is defined, the important question becomes "how do members of the audience derive personally relevant meaning from the communication?" The seven leadership dimensions previously introduced are applicable for all of the strategic audience groups, although the relative importance of each dimension is likely to vary by group. For example, *trustworthy* is more important to employees than is *efficacious*, and *efficacious* is likely more important to lenders than to consumers. Therefore, the audience and the relative importance of the key leadership dimensions should be known before developing and evaluating a company-based strategic message.

Once the strategic elements for companies are identified, we can assess them in advertising much like we can for the product strategy elements. To demonstrate this application, we use the strata model to assess a corporate ad for Food Lion (a grocery chain). The ad, "Say No," doesn't mention any product or service offerings of the company, so in a sense it is "purely" corporate. Our sample included only consumers, which is appropriate for this ad since consumers are an intended target group. "Say No" is described as follows:

> The scenes are entirely from a school auditorium filled with young teenagers of all racial backgrounds. A pop music performer, Loren Stalmaker, is on stage. When Stalmaker is singing, the teens clap and sing along. When he's talking, the teens listen attentively. The ad gives the impression that it was filmed during an actual event.
>
> *Stalmaker (singing):* "Say no . . . say no . . . say no . . ."
>
> *Voice over:* "Almost everyday in school auditoriums across the country, Food Lion people present the pop music and message of Loren Stalmaker."
>
> *Stalmaker (talking):* "You are the future of our country. Without you we have no future."
>
> *Voice over:* "His words are simple . . . say no to drugs."
>
> *Stalmaker (talking):* "For that reason, it's important that you don't get into substance abuse."
>
> *Voice over:* "For young people, Loren's Hang Tough tour means learning how to say yes to life. For Food Lion people it means a chance to share."
>
> *Stalmaker (singing):* "Say yes to life made clean."

The summary strata evaluation scores for "Say No" are shown in Fig. 1.7. This ad communicates only modestly at the Message Elements level—*Motivated Employees* scores a moderate 47 while *Financial Support* is a low 22. At the Societal Benefit level, *Effective Drug Education* comes through clearly with a 63 although *Gets the Community Together*, at 22, is weakly communicated. At the Leverage Point level, *Caring* is communicated only somewhat (43), and *Social Responsibility* at the Driving Force level is communicated less strongly (34). Connections are weak to strong (1 to 5), although each bridge has at least one connection that is moderate (4) or strong (5). Overall, "Say No" is a mediocre ad in terms of its strategic communication ability. This conclusion is reinforced by the Company Affect score of 41, which is slightly below our criteria of 45 for adequate. Although "Say No" communicates *Effective Drug Education*, it doesn't clearly demonstrate personal relevance because it fails to place enough emphasis at the Leverage Point level.

IMPLICATIONS AND FUTURE RESEARCH

We have expanded the strategic assessment of advertising to include three forms of advertising communications used in political elections, social issues, and corporate image campaigns. Considerable resources are allocated in these three areas; thus, a better understanding of the communication

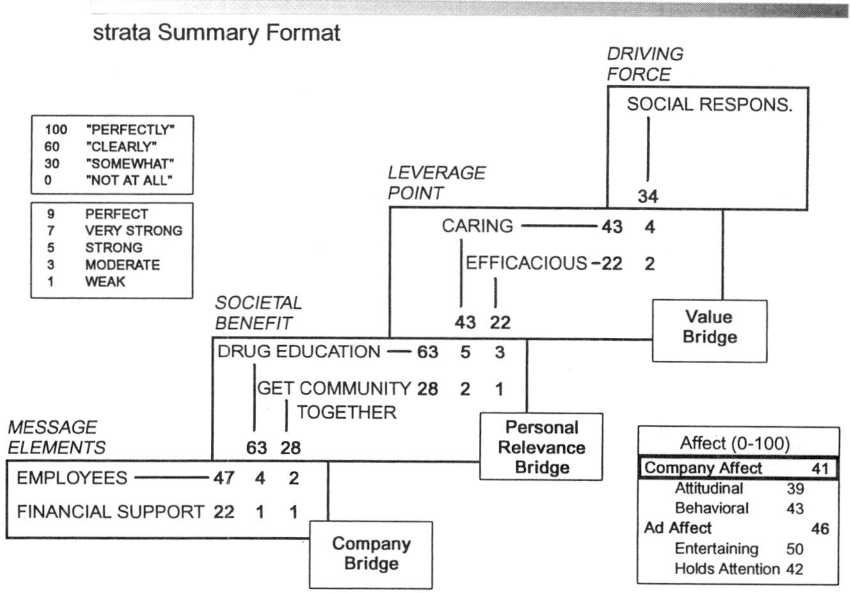

FIG. 1.7. Assessment of advertising: "Say no" (Food Lion).

process holds potentially great rewards. The means-end framework can be applied to political and social issue advertising with only minor terminology changes.

Corporate image advertising, however, requires some modifications in the means-end chain model. Companies can be defined as leaders in society, and as such, the key characteristics of a leader can be assessed as the Leverage Point in company-based communications. Also, company-based communications not only speak to consumers, but to other important stakeholders such as investors or employees who should be evaluated. With this understanding, companies can better manage their company-based advertising to achieve strategic goals relative to their audience stakeholder groups.

We emphasize that applications of the means-end approach need not be limited to advertising. Companies, politicians, and other organizations talk to their audiences via many vehicles including sponsorships, special or "prestige" accounts, and public relations. Further research should seek to expand the means-end framework to all types of communication. Companies that embrace this expanded view of means-end theory, MECCAS, and strata might develop their communication strategies quite differently. For example, corporate sponsorship of the Olympics would seek to involve the consumer or other stakeholder in a personally meaningful way to drive perceptions of the leadership dimensions. Communications surrounding this sponsorship would then use the key dimensions that are associated with the sponsorship to tap into stakeholder values.

Several other areas worthy of investigation have also emerged from our means-end research. Although we described companies as leaders and identified the key characteristics of corporate leaders, we do not yet have a definition of a prototypical or ideal corporate leader. Most likely, the ideal leader will possess different characteristics depending on the situation (Bass, 1981; Vecchio, 1990; Zaccaro, Foti, & Kenny, 1991). In terms of corporate crisis management, how might an understanding of current perceptual beliefs regarding leadership characteristics be used to their fullest advantage? Recall that Exxon spent several million dollars communicating during the Valdez oil spill crisis. Would their communications have been more effective, and hence the penalties later imposed less costly, if Exxon had known which leadership characteristics were attributed to them as well as the relative importance of these characteristics in that situation?

Finally, the corporate image research has not explained the relationship between source credibility and type of communication in terms of the corporate leadership dimensions. Perhaps different forms of communication work better for communicating certain leadership traits. For example, philanthropic giving might better communicate caring than an ad that simply states "we care." Likewise, global sponsorship of the Olympics might convince people that the sponsor is efficacious, while sponsorship of a rock music concert might mean the company is innovative. Our conclusion at this point is that companies should decide what type of leaders they want to be and communicate accordingly.

REFERENCES

Bass, B. M. (1981). *Handbook of leadership: A survey of theory and research.* New York: Free Press.

Bass, F. M., Pessemier, E. A., & Lehmann, D. R. (1972). An experimental study of relationships between attitudes, brand preference, and choice. *Behavioral Science, 17*(6).

Bass, F. M., & Talarzyk, W. (1972). An attitude model for the study of brand preference. *Journal of Marketing Research, 9.*

Fiedler, J. A., & Bahner, L. A. (1985). *The application of MECCAS to advertising strategy development for the 1984 Reagan–Bush campaign.* Paper presented at the 1985 Marketing Educators' Conference, Phoenix, AZ.

Fishbein, M. (1967). Attitude and the prediction of behavior. In M. Fishbein (Ed.), *Readings in attitude theory.* New York: Wiley.

Gengler, C. E., & Reynolds, T. J. (1993). *Consumer understanding and advertising strategy: Analysis and strategic translation of laddering data* (Working paper). Clarkson University.

Gutman, J. (1982). A means-end chain model based on consumer categorization processes. *Journal of Marketing, 46*(2), 60–72.

Gutman, J., & Reynolds, T. J. (1979). An investigation of the levels of cognitive abstraction utilized by consumers in product differentiation. In J. Eighmey (Ed.), *Attitude research under the sun.* Chicago: American Marketing Association.

Gutman, J., & Reynolds, T. J. (1987). Coordinating assessment to strategy development: An advertising assessment paradigm based on the MECCAS approach. In J. Olson & K. Sentis (Eds.), *Advertising and consumer psychology* (pp.). New York: Praeger.

Holbrook, M. B. (1978). Beyond attitude structure: Toward the informational determinants of attitude. *Journal of Marketing Research, 15,* 545–556.

Hollander, E. P. (1978). *Leadership dynamics.* New York: The Free Press.

Homer, P. M., & Kahle, L. R. (1988). A structural equation test of the value-attitude-behavioral hierarchy. *Journal of Personality and Social Psychology, 54*(4), 638–646.

Lehmann, D. R. (1971). Television show preference: Application of a choice model. *Journal of Marketing Research, 8*(1), 47–55.

Myers, J. H., & Shocker, A. D. (1981). The nature of product related attributes. *Research in Marketing, 5,* 221–235.

Olson, J. C., & Reynolds, T. J. (1983). Understanding consumers' cognitive structures: Implications for advertising strategy. In L. Percy & A. Woodside (Eds.), *Advertising and consumer psychology* (Vol. 1, pp. 77–90). Lexington, MA: Lexington Books.

Peters, J. P., & Olson, J. C. (1987). *Consumer behavior.* New York: Irwin.

Reynolds, T. J., & Craddock, A. B. (1988). The application of the MECCAS model to the development and assessment of advertising strategy. *Journal of Advertising Research, 28*(2), 43–54.

Reynolds, T. J., & Gengler, C. (1991). A strategic framework for assessing advertising: The animatic vs. finished issue. *Journal of Advertising Research, 31*(5), 61–71.

Reynolds, T. J., & Gutman, J. (1984). Advertising is image management. *Journal of Advertising Research, 24*(1), 27–36.

Reynolds, T. J., & Gutman, J. (1988). Laddering theory, method, analysis and interpretation. *Journal of Advertising Research, 28*(1), 11–31.

Reynolds, T. J., Gutman, J., & Fiedler, J. A. (1985). Understanding consumers' cognitive structures: The relationship of levels of abstraction to judgments of psychological distance and preference. In L. Alwitt & A. A. Mitchell (Eds.), *Psychological processes and advertising effects: Theory, research and practice.* Hillsdale, NJ: Lawrence Erlbaum Associates.

Reynolds, T. J., & Rochon, J. P. (1991). Means-end based advertising research: Copy testing is not strategy assessment. *Journal of Business Research, 22,* 131–142.

Reynolds, T. J., & Trivedi, M. (1989). An investigation of the relationship between the MECCAS model and advertising affect. In P. Cafferata & A. Tybout (Eds.), *Cognitive and affective responses to advertising.* Lexington, MA: Lexington Books.

Rokeach, M. (1973). *The nature of human values.* New York: The Free Press.

Valette-Florence, P., & Rapacchi, B. (1991). Improvements in means-end chain analysis: Using graph theory and correspondence analysis. *Journal of Advertising Research, 27*(1), 30–45.

Vecchio, R. P. (1990). Theoretical and empirical examination of cognitive resource theory. *Journal of Applied Psychology, 75*(2), 141–147.

Vinson, D. E., Scott, J. E., & Lamont, L. M. (1977). The role of personal values in marketing and consumer behavior. *Journal of Marketing, 41*(2), 44–50.

Zaccaro, S. J., Foti, R. J., & Kenny, D. A. (1991). Self-monitoring and trait-based variance in leadership: An investigation of leader flexibility across multiple group situations. *Journal of Applied Psychology, 76*(2), 308–315.

Chapter 2

Where Perception Meets Reality: The Social Construction of Lifestyles

Basil G. Englis
Berry College

Michael R. Solomon
Auburn University

> *Humanist historians had aimed at individualized portrait. The new social science historians produced a group caricature. . . . Oversimplified sociological concepts—"status," "other-direction," etc.—appealed because they were so helpful in building images. These wide-appealing "modes," expressed in our dominating notions of norms and averages, led us unwittingly to try to imitate ourselves. We have tried to discover what it is really like to be a junior executive or a junior executive's wife,* ***so we can really be the way we are supposed to be, that is, the way we are.*** *(emphasis added; Boorstin, 1961, p. 202)*

Mass media vehicles of popular culture are replete with lifestyle imagery. Indeed, it is often through the strategic depiction of consumption acts that creatives instantiate different "social types" for a mass audience. So, when Roseanne Connor opens a restaurant in the downscale community of Lanford, its specialty is a "loose-meat sandwich" (something on the order of a "Sloppy-Joe"), while the upscale, urban characters in the sitcom *Seinfeld* drink Snapple and dine in trendy Manhattan eateries.

But, are these images accurate? For example, how many members of the audience watching *Beverly Hills, 90210* have directly experienced the lifestyle of a Beverly Hills teenager? So long as creatives' choices match audience expectations, the image will be accepted as real. As a result most viewers may now think of this lifestyle as involving trips to the health spa, wearing a vest with no shirt underneath, and driving a Porsche convertible. These examples highlight the fact that the "truth" about a lifestyle may be less important than its mass-mediated image and the social connotations the image has for the audience/consumer.

Moreover, these images are no mere shadows playing across the screen of popular culture. Consumers incorporate these images into their assumptions of how others live and consume (e.g., Faber & O'Guinn, 1988; Gerbner, Gross, Signorielli, & Morgan, 1980), and this information is available to consumers when they themselves make lifestyle-related product choices. Such media-transmitted lifestyle imagery may be especially relevant in situations involving anticipatory consumption, as when consumers consider the purchase of products they believe to be associated with an aspired-to lifestyle. Ralph Lauren's advertising is emblematic of this process. His campaigns depict a moneyed, "traditional Americana" fantasy world—an idealized lifestyle that is led by very few consumers (*Marketing Insights*, 1989). Yet, his images of affluence and sophistication transmitted via mass media become objects of desire for many who *aspire to* this quasi-mythical lifestyle.

As compelling as these idealized lifestyles may be to media audiences, practitioners and academics alike have paid scant attention to the sources of these images. Yet it is clear that effective evocation of the desired cultural connotation is critical to the success of a lifestyle advertising campaign such as that of Ralph Lauren. In this chapter we present a model of how lifestyle imagery is generated and modified by the "channel intermediaries" whose function is to analyze, instantiate, and transmit lifestyle imagery to consumers.

Typically, marketers construct lifestyle categories on the basis of an analysis of patterns of purchase behavior of consumers (e.g., Wells, 1975; Wells & Tigert, 1971). We argue that marketers and advertisers also need to consider lifestyles as *social constructions* in the minds of consumers. We review a body of research bearing on the complex relationships between marketers' analyses of actual market behavior and the process whereby this information is filtered through the hands of diverse media gatekeepers. This research also touches on the nature of consumers' cognitive representations of lifestyle-relevant consumption patterns and how these representations relate to actual market behaviors. In the process we highlight both theoretical and applied ramifications of the divergence between marketer and consumer construals of lifestyle content and meaning.

In particular, we argue that lifestyles can be understood not only in terms of the *actual* patterns of behavior that marketers measure and use to cluster consumers, but also in terms of the *social categories* that lifestyles represent for consumers and marketers alike (e.g., Englis & Solomon, 1995). The use of a lifestyle-oriented approach to market segmentation (and the resulting promotional strategy) is based on the assumption that a "lifestyle campaign" will provide a more effective means of contextualizing a product in the daily life of the target consumer. But, ultimately, the notion of lifestyle only has meaning if it is meaningful to the customer. It is precisely the issue of what lifestyles *mean* to consumers that in our estimation has been underemphasized by traditional conceptualizations.

THE SOCIAL CONSTRUCTION OF LIFESTYLES

Figure 2.1 illustrates the divergent perspectives of "lifestyle" encoders and decoders. The top half of the figure captures the role(s) played by marketing gatekeepers and the bottom half the role of consumers in the social construction of lifestyle meaning. From the advertiser/marketer perspective, market data are filtered into the creative process, and then lifestyle-oriented communications are channeled through discrete media to separate audiences. In contrast, audiences/consumers integrate messages from a variety of sources, many of which are mass-media vehicles of popular culture. The illustration highlights the peripheral role that actual market behavior may play in consumer, as compared with marketer, formulations of lifestyle categories.

As the consumption patterns that are the bases of lifestyle segmentation schemes are depicted in the context of popular culture, two important processes come into play. The first is that actual market behavior becomes distorted and idealized as creatives offer their own interpretations of a market—often by depicting only selected or stereotypical perspectives on what a prototypic member of a particular lifestyle category "ought" to look like. For example, the definition of a young African-American, urban, entrepreneurial lifestyle may originate in the market analysis of an advertiser wishing to identify and reach this particular audience. Over time, however, this group and its defining attributes will be turned over to the creatives, whose task is to represent the group by a series of images—physical appearance, clothing, hairstyle, make-up, decorating style, and so on—which then become the icons defining the group. In this cultural encoding process a form of stereotyping is inevitable—not necessarily as a negative portrayal of the group, but rather as a simplification and a distortion of its reality and true diversity.

The second process involves how consumers learn about and represent lifestyle groups cognitively. We argue that the pervasive images of popular culture become as, or more, important to the cognitive representation of lifestyle groups as the direct observation of these groups. Direct observation takes a back seat because consumer behavior is often motivated *not* by a desire to emulate the lifestyle group to which the consumer *currently* belongs, but rather by the desire to emulate one that he or she *aspires* to

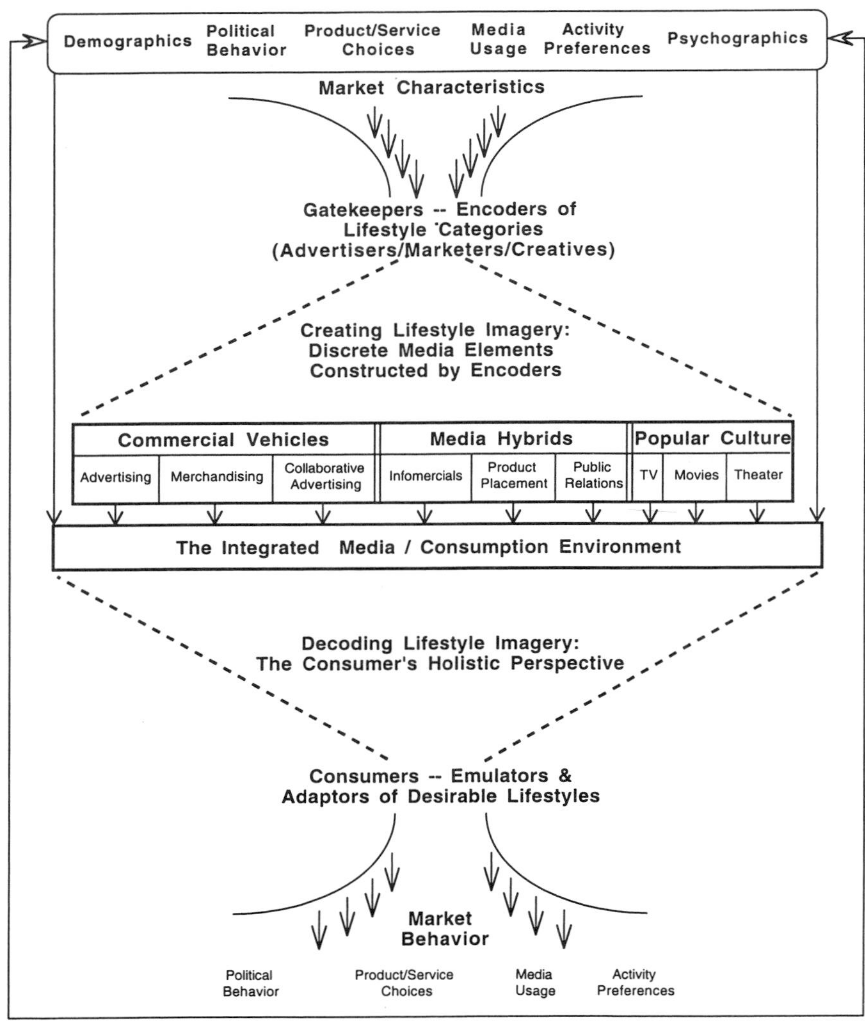

FIG. 2.1. The figure illustrates the divergent perspectives of media gatekeepers—lifestyle encoders and consumers—lifestyle decoders. From the advertiser/marketer perspective, market data are filtered into the creative process and then lifestyle-oriented communications are channeled through discrete media to separate audiences. In contrast, audiences/consumers integrate messages from a variety of sources, many of which are mass media vehicles of popular culture. The illustration highlights the more peripheral role that actual market behavior plays in consumer, as compared with marketer, formulations of lifestyle.

join. Thus, either in their actual or anticipatory (e.g., fantasy) consumption behavior, consumers are oriented toward lifestyle information that in some manner represents an aspirational social group—a desirable ideal. And, at the same time they may orient away from lifestyles that have acquired a negative valuation, and thereby represent an avoidance group—an anti-ideal. In effect, consumers seek to move toward ideal and away from anti-ideal lifestyles (see Englis & Solomon, 1995).

However, information about aspirational and avoidance lifestyle categories is less available to consumers in their day-to-day lives (these are by definition *not* occupied groups). Therefore, consumers must rely on vicarious sources of information—whether the glowing reports of friends who visited the "next-most-upscale" neighborhood *or* the media portrayals of these lifestyles. Just as social observers act to simplify complex social information and to represent social categories by forming stereotypes and prototypes (e.g., Cantor & Mischel, 1979; Rosch, 1978), they should do the same in representing lifestyle categories. Whether acquired from direct or vicarious sources, cognitive representations of lifestyles should be structurally similar to the representations of other social categories (Englis & Solomon, 1995).

Moreover, it is these cognitive representations that may prove more important to marketers and advertisers than actual market data. The ultimate goal of lifestyle advertising and marketing campaigns is for the target customer to *accept* the specific lifestyle portrayal as representing a "real" and desirable ideal, *and* for the customer to accept the appropriateness of the focal product *given* the lifestyle context in which it is placed. In order to garner such acceptance it is important for advertisers to select the appropriate lifestyle category for a specific target market. *And*, it is equally important that the lifestyle be instantiated in a manner that reflects consumers' own cognitive representations. This final point is crucial to the present analysis. All too often it is assumed that lifestyle portrayals that reflect actual market behavior will be the most effective. In contrast, we argue that portrayals reflecting *perceived* market behavior may prove the most effective.

In this chapter we review a program of research that has examined the top-down process employed by advertising, marketing, and media gatekeepers in the instantiation of lifestyle categories and their various accouterments. We also discuss several studies that have explored the question of how the social valuation of lifestyle categories is related to the structure and content of consumers' cognitive representations of those categories. Finally, we describe research that is designed to examine how consumers utilize these representations in their own consumption behavior. Data from these studies encompass such diverse populations as magazine editors and teenage viewers of music television.

GATEKEEPER STUDIES

The gatekeeper studies focus on the processes depicted in the top half of Fig. 2.1. Our emphasis in this series of studies was on the top-down process employed by advertising, marketing, and media gatekeepers in the instantiations of lifestyle categories. These studies represent direct and indirect examinations of the behavior of media gatekeepers and their selection of consumption-related ideals.

Study I

This study was part of a larger project that examines the role of context in the effectiveness of print advertising (Englis & Solomon, 1993). In this pretest study we examined the use of collateral products in print advertisements. One important decision in ad execution is whether or not a focal product appears alone or in a visual context that includes other products and/or consumption activities. We performed a content analysis of magazine advertisements that had footwear, alcoholic beverages, and housewares as the focal products. Context products were defined as "nonessential," nonfocal products that play a role as part of the ad's setting. (For example, clothing on a model or a table upon which an appliance appears were not coded as context products. However, exercise equipment in an ad for athletic shoes or a coffee maker alongside a toaster when the toaster was the focal product were coded as context products.)

Our sample of advertisements was taken from *Playboy, GQ, Vogue, Travel & Leisure, Better Homes & Gardens, Self, People, Bride's, Sports Illustrated,* and *Rolling Stone*—magazines with more than one million readers in the 18–24 years-old age range. We examined a 3-month sample (single quarter) for each magazine, which resulted in a total of 1,730 advertisements. Each ad was coded for the presence/absence of ancillary products, for the target gender of the ad (male, female, or both), and for the setting (indoors or outdoors).

We found that ancillary products were much more prevalent in advertisements for housewares (60% of all housewares ads) than for the other categories—alcoholic beverages (43%) or footwear (33%). In addition, we found that the use of ancillary products as an executional element of these ads was dependent on whether the ad was aimed at a male or female consumer—ancillary products are far more prevalent in ads targeting women.

Although this study is a coarse examination of advertising context, it does reveal that some target products are more likely than others to appear in a visual context that includes other "nonessential" products. As might be expected, houseware products are the most likely to be thus contextualized. It is also noteworthy that ads targeting female consumers are more likely to place the focal product alongside other products than ads targeting males. It would be interesting to determine whether this is a deliberate decision or whether it is merely a serendipitous outcome of the set design process. In what follows, we more closely examine stylistic features of advertising context.

Study II

This study was an attempt to examine directly the choices made by media gatekeepers by interviewing a group of working property masters (Solomon & Greenberg, 1993). The focus of this study was on the specific selection of props chosen by property masters for use in instantiating different "social types." The method involved one-on-one interviews with property masters who responded to a task designed to simulate the sorts of preproduction decisions commonly encountered in designing television advertising sets. Property masters were asked to select props (living room ensembles, house exteriors, coffee mugs) to fit four advertising scenarios that varied in terms of the gender and musical preference of the main character of the ad.

The most notable finding was the high level of agreement among the property masters in how the different "social types" ought to be represented (see Table 2.1 for agreement levels). The property masters who were interviewed in this study have clear *and* shared notions of how to depict these social types. Thus, a female aficionado of classical music is depicted in an "English" styled living room in a Tudor house, and she drinks her coffee from a traditional/floral mug. In contrast, her male counterpart lives in a colonial house and his living room is decorated with contemporary furnishings. He drinks coffee from a plain white coffee mug. Regardless of the specific styles chosen, the operative point here is that the media gatekeepers who construct television commercial settings appear to share common stereotypes regarding the lifestyles of different social types. Fur-

TABLE 2.1
Property Masters' Selections of Props to Instantiate Various Social Types

Social Type	*Living Room*	*House Exterior*	*Coffee Mug*
Female-Country	60% Eclectic	68% Farm	68% Country/Rustic
Female-Classical	72% English	64% Tudor	44%Traditional/Floral
Male-Country	76% Early American	76% Farm	64% Country/Rustic
Male-Classical	76% Contemporary	84% Colonial	64% Plain/White

Note. Figures are the percent of property masters selecting each prop. Random selection levels are 16.67% for living rooms, 25.0% for house exteriors, and 12.5% for coffee mugs. Data adapted from "Setting the Stage: Collective Selection in the Stylistic Content of Commercials," by M. R. Solomon and L. Greenberg, 1993, *Journal of Advertising, 22* (January), 11-24.

thermore, this shared cultural script translates into consensus regarding the media instantiation of these types.

Study III

This study also provides a direct examination of the choices of media gatekeepers in that fashion and beauty magazine editors were the population studied (Solomon, Ashmore, & Longo, 1992). These editors were asked to categorize types of female beauty and to provide their perceptions of the associations of these different looks with various products and magazines. One of the assumptions guiding this study was that beauty is not a unidimensional cultural construct, but is instead comprised of "types" whose specific meaning evolves over time.

Six types of female beauty emerged from a multidimensional scaling solution of the editor judgments (see Table 2.2). These types are distinct in the minds of these gatekeepers and each type is associated with specific perfumes and magazines. It is clear from these data that magazine editors

TABLE 2.2
Six "Types" of Female Beauty Derived From Judgments and Descriptions Provided by Editors of Fashion and Beauty Magazines

Beauty Type	*Characteristics*	*Perfume/ Magazine*
Classic/Feminine[a]	Blond or light hair/WASPish Soft image Feminine apparel	Chanel Charlie *Vogue* *Glamour* **not** *Cosmopolitan*
Sensual/Exotic[a]	Ethnic looking Sexually attractive/understated	*Vogue*
Trendy	Tousled/sexy Current/faddish clothing Provocative/challenging pose	**not** White Linen
Cute	Youthful/petite/casual attire Naturalness/awkwardness Caught off-guard	Charlie *Seventeen*
Girl-Next-Door	Athletic/outdoors/casual/active Wears a bathing suit like a swimmer	**not** Poison White Linen
Sex Kitten	Sexy attire/lingerie/tight clothes Cheesecake poses/looks away from camera	**not** Charlie *Cosmopolitan*

Note. [a]Each of these types is a combination of two categories from the raw sorting data. Data adapted from "The Beauty Match-Up Hypothesis: Convergence Types of Beauty and Product Images in Advertising," by M. R. Solomon, R. D. Ashmore, and L. C. Longo, 1992, *Journal of Advertising, 21* (December), 23-34.

do not conceive of female beauty as unidimensional, and that broad consensus exists as to the cultural meaning associated with each beauty type. Although at a particular time this pattern may reflect the prevailing cultural *Zeitgeist* for female beauty, the choices of these gatekeepers also shape readers' perceptions of valued or devalued beauty types. In order to begin to examine how the connotative meaning of these beauty types evolves, it is important to examine the cultural contexts in which they appear.

Study IV

It is one thing to show that magazine editors distinguish among types of female beauty, but quite another to argue that there are systematic differences in the messages transmitted to consumers about the meaning of these types. One method for examining how cultural meanings become attached to different forms of beauty is to analyze their prevalence as a function of the communications vehicle in which they appear. Since variations in genre and medium relate to differences in market segments, this provides *prima facie* evidence that media gatekeepers are crafting stylistically distinct messages for different consumer groups (Englis, Solomon, & Ashmore, 1994).

In this study, we examined the prevalence of different types of female beauty in print advertising and music television. Both media reach young, fashion-conscious audiences. Fashion magazines represent a traditional print medium that is directly concerned with beauty, and which is an important media vehicle for advertisers who seek to link their products to a particular beauty ideal. In contrast, music television is an electronic medium that is nontraditional in terms of its structure and content (e.g., Fry & Fry, 1987; Kaplan, 1987), and it transmits a great deal of consumption imagery (see also Englis, Solomon, & Olofsson, 1993a, 1993b).

Advertisements. Magazine advertisements were taken from a one-month sample of *Cosmopolitan, Glamour, Mademoiselle, Self, Seventeen,* and *Vogue.* For comparison purposes we also examined advertisements from a group of fashion-oriented men's magazines: *Esquire, GQ,* and *Playboy.* This sampling procedure yielded 195 codeable advertisements showing a female model in a full-face frontal shot. As shown in Table 2.3, the specific types of female beauty portrayed were clearly different as a function of magazine. Most important were the systematic covariations of beauty type, editorial format, and magazine readership. For example, *Glamour* and *Vogue* place great emphasis on "high" fashion and cutting edge trends. In contrast to several of the the other magazines (e.g., *Self* or *Cosmopolitan*), these emphasize Sensual/Exotic and Trendy looks (see Solomon, Ashmore, & Longo, 1992, for a complete description of these looks). The Classic Beauty/Feminine

TABLE 2.3
The Three Most Prevalent Types of Female Beauty in Fashion and Beauty Magazine Advertisements and in Music Videos

Beauty Type	Magazine Ads		Music Videos	
Sensual/Exotic	31.5%	*Vogue*	65.4%	Rap
		Glamour	62.5%	Soft Rock
Trendy	30.6%	*Seventeen*	60.0%	Dance
		Vogue	45.5%	New Wave
Classic/Feminine	54.6%	*Self*	35.0%	Classic Rock
	38.5%	*Cosmopolitan*		
	34.4%	*Mademoiselle*		

Note. Percentages are based on the total number of coded ads in each magazine or music videos in each genre. Data adapted from "Beauty *Before* the Eyes of Beholders: The Cultural Encoding of Beauty Types in Magazine Advertising and Music Television," by B. G. Englis, M. R. Solomon, and R. D. Ashmore, 1994, *Journal of Advertising, 23* (June), 49-64.

look was the most prevalent in *Cosmopolitan, Mademoiselle,* and *Self. Cosmopolitan* and *Mademoiselle* appeal more to a mass market audience and are less likely to be read by "opinion leaders."

Music Videos. We used a 24-hour time sample of music videos, taking 4 hours from each of six genres (see Englis, Solomon, & Olofsson, 1993b, for details about music genres). Of the 267 videos sampled, 113 contained codeable scenes. Even more than in print advertisements, music television presents a stereotyped image of beauty in its emphasis on a single look—Sensual/Exotic (see Table 2.3).

The "face" validity of the fit between genre and type of beauty is quite striking. New Wave music, which emphasizes musical innovation, is associated with the Trendy look. Just as "trendy" exemplifies a cutting-edge look for fashion editors, it seems to carry a similar connotation for those casting music videos. In contrast, Classic Rock radio stations, VH-1, and bands in this genre (e.g., The Grateful Dead) frequently emphasize to their links to the roots of Rock 'n' Roll. It is striking that the women chosen to appear in these videos also represent a Classic Beauty/Feminine look. It is not surprising that Rap and Dance videos, given the multicultural focus of these genres, should emphasize the Sensual/Exotic form of beauty.

It is clear that music television and the ads appearing in currently popular fashion magazines tend to highlight a select subset of beauty ideals. Three types—Sensual/Exotic, Trendy, and Classic—were most prevalent overall in magazine ads (72.9% of all ads) and in music videos (85.2% of all videos). In this manner women are being "told" that some types of beauty are more highly valued than others. The fashion magazines and music genres analyzed in the present study appeal to different audiences (market segments) who can be defined by their shared demographic, lifestyle, and/or aesthetic preferences. An interesting question for future research is to what extent audience members are incorporating these images into idealized images of how they themselves desire to look.

Study V

This study was another indirect assessment of the creative choices of gatekeepers in music television. Our analysis focused on the nature and prevalence of consumption imagery in music television and its covariation with musical genre (Englis, Solomon, & Olofsson, 1993a, 1993b). This study was the first of a series that is designed to empirically assess the impact of fashion-related imagery in music television on viewers' aesthetic preferences and knowledge. In order to isolate the specific contributions of music videos as a source of this fashion imagery, we examined this media vehicle in the United States (where MTV was first aired in 1981) and in Sweden (where MTV was first aired in 1989). In this study we performed a content analysis, which focused on the presence of products and consumption activities in music videos (see Table 2.4). We used a 24-hour time sample with 4 hours from each genre, which yielded 400 music videos for analysis (192 from the United States and 208 from Sweden).

Our analyses revealed several differences in consumption imagery as a function of musical genre. As shown in Table 2.4, Dance music videos contain the most fashion-oriented imagery—including references to and consumption activities involving clothing, jewelry, lingerie, hairstyles, and make-up. In contrast, Classic Rock and New Wave videos were lower than all other genres in imagery concerning fashion. Although Dance videos contained a great deal of fashion-related products, they were lowest in brand appearances (see Table 2.5). Heavy Metal videos contained a large number of brand references, but this was due to the visual emphasis on music instruments in these videos—the brand is often emblazoned on guitars and drum sets.

In sum, the content analysis showed that consumption imagery is pervasive and that the quality of the imagery varies as a function of genre. The results makes more plausible the tacit assumption that exposure to music television may be a mediator of the hypothesized relationship between musical preference and personal style and its related consumption activities.

Conclusions

As a group, these studies represent direct and indirect examinations of the behavior of media gatekeepers and their selection of consumption-related ideals. The studies examined both commercial and cultural media

TABLE 2.4
The Eighteen Forms of Consumption Activity Coded in Study V Are Clustered According to the Results of a Factor Analysis

	Factor Labels					
	Fashion[a]	*Vehicles*	*Darkside*[a]	*The Band*[a]	*Food*[a]	*Toys*
	Clothing Lingerie Hairstyle Make-up Jewelry Earrings (on men)	Cars Motorcycles Trucks	Drugs Weapons Alcohol	Instruments Tattoos	Food Tobacco Beverages	Toys
	Imagery Prevalence					
Genre	*Fashion*[a] *(range 0-6)*	*Vehicles (range 0-3)*	*Darkside*[a] *(range 0-3)*	*The Band*[a] *(range 0-2)*	*Food*[a] *(range 0-3)*	*Toys (0-1)*
Classic	1.44	0.28	0.17	0.62	0.52	0.05
Dance	2.75	0.24	0.16	0.38	0.13	0.02
Metal	1.58	0.48	0.29	1.27	0.15	0.06
New Wave	0.98	0.28	0.17	0.89	0.11	0.08
Rap	1.93	0.47	0.66	0.22	0.42	0.07
Soft/Top 40	1.97	0.33	0.20	0.77	0.17	0.09

Note. The bottom half of the table shows the composite scale means for each category as a function of music genre. Data adapted from "Consumption Imagery in Music Television: A Bi-Cultural Perspective," by B. G. Englis, M. R. Solomon, and A. Olofsson, 1993, *Journal of Advertising, 22* (December), 21-34.
[a]Significant main effects for genre ($p < .0001$).

formats, as well as print and electronic media. Taken as a whole, they demonstrate that media gatekeepers appear to read from a common cultural script and to present consistent lifestyle-related images to their audiences. The content of these images were found to vary systematically by lifestyle portrayal and by characteristics of the medium/audience interface.

CONSUMER STUDIES

The consumer studies focus on the processes depicted in the bottom half of Fig. 2.1. Emphasis is on consumers' cognitive processing of media and market information, and how different lifestyle categories are represented in memory. In addition, we examine consumption behaviors and their relationship to media imagery. A central assumption of our model is that consumers learn about and encode social/lifestyle types in much the same manner as they deal with other forms of cognitive categorization. Thus, consumers should possess cognitive prototypes of the stylistic features of different lifestyle groups, these stylistic features should include patterns of consumption.

A set of symbolically related consumption activities and products associated with a lifestyle has been referred to by McCracken (1988) as "the Diderot effect" and by Solomon as a *consumption constellation* (Solomon, 1988; Solomon & Assael, 1987). A consumption constellation in essence constitutes a prototypical set of products and consumption activities associated with a lifestyle group. Consumption activities and products firmly embedded as category prototypes should be more easily retrieved, and may become emblematic of a particular lifestyle. Because the lifestyle categories generated by quantitative analyses of market behavior are pervasive in popular culture (albeit filtered by media gatekeepers), then consumers' cognitive prototypes should reflect the media images to which the are exposed.

Study I

In this study, we examined consumers' ability to decode the stylistic imagery of music television (see Englis et al., 1993b). The focus of this study was on viewers' ability to accurately associate these stylistic images with the musical genre in which they appeared. We presented viewers with visual images taken from the sample of music videos used in the content analysis reviewed earlier (see Gatekeeper Study V). Twenty-four scenes were sampled (the scenes ranged from 10 to 15 seconds in length).

Another purpose of this study was to relate involvement in (and exposure to) music television and popular music to ability to decode musical genre from exposure to only the visual content of music television. As predicted, there was a strong interaction between decoding accuracy and involvement (see Fig. 2.2). High-involvement respondents were equally accurate at

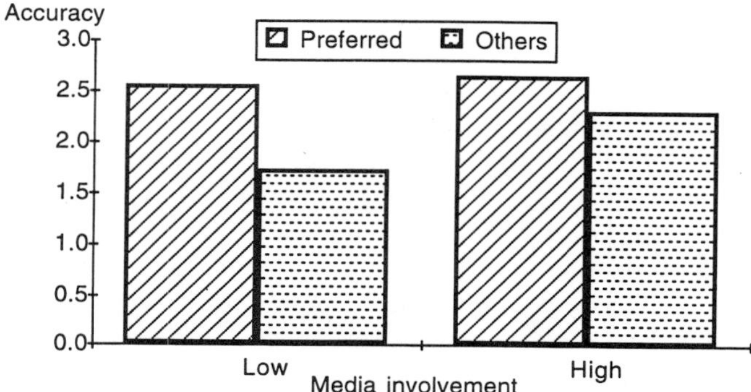

FIG. 2.2. Decoding accuracy for visual images taken from music videos as a function of viewer level of involvement. The interaction was statistically significant. From Englis, Solomon, & Olofsson (1993a).

decoding the visual imagery associated with their preferred musical genre as well as all other genres. In contrast, low-involvement respondents were poor decoders of nonpreferred genres and also performed more poorly at decoding their preferred genre as compared with high-involvement viewers.

Taken together with the results of our content analysis of the consumption imagery present in music videos, these findings lend credence to the assumption that viewers of music television engage in incidental learning of lifestyle cues. The stylistic differences among music genres involve consumption activities—these activities are associated with distinct categories of products and types of products within these categories. The present study shows that the characters depicted (their hairstyles, clothing, and so on), the settings in which they are shown, and their actions all create a stylistic gestalt that is readily decoded by viewers. Most notable was the finding that all viewers, regardless of their involvement in this medium, learn the styles associated with their most preferred genre of popular music.

Study II

Our conceptual framework also assumes that the properties of consumers' cognitive representations of lifestyle information should be influenced by their motivations vis à vis a specific lifestyle category. If lifestyle information is organized cognitively in the form of prototypes (consumption constellations) associated with particular lifestyles, then it is important to understand the structure as well as the content of these cognitive representations. One basic assumption guiding this study was that consumers' motivations to emulate or to avoid particular lifestyles would affect the structure of the consumption constellations associated with each. We used a sorting task to map lifestyle clusters of the widely used PRIZM system (see Weiss 1988) onto *aspirational* and *avoidance* (rejected) lifestyle categories for our subject population (see Englis & Solomon, 1995, for more detail on the experimental conditions tested).

Using a second sample, we assessed the extent of consumers' knowledge of the consumption patterns associated with these lifestyles and how well their perceptions matched PRIZM data. In addition, we examined the degree of consensus among consumer perceptions—to what degree do consumers agree with each other that particular products do (or do not) belong in various consumption constellations. We employed an open-ended product-elicitation task in which respondents generated lists of products that they felt were consumed by the typical person described by each profile shown in Table 2.5. Our analyses focused on derived measure of consensus and accuracy as structural measures of these prototypes (see Englis & Solomon, 1995).

The predicted interaction shows that levels of consensus and accuracy were dependent on whether aspirational or avoidance lifestyles were de-

TABLE 2.5
Profiles of PRIZM Lifestyle Clusters Used as Prompts in the Product-Elicitation Task

Lifestyle Cluster (Reference Group)	*High Usage Products*[a]	*Low Usage Products*[a]
Money & Brains (Aspirational role)	*These people are especially LIKELY to use, buy, or do:*	*These people are especially UNLIKELY to use, buy, or do:*
	Travel/entertainment card Aperitif/specialty wines Classical records Valid passports	Hunting Pickup trucks CB radios Watch roller derby
	These people are especially LIKELY to eat:	*These people are especially UNLIKELY to eat:*
	Natural cold cereal Whole-wheat bread	Presweetened cold cereal Canned stews
	These people are especially LIKELY to watch:	*These people are especially UNLIKELY to watch:*
	"At the Movies" "Murder, She Wrote"	"Super Password" "As the World Turns"
Smalltown Downtown (Avoidance role)	*These people are especially LIKELY to use, buy, or do:*	*These people are especially UNLIKELY to use, buy, or do:*
	Salt-water fishing rods Watch pro wrestling Cafeterias Gospel records/tapes	Money-market funds Racquetball Travel/entertainment cards Chewing tobacco
	These people are especially LIKELY to eat:	*These people are especially UNLIKELY to eat:*
	Canned meat spreads Packaged instant potatoes	Natural cold cereal Mexican foods
	These people are especially LIKELY to watch:	*These people are especially UNLIKELY to watch:*
	"Scrabble" "The Today Show"	"The Tonight Show" "Late Night with David Letterman"

Note. Data adapted from "To Be *and* Not to Be?: Reference Group Stereotyping and *The Clustering of America*," by B. G. Englis and M. R. Solomon, 1995, *Journal of Advertising, 24* (Spring), 13-28.
[a]Consumption data are taken from Weiss (1988).

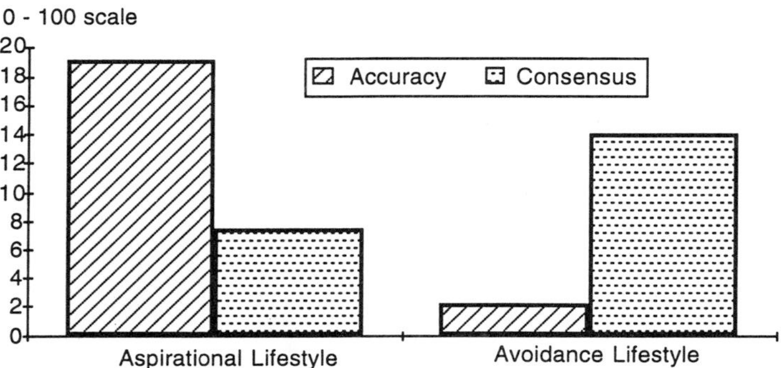

FIG. 2.3. Interaction between measure (accuracy vs. consensus) and lifestyle category (avoidance vs. aspirational). The interaction was statistically significant. *Note.* Data adapted from "To Be *and* Not to Be?: Reference Group Stereotyping and *The Clustering of America*," by B. G. Englis and M. R. Solomon, 1995, *Journal of Advertising, 24* (Spring), 13–28.

scribed (Fig. 2.3 plots the means of this interaction). These data indicate that while consumers are accurate in their perceptions of the products associated with lifestyles to which they aspire, they do not exhibit high levels of agreement with one another about these products. In contrast, consumers form highly stereotyped images of avoidance lifestyles.

Quantification of the data does not capture the connotative richness that emerges from the open-ended protocol used in the present study. In order to illustrate the richness of this content we provide the following descriptions of the constellations associated with aspirational and avoidance groups by more than 15% of the sample. None of these products was "cross-listed" in the consumption constellations associated with other lifestyles.

An Aspirational Lifestyle. The PRIZM cluster "Money & Brains" was the aspirational lifestyle for our sample. It is characterized by Weiss (1988, pp. 272–275) as the lifestyle where ". . . Residents buy investment property, sailboats, classical records and designer telephones at many times the national average. . . . They're big purchasers of salted nuts, snack cheeses and specialty wines—all the ingredients for a cocktail party except stimulating conversation." Our consumers perceived this group as likely to drive BMWs (53.6%), Mercedes (50.7%), Cadillacs (30.4%), Volvos (23.2%), Porsches (21.7%), Acuras(17.4%), and Jaguars (15.9%). This group of products compares well with the top cars in the PRIZM data—BMWs, Jaguars, Mercedes, Rolls Royces, and Ferraris. The aspirational group was perceived as reading travel magazines (21.7%), *Vogue* (21.7%), *Business Week* (20.3%), *Fortune* (17.9%), and *GQ* (15.9%). The actual top magazines/newspapers are *Forbes, Barron's, The New Yorker,* and *Gourmet.* The alcoholic beverages most closely associated with this group are Heineken beer (33.3%), expensive wines (26.1%), Scotch (18.8%), champagne (17.4%), and Beck's beer (15%). Finally, they are perceived as likely users of Polo (27.5%), Obsession (15.9%), and Drakkar Noir (15.9%).

An Avoidance Lifestyle. The avoidance group for our sample presents a sharp contrast to the aspired-to lifestyle. The avoidance group corresponds to the "Smalltown Downtown" cluster in the PRIZM scheme and is characterized as a group that tends ". . . to travel less by plane or train than average Americans . . . Their idea of a vacation is to go camping, fishing, and hiking, and their home-based leisure pursuits would make a preppie blanch: They like to watch wrestling and Roller Derby, go out for a cafeteria dinner or a Tupperware party and listen to gospel and country music" (Weiss, 1988, p. 364). The cars most closely associated with this lifestyle group were pick-up trucks (34.8%), Chevys (23.2%), and Fords (18.8%). As noted by Weiss (1988) this group buys cars at very modest rates and indeed buys no cars at higher than national rates. However, Chevrolet (Chevettes and Spectrums), Isuzus, and Plymouth Gran Furys are among those most likely to be purchased. The magazines associated with this group included *People* (30.4%), *Sports Illustrated* (26.1%), *TV Guide* (24.6%), *Wrestling* (21.7%), fishing magazines (20.3%), and the *National Enquirer* (18.8%). Weiss lists *Sporting News, Colonial Homes, True Story,* and *Southern Living* as the high usage magazines for this group. Budweiser was seen as the most preferred beer for this group (59.4%) followed by Miller (24.6%) and Coors (18.8%). Jack Daniels (15%) was the only distilled spirit, and no wines were associated with this lifestyle. Finally, personal care products included Brut (15.9%), Old Spice (15%), and Mennen Speed Stick (15.1%).

Study III

To the extent that lifestyle categories are associated with specific patterns of contingent consumption, then, we can predict that the conditional probabilities for the consumption of products within the target constellation will be higher than among the population at large. We examined patterns of contingent consumption associated with a particular 1980s media creation known as the "YUPPIE" (Solomon & Buchanan, 1991). For the purposes of this study "YUPPIE" demographics were taken as 25–44 year-old men and women residing in urban areas (more than 100,000 people) earning more than $20,000 annually. We then examined contingent patterns of consumption for a group of products and activities "stereotypically" identified with the yuppie lifestyle, such as deluxe ice creams, imported wines, foreign cars, and playing squash. The data used in this analysis came from the Simmons Study of Media and Markets.

The conditional probabilities for consuming the products in each category selected were higher for the YUPPIE group than for U.S. consumers as a whole. Of course, data of this form can tell us little if anything about causal linkages between the media depictions of YUPPIEs on the one hand and their consumption preferences on the other. However, the contingencies found among this group of symbolically related product categories lends credence to the assumption that consumers organize consumption information and activities along lines of symbolic and not simply functional attributes. The results also support the "grain-of-truth" stereotyping hypothesis (Allport, 1954), insofar as a cluster of distinctive product and media choices was in fact jointly consumed by a (largely marketer-defined) lifestyle group.

Conclusions

The consumer studies reveal that lifestyle-oriented information is readily assimilated from mass-media vehicles. Even though music television is not overtly attempting to "sell" a style to its audience, viewers learn what "looks" do or do not fit a particular music genre. We also find that consumers' cognitive representations of different lifestyles vary in both content and structure as a function of their valuation of these lifestyles. Consumers' motivations to emulate or avoid particular lifestyles mediate their acquisition and cognitive representation of information about that lifestyle.

WORK IN PROGRESS AND FUTURE RESEARCH DIRECTIONS

The studies reviewed in this chapter provide an initial glimpse at the process whereby the lifestyle data collected and analyzed by market researchers are transformed into culturally and psychologically meaningful entities for consumers. Taken as a whole, the results show that media gatekeepers are consistent with each other in their decisions of how to depict particular social types. Gatekeepers' choices are also tied to specific media vehicles and cultural genres. Our two-tiered perspective on the encoding and decoding of lifestyle information from media sources raises a number of issues that need to be addressed in further research.

The overlooked role of cultural gatekeepers in the realm of symbolic encoding needs more exploration. Future work needs to examine the process whereby gatekeepers select and design consumption imagery that is then passed on to consumers. We have focused our preliminary work on a few types of gatekeepers, notably property masters, music video directors, and fashion editors. In addition, other gatekeepers—ranging from casting directors, costume designers, and advertising creatives to retail buyers, window dressers, and fashion journalists—are also deserving of attention.

Another issue relates to the conceptual and practical importance of *contextual congruity*: To what extent is there a perceived "fit" between a target product and the collateral products, settings, and other cues used to position the item in a lifestyle category? Although research on contextual effects by marketers is in its infancy (e.g., Kleine & Kernan, 1991), the current perspective underscores the relevance of this topic. In addition to its possible role in facilitating or inhibiting message acceptance, contextual cues are germane to a host of strategic decisions, including cross-merchandising, product placement, and the design of infomercials.

Similarly, the use of collateral cues by consumers as they decode product messages is worthy of further attention. Again, while little work has been done on advertising context, our research to date indicates that viewers actively incorporate this information in their cognitive representations of product and lifestyle information.

Finally, this research and the resulting data draw our attention to the need to compare the choices of gatekeepers with the idealized images that audience members are themselves striving to achieve. The gulf between perception and reality may be more than academic. This issue may in fact be pivotal when it comes to understanding how consumers structure their consumption activities in light of the (perceived) associations between products and services on the one hand, and social life on the other.

REFERENCES

Allport, G. W. (1954). *The nature of prejudice*. Reading, MA: Addison-Wesley.

Boorstin, D. J. (1961). *The image: A guide to pseudo-events in America*. New York: Vintage.

Cantor, N., & Mischel, W. (1979). Prototypes in person perception. In L. Berkowitz (Ed.), *Advances in experimental social psychology* (Vol. 12, pp. 4–52). New York: Academic Press.

Englis, B. G., & Solomon, M. R. (1993). *The role of context products in the effectiveness of print advertisements*. Rutgers University, unpublished manuscript.

Englis, B. G., & Solomon, M. R. (1995). To be *and* not to be?: Reference group stereotyping and the clustering of America. *Journal of Advertising, 24*, 13–28.

Englis, B. G., Solomon, M. R., & Ashmore, R. D. (1994). Beauty before the eyes of beholders: The cultural encoding of beauty types in magazine advertising and music television. *Journal of Advertising, 23*, 49–64.

Englis, B. G., Solomon, M. R., & Olofsson, A. (1993a). Music television as teen image agent: A preliminary report from the United States and Sweden. In G. Bamossy & F. Von Raij (Eds.), *European Advances in Consumer Research* (Vol. 1, pp. 449–450). Provo, UT: Association for Consumer Research.

Englis, B. G., Solomon, M. R., & Olofsson, A. (1993b). Consumption imagery in music television: A bi-cultural perspective. *Journal of Advertising, 22*(4), 21–34.

Faber, R. J., & O'Guinn, T. C. (1988). Expanding the view of consumer socialization: A nonutilitarian mass-mediated perspective. In E. C. Hirschman & J. N. Sheth (Eds.), *Research in consumer behavior* (Vol. 3, pp. 49–78). Greenwich, CT: JAI.

Fry, D. L., & Fry, V. H. (1987). Some structural characteristics of music television videos. *The Southern Speech Communication Journal, 52,* 151–164.

Gerbner, G., Gross, L., Signorielli, N., & Morgan, M. (1980). Aging with television: Images on television drama and conceptions of social reality. *Journal of Communication, 30,* 37–47.

Kaplan, E. A. (1987). *Rocking around the clock: Music television, postmodernism, and consumer culture.* New York: Methuen.

Kleine, R. E., III, & Kernan, J. B. (1991). Contextual influences on the meanings ascribed to ordinary consumption objects. *Journal of Consumer Research, 18,* 311–324.

Marketing Insights. (1989). A dream world labeled Lauren, June, 9.

McCracken, G. (1988). *Culture and consumption: New approaches to the symbolic character of consumer goods and activities.* Bloomington: Indiana University Press.

Rosch, E. (1978). Principles of categorization. In E. Rosch & B. B. Lloyd (Eds.), *Recognition and Categorization.* Hillsdale, NJ: Lawrence Erlbaum Associates.

Solomon, M. R. (1988). Mapping product constellations: A social categorization approach to symbolic consumption. *Psychology & Marketing, 5*(3), 233–258.

Solomon, M. R., & Assael, H. (1987). The forest or the trees?: A gestalt approach to symbolic consumption. In J. Umiker-Sebeok (Ed.), *Marketing and semiotics: New directions in the study of signs for sale* (pp. 189–218). Berlin: Mouton de Gruyter.

Solomon, M. R., & Buchanan, B. (1991). A role-theoretic approach to product symbolism: Mapping a consumption constellation. *Journal of Business Research, 22,* 95–110.

Solomon, M. R., & Greenberg, L. (1993). Setting the stage: Collective selection in the stylistic content of commercials. *Journal of Advertising, 22,* 11–24.

Solomon, M. R., Ashmore, R. D., & Longo, L. C. (1992). The beauty match-up hypothesis: Convergence of types of beauty and product images in advertising. *Journal of Advertising, 21,* 23–34.

Weiss, M. J. (1988). *The clustering of America.* New York: Harper & Row.

Wells, W. D. (1975). Psychographics: A critical review. *Journal of Marketing Research, 12,* 196–213.

Wells, W. D., & Tigert, D. J. (1971). Activities, interests, and opinions. *Journal of Advertising Research, 11,* 27–35.

Chapter 3

The Value of Understanding the Influence of Lifestyle Trait Motivations on Consumption Beliefs

John P. Murry, Jr.
Case Western Reserve University

John L. Lastovicka
Arizona State University

Jon R. Austin
James Madison University

Over a decade ago, Lutz (1979) observed that consumer research has unfortunately viewed personality and multiattribute belief research "... as alternative 'models' in their own right rather than facets of a more general framework" (p. 37). Although the value of personality theory in attitude research has been recently recognized (Haugtvedt, Petty, & Cacioppo, 1992), the theoretical link between personality traits and consumption beliefs has been largely ignored in empirical marketing research. Therefore, the present research presents a general framework for integrating the personality and multiattribute belief approaches to understanding consumer preferences and behaviors. Specifically, this chapter introduces a motivational approach in which personality or lifestyle traits are used to explain *why* consumers hold specific consumption beliefs. The premise is that understanding *why* these beliefs are held will enable marketers to develop more effective strategies for forming, maintaining, and changing these beliefs.

The next section provides a background on how marketers have traditionally used personality traits and consumption beliefs to examine consumer behaviors. An integrative model is then developed in which lifestyle traits are hypothesized to influence beliefs which in turn influence consumption behaviors; this theoretical model is empirically tested and replicated. Finally, the implications for developing more effective marketing communication programs and avenues for future research are discussed.

BACKGROUND

The "Direct Effects" model in Fig. 3.1 reflects the common practice of examining the impact of lifestyle traits and consumption beliefs on consumer behaviors without considering the potential relationship between traits and beliefs. Thus, this model assumes that lifestyle traits and consumption beliefs have an independent influence on behavior. The following sections review basic ideas and practices that have characterized the lifestyle trait and multiattribute belief research traditions in marketing.

Lifestyle Traits and Behavior

Following from Smith, Brunner, and White (1956), traits are viewed as stable personality characteristics that motivate individuals to achieve some consistency of goal seeking over a variety of behaviors. Whereas traits bring consistency to individual behavior, traits also contribute to differences in

Direct Effects Model

LT1 B1 Beh LT2 B2

Mediated Effects Model

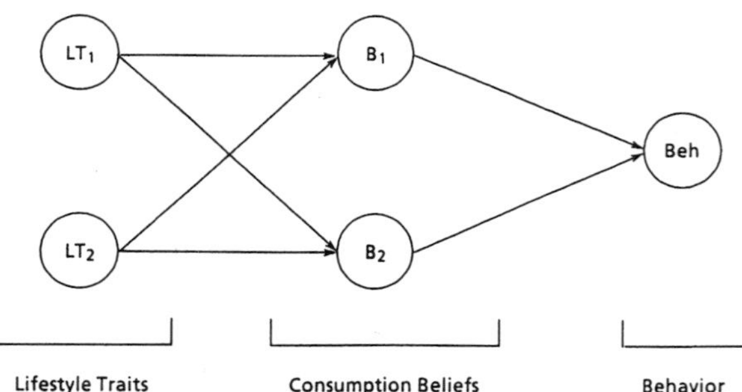

FIG. 3.1. Lifestyle traits, consumption beliefs, and behavior in direct effects and mediated effects models.

behaviors across people. As such, traits are most commonly applied in market research to either form market segments or describe segments formed on other bases (Wells, 1975). Although traits cannot be measured directly, they can be inferred by observing regularities and consistencies in reported behaviors and preferences (Smith et al., 1956). Unlike beliefs about the consequences associated with various behaviors, traits are less action- or outcome-specific; traits reflect more enduring and general dispositions to engage in behaviors.

Empirical research in marketing has found that personality traits are, at best, only modestly good predictors of specific consumption behaviors (Kassarjian & Sheffet, 1991). This is not surprising given that general personality traits are developed to describe modal behavioral tendencies and not specific consumption behaviors. In contrast, lifestyle traits are constructed to be directly relevant to the acquisition, use, and disposition of specific products. As such, lifestyle research has become a cornerstone in many well-informed marketing communications programs. Because lifestyle traits are a specific type of personality trait, lifestyle trait research shares the theory and methods found in the more general personality trait research tradition. The key distinction is that lifestyle traits are secondary dispositions that are operative in limited settings or roles rather than "cardinal" dispositions that influence a broad range of behaviors (Allport, 1961; Lastovicka, 1982).

Market researchers frequently supplement the motivational insights provided by consumer lifestyle research with more concrete and actionable data reflecting consumer beliefs about specific product attributes or consequences (e.g., Lastovicka, Murry, Joachimsthaler, Bhalla, & Scheurich, 1987). In fact, Kassarjian and Sheffet (1991) comment that personality research is bound to fail if it does not account for the *combined effects* of traits *and* other cognitions including more concrete beliefs. While Kassarjian and Sheffet clearly call for research that goes beyond the *isolated* examination of trait effects alone, they do not provide guidance as to how traits and other cognitions like beliefs are related. In fact, consumer theory in general provides little direction on this matter. Therefore, there is a need for an integrative theory to eliminate the current practice of speculating as to how consumer lifestyle traits relate to specific beliefs about products (e.g., Horn, 1991).

Consumption Beliefs and Behavior

Beliefs are interpretations of the environment that people learn, store, and process in order to guide their behaviors. Consumers form consumption beliefs by learning to associate the various attributes and consequences of a product with its use. Marketers have traditionally held that changes in these beliefs are closely related to changes in market related behaviors (Lutz, 1975); hence, marketing strategy is frequently based on the competitive insights that knowledge about these beliefs can provide (Day, 1990, p. 140). As such, research that identifies relevant consumption beliefs is an integral tool in developing and executing effective marketing programs.

In their theory of reasoned action, Ajzen and Fishbein (1980) made an important distinction between the role that beliefs play in *predicting* behavior and *understanding* its causes. They argued that behavior is best predicted by direct measures of one's intention to perform the behavior; however, influencing or changing a behavior requires a deeper understanding of the beliefs that guide behavior intentions. The implication is that marketers should identify and manage the beliefs that guide consumption intentions and behavior. This observation naturally raises two interrelated questions: Why are determinant beliefs held? and How can these beliefs be most effectively formed, reinforced, or changed?

An unfortunate limitation of multiattribute theories is that they do not directly address these two key questions. For example, Ajzen and Fishbein (1980) noted, ". . . a behavior is explained once its determinants have been traced to the underlying beliefs" (p. 90). Nonetheless, other research suggests that attempts to manage these beliefs can be ineffectual if not guided by a clear understanding of *why* these beliefs are held (Locander & Spivey, 1978). Interestingly, although the reasons for holding beliefs is not addressed in their formal theory, Ajzen and Fishbein do comment that personality variables are ". . . sometimes viewed as residues of past experience or are assumed to influence the person's interpretation of the environment and thus the beliefs he holds" (p. 90). Accordingly, personality and lifestyle traits, as representations of past experience, should influence what consumers believe. By examining the relationship between these traits and specific beliefs, marketers might begin to understand why the beliefs are held. This may not improve the ability to predict behavior, but it should enhance the ability to influence it by guiding the development of messages that reinforce or change underlying beliefs. The next section builds on these ideas by developing an integrative model for understanding the relationship between traits, beliefs, and behaviors.

TOWARD AN INTEGRATED MODEL

Motivations for Holding Consumption Beliefs

The functional attitude theories (Katz, 1960; Katz, Sarnoff, & McClintock, 1956; Katz & Stotland, 1959; Smith, 1947; Smith et al., 1956) view humans as organisms striving after certain goals and analyze attitudes in terms of their facilitative or inhibitive effects on attaining these goals. To pick an example not at random, a 20-year-old male could be characterized by a lifestyle trait of general dissatisfaction with life.[1] Further, assume this young man has a variety of beliefs or attitudes consistent with the goal of reversing this dissatisfaction. He may hold utilitarian beliefs toward alcohol, including beliefs that alcohol will serve as a "social lubricant" beneficial for meeting and attracting young women. Other beliefs have the function of giving expression to different aspects of an individual's personality. As such, this same young male may also be characterized as aggressive or "macho" in nature. Consequently, holding the belief that drinking alcohol does not impair his own physical or mental coordination gives expression to his aggressive macho self.

Past consumer research based on the functional theories (Locander & Spivey, 1978; Lutz, 1978, 1979, 1981) has been concerned with identifying or measuring the functions that attitudes perform. The present research will not add to the list of attitude functions as the identified functions apparently serve well for most applications (cf. Herek, 1987; Pratkanis, Breckler, & Greenwald, 1989; Shavitt, 1989, 1990; Snyder & DeBono, 1985). Moreover, it is not clear whether the identification of general attitude functions provides marketing researchers with enough guidance to develop effective messages. For instance, beliefs about alcohol consumption may perform an ego-expressive function, but developing effective advertising copy necessarily requires knowledge about the specific ego or self that the attitude is expressing. Therefore, we agree with Cohen (1978) that consumer research should focus on identifying those motivations and beliefs that are relevant to the specific consumption behaviors being investigated rather than searching for some generic set of attitude functions.

This issue is partially addressed through the network of relationships proposed in Rokeach's (1973) personal values theory. He conceptualizes personality as a hierarchical system of enduring beliefs composed of valued end states (terminal values) and beliefs about preferred modes of conduct for achieving these end states (instrumental values). Hence, the beliefs that consumers hold about the consequences of behaviors are linked to the achievement or expression of valued end states. The similarity between personal values research and functional attitude theory is apparent in Katz' (1989) recent comments on the latter: "It tried to combine beliefs and motives and to take into account the diversity of motivational patterns.

[1]Although the labels given to traits may vary, the satisfaction-with-life trait herein is comparable to trait IV identified in John's (1990) review as one of the "Big Five" personality traits. John's trait IV—which ranges from calm relaxed confidence to anxiety proneness and chronic sadness—is one of five traits that have consistently emerged over several decades of personality research by different investigators. John notes that trait IV has had various labels, including "satisfaction."

Attitudes were seen as a means for meeting some need of the individual including personal *value systems*" (p. xii; emphasis added). Thus, functional attitude theory maintains and reinforces the basic ideas found in personal values theory.

Support for the links between personal values, product beliefs, and behaviors are available from a variety of sources in the marketing literature. Howard (1989) links Rokeach's terminal values to beliefs about the brand and then to brand attitudes and choice behavior. Homer and Kahle (1988) provide empirical support for a hierarchical model that links values, attitudes, and behaviors using the List of Values (LOV). Perhaps the most managerially useful application of this hierarchical approach is found in Gutman's (1982) "means–end chain" model. This approach uses lengthy laddering interviews to build a rich context for understanding why consumers hold consumption beliefs. The dependence of this approach on relatively small sample sizes, however, makes it difficult to generalize the resulting models to more substantial target segments. Therefore, a more useful approach would afford similar insights, yet retain the convenience, efficiency, and representativeness that characterize more traditional survey research.

A Lifestyle Trait → Consumption Belief → Behavior Model

Both functional attitude theory and personal values theory argue that understanding *why* beliefs are held is critical for developing effective programs that develop, reinforce, or change those beliefs. Although theory directs marketing researchers to examine the motivational bases for consumption beliefs, practical problems in implementing these theories have limited their application. Most importantly, the various lists of attitude functions and values are often too circumscribed and abstract to help marketers manage actual communications campaigns. That is, while theory may point to the importance of understanding self-expressive motivations, it does not provide a framework for identifying the specific values or traits that are being expressed.

Reviews of the personality (Pervin, 1990) and consumer research literature (Kassarjian & Sheffet, 1991) reveal that the inventory of human needs and motives is so diverse that it may be myopic to rely on, as in the case of Kahle's LOV, only 9 values. Consumer researchers readily accept that there is no universal set of attributes that characterize all products. Similarly, given the diversity of human motivations, relying on some set of universal person-motivating characteristics for all consumer behaviors may be shortsighted. In response to these problems, the present research proposes an integrated modeling approach which requires researchers to carefully define and measure relevant lifestyle traits, consumption beliefs, and consumption behaviors. As illustrated in the "mediated effects" model in Fig. 3.1, these variables are expected to be hierarchically related with consumption beliefs mediating the effect of traits on behavior. Consistent with multiattribute modeling, the researcher must hypothesize which beliefs will impact behavior. What distinguishes our approach is that the researcher must also hypothesize the relationships between specific lifestyle traits and beliefs by considering the motivational influence of the former on the latter. Although the example in Fig. 3.1 shows *all* traits influencing *all* beliefs, it is more likely that each trait will influence only *some* of the beliefs depending on the behavior being studied.

Our "mediated effects" modeling approach embraces the premise of functional-attitude and personal-values theory that views traits as the motivational underpinnings of consumption beliefs. Thus, the model depicts differences in behaviors as being explained by differences in consumption beliefs; further, consumption beliefs are explained by differences in lifestyle traits. As the bulk of the previous discussion implies, the mediated effects model is hypothesized to better represent the interrelationship of consumers' beliefs, traits, and behaviors than will a "direct effects" model. Specifically, lifestyle traits are predicted to influence consumption behaviors through their influence on consumption beliefs.

The next section provides an empirical comparison of the direct effects and the mediated effects models within the context of young male alcohol consumption. The goal of this investigation is to examine the relative usefulness of these models in explaining drinking behavior and providing information that could be utilized to develop mass media messages for alcohol health education programs.

MODELING YOUTHFUL ALCOHOL CONSUMPTION

The problems associated with young male alcohol abuse are well documented (Koop, 1988). Moreover, there have been numerous calls for consumer and marketing researchers to conduct theoretically rigorous research in the context of important social problems (Andreasen, 1993; Hirschman, 1991; Lutz, 1991). The context of young male alcohol consumption is well suited for studying models of traits and beliefs; in particular, Mooney and Concoran (1989) argue that alcohol studies based on a combination of beliefs and personality variables offer the best insights for developing programs to counter heavy drinking behaviors. The following discussion briefly reviews the expected relationships between the specific traits, beliefs, and alcohol consumption behaviors modeled in this research.

Alcohol Consumption Research

The empirical version of the hypothesized mediated effects model for young male alcohol consumption is depicted in Fig. 3.2. Although the alternative direct effects model is not illustrated with a figure, this model can be derived from Fig. 3.2 by deleting the γs leading from traits to beliefs and then inserting γ's leading from traits to behavior. As is subsequently described, the lifestyle traits and alcohol consumption beliefs used in the empirical version of both models were developed from a review of the alcohol literature and qualitative research with heavy drinking young males.

Consumption Beliefs and Behavior. Qualitative research and past alcohol research indicated that two beliefs are particularly important in understanding the volume of young male alcohol consumption. First, heavy drinkers are more likely to believe that alcohol facilitates social interactions. Young males perceive that alcohol helps them relax, lowers their inhibitions, and makes them more conversant with women (Fitzgerald & Mulford, 1984; Matros & Hines, 1982; Plant, Bagnall, & Foster, 1990). Second, heavy drinkers are also less likely to believe that alcohol diminishes their physical or mental abilities. Thus, they do not associate alcohol consumption with negative outcomes such as diminished motor skills, loss of self-control, or poor judgment (Kline, Canter, & Robin, 1987; Plant et al., 1990).

Lifestyle Traits and Alcohol Consumption Beliefs. Lifestyle research has characterized heavy beer drinkers as being more macho (Wells, 1975) and personality research frequently links male aggression to heavy alcohol consumption and alcohol abuse problems (Knorring, Knorring, Smigan, Lindberg, & Edholm, 1987). In addition, qualitative interviews indicated that aggressive young males were less likely to believe that alcohol impairs either their cognitive or motor abilities. Prior survey research also finds male aggressiveness associated with an increased propensity to engage in risky behaviors such as drinking and driving (Lastovicka et al., 1987). Therefore, the trait "male aggressiveness" should be negatively related to the belief that alcohol diminishes abilities. Qualitative research also indicated that aggressive males considered alcohol consumption to be an integral part of their social activities. As previously noted, alcohol diminishes these young males' inhibitions and helps them express their macho values in social settings. Therefore, the trait male aggressiveness is expected to be positively associated with the belief that "alcohol helps socially."

Past personality research has associated alcohol consumption problems with consumers who generally feel dissatisfied with life (Mayer, 1988). Similar results have been reported in the consumer behavior literature where Mehrota and Wells (1977) characterize heavy drinkers as being

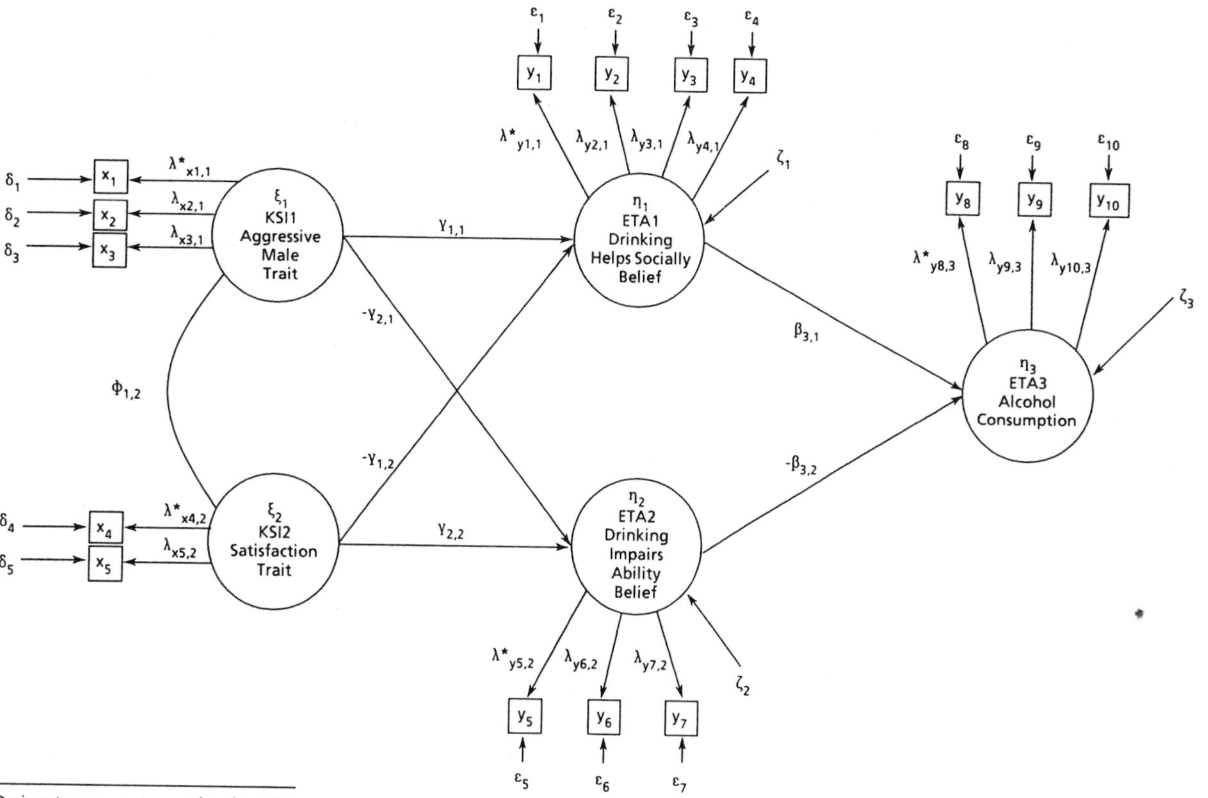

FIG. 3.2. Structural equations model for alcohol consumption.

dissatisfied with life. Apparently, consumers believe that alcohol soothes distress, diminishes arousal, and minimizes negative feelings (Wilson, 1987). These perceived therapeutic benefits are frequently realized in social settings where alcohol's disinhibiting effects facilitate social interactions. In fact, Hover and Gaffney (1991) argue that alcohol abuse problems are frequently a symptom caused by not possessing effective social skills for dealing with life problems. As a result, many alcohol treatment programs include social skills training as an integral component of alcoholism recovery (Wilson, 1987). Based on this literature, the trait "satisfaction with life" is expected to be negatively related to a belief that alcohol facilitates social interactions and positively related to a belief that alcohol impairs cognitive and motor abilities (see fn 1).

RESEARCH METHOD

Data from two independent sample surveys of young male drinkers were used to test the "direct effects" and "mediated effects" models. Identical measures for all concepts in both surveys provided an opportunity to test the stability of findings in a second data set. With the goal of replication in mind, Sample Survey I was used for an initial analysis while Sample Survey II provided an opportunity to conduct a replication test.

Populations and Sampling

Two independent telephone sample surveys were conducted. The sample for Sample Survey I was a telephone survey of 864 18- to 24-year-old males conducted in four midwestern Standard Metropolitan Statistical Areas (SMSA). Within each SMSA, phone subscribing households were selected with random digit dialing and then screened for 18- to 24-year-old males; eligible young males were then randomly selected within household. The response rates at the four sites ranged from 88% to 91%. Overall, 77% of these young males claimed to have consumed alcohol in the past month. The replication data from Sample Survey II was collected in a statewide phone survey of some 700 18- to 24-year-olds from a midwestern state that obtained a 91% response rate. Fully 80% of these young males reported drinking in the past month.

Measurement

The questionnaire inquired about: lifestyle traits, beliefs about alcohol and its effects, alcohol-related behaviors, and demographics. The trait and belief measures used a 4-point "strongly disagree–strongly agree" scale for each questionnaire item. In light of the available methodological literature (Givon & Shapiro, 1984; Groves & Kahn, 1979), the collection of trait or belief data with 4-point scales is justified in telephone surveys. The alcohol consumption questions asked about the frequency of consuming different volumes of alcohol (i.e., 1 or 2 drinks vs. 3 or 4 drinks at a time) during the past month; these questions used a 7-point scale ranging from *never* to *every day*.

Table 3.1 contains the items used to measure the lifestyle traits, consumption beliefs, and behaviors in both sample surveys. At the top of this table are the sets of items used to assess the two traits: Aggressive Male Orientation and Satisfaction with Life. This is followed by the items used to assess the belief that Drinking Helps Socially and the belief that Drinking Impairs Ability. Finally, the alcohol consumption measures are listed at the bottom of Table 3.1.

RESULTS

Overview

The analysis had three steps. First was an examination of the data for necessary distribution assumptions. Next the covariances from Sample Survey I were modeled with LISREL 7 using maximum likelihood estimation (Jöreskog & Sörbom, 1990); these analyses evaluated empirical models guided by the competing ideas represented by Fig. 3.1. Finally, these models' stability were examined with a replication test implemented by LISREL modeling of Sample Survey II's covariances.

Distribution Assumptions

The distribution properties of the data were examined with Jöreskog and Sörbom's (1986) PRELIS program. Mardia's (1970) measure of multivariate relative kurtosis was 1.13 for the initial data and 1.15 for the replication data. Whereas these values were less than 1.96, Mardia's test rejects the hypothesis of excessive kurtosis; thus implying multivariate normality for both sets of data. Consequently, the use of maximum likelihood estimation with LISREL was justified.

Initial Analysis in Sample Survey I Data

In addition to estimating the direct effects and mediated effects models, analysis of the data collected in Sample Survey I included estimating a third model that was termed the *common path* model. Although this research concerns the comparative fit of the direct effects and the mediated effects models, these two models are not nested and thus cannot be directly

TABLE 3.1
Constructs, Empirical Measures, and Standardized Measurement Model Parameters for the Mediated Effects Model

Construct	Empirical Measures[a]		Measurement Model Estimates[b]			
			Survey I		Survey II	
			KSI1	KSI2	KSI1	KSI2
Aggressive male trait (KSI1)	It is important for me to act and dress like a tough guy.	(x1)	.61[c]	.00	.59[c]	.00
	If somebody gives me a hard enough time, I'll punch him.	(x2)	.55	.00	.51	.00
	There should be a gun in every home.	(x3)	.41	.00	.40	.00
Satisfaction trait (KSI2)	I am happier now than I ever was before.	(x4)	.00	.59[c]	.00	.57[c]
	Overall, I'd say I'm very happy.	(x5)	.00	.71	.00	.68
Fornell-Larcker average variance extracted			.76	.67	.78	.80

			ETA1	ETA2	ETA3	ETA1	ETA2	ETA3
Drinking helps socially belief (ETA1)	People who drink have more fun than people who don't.	(y1)	.58[c]	.00	.00	.42[c]	.00	.00
	Drinking helps a guy do better with girls.	(y2)	.60	.00	.00	.60	.00	.00
	People who drink have more friends than those who don't.	(y3)	.46	.00	.00	.35	.00	.00
	Having something to drink at a party helps you talk to other people.	(y4)	.57	.00	.00	.49	.00	.00
Drinking impairs ability belief (ETA2)	Even if you only have a little bit to drink, you start to lose your self-control.	(y5)	.00	.57[c]	.00	.00	.43[c]	.00
	Having only a few drinks can noticeably impair your speaking and coordination.	(y6)	.00	.69	.00	.00	.59	.00
	You can make a fool of yourself in front of your buddies from drinking too much.	(y7)	.00	.35	.00	.00	.37	.00
Alcohol consumed (ETA3)	How many times during the past month did you have . . .							
	5-6 drinks at a time?	(y8)	.00	.00	.80[c]	.00	.00	.81[c]
	3-4 drinks at a time?	(y9)	.00	.00	.97	.00	.00	.97
	1-2 drinks at a time?	(y10)	.00	.00	.71	.00	.00	.66
Fornell-Larcker average variance extracted			.83	.74	.65	.77	.77	.63

[a]Coding for x1-x8 and y1-y7 was 1 = strongly disagree, 2 = disagree, 3 = agree, 4 = strongly agree; for y8-y10: 0 = never, 1 = once a month, 2 = 2-3 times a month, 3 = 1-2 times a week, 4 = 3-4 times a week, 5 = almost every day, and 6 = daily.
[b]Values shown as .00 were restricted to zero during estimation
[c]Corresponding values were restricted to 1.00 in the nonstandardized model.

compared. Therefore, it was necessary to estimate a third model, labeled the "common path model," in which the traits had *both* mediated and direct effects on behavior because both the direct effects and mediated effects are nested in this model. That is, this third model had γs from traits to beliefs and γs from traits to behaviors; thus, it allows an indirect comparison of the direct and mediated effects models, but is not intended as an additional theoretical model.

The maximum likelihood estimates for the structural parameters of the direct effects and mediated effects models are presented in Table 3.2. Due to space constraints and redundancy in results, measurement parameter estimates for both models are not reported in Table 3.2. However, Table 3.1 does contain measurement model estimates for the hypothesized mediated effects model.

Preliminary Evaluation. Before examining the relative merits of the alternative models, some properties of the individual parameters and some aspects of the models' measurement properties are briefly described. To begin, all estimated models were free from anomalies like negative variances or extremely large parameter values; this suggests freedom from model specification and identification problems. Second, with respect to the measurement model properties, all estimated factor loadings had t values with absolute values greater than 1.96. Third, again with respect to the measurement models, the Fornell–Larcker (1981) average variance extracted coefficient was computed for the constructs; this coefficient measures the variance captured by the construct in relation to the variation due to measurement error. These coefficients were all above 0.50, the threshold of "adequacy" for this measurement statistic, suggesting the measures were sufficiently reliable. Fornell–Larcker coefficients for the mediated effects model are reported in Table 3.1.[2]

Evaluation of Alternative Models. The top half of Table 3.2 contains the estimated structural parameters for the two competing theoretical models. The parameter estimates for the direct effects model performance in Sample Survey I are presented in the first column of Table 3.2. These results show that beliefs influenced behavior as predicted. Specifically, the sign and size of the t value associated with $\beta_{3,1}$ reveals that holding the drinking-helps-socially belief is associated with more frequent drinking; and the sign and size of the t value associated with $\beta_{3,2}$ means that believing that drinking impairs ability is associated with less frequent drinking behavior. The nonsignificant estimates for $\gamma_{3,1}$ and $\gamma_{3,2}$ reveal no direct effect of traits

[2]The structural models of the Sample Survey II data were also all characterized as having: (1) a lack of anomalous values, (2) significant t values for all factor loadings, and (3) satisfactory values for the Fornell–Larcker coefficient.

TABLE 3.2
Structural Parameter Estimates and Goodness-of-Fit Indices

	Standardized Estimates (t-Values)			
	Sample Survey I Estimates for Models:		*Sample Survey II Estimates for Models:*	
Parameter	*Direct Effects*	*Mediated Effects*	*Direct Effects*	*Mediated Effects*
BETA 3,1 Facilitating Belief ->Drinking	.36 (7.2)	.37 (7.4)	.29 (6.4)	.32 (5.9)
BETA 3,2 Impair Belief ->Drinking	-.20 (-4.2)	-.16 (-3.5)	-.13 (-2.4)	-.08 (-1.5)
GAMMA 1,1 Aggressive Trait ->Drinking Helps Belief	.00	.52 (6.8)	.00	.32 (3.8)
GAMMA 2,1 Aggressive Trait ->Drinking Impairs Belief	.00	-.35 (-4.7)	.00	-.23 (-2.3)
GAMMA 1,2 Satisfaction Trait ->Drinking Helps Belief	.00	-.20 (-3.3)	.00	-.43 (-5.0)
GAMMA 2,2 Satisfaction Trait ->Drinking Impairs Belief	.00	.13 (2.0)	.00	.45 (4.2)
GAMMA 3,1 Aggressive Trait -> Drinking	.06 (1.2)	.00	.21 (3.1)	.00
GAMMA 3,2 Satisfaction Trait ->Drinking	-.06 (-1.3)	.00	.09 (1.5)	.00
Fit Indices				
X^2	409.72	232.00	534.02	274.60
df	85	83	85	83
p	.00	.00	.00	.00
T-L rho	.91	.96	.89	.96
B-B delta	.93	.96	.90	.95
AGFI	.91	.95	.89	.94
RMR	.06	.03	.06	.04

Note. Parameters omitted above (e.g., BETA 2,2 or GAMMA 1,3) were restricted and set to zero for all models estimated. Parameters with values shown as .00 were also restricted and set to zero during estimation; these parameters have no standard errors associated with them.

on behavior. Such results for the γs, of course, do not mean that the traits have *no* effect on behavior whatsoever; such results, however, *are* consistent with an effect of traits on behavior that is fully mediated through beliefs.[3]

The second column in Table 3.2 contains information about the performance of the mediated effects model. The βs show the same pattern of significant direct effects of beliefs on behavior as found in the direct effects model. In addition, the γs are all significant and conform to expectations in sign; suggesting that the effect of traits on behavior is mediated through beliefs. Specifically, the following trait effects were supported: Macho-aggression is associated with believing that alcohol helps socially ($\gamma_{1,1}$); macho-aggression is negatively associated with believing that alcohol impairs motor and cognitive ability ($\gamma_{2,1}$); satisfaction with life is negatively associated with believing that alcohol helps socially ($\gamma_{1,2}$); and satisfaction with life is positively associated with believing that alcohol impairs motor and cognitive ability ($\gamma_{2,2}$).

Absolute Fit. Attention now turns to the absolute fit of these two competing models in the data from Sample Survey I. Because of the large samples obtained herein, and the well-known problems associated with using the χ^2 test to assess fit with large samples, the models' absolute fit to the data was assessed primarily with indices like the Tucker–Lewis (1973) ρ and the Bentler–Bonnet Δ. Unlike the χ^2 test, these indices are unaffected by sample size. Like comparable fit indices, ρ and Δ values near unity indicate good fit.

The absolute fit indices are reported in the bottom of columns one and two in Table 3.2. Examining ρ and Δ in light of a standard value of 0.95 or better for an acceptable model suggests that the mediated effects model represents the data better than the direct effects model. The merits of the mediated effects model over the direct effects model are also corroborated by a higher value on the Jöreskog–Sörbom adjusted goodness-of-fit index. Finally, the root mean-square residual (RMR) is smaller for the mediated effects model and is under the recommended 0.05 criterion.

Relative Fit. The mediated effects and direct effects models are both hierarchically nested in a third model termed the *common paths* model. As previously discussed, this latter model is not of theoretical interest, but is of *empirical* value in allowing an indirect comparison of the direct effects

[3]A regression-based approach for testing whether beliefs mediate the influence of traits on behavior requires evidence that traits have a significant influence on behavior prior to modeling the beliefs-to-behavior relationships. Consistent with this approach, a structural model was estimated in which the beliefs-to-behavior paths were fixed to 0.0; both the "aggressive male" trait ($t = 3.54$) and the "satisfaction with life" trait ($t = -2.52$) had a significant effect on behavior.

TABLE 3.3
Relative Fit of Competing Models

	X^2 *Difference, df*	
Comparison	*Sample Survey I*	*Sample Survey II*
Direct Effects Model vs. Common Path Model	187.90,[a] $df = 4$	266.73,[a] $df = 4$
Mediated Effects Model vs. Common Path Model	10.18, $df = 2$	6.71, $df = 2$

[a] $p < 0.01$.

and mediated effects models. This third model is a nonparsimonious, biased-to-fit, model because it estimates all possible path coefficients. The relative fit of the direct effects and mediated effects models were evaluated by way of χ^2 difference tests with this common path model (Table 3.3).

The chi square difference between the direct effects model and the common paths model is significant ($\Delta\chi^2 = 187.90$, $df = 4$, $p < .01$), indicating that not having the mediating paths leading from the traits to the beliefs causes the model to fit less well. In comparison, the difference between the mediated effects model and the common paths model is not significant ($\Delta\chi^2 = 10.18$, $df = 2$, $p > .01$). This indicates that the mediated effects model fits the data as well as a more complicated model and that adding paths from traits to behavior does nothing to improve goodness of fit. Consequently, both the absolute and relative goodness-of-fit tests suggest the mediated effects model is superior to the direct effects model in the data from Sample Survey I.

A Replication Test With Sample Survey II Data

In these replication analyses, the models examined in the Sample Survey I data were re-estimated with independent data collected in Sample Survey II. The objective was to determine whether the general pattern of parameters developed in Sample Survey I (i.e., which pattern of zero-valued, positive-valued, and negative-valued parameters implied by the alternative models) would be representative of Sample Survey II's covariances. The magnitude of the parameter estimates from Sample Survey I were not expected to be precisely replicated in the Sample Survey II data. Rather, the purpose was to test if the basic pattern of findings from the analysis of Sample Survey I would be replicated in Sample Survey II covariances.

The right-most columns of Tables 3.1, 3.2, and 3.3 contain the replication results estimated by LISREL 7 in the Sample Survey II data. Table 3.1 contains the replicated measurement model estimates for the mediated effects model; like the earlier findings, these results suggest adequate measurement in Sample Survey II. Table 3.2 contains the replicated structural parameter estimates which are generally comparable to those found in the analysis of Sample Survey I. Once again, the goodness-of-fit indices suggest that the mediated effects model represents the data better than does the direct effects model. The sole difference in the replication analysis was the inability to replicate the path representing the negative effect of the alcohol-impairs belief on alcohol consumption; this was the only path that was not replicated. Despite the nonreplication of this one path, the basic characteristics of the mediated effects model remain unaltered in the validation data. Finally, Table 3.3 reports the χ^2 difference tests for the replication effort; again, like the Sample Survey I results, the mediated effects model provides a statistically better fit than the direct effects model.

DISCUSSION

The mediated effects model explained the interrelationship between lifestyle traits, consumption beliefs, and behavior better than did the direct effects model. Thus, these results support Lutz' (1979) recommendation to integrate lifestyle traits and multiattribute belief models into a more general framework for analyzing consumers' preferences and behaviors. The mediated effects model views differences in consumption beliefs as based in differences in consumers' enduring personality or lifestyle traits. Moreover, it is a hierarchical model which sees traits as underpinning beliefs such that the effects of traits on behavior are mediated through beliefs.

Implications for Designing Persuasive Messages

Multiattribute based insights for developing persuasive messages have focused marketers' attention on the relationship between consumer beliefs and subsequent behaviors. Accordingly, a common marketing communication strategy is to provide consumers with new information to alter consumers' beliefs about the different aspects of multidimensional social objects in order to promote targeted behavior changes. However, this approach may be myopic as it is necessary to understand *why* beliefs are held in order to anticipate how to change them (Ajzen & Fishbein, 1980; Gutman, 1982; Locander & Spivey, 1978). The present research demonstrates how structural equation modeling can be used to integrate multiattribute and lifestyle theory to acquire this deeper understanding. With knowledge about these underlying motivations, marketers should be better equipped to develop more persuasive advertising messages.

The advantages our approach offers relative to traditional multiattribute research can be illustrated using the young male alcohol consumption model portrayed in Fig. 3.2. Assuming the goal of reducing young male alcohol consumption, the belief–behavior section of the model implies that an appropriate persuasion strategy would be to provide information that counters the current "ability-is-impaired" belief. For example, a message might document laboratory research demonstrating how increased blood alcohol level impairs cognitive and motor performance. Such messages appear sterile when compared to the insights provided by the complete treatment of beliefs as underpinned by lifestyle traits. To continue the example, the empirical results show that young males with aggressive/macho orientations are less likely to believe that alcohol impairs their abilities. A functional interpretation is that this belief reflects these youths' deeper and more general sense of masculinity. Therefore, persuasive messages should show that alcohol consumption can detract from these youths' masculinity by impairing their cognitive and physical ability to be masculine. Persuasive messages based on the advocated approach would contain information about how alcohol impairs performance, but more importantly, they would go on to convey how avoiding such impairment helps express a desired lifestyle trait. This could be accomplished by demonstrating how the current drinking-impairs-ability belief does not express their macho conception of self or how changing this belief can aid in a more successful presentation of self. In either case, the persuasive message focuses on the reason the belief is held rather than the belief in isolation. The relative effectiveness of these persuasion approaches should be examined in future research.

The advocated lifestyle trait → consumption belief → behavior model should also provide more actionable direction for copywriters relative to approaches that rely on more abstract motivations for beliefs. For example, the meaning of Homer and Kahle's (1988) external values orientation (which was derived from a factor analytic distillation of the nine abstract LOV measures) is, at first glance, less clear than a more concrete lifestyle trait like the "aggressive male" trait examined in the present research. Moreover, since this trait was specifically developed to understand alcohol related behaviors, the scale's items are saturated with the details and context in which the behavior occurs. In pragmatic circumstances, this approach is preferable to using more abstract values or personality traits because it provides the practitioner with a more concrete and detailed understanding of the motivations that are relevant to purchasing and using their specific products.

Implications for Theory and Future Research

The results have implications for future research agendas in consumer behavior and applied marketing research.

Lifestyle Research. Although the literature has called for more complete examinations of how lifestyle or personality traits influence various mediators of trait–behavior relationships (e.g., Engle, Blackwell, & Miniard, 1993, p. 362), precious little research has taken that approach (Haugtvedt et al., 1992). The current research clearly begins to fill this void. More specifically, the present research illustrates how consumer lifestyle research can benefit from using the integrative framework suggested by functional attitude and personal values theory. The framework advances lifestyle research beyond more limited examinations of only trait–behavior relations (e.g., Lastovicka & Joachimsthaler, 1988) that have often forced lifestyle researchers into guessing exactly how consumers' known and measured lifestyle traits are related to beliefs about product attributes (e.g., Horn, 1991). In contrast to such guess work, the current research provides a useful integrative structure for guiding data collection, analysis, interpretation, and implementation to obtain generalizable and managerially useful hierarchical models of traits, beliefs, and behaviors.

The hierarchical modeling approach also provides a more refined understanding of market segment preferences. For example, while market researchers frequently form benefit segments by clustering on consumers' product beliefs, these researchers typically have no explanation for why specific benefit segments emerge. The framework demonstrated in the present research can address the motivational differences behind these segments. Moreover, this approach suggests that additional analyses should be conducted within benefit segments to determine if consumers value attributes for the same reasons. For example, consumers in a benefit-defined segment may be motivated to purchase alcohol because they believe that alcohol helps socially. However, individuals belonging to this segment may differ with respect to why they believe alcohol helps socially. The present research suggests that one subsegment may consume alcohol to enhance their aggressive/macho self in social settings. Alternatively, a second subsegment may be dissatisfied with life and believe that alcohol provides positive benefits by helping them socially. Hence, developing an effective communication strategy for a benefit-defined segment may require multiple messages if different groups of consumers hold the same belief for different reasons. Analyzing either lifestyle traits or consumption beliefs in isolation will not uncover this important distinction.

Lifestyle and Multiattribute Modeling. In terms of multiattribute modeling, our research has applied a belief-only model (Wilkie & Pessemier, 1973). Importance weights or attribute values were not collected; however, these weights can be inferred from the LISREL model standardized beta estimates. Successfully modeling such belief-only data along with lifestyle trait measures may be limited to those cases where beliefs about the outcome of some choice are *heterogeneous* over respondents and market segments. However, sometimes almost all of some population will believe that a brand possesses some characteristic or behavioral outcome. This is especially true for highly advertised, well established packaged good brands that "own" some attribute (e.g., Crest and the benefit of decay prevention). For such circumstances, it may be more fruitful to model the relationship between traits and directly measured attribute importance measures rather than relying exclusively on belief measures.

To illustrate, in the research reported herein there was variance in young male beliefs about alcohol's effects. Some believed alcohol is a social lubricant while others saw alcohol as an impairment to enjoying others' company. Nevertheless, beliefs about other alcohol consumption outcomes may be more homogeneous. For these beliefs, this lack of variation makes it unlikely that they can be empirically linked to either lifestyle traits or consumption behaviors. For such *homogenous* beliefs, it may be more fruitful to examine the importance attached to these outcomes rather than the beliefs themselves. For example, consider consumers' beliefs about the relationship between heavy alcohol consumption and the likelihood of experiencing a "hangover." It is likely that this belief is so widely held that it would provide little explanation for differences in alcohol consumption level. But, as Howard (1989, p. 280) noted, the importance that consumers attach to consumption outcomes is largely determined by abstract dispositions such as values and traits. Consequently, consumers who ascribe to a health-oriented lifestyle should attach more importance to a negative health consequence such as a hangover than would those who are less health conscious. Because the present research only collected belief data, it remains for future research to examine the relationships between consumer traits, consumption beliefs, importance dimensions, and behaviors.

CONCLUSION

Past lifestyle research and multiattribute belief research have made significant independent contributions to marketers' ability to understand and predict consumption behaviors. The present research builds on these traditions by proposing a new and integrated approach for examining consumer preferences and knowledge. The simultaneous examination of lifestyle traits and consumption beliefs is compatible with the practice of collecting both lifestyle and belief information. The significant difference is that this approach argues for a more "holistic" understanding of consumers in which the researcher should be concerned about both what consumers believe and *why* they hold these beliefs.

ACKNOWLEDGMENTS

The authors are grateful for the helpful suggestions provided by Christine Moorman and Peter Reingen. This research was supported, in part, by research contracts awarded to the second author by U.S. Department of Transportation, National Highway Traffic Safety Administration and the State of Kansas, Department of Transportation, Traffic Safety Office.

REFERENCES

Ajzen, I., & Fishbein, M. (1980). *Understanding attitudes and predicting social behavior.* Englewood Cliffs, NJ: Prentice-Hall.

Allport, G. W. (1961). *Pattern and growth in personality.* New York: Holt, Rinehart & Winston.

Andreasen, A. (1993). Presidential address: A social marketing consumer research agenda for the 1990's. In L. McAlister & M. R. Rothschild (Eds.), *Advances in consumer research* (Vol. 20, pp. 1–5). Provo, UT: Association for Consumer Research.

Cohen, J. B. (1978). New directions in attitude research: A critical review. In H. K. Hunt (Ed.), *Advances in consumer research* (Vol. 5, pp. 370–376). Provo, UT: Association for Consumer Research.

Day, G. S. (1990). *Market driven strategy.* New York: The Free Press.

Engle, J. F., Blackwell, R. D., & Miniard, P. W. (1993). *Consumer behavior* (7th ed.). Fort Worth, TX: Dryden Press.

Fitzgerald, J. L., & Mulford, H. A. (1984). Factors related to problem-drinking rates. *Journal of Studies on Alcohol, 45*(5), 424–432.

Fornell, C., & Larcker, D. F. (1981). Evaluating structural equation models with unobservable variables and measurement error. *Journal of Marketing Research, 18*(1), 39–50.

Givon, M. E., & Shapiro, Z. (1984). Response rating scales: A theoretical model and its application to the number of categories problem. *Journal of Marketing Research, 21*(4), 410–419.

Groves, R. M., & Kahn, R. L. (1979). *Surveys by telephone: A national comparison with personal interviews.* New York: Academic Press.

Gutman, J. (1982). A means-end chain model based on consumer categorization processes. *Journal of Marketing, 46*(2), 60–72.

Haugtvedt, C. R., Petty, R. E., & Cacioppo, J. T. (1992). Need for cognition in advertising: Understanding the role of personality variables in consumer behavior. *Journal of Consumer Psychology, 1*(3), 239–260.

Herek, G. M. (1987). Can functions be measured? A new perspective on the functional approach to attitudes. *Social Psychology Quarterly, 50,* 285–303.

Hirschman, E. C. (1991). Presidential address: Secular mortality and the dark side of consumer behavior—or how semiotics saved my life. In R. H. Holman & M. R. Soloman (Eds.), *Advances in consumer research* (Vol. 18, pp. 1–6). Provo, UT: Association for Consumer Research.

Homer, P. M., & Kahle, L. R. (1988). A structural equation test of the value-attitude-behavior hierarchy. *Journal of Personality and Social Psychology, 54*(4), 638–646.

Horn, M. I. (1991, October). *How life style research is conducted at DDB Needham.* Paper presented at the EIASM workshop on values and lifestyle research in marketing held in Brussels, Belgium.

Hover, S., & Gaffney, L. R. (1991). The relationship between social skills and adolescent drinking. *Alcohol and Alcoholism, 26*(2), 207–214.

Howard, J. A. (1989). *Consumer behavior in marketing strategy.* Englewood Cliffs, NJ: Prentice-Hall.

John, O. P. (1990). The 'Big Five' factor taxonomy: Dimensions of personality in the natural language and in questionnaires. In L. A. Pervin (Ed.), *Handbook of modern personality theory and research.* New York: Guilford.

Jöreskog, K. G., & Sörbom, D. (1986). *PRELIS User's Guide.* Mooresville, IN: Scientific Software.

Jöreskog, K. G., & Sörbom, D. (1990). *LISREL 7 User's Reference Guide.* Mooresville, IN: Scientific Software.

Kassarjian, H. H., & Sheffet, M. J. (1991). Personality and consumer behavior: An update. In H. H. Kassarjian & T. S. Robertson (Eds.), *Perspectives in consumer behavior* (pp. 281–303). Englewood Cliffs, NJ: Prentice-Hall.

Katz, D. (1960). The functional approach to the study of attitudes. *Public Opinion Quarterly, 24,* 163–204.

Katz, D. (1989). Foreword. In A. R. Pratkanis, S. J. Breckler, & A. G. Greenwald (Eds.), *Attitude structure and function* (pp. 339–360). Hillsdale, NJ: Lawrence Erlbaum Associates.

Katz, D., Sarnoff, I., & McClintock, C. (1956). Ego defense and attitude change. *Human Relations, 9,* 27–46.

Katz, D., & Stotland, E. (1959). A preliminary statement to a theory of attitude structure and change. In S. Koch (Ed.), *Psychology: A study of a science: Formulations of the person and the social context* (Vol. 3, pp. 423–475). New York: McGraw Hill.

Kline, R. B., Canter, W. I., & Robin, A. (1987). Parameters of teenage alcohol use: A path analytic conceptual model. *Journal of Consulting and Clinical Psychology, 55*(4), 521–528.

Knorring, L. von, Knorring, A. V., Smigan, L., Lindberg, U., & Edholm, M. (1987). Personality traits in subtypes of alcoholics. *Journal of Studies on Alcohol, 48*(6), 523–527.

Koop, C. E. (1988). Opening and closing remarks. In *Proceedings of the Surgeon General's Workshop on Drunk Driving.* U.S. Dept. of Health and Human Services, Washington, DC: U.S. Government Printing Office.

Lastovicka, J. L. (1982). On the validation of lifestyle traits: A review and exposition. *Journal of Marketing Research, 19*(1), 126–138.

Lastovicka, J. L., Murry, J. P., Jr., Joachimsthaler, E. A., Bhalla, G., & Scheurich, J. (1987). A lifestyle typology to model young male drinking and driving. *Journal of Consumer Research, 14*(2), 257–263.

Lastovicka, J. L., & Joachimsthaler, E. A. (1988). Improving the detection of personality-behavior relations in consumer research. *Journal of Consumer Research, 14*(4), 583–587.

Locander, W. B., & Spivey, W. A. (1978). A functional approach to attitude measurement. *Journal of Marketing Research, 15*(4), 576–587.

Lutz, R. J. (1975). Changing brand attitudes through modification of cognitive structure. *Journal of Consumer Research, 1*(4), 49–59.

Lutz, R. J. (1978). A functional approach to consumer attitude research. In H. K. Hunt (Ed.), *Advances in consumer research* (Vol. 5, pp. 360–376). Provo, UT: Association for Consumer Research.

Lutz, R. J. (1979). A functional framework for designing and pretesting advertising themes. In J. C. Maloney & B. H. Silverman (Eds.), *Attitude research plays for high stakes* (pp. 37–49). Chicago: American Marketing Association.

Lutz, R. J. (1981). A reconceptualization of the functional approach to attitudes. In J. N. Sheth (Ed.), *Research in marketing* (Vol. 5). Greenwich, CT: JAI.

Lutz, R. J. (1991). Editorial. *Journal of Consumer Research,* 17(4).

Mardia, K. V. (1970). Measures of multivariate skewness and kurtosis with applications. *Biometrika, 57,* 519–530.

Matros, R., & Hines, M. (1982). Behavioral definitions of problem drinking among college students. *Journal of Studies on Alcohol, 43*(7), 702–713.

Mayer, J. E. (1988). The personality characteristics of adolescents who use and misuse alcohol. *Adolescence, 90,* 383–404.

Mehrota, S., & Wells, W. D. (1977). Psychographics and consumer behavior: Theory and recent empirical findings. In A. G. Woodside, J. N. Sheth, & P. D. Bennett (Eds.), *Consumer and industrial buying behavior.* New York: New-Holland/Elsevier.

Mooney, D. K., & Corcoran, K. J. (1989). The relationship between assertiveness, alcohol-related expectations for social assertion and drinking patterns among college students. *Addictive Behaviors, 14,* 301–305.

Pervin, L. A. (1990). A brief history of modern personality theory. In L. A. Pervin (Ed.), *Handbook of modern personality theory and research.* New York: Guilford.

Plant, M. A., Bagnall, G., & Foster, J. (1990). Teenage heavy drinkers: Alcohol related knowledge, beliefs, experiences, motivation, and the social context of drinking. *Alcoholism and Addiction, 25*(6), 691–698.

Pratkanis, A., Breckler, S. J., & Greenwald, A. G. (1989). *Attitude structure and function.* Hillsdale, NJ: Lawrence Erlbaum Associates.

Rokeach, M. (1973). *The nature of human values.* New York: The Free Press.

Shavitt, S. (1989). Product, personalities, and situations in attitude functions. In T. K. Kinnear (Ed.), *Advances in consumer research* (Vol. 16, pp. 300–305). Provo, UT: Association for Consumer Research.

Shavitt, S. (1990). The role of attitude objects in attitude functions. *Journal of Experimental and Social Psychology, 26,* 124–148.

Smith, M. B. (1947). The personal setting of public attitudes: A study of attitudes toward Russia. *Public Opinion Quarterly, 10,* 507–523.

Smith, M. B., Bruner, J. S., & White, R. W. (1956). *Opinions and personality.* New York: Wiley.

Snyder, M., & DeBono, K. G. (1985). Appeals to image and claims about quality: Understanding the psychology of advertising. *Journal of Personality and Social Psychology, 49*(3), 586–597.

Tucker, L. R., & Lewis, C. (1973). A reliability coefficient for maximum likelihood factor analysis. *Psychometrika, 38,* 1–10.

Wells, W. D. (1975). Psychographics: A critical review. *Journal of Marketing Research, 12*(2), 196–213.

Wilkie, W. L., & Pessemier, E. A. (1973). Issues in marketing's use of multi-attribute attitude models. *Journal of Marketing Research, 10*(4), 428–441.

Wilson, G. T. (1987). Cognitive studies in alcoholism. *Journal of Consulting and Clinical Psychology, 55,* 325–331.

Chapter 4

Advertising, Values, and the Consumption Community

David Prensky
Trenton State College

Christine Wright-Isak
Young and Rubicam

Understanding the social context in which values are enacted is vital for broadening the application of values research in advertising. Although values are societally shared, their expression as attitudes and behaviors varies by subcultural groups within the larger society. Community is the social institution that mediates between subculture and larger society by providing a shared ethos that influences individual expressions of societal values in local, mutually agreed-upon ways. Members of a community share similar conceptions of how a particular value should be enacted, and the community provides examples as well as feedback about the appropriateness of its members' attitudes and behavior.

Drawing a distinction between values and their enactments is necessary because current research has not succeeded in establishing a relationship between values, attitudes, and behaviors. This lack of success has been noted by others in this volume (see chapters by Kahle, Homer, O'Brien, & Boush; Shrum & McCarty). We think that it stems from a failure to understand that values themselves are largely shared by members of a national society, but what are considered appropriate attitudes and behaviors to express them vary within a society. What are commonly measured as values in marketing research and in the psychological and sociological literatures are believed to be underlying values that, it is hoped, will predict attitudes and behaviors. We take the perspective that values are not direct predictors of attitudes and behaviors. We believe that attitudes and behaviors are enactments of values and that enactment is a sociocultural process that occurs in the context of a community. Then, understanding the community contexts in which similar values are expressed as different attitudes and behaviors becomes the important task for our research.

In distinguishing enactments from values themselves we can examine how the community an individual belongs to mediates between personal inclinations and social reinforcement of shared attitudes and behaviors. A community provides models of what its members believe are appropriate attitudinal and behavioral interpretations of values, places emphasis on certain values over others, and is a source of regular, often prosaic, feedback about the individual's conformity or departure from its norms and customs.

SHIFTS IN COMMUNITY AS THE BASIS OF VALUE ENACTMENT

In the last 100 years Americans have shifted from the traditional residential and occupational communities to consumption communities as a significant basis for expressing values (Boorstin, 1974). This shift has its causes in the decreasing salience of communities of geographic residence and occupational identification and the increasing importance of consumption to Americans in today's world. This shift occurred in two phases: the addition of occupation to residence as a separate basis for value enactment, and the subsequent addition of consumption communities to those of residence and occupation. In each case, the additional form became the most salient one, but the existing forms continued to be relevant. Thus, residence and occupation are not dispensable, but they have diminished in importance relative to consumption.

The Concept of Community

Central to this discussion is the concept of community. Community consists of a group of individuals who share a central ethos, or set of values *and* common understandings about how these shared values will be enacted in attitudes and behaviors. The consensus of the members of a community about how given events are to be interpreted, what they mean for the values held by the community, and the social actions taken to praise and reward, or condemn and punish, fellow members are all part of the social dynamic that constitute a viable community. Often the values and their significance for daily attitudes and behaviors are represented by symbols that serve as signs that both unite members who know what they stand for and alert outsiders that there is a community of persons they must take into account.

When we speak of the medical community, the gay community, or retirement communities, we are thinking of communities whose members are united by some commonly shared attitudes and behaviors. Despite the differences between these communities, the members of each share some basic American values. The general tenets of the work ethic that center on deferred gratification and success based on accomplishment, not lineage or caste, are among the ideal values of this society, explicitly encoded in its founding documents (Burlingame, 1957; DeTocqueville, 1945; Weber, 1958). The United States Constitution and the Declaration of Independence enshrine our national affirmation of individualism, the healthy benefits of free enterprise, and a list of rights intended to protect both. Yet our social and political processes often contain acrimonious arguments about them. If we scrutinize these opposing arguments they almost always affirm the value but condemn one or another interpretation of it. Such condemnations often criticize the opposing community as a "special interest group" that espouses an enactment we deplore.

Members of different communities may share an underlying value but hold very different conceptions of the attitudes and behaviors required to enact it. Within communities, members mutually reinforce their shared conception of how a given value should be expressed in attitude and behavior. As observers of our fellow Americans, in everyday life we identify each other as belonging to particular communities and shorthand whole sets of expectations on the basis of these assignments. We derive much of our sense of social order from the assumptions we make about members of other communities.

The abortion rights issue is perhaps the most vivid example of how two women who share identical values, demographic characteristics, and psychological profiles may nevertheless be members of two communities of interest with very different understandings of how these values should shape personal attitudes, individual behavior, and legislation. All in American society affirm the right to "life, liberty, and the pursuit of happiness." But whose life, when life begins, whose liberty, and what constitutes happiness, are all questions on which we have no national consensus. What we do have are communities of Americans who at times take diametrically opposed views of *how these values are to be enacted.*

Differentiation of Community and Its Common Forms

The development of consumption communities parallels the trend from local markets, to mass markets, and finally to market segmentation (Boorstin, 1974; Tedlow, 1990). Initially, consumption occurred in local markets that were fragmented by the inability of producers to manufacture sufficient quantities for a national market, by the lack of an effective transportation system to distribute to wide market, and by the absence of national media that would allow producers to communicate with a national market. In this context, consumers in a particular geographic community enacted the common values they held together with their neighbors.

The prototypical rural community of the early 19th century frontier was self-sufficient. The inhabitants of the community lived and worked there, and all of the things that they consumed were produced there. Social agreement about appropriate behavior ensured that shared values were enacted in the same way by all members of the community. Until the late 19th century, classic small towns, farming communities, and urban neighborhoods were still the site of their inhabitants' housing, workplace, and consumption (Boorstin, 1974; Kammen, 1991; Schlesinger, 1933). There was some differentiation among residential, occupational, and consumption spheres of social life, but individuals satisfied most of their basic needs and behaved within a shared set of values, norms, and customs in the same place. The economic and technological constraints of small-scale manufacturing and limited transportation ensured that these functions would be carried out in a local geographic area.

The major economic and technological changes of late 19th and early 20th century industrialization allowed the unification of local markets into a national mass market and increased the importance of occupational communities. Mass production technology allowed a producer to manufacture enough product to satisfy national demand; indeed, the economies of scale required by new production technologies demanded the large sales that could be provided by only a national market. Producers could use the rapidly developing transportation system to distribute products nationally, and the development of newspapers, magazines, radio, and television allowed them to communicate with that national mass market. These developments, along with the increase in educational and occupational opportunities, loosened the monopoly of traditional geographic communities in illustrating customary ways of enacting values.

Increasing integration of traditional social and cultural groups accompanied the massive economic and technological change that occurred during this period. These traditional groups, rooted in residential community and related to ascribed characteristics like religion and ethnicity, lost influence over what was commonly understood to be proper value enactment. Consumers were increasingly influenced by their occupational communities and their enacted values found daily expression based on work norms and formal rules. The differentiation of men's work, defined as occurring outside the home, and women's work, defined as family centered, took place at this time (Demos, 1986; Mintz & Kellogg, 1988). The democratization of educational and employment opportunities decreased the primacy of residential community with its ascribed characteristics, as occupational community based on educational achievements and work roles grew in importance.

The rise of movies, magazines, radio, and television, as illustrations of the American way of life, combined with the increased democratization of consumption opportunities, offered consumers the chance to learn about and adopt new attitudes and behaviors with fewer social or occupational constraints. Branded products were distributed and advertised nationally and portrayed in the context of various sets of attitudes and behaviors that gave them social significance. Individuals from different parts of the country meeting by chance might recognize that each was drinking Coca-Cola and not Pepsi, or they were wearing a Sears watch and not an expensive Hamilton. Even if they never met, both were members of a consumption community by virtue of the same brand selection.

The decreasing salience of residential and occupational communities as the basis for value enactment, resulting from increasing differentiation among the forms of community, meant that they no longer provided all-encompassing examples of appropriate value enactments. As occupation superseded residence, and then consumption superseded occupation, the growing differentiation among them meant that the relative salience of the older forms of community diminished. Increasing residential and occupational mobility loosened the attachment of individuals to specific living or work places at the same time that technological changes in media offered individuals easy access to symbols of value enactment through modern consumption communities.

The Increasing Salience of the Consumption Community

A steady rise in the American standard of living afforded consumers economic power and rapidly expanding mass media provided examples of consumption styles that spanned both residential and occupational communities. This rising affluence and universal access to media-based demonstrations of alternative value enactments has resulted in opportunities for consumers to subscribe to "virtual" consumption communities and the attitudinal and behavioral enactments that they convey. Today, consumption communities do not require face-to-face contact with other community members because media, both mass and individualized, provide examples and feedback about appropriate behavior.

Boorstin (1974) first coined the term *consumption communities* in describing the cultural changes brought about by the rise of mass media advertising and the early mail order catalog businesses of the last century: Sears, Roebuck and Company and Montgomery Ward. At the turn of the century, the two most salient forms of community for most individuals remained their geographic community of residence and the occupational community of workmates and employer. Such communities communicated examples of the shared conceptions of what is proper and improper by means of face-to-face interactions channeled through customs, norms, and formal rules to demonstrate appropriate behavior.

On the other hand, individuals in consumption communities learn through the media, since their members are united through the process of consumer choice and acquisition rather than propinquity of residence or workplace. Mail order catalogs conveyed examples of value enactments through pictures and descriptive copy that was explicitly value laden. However, the catalogs were episodic and changed little from one issue to the next.

Today, technology has made media an even more salient source for demonstrations of appropriate behavioral enactments of values. Television is the primary source of entertainment for most Americans on most evenings of the week. The enactments portrayed take place with motion, drama, and sound, unlike the early catalogs. Also unlike the catalogs, they require no reading to absorb the value enactments they convey.

Marketers, the media, and advertisers developed both new products and new media vehicles to satisfy the differentiated needs of these new consumption-based communities. After World War II they showed widespread interest in incorporating measures of consumption as the basis for understanding and appealing to consumers. New segmentation methods that would move beyond the traditional ascribed characteristics were developed. Lifestyle and psychographics were used as additional factors to help explain the differences in consumption among consumers who shared common demographic characteristics (Plummer, 1974; Wells, 1975).

Advertising and marketing scholars have also responded to this consumption segmentation by developing new theories and methods for understanding value-based segments. Several research traditions emerged to address cultural values. Rokeach's (1973, 1979) work on instrumental and terminal values has been applied to some consumer and advertising settings (Becker & Connor, 1981; Kamakura & Mazzon, 1991; Vinson, Scott, & Lamont, 1977). The list of values approach (Beatty, Kahle, Homer, & Misra, 1985; Kahle, 1983) attempts to provide a less abstract value measurement approach that is more directly applicable to consumer issues. This approach has been applied extensively in both original and modified forms (Kamakura & Novak, 1992; Kennedy, Best, & Kahle, 1988; Novak & MacEvoy, 1990). Other work has investigated the links between specific product attributes and consumer values (Reynolds & Craddock, 1988; Reynolds & Gutman, 1988) and, of particular relevance for consumption communities, the underlying symbolic value of product consumption (Solomon, 1988; Solomon & Buchanan, 1991).

ADVERTISING, MEDIA CONSUMPTION, AND VALUES

The historical shift from traditional social and cultural communities as the basis for value enactment to the predominant influence of consumption communities is accompanied by significant changes in the way that individual members obtain information about appropriate value enactments. The traditional cultural and social communities were based in residence and occupation, with face-to-face interaction and value enactments channeled by customs, norms, and formal rules to demonstrate appropriate behavior. The shift to consumption communities gives increasing importance to markets, the consumer behavior that comprises them, and the communications channels that provide examples of appropriate value enactments.

This shift makes understanding how consumers receive messages from various media, especially television, particularly important in understanding new generations of consumers. Individuals learn about their consumption communities through media demonstrations of appropriate attitudinal and behavioral enactments. We suggest that consumption communities consist of individual consumers who reaffirm their membership in the community in a variety of ways, including regularly viewing a set of television programs that are chosen for common attitudinal and behavioral enactments. Examination of television programming both for its influence on social norms and customs as well as its effects on consumer interpretations of its advertising messages can tell us a great deal about the relationship between values and attitudes and behaviors. Moreover, we must understand this shift to media-based consumption communities if we are to fully appreciate the apparent unpredictability of consumer adaptations to the cumulative effects of commercial messages and programming content.

Media choice itself is a particularly powerful enactment of the consumer's underlying values because it offers opportunities for value expression through both symbolism and cognition. The consumer can simultaneously affirm and communicate his or her membership in a community of values through consuming media that clearly espouse those values. Examples include new managers ostentatiously reading the *Wall Street Journal* or the viewers of a particular televisions program discussing the latest episode with each other. The consumer can express affiliation with a program symbolically by using products that contain program logos, as shown by the new line of *Northern Exposure* clothing.

Media consumption provides information to consumers that they use in learning about their consumption community and also about the broader society. Whether through programs and articles with an overt educational purpose, or through assimilation of information presented incidentally, consumers can gather information that will deepen their knowledge and increase their commitment to the community. Examples include adolescents' use of television as a source of role models (Faber & O'Guinn, 1988) and the well-known Trekkie phenomenon.

In these new consumption communities, products and services are bought in community rituals such as country club dances, garage sales, and Star Trek conventions, and serve as direct behavioral affirmation of the community and its values. Consumers can show their symbolic expression of the community's values through the product itself or through the process used to purchase the product. The consumer who buys a Volvo uses the product itself to symbolize responsibility and security, while the consumer who can afford to purchase a Mercedes shows evidence of accomplishment and salvation (Weber, 1958).

How does advertising function in the context of media consumption that expresses consumers' values? Given the power of television programming in presenting images of value enactments, advertisers must concern themselves with how the values expressed in the advertisements that are placed in those programs will interact with those that are expressed by the program content. This is commonly recognized in practice, although usually in extreme cases where the program's content is so offensive to some viewers that they threaten advertisers in those programs. The effect of such extreme negative cases is that advertisers refuse to advertise in those programs. In less extreme cases, most advertisers use guidelines for creative development and media planning that uses informal knowledge about advertising and program content to ensure that their respective values are consistent. There has been some research into the contextual effects of program content on advertising response, although they have not explicitly examined the interaction of values in program and advertisement (Kamins, Marks, & Skinner, 1991; Murry, Lastovicka, & Singh, 1992).

We anticipate that the relationship between the values expressed in television programs and the values expressed in the advertising in those shows will affect consumers' response to advertising. Much of the investigation of characteristics of ads and the reception processes of consumers needs to be reviewed for its relevance to value consistency (Belch, Belch, & Villarreal, 1987). Basic elements of advertising, such as type of appeal (Johar & Sirgy, 1991), emotion (Holbrook & Batra, 1987), and feelings (Edell & Burke, 1987) have already been shown to affect the relationship between program and advertising values.

OUR RESEARCH PROGRAM

We are beginning a research program with two key goals. The first goal is empirical: We want to examine the media choices of individuals in order to identify consumption communities that are composed of members who look to the same programs and advertisements for symbols of appropriate behavior. Our second goal is to achieve theoretical clarity about the role that programming and advertising play in providing such symbols.

The empirical identification of consumption communities will be done by grouping individual consumers on the basis of a behavioral measure of regular media consumption over an extended time frame. We will examine individual consumers, not household media consumption patterns, because our basic assumption is that the residential basis for community is decreasing. Just as the residential community no longer provides the strong basis for its members value enactments, the household no longer serves that function either. Because individual members of a household may enact commonly held values in very different behaviors, we do not expect that household members will consume the same media. In other words, the members of a particular family are not necessarily members of a common consumption community and therefore do not watch the same television programming, so we must examine individual-level television viewing data.

We require a behavioral measure of regular media consumption over an extended time period if we are to assume community membership. Behavioral measures are more reliable than self-reported measures gathered through survey research, particularly over extended viewing periods. The behavioral measure will eliminate problems such as memory lapses, telescoping, and social desirability response biases. We want regular media consumption over a substantial viewing period in order to reduce the situational effects that would obscure accurate identification of value enactment. Patterns of viewing are an appropriate measure despite criticisms that fear the effects of inertia in viewing combinations of shows (Rust, Kamakura, & Alpert, 1992). Television programmers expend much effort to place shows together that will attract compatible audiences, and viewers can certainly validate or undermine such efforts with great ease in today's world of remote controls, videocassette recorders, and multiple channel cable systems. We begin with an analysis of television viewing behavior based on Arbitron ScanAmerica viewing data. This will allow us to define specific media consumption communities and compare them to traditional demographically based media segmentation schemes.

Arbitron, through its ScanAmerica service, conducts an in-depth data collection effort in Denver among a sample of television viewers. These viewers record every time that they begin to watch television, change channels, and end viewing. The data are in 15-minute time segments, and we will identify each program and then create consumption communities based on evening viewing patterns for the sample for a 13-week period. We will group viewers who watch the same pattern of programs into consumption communities. Once these consumption communities have been created, we will search for viewer and program characteristics that will help us to derive the underlying value enactments of each community.

Our second goal is to understand the role that programming and advertising play in providing symbols of appropriate value enactment. To achieve that understanding, we must investigate issues of consumer initiative in receiving and processing symbols, the respective role played by programming and advertising in providing symbolic norms for value enactment, and the contextual effects of programming symbols on advertising response. We will build on the limited amount of work done in this area, which we cited earlier, as well as considering the underlying relationship between television programming and its audience. This relationship has been discussed in the context of advertising (Holbrook, 1987; Pollay, 1986, 1987): Do programmers attempt to change their intended audience or do they reflect already existing value enactments? To achieve this goal we will need to conduct qualitative research with members of various consumption communities. We need to understand how they learn value enactments and how they view programming and advertising as providers of symbolic enactments. We will also need to investigate the process by which programming and advertising creators embed symbols in both, as well as the actual use of such symbols through content analysis of programming and advertising. Underlying this is our assumption that the judgments of those who produce programming and advertising are influenced by the same national values and social processes as those who perceive them (Becker, 1982).

IMPLICATIONS FOR THEORY AND PRACTICE

Our approach to understanding the relationship of advertising and values is based on investigating the role of the consumption community in mediating between societally shared values and subcultures' varying interpretations of them, expressed through community-specific enactments. Consumption communities provide examples of appropriate attitudinal and behavioral enactments through media programming and advertising. This distinction between values and their enactments sensitizes values researchers to understand that consumers who share values may express very different attitudes about specific issues and exhibit different behaviors in specific contexts. We seek to widen the scope of current research on values first by identifying community as the social institution that nourishes that distinction between values and enactments, and then by examining how they are enacted in today's fragmented and rapidly changing consumption communities. Insights about the ways that values are symbolized in programming and in advertisements, and how they influence each other, will extend existing scholarship on values segmentation.

An understanding of the evolving role of programming and advertising as the enabling device for consumption communities will offer significant benefits to advertising and media practitioners as well as researchers in those areas (Englis & Solomon, this volume; MacEvoy, this volume). An examination of television viewing patterns within consumption communities will provide advertisers with the practical knowledge that they need to select media programming and to create advertising that is effective in the context of those vehicles. Television advertising is a very important communication tool for marketers. Yet, marketers and advertising agencies have little systematic knowledge of the programming environment in which they place their advertising. Such knowledge would be very useful for choosing the best combination of programs for their advertising and for the creation of advertising that would capitalize on the programs in which it appears.

How consumers select and use media is also important because it will deepen our conceptual understanding of consumer behavior in response to advertising. The analysis of media consumption provides a powerful method for identifying the values that a consumer's consumption community gives to him. Advertisers and advertising scholars alike must understand the underlying values of consumption communities, how consumers express their values through media consumption, and how advertising functions in the context of program choices that express consumers' values.

For advertising practice, understanding the relationship among advertising, value enactment, and consumption communities is necessary to develop creative executions that work together with both the value enactments of the target market and their enactment during media consumption. Advertising must be developed with an understanding of how it works within the value context in which it will be viewed, so that it can be placed in media vehicles that will support the values that it symbolizes. Our work will add substantive support to the experiential knowledge that creatives and media planners use currently.

REFERENCES

Beatty, S. E., Kahle, L. R., Homer, P., & Misra, S. (1985). Alternative measurement approaches to consumer values: The list of values and the Rokeach value survey. *Psychology and Marketing, 2,* 181–200.

Becker, B. W., & Connor, P. E. (1981). Personal values of the heavy user of mass media. *Journal of Advertising Research, 21,* 37–43.

Becker, H. S. (1982). *Art worlds.* Berkeley: University of California Press.

Belch, G. E., Belch, M. A., & Villarreal, A. (1987). Effects of advertising communications: Review of research. In J. N. Sheth (Ed.), *Research in marketing* (Vol. 9, pp. 59–117). Greenwich, CT: JAI.

Boorstin, D. (1974). *The Americans: The democratic experience.* New York: Vintage.

Burlingame, R. (1957). *The American conscience.* New York: Knopf.

Demos, J. (1986). *Past, present, and personal: The family and life course in American history.* New York: Oxford University Press.

DeTocqueville, A. (1945). *Democracy in America* (P. Bradley, Ed.). New York: Vintage.

Edell, J. A., & Burke, M. C. (1987). The power of feelings in understanding advertising effects. *Journal of Consumer Research, 14,* 421–433.

Faber, R. J., & O'Guinn, T. C. (1988). Expanding the view of consumer socialization: A nonutilitarian mass-mediated perspective. In E. C. Hirschman & J. N. Sheth (Eds.), *Research in consumer behavior* (Vol. 3, pp. 49–77). Greenwich, CT: JAI.

Holbrook, M. B. (1987). Mirror, mirror, on the wall, what's unfair in the reflections of advertising? *Journal of Marketing, 51*, 95–103.

Holbrook, M. B., & Batra, R. (1987). Assessing the role of emotions as mediators of consumer responses to advertising. *Journal of Consumer Research, 14*, 404–420.

Johar, J. S., & Sirgy, M. J. (1991). Value-expressive versus utilitarian advertising appeals: When and why to use which appeal. *Journal of Advertising, 20*, 23–33.

Kahle, L. R. (1983). *Social values and social change: Adaptation to life in America.* New York: Praeger.

Kamakura, W. A., & Mazzon, J. A. (1991). Values segmentation: A model for the measurement of values and value systems. *Journal of Consumer Research, 18*, 208–218.

Kamakura, W. A., & Novak, T. P. (1992). Value-system segmentation: Exploring the meaning of LOV. *Journal of Consumer Research, 19*, 119–132.

Kamins, M. A., Marks, L. J., & Skinner, D. (1991). Television commercial evaluation in the context of program induced mood: Congruence versus consistency effects. *Journal of Advertising, 20*, 1–14.

Kammen, M. (1991). *Mystic chords of memory: The transformation of tradition in American culture.* New York: Knopf.

Kennedy, P. F., Best, R. J., & Kahle, L. R. (1988). An alternative method for measuring value-based segmentation and advertising positioning. *Current Issues and Research in Advertising, 11*, 139–155.

Mintz, S., & Kellogg, S. (1988). *Domestic revolutions: A social history of American family life.* New York: The Free Press.

Murry, J. P., Jr., Lastovicka, J. L., & Singh, S. N. (1992). Feeling and liking response to television programs: An examination of two explanations for media-context effects. *Journal of Consumer Research, 18*, 441–451.

Novak, T. P., & MacEvoy, B. (1990). On comparing alternative segmentation schemes: The list of values and values and life styles. *Journal of Consumer Research, 17*, 105–109.

Plummer, J. T. (1974). The concept and application of life style segmentation. *Journal of Marketing, 38*, 33–37.

Pollay, R. W. (1986). The distorted mirror: Reflections on the unintended consequences of advertising. *Journal of Marketing, 50*, 18–36.

Pollay, R. W. (1987). On the value of reflections on the values in the distorted mirror. *Journal of Marketing, 51*, 104–110.

Reynolds, T. J., & Craddock, A. B. (1988). The application of the MECCAS model to the development and assessment of advertising strategy, *Journal of Advertising Research, 28*, 43–54.

Reynolds, T. J., & Gutman, J. (1988). Laddering theory, method, analysis, and interpretation. *Journal of Advertising Research, 28*, 11–34.

Rokeach, M. (1973). *The nature of human values.* New York: The Free Press.

Rokeach, M. (1979). *Understanding human values.* New York: The Free Press.

Rust, R. T., Kamakura, W. A., & Alpert, M. I. (1992). Viewer preference segmentation and viewing choice models for network television. *Journal of Advertising, 21*, 1–18.

Schlesinger, A. M. (1933). *Political and social growth of the United States 1852–1933.* New York: Macmillan.

Solomon, M. R. (1988). Mapping product constellations: A social categorization approach to symbolic consumption. *Psychology and Marketing, 5*, 233–258.

Solomon, M. R., & Buchanan, B. (1991). A role-theoretic approach to product symbolism: Mapping a consumption constellation. *Journal of Business Research, 22*, 95–110.

Tedlow, R. S. (1990). *New and improved: The story of mass marketing in America.* New York: Basic Books.

Vinson, D. E., Scott, J. E., & Lamont, L. R. (1977). The role of personal values in marketing and consumer behavior. *Journal of Marketing, 41*, 44–50.

Weber, M. (1958). *The Protestant ethic and the spirit of capitalism.* New York: Scribner.

Wells, W. D. (1975). Psychographics: A critical review. *Journal of Marketing Research, 12*, 196–213.

Chapter 5

Value and Values: What Is the Relevance for Advertisers?

Geraldine Fennell
Consultant

To consider the relevance of any psychological construct for those who spend the portion of a firm's resources earmarked for advertising, it is necessary to understand the nature of the behavioral task that management assigns to advertising. Accordingly, in the first of three main sections of this chapter, I examine the behavioral implications of the advertiser's task. In a second section, I use that analysis to comment on views of selected theorists of values and, in a third section, I discuss from the present theoretical perspective the relevance of value and values to the advertiser's task.

BEHAVIORAL IMPLICATIONS OF ADVERTISING'S TASK

The time is long overdue to acknowledge what the advertiser's task entails in behavioral terms. With its behavioral implications in front of us, we can then address questions such as: What role, if any, do values, lifestyles, psychographics—or traits, attitudes, emotions—play in helping to accomplish advertising's assignment?

Spelling out what the advertiser's task entails behaviorally is not a matter of a single sentence. As a first approximation, it has aspects that may be stated as follows. Advertisers, and the consumer psychologists who advise them, want some ground for believing that an ad campaign is a worthwhile use of scarce resources. For that to be the case, minimally, the following must occur: (a) An ad containing the right message is exposed in the environment of, and its message is processed by, the right people, so that brand name linked to brand claim/promise[1] is available at the right moment; (b) The brand itself is available for sale at the right place, time, and price; (c) The brand-in-use gives the right degree of satisfaction relative to its competitors; (d) The brand is available for reordering at the right place, time, and price; (e) Brand purchase occurs at a level that provides a satisfactory return on investment.

Given the complex ramifications of achieving such objectives, a high degree of collaboration is called for, to the extent that neither the success or failure of a brand can readily be laid at the door of any one of the relevant functional specialties. The part of such a sequence that custom assigns most directly to advertising is the first, that is, announcing the right offering to the right people, so that brand name and claim/promise are available at the right moment. Moreover, it is clear that difficult and crucial strategic choices have taken cover under the word "right." So, let me bring some of them into the open, particularly as regards the part most closely associated with advertising. As regards objective (a), to announce the *right* offering to the *right* people, advertisers must:

1. Identify in a naturally occurring population the kind(s) of people to study. These are one's *prospects*, that is, people who give grounds for believing that they may be in the market for the kind of good/service that an advertiser considers offering, which I refer to as the *focal product category*. In practice, to qualify individuals as prospects, marketers usually rely on evidence of engaging in activity that corresponds to the focal product category. Examples of such *focal activities* are, for a food advertiser, people who prepare meals; for an airline or tour operator, people who plan a winter vacation (see Fennell, 1985a, for a discussion of screening criteria).[2]

2. Given competitive offerings and the advertiser's own capability, identify the features of an offering and ad campaign that are right for some defined set of conditions that some prospects experience, that is, advertisers

---

[1]"Claim/promise" includes whatever advertisers want to associate with their brand's name, ranging from claimed attributes to promised benefits and, in each case, whether executed via "plain facts" or "atmospherically." Note that the present analysis is unchanged in essentials whether a new or existing brand is at issue. In principle, the firm may always change the features of its offering. Hence, its decision to continue a brand in existence unchanged indicates that management concludes, implicitly or explicitly, that the brand's current formulation is optimal.

[2]"Focal" is intended to remind the reader that, in any project, advertisers are concerned with one from all possible substantive domains, which they select because of their own expertise or interest. The focal domain spans the worlds of user (e.g., context for activity) and producer (e.g., materials and process).

select the conditions to be targeted, and the prospects who experience them. As to conditions, what is at issue are the differing kinds of personal and environmental context for engaging in the focal activity. *Targeted prospects*, for brevity referred to as targets, are prospects who experience the *targeted conditions*.

3. Place in their environment a message that targets will process and store accurately enough so that they will consider the advertised brand's name and features when they make purchase and use decisions for the targeted conditions.

When I unpack my original objective (a) into these three steps, step 3 is assigned to advertising professionals. However, in order to implement step 3, advertising professionals must understand how targets and targeted conditions are defined, that is they must be thoroughly conversant with the evidence and analysis of steps 1 and 2. They need such understanding for two aspects of the task of securing the ad's communicative objectives (Fennell, 1979): exposing the ad in the environment of targets (for which choosing media vehicles is at issue); having targets process, and appropriately store the ad's message (for which gaining the attention of targets in the audience of a media vehicle is at issue).

Choosing Conditions to Target

As noted, advertisers seek to communicate, not with an entire population, but with prospects for their offering. After analysis, an advertiser may choose some, most, or all prospects as targets, depending on the degree of specificity that is strategically appropriate for the offering. Essentially, the targeting decision addresses the degree to which one's offering is tailored for one or more *kind of context* in which prospects engage in the focal activity. For example, if prospects are defined as "individuals planning to take a winter vacation," the Suntown tourist office may advertise to all prospects with a message like, "Suntown is the best for your winter vacation," or it may plan to develop its services and tailor its message for *some* prospects, for example, those for whom one among conditions such as the following is a significant part of their context for a winter vacation: exhaustion from overwork, impressing one's coworkers, exploring ski slopes whose features are technically interesting, enjoying the sensory experiences of a favorite hobby. In fact, the analysis is yet more complex in that different conditions may feature significantly in the context for a winter vacation depending on whether an individual plans to vacation alone, with spouse, or in a family group, that is, variation in the context for a focal activity may occur intraindividually as well as interindividually.

Summary: Three Implications

The preceding way of thinking about strategic alternatives is commonplace among advertising professionals. In many respects, however, such analysis is not reflected in the academic literature which, by and large, has overlooked the advertiser's underlying conceptual model. For simplicity here let me note three significant points.

1. The analysis starts by focusing on one small part of the users' world. Advertisers identify prospects, that is, individuals who engage in a focal activity. They study the conditions that give rise to such activity, which, along with other information, provides a basis for judging if there is an opportunity to compete with existing brand offerings.
2. Once intraindividual variation is recognized, the relevant universe changes from individuals to occasions for action.
3. However desirable it may seem, on grounds of analytic convenience, to be able to characterize individuals across activities and contexts within activity, users come to know and evaluate brand performance in individual instances of use. That means that marketing research and analysis must be conceived in light of representations of a single occasion for action.

I now discuss each of these considerations in turn.

Analysis Begins in the User's World

Instead of focusing first on the user's world, available formulations, whether originating in mainstream psychology, consumer behavior, or academic marketing, typically start by obtaining reactions to existing or candidate goods/services. Consider attitude formulations, which are cast in terms of cognitions (for example, expectations, information) and affect (for example, evaluations, feelings) in regard to an attitude object (e.g., good/service, or act in relation to a good/service). Similarly, in "laddering" (e.g., Reynolds & Gutman, 1988) researchers follow a procedure of repeated questioning regarding reactions to examples of goods/services; in market structure analysis (e.g., Shocker, Stewart, & Zahorik, 1990) researchers ask respondents to mention activities or situations for which they consider examples of goods/services to be appropriate; and in benefit segmentation (e.g., Haley, 1968) researchers inquire into individuals' reactions to the benefits associated with examples of goods/services. Moreover, extending such approaches—principally, attitudinal approaches—by first classifying respondents, researchers use classificatory schemes that characterize individuals across activity domains and/or occasions within domain (using, for exam-

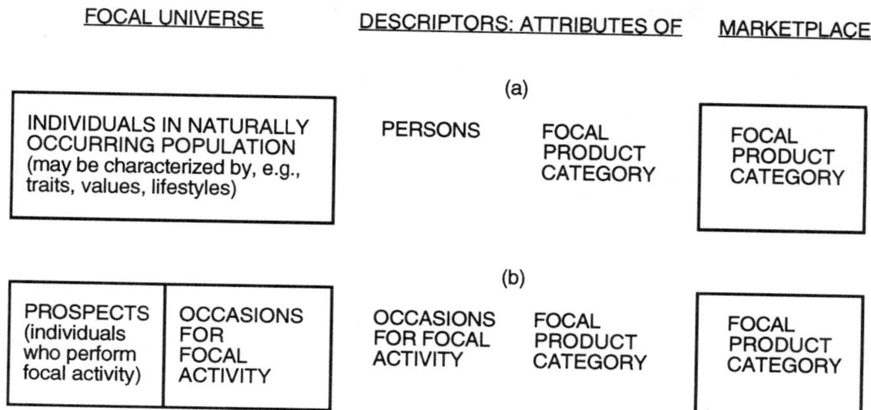

FIG. 5.1. (a) Essentials of existing formulations and research approaches; (b) essentials of formulation that reflects advertiser's task.

ple, traits, values, lifestyles). The essentials of these approaches are shown in Fig. 5.1a, where two basic flaws may be noted: (a) From the universe of marketplace offerings (or, more broadly, attitude objects) researchers select some for study, usually asking questions about attributes of, and/or associations for, the selected offerings. However, researchers obtain such reactions without selecting respondents in a manner that is appropriate to the marketplace offerings being studied. In particular, the scope of personal descriptors such as traits, values, or lifestyles, which researchers sometimes use, is too broad in comparison with the narrow range of relevance of a focal brand. Moreover, available models and formulations fail to raise the issue of identifying in the users' world the behavioral counterpart to a brand. (b) The absence of conceptual development of the conditions that give rise to value in marketplace offerings makes it difficult for advertisers to investigate such conditions systematically, as a basis for (i) assessing, from an independent vantage point, the attributes of existing offerings, and respondents' reactions to such attributes in light of the conditions that they experience, or (ii) generating and proposing attributes for modified or new offerings.

In contrast, the advertiser's task requires an approach that first studies the conditions affecting prospective users that may predispose them to buy/use a focal product category. As depicted in Fig. 5.1b, advertisers first identify prospects in the general population (i.e., individuals who engage in an activity that corresponds to the focal product category), and then study the varying contexts in which they perform such activity, thus identifying attributes of the conditions in which the focal product category may be used. In this way, planners and researchers may assess attributes of the focal product category and of candidate brands in light of attributes of *relevant conditions in the user's world* (i.e., of occasions for performing the focal activity), which also constitute an independent basis for proposing features for modified and new offerings.

A Universe of Occasions for Action: Sources of Intraindividual Variation

Considering intraindividual variation, we may distinguish variation across and within activity domain. Marketing research practice has long taken a position on each kind of variation.

Variation Across Activity Domain

Recall that the outside limit of an advertiser's interest extends to individuals who currently give grounds for believing that they may be interested in a focal product category. To qualify such prospects, researchers usually accept an affirmative answer to a question about engaging in a focal activity. In other words, selecting individuals who engage in a focal activity, professional marketing researchers sideline the issue that so exercises personality psychologists, that is, whether behavior is or is not consistent across activity domain. As a first step in defining their market, advertisers select individuals who engage in the focal activity, for example, for laundry detergent, all individuals who do laundry.

Variation Within Activity Domain

Exploring the context for the focal activity in qualitative research, marketing researchers have known to probe for intra- as well as interindividual variability within activity. Specifying the relevant universe in terms of *occasions* for engaging, rather than *individuals* who engage, in a focal activity, acknowledges that, within the one individual, conditions for performing a focal activity may change over the course of a focal time period: Change may occur in conditions of the *external* environment (e.g., seasonally, with associated change in weather conditions; change of physical location due to work or family obligations, or leisure pursuits); and in conditions of the *personal* environment (e.g., mood, available information). Beneficial consequences that arise when the model is stated in terms of occasions rather than individuals, include these two: (a) Planners and researchers are directed to deal explicitly with the fact of intraindividual variation *within* activity domain, for example, they are reminded to investigate the sources

FIG. 5.2. Universe of occasions for action.

of such variation systematically; (b) Estimating the contribution of different contexts for a focal activity to total volume of use is facilitated.[3] Accordingly, for strategic analysis and planning, the relevant universe is one of occasions for a focal action (Fig. 5.2) such as feeding the baby (baby food), shaving one's beard (razors), doing the laundry (laundry detergent).[4] Let me clarify a small point here without allowing it to distract from the main thread of my argument. While marketing researchers usually phrase screening questions in terms of actions actually performed, such as "preparing a meal," "planning a winter vacation," "feeding the cat," or "doing the laundry," research interest extends to all the occasions on which the focal activity may arise, that is, occasions on which qualified individuals may consider, but not actually perform "preparing a meal." Researchers may examine such occasions in qualitative research and later, in the quantitative phase, investigate incidence of the information obtained.

---

[3]To clarify my use of "occasions," let me note that: (a) "occasions" are the units in which the size of a focal universe is enumerated, that is, instead of the number of individuals who engage in a focal activity, for example, prepare breakfast for self/family, what is at issue here is the number of occasions for breakfast preparation (in a focal geographic region and period of time); (b) my theoretical taxonomy of "kinds of occasions" classifies the conditions that allocate people's resources into five simple and two complex categories; and (c) my model of a behavioral episode represents motivational (i.e., resource allocating) and instrumental (i.e., resource using) aspects of an occasion on which action may occur. Use of "occasions" elsewhere in the literature (e.g., as in the phrase "occasion segmentation," or "kinds of use occasion" in market structure analysis), is broadly similar to my use at (b), in that kinds of occasion is at issue, but differs, among other respects, in that the categories of occasion are not, as in my approach, theoretically specified, nor are considerations such as (a) and (c) discussed.

[4]Practical considerations, and clear strategic thinking, require more specificity than this so that the focal universe is stated to indicate a focal geographic region and period of time and whether or not some individuals who engage in the focal activity are to be omitted, on grounds, for example, of low frequency, family or personal relevance of the activity, communicative, or competitive considerations, for example, "all occasions for doing personal laundry in the United States in 1994 for adult females who do laundry at least once a week." (See discussion of market definition in Fennell, 1982a.)

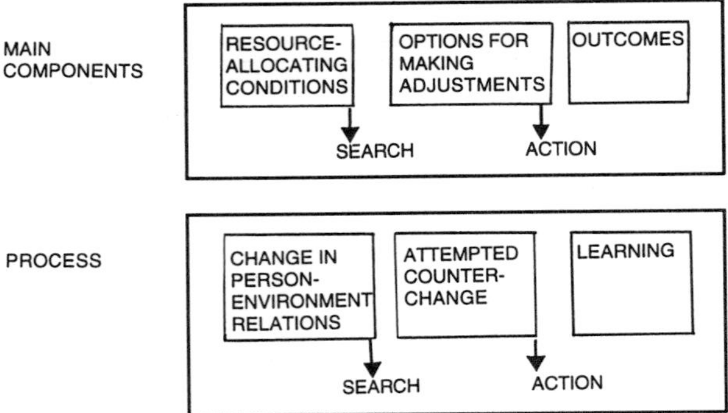

FIG. 5.3. A behavioral episode: components and process.

A Behavioral Episode: Behavioral Scope of a Single Good/Service

It is in individual instances of use that a brand does or does not deliver its promised satisfaction. Hence, research interest is focused on a small region of an individual's tasks and interests that must be studied in concrete detail. The qualifying questions that I referred to earlier as well as exploratory[5] qualitative research are procedures that permit researchers to investigate the varied contexts in which people perform a focal activity. In order to do so systematically, attention is directed to conceptualizing and describing a single instance in which an individual may perform a focal action. Let me note in passing, that, as behavioral scientists, we may have resisted focusing on the single instance, afraid that we must then open the door to a deluge of minutiae. However, being true to the nature of the phenomenon that we study means finding order in behavior as it naturally occurs, including representing the conditions of actual experience. Moreover, the mere fact of modeling an occasion for action does not compel one to investigate all such occurrences. Most significantly, it places an investigator in a position to choose research strategies, systematically, in light of the relevant conditions. Let me now be more specific about the nature of the conditions to which marketers and advertisers are responsive.

The advertiser's need to investigate single instances of everyday human activities poses a conceptual question of great interest: What kinds of conditions are common to all instances in any universe of action? One approach to modeling the single instance is to conceive of a behavioral episode, which is represented here by just three main components. Figure 5.3 represents any occasion for action in the universe shown in Fig. 5.2. It is a greatly simplified version of a more detailed model (e.g., Fennell,

[5]As noted elsewhere (Fennell, 1985b, p. 547 note, 1991b), researchers are exploring, not for constructs (Calder, 1977), but for specific information about the real world.

1988). In what follows, I focus first on structural aspects and then on process.

Structure

Very briefly, because I have discussed this elsewhere (e.g., Fennell, 1980, 1988, 1991a), action may occur as part of a behavioral episode. For those accustomed to think in terms of expectancy-value models, the two components to the right will be familiar—options for action, and outcomes. To the left, is the less familiar "resource-allocating conditions" (RAC). RAC initiate a behavioral episode by instating the substantive domain in which cognitive processing occurs. They comprise an individual's domains of sensitivity and environmental circumstances which, at above threshold values, specify the domain (e.g., body temperature) in which cognitive activity occurs, and the desired adjustment within that domain (e.g., becoming warmer).

One way to think of this model is that it is extending upstream the behavioral terrain that expectancy-value models represent, which, typically, envisage an individual who is already considering one or more options that the researcher has presented. Expectancy-value models are not designed to study an individual allocating his or her resources to a substantive domain and criterion of value, and generating relevant instrumental options. Investigating such questions, however, is necessary if one wants to guide creating offerings appropriate to the conditions that prompt individuals to value certain outcomes, and generate and consider relevant options. Accordingly, I want to represent the naturally occurring conditions that select the domain (e.g., body temperature) and criterion of value within that domain (e.g., making warmer) for cognitive activities such as the following: searching memory and the current environment for instrumental acts/objects; generating and judging one or more candidate acts/objects and, if more than one is being considered, selecting one to judge for costworthiness and, possibly, to perform; if the individual performs an action and unfavorably evaluates the outcome, further cognitive processing along the same lines may occur leading to trying another option; if she or he favorably evaluates the outcome, the episode ends.[6]

---

[6]In the interest of clarifying differences between the present approach and others, let me say that precisely because expectancy-value formulations do not include a term comparable to RAC, they cannot be regarded as addressing the topic of motivation, as Feather (1988a, p. 381) claims: "For many years now, expectancy-value theory has been a key theoretical approach in the psychology of motivation." Similarly, because they omit a resource-allocating term, expectancy-value formulations are deficient as models of action. Feather (idem.) continues: "The distinctive characteristic of this (i.e., expectancy-value) theoretical approach is the attempt to relate action (choice, performance, and persistence) to the perceived attractiveness and aversiveness of expected outcomes. A person's actions are assumed to bear

Such cognitive activities implicate some variables that expectancy-value theorists study, especially the degree to which outcomes are valued, and the likelihood/expectation that performing a particular act in regard to a particular object will lead to a valued outcome. However, from the upstream vantage point of a behavioral episode, such cognitive variables assume a different role in my model compared with expectancy-value formulations. In a behavioral episode, interest focuses on the upstream conditions to which an individual is sensitive that allocate his or her resources to a substantive domain, and specify a criterion of value, which in turn selects the options that an individual generates within the focal domain. Accordingly, degree of association with a valued outcome is a variable that affects (via noncompensatory processing) the options that an *individual generates*, and assesses (via compensatory processing). This is, of course, in sharp contrast to expectancy-value formulations, where subjects' expectations and values associated with *researcher-presented* options are investigated with a view to explaining preference among such options.

In sum, the first component of a behavioral episode (RAC), represents the conditions that determine the domain and criterion of value to which cognitive resources are allocated; the second component has to do with the options within that domain that an individual may generate and consider using in trying to effect the adjustment. The third component focuses on the outcome of engaging in action, for example, the extent to which the individual believes that she or he has been successful in making a desired adjustment. Note that, specifying the domain and kind of adjustment that the individual considers, RAC are influential throughout a behavioral episode. Accordingly, marketplace offerings (competing products and brands), which, along with nonmarketplace options, are represented by the second component, enter the model if the individual considers them relevant to effecting an adjustment that is underway.

Resource-Allocating Conditions (RAC). Given that an individual's resources are always allocated in one way or another, interest focuses on the conditions that select the substantive domain and criterion of value to which resources are allocated. RAC comprise personal and environmental conditions, whether enduring or transitory, that bring a particular substantive domain to center stage for an individual. They interrupt what is ongoing, bringing concerns and opportunities to focal attention. Appraising

---

assumed to bear some relation to the expectations that the person holds and to the subjective values (or valences) of the outcomes that might occur after the actions." An expectancy-value formulation does not, however, reach to the (motivating) conditions that select the substantive domain and criterion of valued outcome for action, which are represented by RAC in my model. Further points on which my position differs from Feather's are discussed later in this chapter.

the newly-in-focus state of affairs, an individual may decide that the interruption was unwarranted, and return to whatever had been ongoing. On the personal side, RAC include domains of sensitivity whether sensory (e.g., sensations of cold, heat, pressure), or cognitive (e.g., information regarding threats or opportunities), and the notion of threshold values of variables in such domains. On the environmental side, they comprise the presence of above threshold values of variables in domains to which individuals are sensitive. It is much easier to point to a few categories of stimulus that are not, than to list all those that are, capable of allocating an individual's resources. Stimuli that are outside the range of human sense organs (such as dog whistles, whose frequency is too high for human ears to detect), and names of celebrities in unfamiliar fields do not normally reallocate individuals' resources. On the other hand, individuals sitting quietly in an unchanging external environment may find their resources reallocated. For example, they may: (a) understand in a new and personally significant way a remark heard a few days previously; (b) realize that there is a means of improving some condition that they had previously considered intractable; or (c) feeling tired and irritable at having missed lunch, now see as grossly unjust a comment that yesterday they had heard with indifference.

We can distinguish classes of RAC, depending on considerations such as whether experienced discomfort: is actual or signaled; if actual, whether experienced as severe and likely to continue, or mild and worsening; arises because of uninterpretable information; arises from perceived opportunity for sensory pleasure (Fennell, 1978, 1980). Perhaps what I can point to most concretely to orient a reader to the notion of RAC are the classic procedures for getting behavior started in the instrumental learning laboratory—the experimental *arrangements* that determine, for example, if behavior labeled escape, avoidance, maintenance (e.g., using food/water deprivation), exploratory (e.g., using stimuli varying in complexity), or sensation-seeking (e.g., using taste-appealing nonnutritive substances; sexual lures) is being studied. Much of the work there, of course, is concerned with detailed investigations *within* one or other of the classic kinds of resource-allocating operation. Here, interest focuses on looking across the different kinds, with the assumption that each represents a class of real world conditions that allocate resources in characteristic ways (see Fig. 5.4).

For present purposes, the significant point about RAC is that individuals have domains of sensitivity: Certain conditions rivet their attention and allocate their cognitive processing to a particular substantive domain. Virtually all people who speak the same language may have a particular sensitive domain in common, as in the case of the sound, "fire." In other cases, only individuals who share a common interest or concern may share particular sensitive domains. Some sensitive domains may be totally unique

SIMPLE

ESCAPE. (Believed) presence of grave, unpleasant circumstances whose occurrence is outside the actor's control in the short run. The actor must deal with them in some way. "Grave" may refer to physical intensity, speed on onset, or frequency, of something an individual dislikes.

Essential idea: Unpleasantness will continue, unless I act.

PREVENTION. (Believed) future presence of unpleasant circumstances whose occurrence, being contingent on the actor's behavior, may be prevented. Negative evaluations are significant here--whether the source is oneself or another, and whether the other is a human being, an infant, or some nonhuman entity whom the actor imbues with human capacities.

Essential idea: Future unpleasantness is assured unless I act (appropriately).

MAINTENANCE. (Believed) presence of a state of affairs that requires action--maintenance of some sort--to keep it functioning. Deterioration is outside the actor's control in the short run, and all the actor can do is periodically make good whatever deficit has occurred.

Essential idea: Unpleasantness will worsen, unless I act.

EXPLORATORY INTEREST. Experienced difficulty in processing information. The actor becomes aware that insufficient, too much, contradictory, unexpected, information is impeding his/her ability to process information and that steps must be taken to remove this impediment.

Essential idea: Impediment to information processing must be removed.

SENSORY PLEASURE OPPORTUNITY. (Actual or imagined) opportunity for sensory pleasure that the actor is not yet enjoying.

Essential idea: Deficiency will continue, until I experience these sensations.

More than one of the above classes may coexist. Moreover, any one may become a complex case should the indicated action be seen to entail an added source of activation, such as:

COMPLEX CASES

CONFLICT. Effecting the adjustment that the activating change calls for entails its own source of activation. It is seen to entail some disproportionate cost.

FRUSTRATION. Counterchange is called for but no means of effecting it is available.

FIG. 5.4. Classes of motivating condition.

to an individual, such as a distinctively patterned leaf that has personal significance. While I may seem to be saying that people are sensitive to what people are sensitive to, I am saved from useless circularity by the fact that, if they are to produce and promote responsive offerings, advertisers must start by investigating attributes of the conditions to which people are sensitive. So that advertisers may do so systematically, an appropriate model must represent the various kinds of condition that people use their resources to try to adjust, possibly using a good/service to help do so.

Process

We may also think of a behavioral episode as a process that begins when a *change* in person–environment relations (i.e., variables in domains of sensitivity are at above-threshold values) prompts an individual to consider, and try to effect, *counterchange* (i.e., a substantive domain is brought to focal attention for possible adjusting); whatever the outcome, *learning* occurs (Fig. 5.3).

One Mechanism for Behavioral Adjusting. Although I have identified motivational classes that are structurally different from each other and although adjusting may be occasioned by high or low nonequilibrial values, it does not follow that there is more than one motivational mechanism (Fennell, 1992). To the contrary, I postulate a single mechanism in all cases: Nonequilibrial values of variables in domains of sensitivity bring the domain to focal attention, raising the possibility of spending resources to effect an adjustment in that domain (Fennell, 1988). The individual allocates further resources if, comparing actual and imagined states, there is a disparity favoring the imagined state that justifies spending resources to try to improve matters. Whether the imagined state *lacks* attributes that are present in the actual state or *possesses* attributes that are absent in the actual state, that is, whether the individual wants *not to have* or *to have*, the behaviorally significant element is that she or he may be able to improve her or his state of being. In the sense of not being as good as it might be, the individual's actual state appears deficient—lacking in some particular way, and to a degree that warrants spending resources.

A Nested Model of Action

Even in the abbreviated form of the model that I am using here, it is plain that the present is a view of action that sharply contrasts with a simple stimulus–response view. For a long time, psychologists have been dissatisfied with the notion that action is related in some simple manner to a stimulus. The present perspective offers a concrete alternative to such a simple S–R view. If action is observed, it has arisen in a two-step manner: A first stage instates a particular domain and subdomain of the psychological environment, within which a second stage of constructing and attempting one or more candidate acts may occur. The second stage is nested within the first. In contrast to a universal S–R behavioral unit, such a nested view requires that we ask regarding any stimulus whether its role is *motivational*, that is, participating in allocating resources to a substantive domain and kind of outcome, or *instrumental*, that is, within a focal substantive domain, participating in directing instrumental behavior (more accurately,

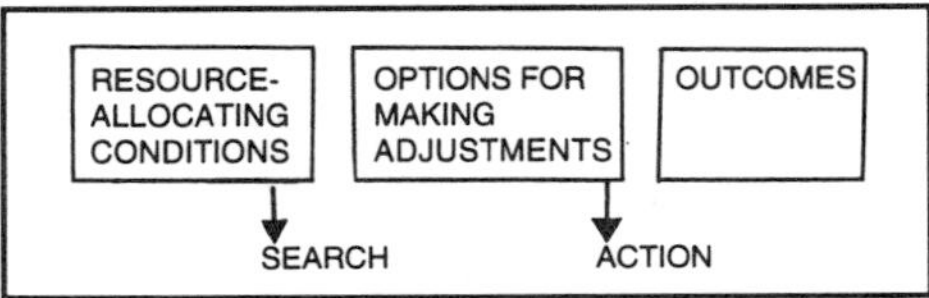

FIG. 5.5. Personal and environmental variables.

participating in directing behavior expected or hoped to be instrumental in producing a valued outcome).

Contribution From Person and Environment

Personal and environmental conditions, each of which may be enduring or transitory, are jointly implicated throughout a behavioral episode (Fig. 5.5). A specific action that is observed arises from enduring and transitory personal conditions combining with enduring and transitory environmental conditions to allocate an individual's resources to a particular substantive domain and subdomain (criterion of value) and, within that domain, from enduring and transitory personal conditions combining with enduring and transitory environmental conditions to generate, select, assess for costworthiness, and try to perform an instrumental act.

It is of interest to consider the present in light of Lewin's (1936) formulation, $B = f(S)$; $S = f(P, E)$, which, as I discussed elsewhere (Fennell, 1987), is often mistakenly stated as: $B = f(P \times S)$. Although Lewin did not represent the behavioral domain upstream from the options being considered, and did not have a construct comparable to RAC, my formulation is congruent with his thinking in three respects: It views behavior as situational (cf. $B = f(S)$), with both personal and environmental conditions contributing to the situation (cf. $S = f(P, E)$), and it distinguishes between concrete (e.g., eye color) and abstract (e.g., trait label) characteristics (Fennell, 1987).

Inadequacy of Trait Approaches. Two additional points follow fairly obviously: The present formulation clarifies why trait approaches to explaining action have produced disappointing results. Traits are thought of as attributes of the person that are present over time, and across activities. So construed, they are one—enduring personal—of four kinds of variable that may contribute to action. Moreover, in the present approach personal and environmental conditions combine in a nested manner—first to allocate resources to a substantive domain for possible adjusting and then, *within* that domain, to direct resources among ways of effecting the adjustment—a complexity that is not reflected in a procedure that would predict observed behavior from an enduring attribute of the person.[7]

RECENT DISCUSSION OF THE ROLE OF VALUES

In one respect, my analysis is broadly congruent with recent discussion of the role of values in explaining observed behavior (e.g., Feather, 1988b; Homer & Kahle, 1988; Williams, 1979). Specifically, the notion that, to predict action, values require the mediation of other constructs such as attitude (e.g., Feather, 1988; Homer & Kahle, 1988) is consistent in a general way with the two-step form of my model of a behavioral episode. Admittedly, such congruence with other authors as I detect may partly trace to the relative ambiguity of what other authors have stated regarding values, given that they do not distinguish, as does my model of a behavioral episode, between the conditions that allocate resources *to*, and direct behavior *within*, a substantive domain. On the other hand, Fischhoff's (1991) view of values contrasts sharply with my own, in that he may consider values only in the context of the instrumental aspect of a behavioral episode. In what follows I discuss reactions to the words of three values theorists that arise from the perspective of a behavioral episode.

Williams

Consider, for example, Williams' (1979) statement: "Actual selections of behavior result from concrete motivations in specific situations: Both the motivations and the definitions of the situation are partly determined by the prior beliefs and values of the actor" (p. 20).

The "actual selections" are represented in my model as a choice among options (second component of Fig. 5.3), and "the prior beliefs and values" that "partly determine(d) both the motivations and the definitions of the situation" are represented among RAC (first component of Fig. 5.3). The two-step form of my model provides explicitly for additional variables to enter at the stage of generating options, notably, the individual's beliefs concerning what is currently available in the environment. Williams also stated: "Values serve as criteria for selection in action" (p. 16), leaving

[7]An example, present in marketing and advertising practice for decades, is the pattern of association for the personal descriptors of demographic classification, that is, some relationship with reported product use/purchase, and frequency of product use/purchase (domain of resource allocation) compared with virtual independence as regards reported brand use/purchase (actual behavior).

ambiguous whether he refers to selecting a substantive domain in which action may occur, choosing among options, or both.

Ambiguity on another topic is evident when Williams (1979) indicates his unwillingness to reject a view of values "as significant causes of behavior" (p. 23), in light of findings on the relationship between values, measured in the manner of traits, and behavior. However convenient it may be for researchers to develop instruments that permit them to characterize individuals across activity domains and contexts, hoping thereby to predict observed action, the resulting categories and labels cannot reasonably be regarded as "causing" behavior. Only events that are present in the contemporaneous context can be considered to cause or, more weakly, affect behavior. It is, for example, the perceived presence of concrete violation of, or opportunity to enjoy, some valued condition that places a substantive domain and criterion of value in focal attention, thus enabling the individual to consider allocating further resources to trying to effect a corresponding adjustment. Later, an analyst may classify under a common label what an individual reports about such an event and others, along with reports from other individuals. However, it is the event itself rather than the subsequent label or abstract category that has affected behavior. A description of the context in which people make decisions about food buying that remains close to actual experience consists of sensations, beliefs, feelings relative to the *conditions that lead to meal preparation*. Rather than the abstract labels of theorists, it is such concrete elements that determine the substantive domain and criterion of value that pertain during a behavioral episode.

Feather

Let me begin by noting some points at which Feather's views are broadly congruent with my own. When Feather (1988a) extended the theoretical reach of expectancy-value formulations by including the effect of values on behavior, he seemed to recognize the deficiency in expectancy-value formulations to which I referred above when discussing structural aspects of a behavioral episode. However, as noted (see Footnote 6), he did not, as I do, express the deficiency as the absence of a motivational term in expectancy-value formulations:

> This extension can be made if one assumes that personal values, like needs or motives, function to influence a person's subjective definition of a situation so that certain objects, activities, and states of affairs within the immediate situation acquire either positive valence (become attractive) or negative valence (become aversive), to use Lewin's (1936) terminology. Like needs and wants, a person's values may selectively sensitize the individual to certain objects and activities within a situation . . . Just as food and ways of getting food will become salient and acquire demand characteristics when a person

is hungry, so too will a person's values sensitize the person "to perceive some potential events and activities as desirable and worth approaching or continuing with, and other aspects as undesirable, to be avoided or terminated" (Feather, 1982, p. 277). (p. 381)

In postulating that "values . . . sensitize the person to perceive some potential events . . . as desirable . . . ," and that "food . . . will become salient . . . *when a person is hungry* (emphasis added)," Feather's words are consistent with my position that expectancy-value formulations lack a motivational term, that is, one that represents selecting a substantive domain within which to generate, assess, choose among, and try to perform, options for action. Moreover, some of Feather's (1988b, pp. 119–120) suggestions for developing a values-action model are addressed within my formulation. His calling for greater specificity in the behavior studied is congruent with my own interest in going beyond the abstraction inherent in the names of activities (e.g., Feather's "finding employment") to the concrete context in which action occurs (Feather's "how an unemployed person handles an interview for a specific job"). Further, my concept of RAC may address what Feather seeks when he calls for a "comprehensive theory about the processes that determine valences or demand characteristics in particular situations," and for "theoretical analysis of how needs and values are engaged in a situation." Notwithstanding such possibilities for common ground between Feather's position and my own, in addition to the differences that I already noted (see Footnote 6), let me make the following points by way of sharpening a distinction between my approach and Feather's.

First, Feather (1988a, p. 381) has not stated the conditions under which "values" may "sensitize the person . . ." Second, in the previous sentence, I have placed "values" in quotation marks to indicate that the term is ambiguous when it comes to real world applications—for two related reasons. If abstract "values" is intended then, as noted, values cannot reasonably be regarded as affecting behavior. If "values" means a cognition stated in the concrete terms of a focal substantive domain, and present during a real world behavioral episode, it will be helpful if values theorists so specify and clarify the distinction between values and other kinds of term (e.g., values terms contain/imply an "ought" word; are rules of thumb as articulated in everyday circumstances).

Third, there is much to recommend reverting to the Lewinian (1936) formulation: $B = f(S)$; $S = f(P, E)$, which, as noted, seems to have all but disappeared from general discourse, having been replaced by the misleading, $B = f(P \times S)$. Let me state two implications that are relevant here. The first is that the Lewinian formulation readily permits distinguishing between the variables that constitute the totality of person and environment, on the one hand and, on the other, those personal and environmental variables that receive focal attention through the course of a situation, or behavioral episode. If Feather thus distinguished "situation" from "environment," he would likely have written "environment" in place of the second "situation" in the following sentence, which I quoted earlier: ". . . personal values, like needs or motives, function to influence a person's subjective definition of a situation so that certain . . . states of affairs within the immediate situation (substitute "environment") acquire either positive . . . or negative valence . . . ," and, similarly, in the following sentence, "Like needs and wants, a person's values may selectively sensitize the individual to certain objects and activities within a situation" (substitute "the environment"). The second implication is that Feather's words need more radical revision to reflect the joint contribution of person and environment to establishing a situation, or behavioral episode. In my formulation, as in Lewin's, there is an explicit place for environmental variables, as perceived and as available, along with personal variables (e.g., Feather's "personal values . . . needs . . . motives"). In fact, extending an expectancy-value model by adding "personal values," Feather has a formulation that is roughly in the form: $B = f(P[\text{values}] \times S[\text{attitude}])$. In contrast, in a behavioral episode as in Lewin's $S = f(P, E)$, environmental conditions (e.g., time since last meal) combining with a personal domain of sensitivity (hunger sensations) may cause departure from a state of well-being and bring the domain of nourishment to focal attention. The individual considers effecting an adjustment within that domain, finding his or her attention selectively focused on aspects of the environment that have acquired value by virtue of their relevant instrumentality.

Fourth, a fundamental difference between Feather's approach and my own lies in our respective immediate interests, hypothesis-testing in Feather's case and systematic description in my own. Such objectives are not basically in competition with each other. In fact, a model that has been developed to aid those who wish to describe systematically an aspect of the behavioral universe may be of interest to theorists whose empirical work has focused on developing psychology's traditional constructs. It remains to be seen if Feather will make explicit, in the context of an individual instance of behavior, his statement of the role of values in explaining behavior. The first of two additional points, related to the preceding, is the advertiser's need for concrete description. As noted, advertisers want to (a) imbue offerings with attributes that are responsive to the attributes, personal and environmental, of the conditions in which people may use brands, as well as (b) depict such targeted conditions in ads in order to engage the attention of targets, informing them that a brand responsive to conditions that they experience is available (Fennell, 1979). Information at the requisite level of concreteness is not to be found in the names of values, in the sense of the classificatory terms that analysts create when they abstract across activities and contexts. Whatever use such abstract terms have elsewhere, advertising's task requires obtaining information at the concrete level of the single event. The second related point is a corresponding requirement that an appropriate formulation specify the unit of analysis (e.g., an occasion on which a focal action may occur) and the outside limits of the relevant universe (e.g., all occasions on which a focal action may occur in a given period of time and geographic region).

Finally, as regards Feather's suggestion (e.g., Feather, 1988a, p. 321) that the construct of values enhances behavioral understanding by extending the scope of expectancy-value formulations, I have noted some congruence with my own theoretical position. It may already be obvious why I find the attitude construct unsatisfactory as a starting point for advertising-relevant analysis, but let me briefly make the problem explicit. As long as attitude research fails to provide for the construct's ambiguity as regards domains of sensitivity, attitude's explanatory power will remain low (Fennell, 1990). The point is that one may learn that an individual has a favorable attitude to a particular car because of its "reliability," yet, without knowing if the individual has in mind traveling on lonely roads, operating on an extremely tight budget, living in the rust belt, daily contending with fast-moving traffic, being thought of as a discerning car purchaser, or other sensitivities, an investigator has gained no information on the concrete conditions that pertain for the individual. Note, however, that adding "values," in the sense of an abstraction across activity domains and contexts, does nothing to bring such specific domains of sensitivity to the fore, and thus fails to repair the limitation of the attitude construct, which remains as ambiguous, motivationally, as before. That is not to say that the cognitive and affective components of attitude, stated with a degree of specificity appropriate to real world actions, are not relevant in explaining behavior. To the contrary, as a behavioral episode unfolds, it is apparent that various kinds of cognition (e.g., beliefs about: technical requirements of an adjustment under way, the properties of specific acts/objects, one's own abilities and those of potential helpers in relation to such requirements, the availability of assistance through objects/persons, costworthiness) and affect (e.g., not only liking/disliking but hope; not only satisfaction/dissatisfaction but relief, joy, delight, anger, rage; Fennell, 1981) are present in the instrumental context for action. Indeed, when one's objective is description, interest focuses on just such concrete cognitions and affects as well as those that pertain to the motivational context, that is, the domains of sensitivity that are activated.

Fischhoff

Questions more fundamental than the author raises may present themselves to a reader of Fischhoff's (1991, p. 835) commentary on "value [*sic*] elicitation" in a variety of disciplines. Such questions relate to the nature of values and the role that values may play in real-world behavior. I have selected two topics for discussion here, namely, Fischhoff's failing to distinguish between value and values, and his linking value(s) to "possible," to the exclusion of actual, events (Fischhoff, 1991; Fischhoff, Slovic, & Lichtenstein, 1980, pp. 117–118).

Value Versus Values

A first question is prompted by Fischhoff's use of "value" in the paper's title, and "values" in the opening sentence of the abstract ("Eliciting people's values is . . . ," p. 835). Fischhoff does not develop a distinction between value elicitation and values elicitation and, to cast light on this matter, I turn to an earlier statement of what "values" means (Fischhoff, Slovic, & Lichtenstein, 1980).

> By "values," we mean evaluative judgments regarding the relative or absolute worth or desirability of possible events. Such events may be general (being honest) or specific (winning a particular lottery). Their consequences (or outcomes) may have one or many salient attributes and may be certainties[8] or possibilities. Such a broad definition captures just about any task ever included under the topics of value, choice, or preference, as well as many that would fit comfortably under attitudes, opinions, and decision making. (pp. 117–118)

Here too, it may be fair to say that the authors see no need to distinguish "values" and "value." In contrast, from the perspective of a behavioral episode, "values" (in two senses) and "value" must be distinguished. As regards the former, let me first remind the reader that earlier I contrasted abstract values (i.e., the category labels that analysts create in combining across activities and contexts) with concrete cognitive and affective elements present in the context for real world action, including the individual's devaluing a currently experienced state. Value in the latter sense, but not abstract values may affect behavior. Second, there are the relatively low level rules of thumb, noted by values theorists, that may be present in the context for real world action, for example, "cleanliness is next to godliness" (Fischhoff et al., 1980, p. 118). Research is needed to investigate the role that such sayings play in actual behavior. Just how little guidance

[8]Elsewhere (e.g., Fennell, 1986, 1988), I have taken the position that, in advance of acting, the outcome (i.e., effecting a desired adjustment) is always uncertain for the actor—for a variety of reasons, including the fact that the actor may be unable to effect the intended act (e.g., the environment may not be as the actor believes it to be), the outcome may not be what the actor expects, the expected outcome may not effect the desired adjustment. I would welcome the authors' clarifying their view that the "outcomes" of "possible events" may be "certainties."

they provide from an advertiser's perspective may be apparent when one reflects that the phrase could be used in the context, among others, of getting clothes clean (e.g., laundering, dry cleaning), personal hygiene (e.g., body, hair, teeth), household cleaning (e.g., baths, tiles, toilets, food preparation surfaces, floors, carpets), pest control, and dishwashing. Not only do such activities differ from each other in their physical circumstances and personal sensitivities, as well as the array of goods/services offered for each, but a consistent finding from exploratory qualitative research is one of heterogeneous conditions *within* activity.

Behavioral Role of Value: Possible Versus Actual Events

Of particular interest here is the authors' view that the place in behavior of value(s) is in regard to *possible* events, "evaluative judgments regarding . . . worth . . . of possible events" (Fischhoff et al., 1980, p. 117). "Possible events" raises at least two issues, the more obvious of which is that it links value(s) only to the instrumental aspect of a behavioral episode. It is necessary to consider an effect on behavior both as regards resource allocation (i.e., actual events) and choosing among instrumental options (i.e., possible events).

Relevance to Resource Allocation. Instrumental options present themselves to the actor as candidate acts with possible outcomes, whereas the actor experiences resource allocation as an existing state of affairs. The effect of value on behavior includes allocating resources to a substantive domain—as when conditions are such that a criterion of value within that domain is not being met. In the context of a behavioral episode, "value elicitation" would mean investigating (a) the personal sensitivities and environmental circumstances that bring substantive domains and criteria of value to focal attention raising, for the individual, the question of allocating resources further to try to effect an adjustment, and (b) the specific options and outcomes that the individual generates and values.

Motivational Ambiguity. "Possible" events raises a second issue in that it may refer to an individual's being asked to choose among researcher-presented options without regard to the conditions of resource allocation that give rise to the options. First, what is at issue here, in part, is a distinction between asking individuals to provide information about, on the one hand, the activities that they engage in, in their everyday life and, on the other, issues that go beyond direct personal experience. The two tasks differ in that, as regards the everyday activities in which individuals actually engage, their resources have been allocated by conditions that they experience at first hand, namely, their personal sensitivities in conjunction with environmental circumstances. This means that the candidate acts that they consider have been generated by the naturally occurring resource-allocating conditions. In the case of activities that go beyond direct personal experience, individuals are being asked to comment on scenarios that are presented to them symbolically—usually in words. In such instances, naturally occurring conditions of resource allocation are relevant to the individual's offering an opinion and only incidentally, if at all, to the specific options among which the individual is asked to choose. Consider also the parallel case of everyday versus expert decisions. Experts or professionals are asked to advise in the context of the lives of other people, their clients. Typically, whether or not in their own lives they themselves have experienced comparable conditions is not at issue. In part at least, their specialized training attempts to equip professionals with approaches to generating, and advising regarding, options in circumstances where they must act without experiencing the naturally occurring resource-allocating conditions. Undoubtedly, such training will be enhanced when it explicitly acknowledges the behavioral implications, in this respect, of expert versus client roles. It is beyond this chapter's scope to discuss in detail the conditions of resource allocation that experts and professionals experience in performing their professional assignments. For present purposes, it is sufficient to point out that, behaviorally, there are systematic differences between their roles as laypeople making the decisions of their everyday lives, and as professionals providing expert opinion. Second, consider now the implications of values researchers asking individuals for responses to questions stated solely in terms of instrumental options. Even for domains with which respondents are familiar, such a task places people in circumstances that are systematically different from those that they experience when naturally occurring conditions allocate their resources to considering action.

This is not to say that people are explicitly aware of, or readily able to articulate, the conditions that give rise to their everyday actions (see e.g., Fennell, 1982b, 1986, for a discussion of reasons and countermeasures), as advertisers discover when conducting exploratory qualitative research concerning everyday activities. However, the purpose of such research is clear. It is to obtain as much information as possible on the actual conditions that the respondents experience, as they view that experience. In contrast, whether in familiar or unfamiliar domains, when people are asked to choose among candidate acts without being provided with information on the naturally occurring context in which such acts come up for consideration, the purpose of the investigation is unclear. Plainly, its purpose is not to obtain information on the conditions of actual experience, or to investigate preferences among well-specified alternatives. Presumably, to provide the missing context (RAC), respondents search for something comparable in their own experience. The context that they construct may not be the same as the researchers had in mind, is likely to vary across respondents and, in any case, is not routinely made available for analysis within the research design. Given such ambiguity, it is not clear that the research can claim relevance to any aspect of real world behavior.

Let me distinguish what I have just been discussing from Fischhoff's (1991, p. 835) "philosophy of basic values," which holds that "people lack well-differentiated values for all but the most familiar of evaluation questions, about which they have had the chance, by trial, error, and rumination, to settle on stable values," which he places at the opposite end of a continuum from a "philosophy of articulated values." The only point of contact here is that both Fischhoff and I draw attention to an actor's first-hand experience with the substantive domain at issue. Beyond that, my model of a behavioral episode permits me to be much more specific than is Fischhoff in discussing what personal experience means behaviorally both for the actor, and for the nature of the question to which a researcher may require a response. For example, I can point out that the mere fact that one's respondents are prospective car buyers (i.e., are likely to have relevant first-hand experience in the substantive domain) does not obviate problems when researchers ask for reactions to an attribute such as "reliability," or to a question such as "Just how much worse is breaking down once a month than breaking down twice a year?" both of which are examples that Fischhoff (1991, p. 836) uses to illustrate a "philosophy of basic values." Considering the range of relevant RAC, "reliability" and "breaking down" are motivationally ambiguous (Fennell, 1978).

In sum, not only theorists of values and researchers who use inventories of values, but the rules of thumb, nouns, and activity names of everyday language, abstract across the personal and environmental conditions that constitute a behavioral episode. Research that presents such abstractions as stimuli may be useful in its own right, but its findings cannot be unambiguously related to behavioral events outside the investigative context. As they select stimuli for research, values theorists may find my model of a behavioral episode useful in clarifying the kind of ambiguity that is present when one states options for action without providing information on the corresponding conditions of resource allocation. In large measure, Fischhoff (1991) may be viewed as chronicling the anomalies that result from conducting research that is thus motivationally ambiguous.

VALUES AND ADVERTISING

Value(s) From the Perspective of a Behavioral Episode

From the perspective of a behavioral episode, I have been considering the work of selected theorists of values. Given various uses of the term, values, a first point that must be made is that there can be no single view on the relevance of values to advertising. It depends on what is meant by value(s).

Value: Worth Spending Resources to Restore

The meaning of value in a behavioral episode is clear and basic. It reflects the economics of the organism. What is valuable is what the individual is ready to spend resources for, believing such expenditure will help to effect *counter*change, that is, *restore* an acceptable state of being.

Motivational and Instrumental Aspect of Value

Note that there is both an instrumental and a motivational (cf. "terminal" Rokeach, 1973) aspect of value in a behavioral episode. The motivational aspect arises from the sense of unease that is the means by which a particular domain of sensitivity gains focal attention, permitting the individual: to review the state of affairs in that domain, to conclude that conditions are or are not acceptable and, if the latter, to assign further resources to trying to effect counterchange. The individual is then trying to bring about a state of being in which an unacceptable state of affairs in the focal domain has been rectified, that is, she or he considers that the focal domain no longer needs adjusting. If one were to name such states, it would have to be by referring to an individual's domains of sensitivity, that is, the fact that individuals have criteria for an acceptable state as regards body temperature, food/liquid intake, particular social relationships, personal hygiene, grooming, and so on. From the present perspective, these are values for the individual—conditions that it is worth spending resources to regain. The *instrumental* aspect of value arises from the fact that the individual believes that certain acts and objects will help to restore an acceptable state. Acts and objects and, in the context of relevance to advertisers, brands of goods/services that the individual believes likely to be helpful take on value, in the sense that they are candidates for a further allocation of the individual's resources. If they in fact prove to have been helpful, they likely come to mind when similar conditions recur. Note that, by definition, what has instrumental value is worth some of one's resources because it is believed useful for something beyond itself, that is, the valued state that it will likely restore.

Relevance for Advertisers: Three Aspects of Value

Relying, as they must, on tendencies that are already in place, if targets are to process, store, and use their message at the appropriate time, advertisers are interested in three aspects of value in a behavioral episode: the conditions that lead to a loss of value; the individual's judgment that using resources to restore value is warranted; and the conditions that an individual believes likely to restore value. Let me recap the advertising relevance of each of these three aspects, starting for convenience with the second.

The judgment that it is worth using resources to restore a valued state warrants allocating an advertiser's resources only when individuals so judge in a domain that corresponds to the advertiser's interest/expertise. Finding such correspondence is of critical importance, because it is the advertiser's ground for believing that an individual will process and store messages about an offering. I noted earlier that, as initial evidence of such correspondence, advertisers accept individuals' affirmative response when asked about engaging in a focal activity. However, knowing only that an individual engages in an activity does not provide information that helps to design or promote an appropriate offering. Advertisers seek such information through exploratory qualitative research, often followed by quantification. From a universe of qualified individuals, and for a focal domain, the information that advertisers want from prospects includes details of the conditions that lead to a loss of value and of the conditions that prospects believe likely to restore value.

The conditions that lead to losing a valued state (RAC) occur outside the control of an individual, who may become aware of them only after they have gained focal attention for the substantive domain and criterion of value that is implicated. Across domains, individuals' degree of understanding of the resource-allocating conditions may vary from, for example, some understanding of the conditions that give rise to a headache, to minimal or no understanding of the conditions that lead to an occasional sense of boredom or anxiousness.[9] Note, however, that for someone who frequently experiences a condition such as bothersome headaches and who may, even, have obtained medical advice, there remains a difference between the sense in which layperson and relevant experts understand the precipitating conditions. The same is true for the broad spectrum of conditions that lead to the activities for which people may use goods/services. There is always the view of the layperson, on the one hand, and of the specialist, on the other. Both are essential to creating appropriate offerings—the layperson's understanding is the specialist's point of entry into the prospective user's world, and the specialist's understanding may bring the best of science and technology to bear in creating appropriate brands. Moreover, to communicate the availability of a relevant offering to individuals in the audience of media vehicles, who experience the targeted conditions, advertisers create scenarios that use information about the RAC, as the prospective user understands such conditions.

---

[9]Conditions likely to affect such understanding include not only those that are relevant to the individual and the nature of the domain, such as familiarity and technical complexity, respectively, but the extent to which the cultural and social environment has articulated ready-made explanations that may or may not be accurate.

A third aspect of value in a behavioral episode that is of interest to an advertiser is the conditions that prospects believe likely to restore an acceptable state of affairs. These are the acts and objects, and their consequences that a prospect generates, from memory and the current environment, and considers using in trying to effect an adjustment in a focal domain. Advertisers want to obtain such information, always in the context of the operative RAC, for the insight it provides, indirectly, into the conditions that a prospect is trying to deal with and, directly, into the prospect's view of the competitive frame. Additionally, and for the same two reasons, advertisers are usually interested in obtaining information on prospects' reactions, again in light of the operative RAC, to selected marketplace offerings beyond those that prospects mention spontaneously.

Values Measured as Traits

Authors who use "value(s)" in senses different from mine are better situated than am I to elucidate the relevance to advertising of the construct as they use it. At the beginning of this chapter, I mentioned three behavioral implications of the advertiser's task: The analysis must begin by investigating a region of the user's world that preexists goods/services yet corresponds to the advertiser's domain of interest/expertise; given intra-individual variability, the relevant universe is one of occasions for action rather than individuals; for congruence with the context in which a brand is used, the behavioral event that must be represented is a single occasion for action. Regarding the first implication, the notion of values, as reflecting individuals' preference among various states of affairs, customs, institutions, at least has going for it that it represents reactions of an individual that preexist the marketplace and current or candidate offerings. In that sense, values as traits is a better place to start an advertising-relevant investigation than is the construct of attitude, for example, which is usually studied in the form of reactions to existing or candidate goods/services. Such a trait approach to values is, however, deficient in other respects. Reflecting relatively enduring personal attributes, values is but one of four major classes of variable affecting behavior, the others being transient personal, and enduring and transient environmental. Moreover, as regards the second and third implications, a concept of values that is operationalized by asking people to generalize their preferences across domains of activity and contexts within activity is not well-suited to investigating a universe of occasions for action, or to explaining what may occur on individual occasions for action. It remains for values theorists to elucidate the relevance of such a trait concept of values to the value: (a) that regulates the economy of a self-organizing system as it allocates and uses its resources, and (b) that advertisers want to embody in their offerings, and promise in their communications, so that they, too, may survive and obtain a satisfactory return on their resources.

REFERENCES

Calder, B. (1977). Focus groups and the nature of qualitative marketing research. *Journal of Marketing Research, 14,* 353–364.

Feather, N. T. (1982). Human values and the production of action: An expectancy-valence analysis. In N. T. Feather (Ed.), *Expectations and actions: Expectancy-value models in psychology* (pp. 263–289). Hillsdale, NJ: Lawrence Erlbaum Associates.

Feather, N. T. (1988a). Values, valences, and course enrollment: Testing the role of personal values within an expectancy-valence framework. *Journal of Educational Psychology, 80,* 381–391.

Feather, N. T. (1988b). From values to actions: Recent applications of the expectancy-value model. *Australian Journal of Psychology, 40,* 105–124.

Fennell, G. (1978). Consumers' perceptions of the product-use situation. *Journal of Marketing, 42,* 38–47.

Fennell, G. (1979). Attention engagement. In J. H. Leigh & C. R. Martin, Jr. (Eds.), *Current issues & research in advertising* (pp. 17–33). Ann Arbor: University of Michigan.

Fennell, G. (1980). The situation. *Motivation & Emotion, 4,* 299–322.

Fennell, G. (1981). Emotion: A neglected aspect of consumer behavior. In R. J. Lutz (Ed.), *Proceedings of Division 23, 89th Annual Convention of the American Psychological Association* (p. 9). Nashville, TN: Owen Graduate School of Management, Vanderbilt University.

Fennell, G. (1982a). Terms v. concepts: Market segmentation, brand positioning, and other aspects of the academic-practitioner gap. In R. Bush & S. Hunt (Eds.), *Marketing theory: Philosophy of science perspectives* (pp. 97–106). Chicago: American Marketing Association.

Fennell, G. (1982b). The unit to be classified: Persons v. behaviors. In *Consumer classification: A need to rethink.* Brugge, Belgium: ESOMAR.

Fennell, G. (1985a). Persuasion: Marketing as behavioral science in business and nonbusiness contexts. In R. Belk (Ed.), *Advances in nonprofit marketing* (pp. 95–160). Greenwich, CT: JAI.

Fennell, G. (1985b). Things of heaven and earth: Marketing, phenomenology, and consumer research. In E. Hirschman & M. Holbrook (Eds.), *Advances in consumer research* (Vol. XII, pp. 544–549). Provo, UT: Association for Consumer Research.

Fennell, G. (1986). Extending the thinkable: Consumer research for marketing practice. In R. Lutz (Ed.), *Advances in consumer research* (Vol. XIII, pp. 427–432). Provo, UT: Association for Consumer Research.

Fennell, G. (1987). Reculer pour mieux sauter or, why consumer psychologists need a general model of action. In J. Saegert (Ed.), *Proceedings of Division 23, 94th Annual Convention of the American Psychological Association* (pp. 57–65). Washington, DC: Society for Consumer Psychology (Division 23) American Psychological Association.

Fennell, G. (1988). Action as counterchange: Identifying antecedents of the domain and goal of action. In L. Alwitt (Ed.), *Proceedings of Division 23, 95th Annual Convention of the American Psychological Association* (pp. 122–129). Washington, DC: Society for Consumer Psychology (Division 23) American Psychological Association.

Fennell, G. (1990). Is psychology ready for the marketing concept? In M. Gardner (Ed.), *Proceedings of Division 23, 97th Annual Convention of the American Psychological Association* (pp. 44–49). Washington, DC: Society for Consumer Psychology (Division 23) American Psychological Association.

Fennell, G. (1991a). Context for action = context for brand use = source of valued brand attributes. In K. Haugtvedt (Ed.), *Proceedings of Division 23, 98th Annual Convention of the American Psychological Association* (pp. 73–79). Washington, DC: Society for Consumer Psychology (Division 23) American Psychological Association.

Fennell, G. (1991b). The role of qualitative research in making what the customer wants to buy. In R. Holman & M. Solomon (Eds.), *Advances in consumer research* (Vol. XVIII, pp. 271–279). Provo, UT: Association for Consumer Research.

Fennell, G. (1992). Is "positive" motivation a useful concept? In M. Lynn & J. M. Jackson (Eds.), *Proceedings of Division 23, 99th Annual Convention of the American Psychological Association* (pp. 63–70). Washington, DC: Society for Consumer Psychology (Division 23) American Psychological Association.

Fischhoff, B. (1991). Value elicitation: Is there anything in there? *American Psychologist, 46,* 835–847.

Fischhoff, B., Slovic, P., & Lichtenstein, S. (1980). Knowing what you want: Measuring labile values. In T. Wallsten (Ed.), *Cognitive processes in choice and decision behavior* (pp. 117–141). Hillsdale, NJ: Lawrence Erlbaum Associates.

Haley, R. (1968). Benefit segmentation: A decision oriented tool. *Journal of Marketing, 32,* 30–35.

Homer, P. M., & Kahle, L. R. (1988). A structural equation test of the value-attitude-behavior hierarchy. *Journal of Personality and Social Psychology, 54,* 638–646.

Lewin, K. (1936). *Principles of topological psychology.* New York: McGraw Hill.

Reynolds, T. J., & Gutman, J. (1988). Laddering theory, method, analysis and interpretation. *Journal of Advertising Research, 28,* 11–31.

Rokeach, M. (1973). *The nature of human values.* New York: The Free Press.

Shocker, A. D., Stewart, D. W., & Zahorik, A. J. (1990). Market structure analysis: Practice, problems, and promise. In G. Day, B. Weitz, & R. Wensley (Eds.), *The interface of marketing and strategy.* Greenwich, CT: JAI.

Williams, R. M., Jr. (1979). Change and stability in values and value systems: A sociological perspective. In M. Rokeach (Ed.), *Understanding human values individual and societal* (pp. 15–46). New York: The Free Press.

Chapter 6

Maslow's Hierarchy and Social Adaptation as Alternative Accounts of Value Structures

Lynn R. Kahle
University of Oregon

Pamela M. Homer
California State University—Long Beach

Robert M. O'Brien
David M. Boush
University of Oregon

It is generally accepted that values have a pervasive influence on many aspects of human life (Rokeach, 1973). One of the most well-known, pervasive, and frequently cited theories of values is Maslow's (1954, 1970) hierarchy, which is taught in a wide variety of college courses in the social and behavioral sciences (cf. Mowen, 1987). Although some scholars may view Maslow's theory as out of date, its pervasive influence on contemporary scholarly thought implies that it is highly relevant. As with the proverbial restaurant that is "so unpopular that nobody goes there anymore because it is always too crowded," Maslow's theory may "not interest very many people because so many are writing about it." Many value scholars are surprised to learn that in a recent issue of Social Science Citation Index Maslow's (1954) classic book was cited more than twice as often as Rokeach's (1973). Clearly any theory with this level of influence ought to be examined empirically.

According to Maslow, values are essentially equivalent to needs, and they are hierarchical in nature. (He used *values* and *needs* interchangeably.) His perspective postulates that values become salient in a sequential order that progresses from primitive (i.e., survival) to advanced (i.e., self-actualization). These levels are based on deficits in that people tend to value what they lack at the next highest level. In order for a higher level to become salient, each lower-order level must be at least partially satisfied. Only one value is prepotent at any time, and once satisfied, that value takes a subordinate role to an emerging, higher-order value. Presumably the higher an individual is in the hierarchy, the greater the subjective life satisfaction. All individuals are motivated by a desire to fulfill their potential and to seek self-actualization. As Maslow (1954) stated, "search for identity is search for one's own . . . values" (p. 257).

Alternatively, in social adaptation theory values represent a type of social cognition that functions to facilitate adaptation to one's environment (Homer & Kahle, 1988; Kahle, 1983; Kahle, Beatty, & Homer, 1986; Kahle, Kulka, & Klingel, 1980; Piner & Kahle, 1984). Values resemble attitudes in that both are adaptation abstractions that emerge continuously from the assimilation, accommodation, organization, and integration of environmental information, in order to promote interchanges with the environment favorable to the preservation of optimal functioning (Kahle, 1983). As the most abstract of social cognitions, values function as prototypes from which attitudes and behaviors are manufactured (Homer & Kahle, 1988). Furthermore, all cognitions, including values and attitudes, are affected by the situational context (Kahle, 1980); therefore, the salience of specific values may vary across environmental situations. Whatever dominates an individual's attention dictates what values are important in terms of influencing judgments and behavioral patterns. As a result, this line of reasoning calls into question the existence of hierarchically "better" values and implies that individual values may not be ranked in the same order when situational circumstances change, in contrast to what has been proposed by Maslow. Social adaptation theory argues that the "best" or most adaptive value depends on the situational context.

Empirical Evidence

In spite of the intuitive appeal and widespread didactic application of Maslow's theory, it has little empirical support (Kahle, Boush, & Homer, 1989; Wahba & Bridwell, 1973). Assuming the theory purports to be scientific and testable, the consequences of attempts to operationalize and test it should have a major bearing on its viability. In fact, results that are inconsistent with Maslow's theory have been identified for a wide variety of factors ranging from broad societal concerns to specific personal issues (Kahle, 1983).

Some of the earliest studies whose results bear on the hierarchy of values employed cross-sectional data and prestructural equation statistics to examine organizational issues. Vroom (1964) reviewed studies demonstrating that concern with higher order values is greater among top-level managers than among those people in lower levels of organizations. These studies seemed to support the notion of a need or value hierarchy. For example, Davis (1946) found a lack of ambition and concern with the nature of their work among underprivileged workers. Centers (1948), Lyman (1955), and Moore and Weiss (1955) found that importance ratings for accomplishment and self-expression in work were directly related to job level. Pellegrin and Coates (1957) reported that top executives defined success as career accomplishment, while first-level supervisors defined it more in terms of security and income. Consistent with these findings, Porter (1963) evidenced greater concern for esteem and self-actualization among high level managers than managers at lower levels.

Each of these studies is compatible with a hierarchy based on the argument that lower status occupational groups are not concerned with higher level values because they have not satisfied lower level ones; however, the studies described earlier are all based on cross-sectional data analyzed with prestructural equation statistics. Consequently, the concern for higher order values demonstrated by people at higher occupational levels could have been present before they were promoted. Their values for achievement and interest in intrinsic satisfaction in work could reflect situational or personality differences rather than progression through a hierarchy. Hall and Nougaim (1968) conducted a longitudinal study in direct response to this limitation. Contrary to predictions based on Maslow's hierarchy, they found that concern with higher order values depended more on age and situational role than on satisfaction with lower order values. Also contrary to Maslow's theory, the degree to which a given value was satisfied was correlated with the intensity with which the value was held.

Similarly, Alderfer (1969) examined the simple correlations between satisfaction with lower order values and desire for higher order values as a test of Maslow's hierarchy. He reasoned that the hierarchy predicts desire for higher order values once lower order values are satisfied. The resultant low correlations between satisfaction with values such as belongingness and desire for values such as esteem did not support Maslow's theory.

Trexler and Schuh (1971) attempted to test the value hierarchy via changes in satisfaction with values among people who were made to experience deprivation. Over a 9-week training period, Marine flight students in an intentionally deprived environment gravitated toward lower level values. Presumably, such a regression under conditions of deprivation is a kind of mirror-image of progression through Maslow's hierarchy under normal conditions; however, the relative differences in the types of deprivation experienced by the subjects was not taken into account. One interpretation of the data is simply that people deprived of food and sleep become more concerned with food and sleep.

Graham and Balloun (1973) examined relative satisfaction with physiological, security, social, and self-actualization needs. In general, satisfaction with lower order needs was greater than with higher order needs. These results arguably support Maslow's hierarchy, but the conceptual issues were obscured by data quality problems. The same sample ($n = 37$) and the "low to moderate" agreement across measures of relative satisfaction suggest uncertainty about what was actually measured. Other evidence has also questioned the exact sequence of values. For example, Kahle et al. (1980) surveyed adolescents' self-esteem and their interpersonal relationships annually for 3 years. The Maslow hierarchy suggests that interpersonal needs must be satisfied before self-esteem needs become salient. In direct contrast to the sequence implied by Maslow, low adolescent self-esteem led to multiple interpersonal problems in this longitudinal study.

Maslow's hierarchy also conflicts with current information processing theory, particularly in its implications for attention. According to Maslow's theory (e.g., Srull & Wyer, 1986), the most basic unsatisfied need dominates attention until it is at least partially fulfilled. This view poses two problems. First, it does not accommodate interruptions in the execution of goal hierarchies that are due to factors other than the satisfaction of a need. Examples of such interruptions are physiological arousal (e.g., hunger and thirst), environmental events (e.g., surprises), and cognitive events (e.g., remembering a forgotten task). Second, the execution of plans according to Maslow's hierarchy would be extremely inefficient. Some aspects of the plans that result in need satisfaction are faster and easier to execute than are others, and some basic needs are satisfied on varying schedules. In order to execute plans according to a rigid sequence, opportunities to complete portions of different goal hierarchies would be ignored. Social adaptation theory allows a more flexible view of attention and poses no such problems for currently accepted approaches of information processing.

This research seeks to assess whether the underlying factor structure of value systems is consistent with the low/high continuum proposed by Maslow. Furthermore, we examine the relative effectiveness of Maslow's hierarchical conceptualization and social adaptation theory, a nonhierarchical approach to values, to account for variations in individuals' attitudinal responses.

The List of Values (LOV)

In an effort to overcome limitations associated with the most widely used method of values measurement (i.e., Rokeach, 1973), a more parsimonious alternative, the List of Values (LOV), was developed and shown to relate to a variety of phenomena in a test on a national sample (Kahle, 1983; Veroff, Douvan, & Kulka, 1981). Specifically, the LOV consists of nine values (i.e., a sense of belonging, excitement, fun and enjoyment in life, warm relationships with others, self-fulfillment, a sense of accomplishment, being well-respected, security, and self-respect).

Each of the values in the LOV can be matched directly with a stage in Maslow's hierarchy except for the two pleasure LOV values, which Maslow's hierarchy does not represent, and the hierarchy's physiological stage, which the LOV does not represent. Both people who value the LOV enjoyment-related values and people at Maslow's physiological level are rare among survey respondents in the contemporary United States (Kahle, 1983).

Safety, the second value level in the hierarchy, was described by Maslow (1970) as "security; stability; dependency; protection; freedom from fear, from anxiety and chaos; need for structure, order, law, limits, and so on" (p. 39). Because Maslow used the word "security" as one of the synonyms for safety, the LOV component "security" represents the safety stage.

Once safety needs are fulfilled, Maslow (1970) predicted that belongingness would dominate a person's attention. "Now the person will feel keenly, as never before, the absence of friends, or a sweetheart, or a wife, or children. He will hunger for affectionate relations with people in general, namely, for a place in his group or family" (p. 43). The LOV components "a sense of belonging" and "warm relationships with others" visibly address the belongingness stage.

Regarding esteem, the next level of the hierarchy, Maslow (1970) wrote, "All people in our society (with a few pathological exceptions) have a need or desire for a stable, firmly-based, usually high evaluation of themselves, for self-respect, or self-esteem, and for the esteem of others" (p. 45). Clearly this value level maps directly onto "self-respect" and "being well-respected" in the LOV. Once again, an identical word is employed by both theories.

The highest level in Maslow's hierarchy, self-actualization, "refers to man's desire for self-fulfillment, namely to the tendency for him to become actualized in what he is potentially" (p. 46). The LOV components "self-fulfillment" and "sense of accomplishment" represent the self-actualization value level. Each of these implies a high level of attainment.

This high degree of correspondence between the two conceptual approaches allows the use of the LOV to measure how well Maslow's hierarchy accounts for attitudes. Previous research into social adaptation theory has empirically identified other underlying dimensions within the nine values (Homer & Kahle, 1988; Kahle, 1983), including external/internal (e.g., Rotter, 1966) and personal/apersonal dimensions. These underlying dimensions suggest a view of values that is quite different from Maslow's hierarchical theory. Because each theoretical approach offers unique predictions, conflicting hypotheses can be developed and tested.

Hypotheses and Theoretical Rationale

Maslow's concept of a value hierarchy postulates that the basic human values belong to one of five distinct, enduring levels that can be ranked from low to high. In other words, regardless of situational context or sample variations, similar structural patterns (consistent with the idea of a low/high continuum) will be identified empirically. If, however, values emerge continuously from interactions between persons and their environments with situation-specific levels of salience, different structural patterns may emerge. Furthermore, these patterns may not resemble the hierarchy levels proposed by Maslow. Several underlying value dimensions have been identified that are ignored by the Maslow system, including an external/internal dimension (Homer & Kahle, 1988; Kahle, 1983). The LOV values can be associated with either internal or external sources of control which suggests alternative hypotheses:

H1A: The factor structure of the LOV values will resemble levels in Maslow's hierarchy (i.e., a low order versus high order continuum).

H1B: The LOV values will possess an external/internal factor structure that varies from that proposed by Maslow.

The preceding rationale can be extended to include value influences on attitudinal responses. Theoretical arguments suggesting that values have a causal influence on subsequent attitudes and behaviors have been voiced by many (e.g., Carman, 1977; Williams, 1979). Recently, these causal inferences were examined and empirically supported (Homer & Kahle, 1988). Specifically, Homer and Kahle (1988) demonstrated that three value factors identified by an exploratory factor analysis influenced attitudes, which subsequently influenced self-reported behaviors. These underlying value factors resembled the internal and external dimensions previously identified in a national sample (Kahle, 1983), not those factors predicted by Maslow's hierarchy. To assess the relative effectiveness of a Maslow-predicted factor structure and the external/internal factor structure, the following alternative hypotheses are offered:

H2A: A factor structure that represents Maslow's low/high value continuum will have more influence on attitudinal responses than an external/internal factor structure.

H2B: An external/internal factor structure will have more influence on attitudinal responses than the Maslow-related low/high factor structure.

If the relative importance of Maslow's proposed needs/values levels are consistent across different situations and differing types of personal attitudes, specific attitudinal responses of individuals who rank the same (or "Maslow-related") value primary should be similar. These responses should, in turn, vary from those of individuals who place utmost importance on values from distant levels of Maslow's hierarchy. Furthermore, individuals should be more worried about issues that are close reflections of their reported value orientation (and less worried about more value-distant issues) than those with opposing value orientations. If Maslow's hierarchy is not an accurate representation of human value structures, these predictions will not be consistent with the data. Hypotheses suggested by the opposing perspectives are:

H3A: The pattern of attitudinal responses among the primary value groups will cluster in a pattern that resembles Maslow's hierarchy.

H3B: The pattern of attitudinal responses among the primary value groups will not resemble Maslow's hierarchy.

METHOD

Sampling Procedure

A systematic probability sample of 577 residents in a medium-sized city in the Southwestern United States completed a telephone survey on pet care. Telephone numbers were randomly generated for the initial 2 days (out of 9) of the phone calling sessions. Due to the enormous rate of nonworking numbers, disconnected phones, and business numbers included in the random list, the final portions of the survey relied on the local phone directory. Every tenth phone number was contacted, and when necessary, a second or third callback was made (on a different day) in an attempt to locate the initial nonrespondents. All calls were supervised at a central location on nine consecutive days between the hours of 6 p.m. and 10 p.m. on the seven weekdays and between 10 a.m. and 10 p.m. on the two weekend days. A total of 1,876 individuals were contacted, of which 26.4% were unqualified (only persons at least 25 years old who owned a pet were surveyed) and of which 42.8% refused to cooperate. The final sample ($n = 577$) represented a response rate of 41.8% of qualified contacts. The mean age of the sample was 38.6; the mean reported income level was $43,393; 63% were females; and the mean household size was 2.9 persons.

Survey Instrument

The initial questions on the survey related to pet care. After answering those items, respondents rated the nine individual values in terms of importance on 9-point scales and then selected the single most important value. A three-stage process was used to measure this "first-value" in which subjects first selected the most important value from five-value and four-value subsets. Each respondent then identified the most important of these two values. A series of 10 additional items were designed to reflect affective responses that would directly correspond to the LOV items and to the five levels proposed by Maslow. One item was designed to represent each LOV value, which resulted in a pair of items for each level in the Maslow hierarchy. Specifically, respondents were asked how much time they spent worrying about buying food and shelter (physiological), being burglarized and being fired or laid off (security), friends and being popular (esteem), competence and their own achievements (respect), and their inner self and being happy with oneself (actualization).

RESULTS

The two pleasure values (i.e., fun and enjoyment in life and excitement) were excluded from the analyses reported here because they are not directly represented in Maslow's theory. It may be argued that we have not captured self-actualization with our measures of self-fulfillment and a sense of accomplishment because according to Maslow's original conceptualization, very few people reach this superior level. Because self-fulfillment and a sense of accomplishment can be positioned relatively on a low/high and an external/internal continuum, failure to capture optimally Maslow's highest stage is not particularly problematic. In addition, the primary distinctions between the alternative conceptualizations are associated with two other pairs of values, a sense of belonging and warm relationships with others as well as being well-respected and self-respect.

Value ratings may suffer from inherent positive intercorrelations due to response biases (e.g., Alwin & Krosnick, 1985). Therefore, an accurate assessment of the factor structure of the value ratings must permit positive correlations that result from correlated response errors. This difficulty can be ameliorated by including a method factor, uncorrelated with the other latent factors, upon which all items load equally (Alwin & Krosnick, 1985). Following Alwin and Krosnick, we examined the factor structure of the value ratings using multiple types of common factor models. All confirmatory factor and structural equation models are estimated via LISREL 7.16 (Joreskog & Sorbom, 1989) and are based (due to item nonresponse) on a sample of 530.

Hypothesis One

The first model has a single latent factor. The second model contains a single latent factor and a method factor that is uncorrelated with that latent factor. Each item is constrained to have the same loading on the method factor. The factor loadings and goodness-of-fit statistics for these two solutions are displayed in Table 6.1. The single factor model does not demonstrate an impressive fit based on the chi-square statistic and *p* value. In this case, the hypothesis of an adequate fit of the data is rejected, but the chi-square statistic can be deceptive, because of its dependence on sample size. "In very large samples virtually all models that one might consider would have to be rejected as statistically untenable" (Bentler & Bonett, 1980, p. 591). Each of the factor loadings is statistically significant and, according to the goodness-of-fit (GFI) and adjusted goodness-of-fit (AGFI) indices, the single factor model does indicate an acceptable fit.[1] Although these results are inconclusive, when the magnitudes of the factor loadings are ranked from low to high, an external/internal continuum is visible. The external values (i.e., a sense of belonging, being well-respected, and security) cluster at one end of the continuum, and the remaining internal values (i.e., warm relationships with others, a sense of accomplishment, self-fulfillment, and self-respect), which possess relatively lower factor loadings, form the opposing anchor.

As expected, inclusion of a method factor improves the model's fit substantially (change in chi-square = 21.08 with the loss of only 1 *df*). As in the single factor model, the rank order of the factor loadings is more consistent with an external/internal distinction than with a lower/higher order dimension. The most apparent evidence is in the vastly different loadings associated with pairs of values that Maslow predicts are of similar rank order: warm relationships with others (= .377) and a sense of belonging (= .939), and being well-respected (= .675) and self-respect (= .094).

Overall, these findings do support the alternative hypothesis that values possess a distinct external/internal dimension that is not represented in Maslow's hierarchy.

Hypothesis Two

The first set of causal analyses performed to test hypothesis two modeled a single value factor or a single value factor with a method factor leading to the attitudinal construct. Figure 6.1 depicts the causal relationships in these models, and Table 6.2 summarizes the parameter estimates.

Attitudes toward pet medical care facilities were assessed. The three attitudinal measures were each created by summing five individual items in

---

[1]One measure of overall model fit is the goodness-of-fit (GFI) index calculated by LISREL. GFI is a measure of the relative amount of variances and covariances jointly accounted for by the model, and unlike chi-square, is independent of the sample size and relatively robust against departures from normality (Joreskog & Sorbom, 1986, 1989). LISREL also computes an index that is adjusted for degrees of freedom (AGFI). According to the decision rule proposed by Bentler and Bonett (1980), a model does not represent an acceptable fit if it is less than .90.

TABLE 6.1
Parameter Estimates of Factor Structure Models

Single Factor Model	
Value Item	*Factor Loadings*
Sense of belonging	0.983*
Warm relationship with others	0.740*
Being well-respected	0.967*
Security	0.917*
Self-respect	0.527*
Sense of accomplishment	0.690*
Self-fulfillment	0.695*
Factor covariances	1.000[f]
Goodness-of-Fit	
Chi-square	91.76
df	14
p <	.001
GFI	.953
AGFI	.906

Single Latent Factor and Method Factor		
	Factor Loadings	
Value Item	*Factor 1*	*Method*
Sense of belonging	0.939*	0.623*
Warm relationships	0.377*	0.623*
Being well-respected	0.675*	0.623*
Security	0.906*	0.623*
Self-respect	0.094	0.623*
Sense of accomplishment	0.257*	0.623*
Self-fulfillment	0.234*	0.623*
Factor covariances	1.000[f]	
	0.000[f]	1.000[f]
Goodness-of-Fit		
chi-square	70.68	
df	13	
p <	.001	
GFI	.964	
AGFI	.922	

Notes. *f* Fixed parameter. *Factor loading is at least twice its standard error.

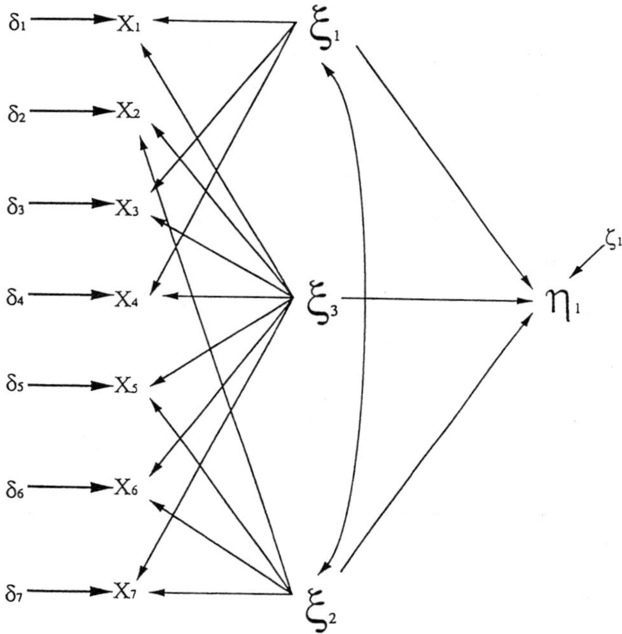

ξ_3 is the methods factor and is constrained to be uncorrelated with the values factors (ξ_1 and ξ_2) and to have each X load equally on it.

FIG. 6.1. General structural equation model.

an effort to construct a parsimonious model (the 15-item scale had a coefficient alpha of .83). These initial structural models were examined to determine whether social values influence attitudinal judgments. The values factor demonstrated a significant influence on attitudes. Inclusion of a method factor improved the model fit (change in chi-square = 46.52 with the loss of 2 *df*) and this was also accompanied by an increase in the absolute magnitude of the causal path linking values and attitudes. These patterns support the importance of taking the correlation among items that is due to the measurement process explicitly into account in the modeling process.

A second procedure was designed to compare the causal impact of the dimensional structure predicted by Maslow with the external/internal value dimension. A causal model in which the measurement model coincided with Maslow's low/high order values (i.e., security, a sense of belonging, and warm relationships with others loaded on the first factor, and the remaining esteem and self-actualization values loaded on a second factor) was compared to a model indicative of the external/internal dimensions described earlier (i.e., security, being well-respected, and a sense of belonging loaded on factor one and the remaining internal values loaded on factor two). This

TABLE 6.2
Parameter Estimates of General Causal Models

	Factor Loadings		
Value Item	Single Latent Factor Model	Latend and Methods Factor Model	
Sense of belonging	0.994*	0.835*	0.655*
Warm relationships	0.748*	0.347*	0.655*
Being well-respected	0.967*	0.613*	0.655*
Security	0.890*	0.855*	0.655*
Self-respect	0.520*	0.015	0.655*
Sense of accomplishment	0.700*	0.212*	0.655*
Self-fulfillment	0.697*	0.164*	0.655*
Gamma path	0.429*	0.513*	0.213*
Goodness-of-Fit			
chi-square	139.42	92.92	
df	34	32	
p <	.001	.001	
GFI	.947	966	
AGFI	.915	.941	

Note. f Fixed paremeter. *Factor loading is at least twice its standard error

procedure was performed for two sets of models, one with and one without the method factor. Figure 6.2 provides a diagram of the alternative models, and Table 6.3 presents the results of this set of analyses.

There was little difference in the chi-square and goodness-of-fit indices associated with the two model specifications. Not surprisingly, only the external or low order factor had a significant impact on persons' attitudes toward pet care. The path from the second factor did not reach significance in either of the alternative models, but both of the value factor → attitude paths had higher magnitudes and *t* values in the external/internal solution. The signs of the significant path estimates for the factor loadings and the values → attitudes link in these models reflect past theoretical and empirical evidence. Those who place more importance on belonging and security also hold more favorable attitudes toward pet care. These patterns are consistent with expectations derived from an external/internal distinction (Homer & Kahle, 1988; Kahle, 1983), but it may also be argued that the findings coincide with predictions based on Maslow's lower order/higher order hierarchy.

As expected, inclusion of a method factor improved the chi-square and "fit" of each of the alternative models (see Table 6.3). Based on these statistics, it appears that the lower-higher order specification proposed by

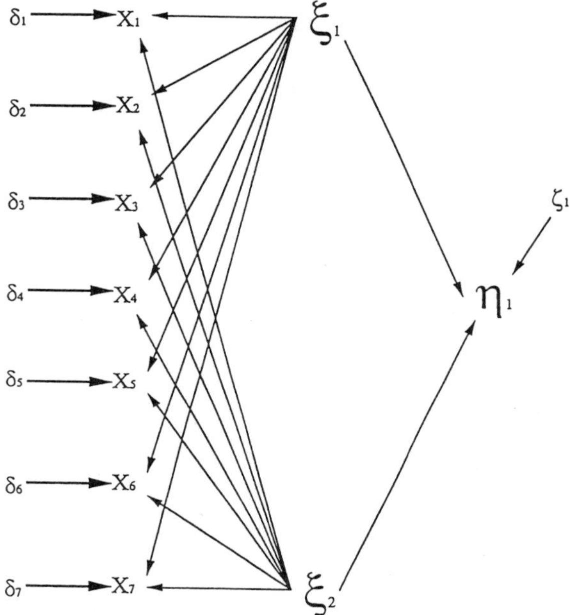

ξ_2 is the methods factor and is constrained to be uncorrelated with the values factor (ξ_1) and to have each X load equally on it.

FIG. 6.2. Structural equation model for tests comparing internal/external and high order/low order specifications.

Maslow is a more accurate representation. However, the two value items that determine the differences in factor structures between the adaptive and hierarchical models (i.e., warm relationships with others and being well-respected) had high modification indices in the low/high order model. These indices (= 11.89 and 6.76 for warm relationships with others and being well-respected, respectively) indicate that the model could be improved by allowing these items to load on both of the value factors (i.e., warm relationships with others and being well-respected would be loaded on both the low order and high order factors).[2] Such occurrences are

[2]Chi-square and GFI assess the overall fit of the model to the data and do not assess whether each relationship is accurately determined. The modification indices provide a more detailed means to assess the accuracy of specific fixed and constrained paths in a model. The modification index associated with a parameter indicates the expected reduction in chi-square that would result if that single parameter alone would be freed. Therefore, the modification indices can be examined in relation to a chi-square distribution with one degree of freedom (Joreskog & Sorbom, 1986, 1989).

TABLE 6.3
Causal Models Relating Values to Attitudes

Low/High Order Specification

	Factor Loadings	
Value Item	*Lower*	*Higher*
Sense of belonging	1.048*	0.000[f]
Warm relationships	0.800*	0.000[f]
Being well-respected	0.000[f]	0.990*
Security	0.998*	0.000[f]
Self-respect	0.000[f]	0.531*
Sense of accomplishment	0.000[f]	0.746*
Self-fulfillment	0.000[f]	0.746*
Factor covariances	1.000[f]	
	0.788*	1.000[f]
Gamma paths	0.570*	-0.097
Goodness-of-Fit		
chi-square	97.54	
df	32	
p <	.001	
GFI	.963	
AGFI	.937	

Internal/External Specification

	Factor Loadings	
Value Item	*External*	*Internal*
Sense of belonging	0.998*	0.000[f]
Warm relationships	0.000[f]	0.764*
Being well-respected	1.009*	0.000[f]
Security	0.978*	0.000[f]
Self-respect	0.000[f]	0.559*
Sense of accomplishment	0.000[f]	0.723*
Self-fulfillment	0.000[f]	0.732*
Factor covariances	1.000[f]	
	0.827*	1.000[f]
Gamma paths	0.787*	-0.323

TABLE 6.3
(Continued)

Goodness-of-Fit	
chi-square	102.00
df	32
$p <$	.001
GFI	.961
AGFI	.933

Low/High Order Specification

Factor Loadings

Value Item	*Lower*	*Higher*	*Method*
Sense of belonging	0.849*	0.000[f]	0.662*
Warm relationships	0.356*	0.000[f]	0.662*
Being well-respected	0.000[f]	1.056*	0.662*
Security	0.964*	0.000[f]	0.662*
Self-respect	0.000[f]	0.072	0.662*
Sense of accomplishment	0.000[f]	0.330*	0.662*
Self-fulfillment	0.000[f]	0.306*	0.662*
Factor covariances	1.000[f]		
	0.474*	1.000[f]	
	0.000[f]	0.000[f]	1.000[f]
Gamma paths	0.426*	0.084	0.212*

Goodness-of-Fit	
chi-square	66.16
df	30
$p <$	.001
GFI	.976
AGFI	.956

Internal/External Specification

Factor Loadings

Value Item	*External*	*Internal*	*Method*
Sense of belonging	0.836*	0.000[f]	0.640*
Warm relationships	0.000[f]	0.456*	0.640*
Being well-respected	0.695*	0.000[f]	0.640*
Security	0.896*	0.000[f]	0.640*
Self-respect	0.000[f]	0.111	0.640*
Sense of accomplishment	0.000[f]	0.367*	0.640*
Self-fulfillment	0.000[f]	0.355*	0.640*

TABLE 6.3
(Continued)

Factor covariances	1.000[f]		
	0.747*	1.000[f]	
	0.000[f]	0.000[f]	1.000[f]
Gamma paths	0.436*	0.129	0.152
Goodness-of-Fit			
chi-square	86.31		
df	30		
p <	.001		
GFI	.968		
AGFI	.941		

Note. f Fixed parameter. * Factor loading is at least twice its standard error.

indicative of a mixed loading pattern, which in our case indicates a model misspecification. No equally large modification indices appeared in the value factors in the external/internal solution and, in this respect, the solution was less complex. When a method factor is added to these models, the relationships between the internal and high order factors and attitudes still failed to attain significance, but the signs of the path estimates were positive (in contrast to the negative estimates in the solutions without a method factor).

The affective measures collected for the study were designed as a direct assessment of the robustness of the Maslow hierarchy. Two affective responses were created to correspond with each of the five Maslow value/need levels. More specifically, concern about food and shelter represent the survival level, concern about being burglarized and being fired/laid off represent the safety level (security), concern about friends and being popular represent the belongingness level (warm relationships with others and a sense of belonging, respectively), concern about one's own achievements and competence represent the respect level (self-respect and being well-respected, respectively), and concern about one's inner self and being happy with oneself represent the self-actualization level. Three sets of analyses were performed using these affective measures to test the predictions offered in the second and third set of hypotheses. If Maslow's theory accurately explains individuals' affective responses, the associated value rating should be most highly correlated with the representative affective measure (e.g., the rating of the importance of warm relationships with others should be highly correlated with worrying about one's friends). Similar to the patterns tested previously, we also expect that the external/internal factor structure will provide a meaningful explanation when the underlying value constructs are correlated with lower order affect. Lastly, as stated in H3A, the means of the first-value groups should behave in a similar hierarchical manner (e.g., those who value warm relationships with others most should resemble those who value a sense of belonging).

The correlational patterns among the 10 affective responses were inconsistent with Maslow's five distinct value levels. Not only were the within-value level correlations often lower than the between-value level correlations (for 7 of the 10 items), but an exploratory factor analysis revealed two underlying factors (that explained 55.3% of the variance) in which all but one of the five pairs of affective responses were separated. That is, only the two self-actualization affective measures loaded on the same factor—for all other pairs, one item loaded on each of the two factors. Factor one was composed of being concerned about shelter, being burglarized, being popular, competence, one's inner self, and being happy with oneself. The remaining items, buying food, being fired/laid off, friends, and one's own achievements comprised the second factor.

The external/internal and lower/higher order factors depicted in Fig. 6.1 were correlated with the items designed to represent Maslow's basic needs (i.e., food, shelter, and being burglarized) as an extension of the relationships discussed in the previous paragraph. Table 6.4 presents the LISREL estimates for the correlations among the underlying constructs. As expected, the external and internal value factors are both related to the affect construct. In the Maslow-based model, the chi-square statistic is lower than that for the external/internal solution; but only the lower order values' construct impacts affect ($p < .05$), the higher order factor correlation is positive, and the method factor correlation is significant. Furthermore, examination of the modification indices in the Maslow-based model indicated that warm relationships with others does not represent the same underlying construct as a sense of belonging and security. In fact, the modification index for the second value factor was the only troublesome one (= 12.54). None of the modification indices associated with the values factors in the lambda_x matrix of the external/internal model attained this level, however all were less than 2.54. In addition, the relationships between the values and affective factors in the external/internal model are enhanced, thus further supporting the basic relationships proposed in H2B.

Hypothesis Three

The final set of analyses investigated the relationship between the most highly ranked value and the 10 affective measures. Subjects were classified into a first-value group according to which of the LOV items they indicated

TABLE 6.4
Correlations of Latent Value Factors With Affective Factor

	Lower/Higher Order Model	
I.	Lower order factor	0.217*
II.	Higher order factor	0.047
III.	Differential bias	0.127*
	chi-square	121.84
	df	30
	p <	.001
	GFI	.957
	AGFI	.921
	External/Internal Model	
I.	External factor	0.252*
II.	Internal factor	0.360*
III.	Differential bias	0.015
	chi-square	155.14
	df	30
	p <	.001
	GFI	.941
	AGFI	.893

Note. *Correlation is at least twice its standard error.

was most important in their daily lives. ANOVAs were then performed for each of the 10 dependent affective measures using the first-value assignments as the independent variable. Because the two fun-related values are not represented in Maslow's hierarchy, those who valued fun and enjoyment in life or excitement most (= 28 Ss) were eliminated in these analyses. Afterwards, post hoc comparisons using Duncan's Multiple Range Test (Duncan, 1955; Steel & Torrie, 1960) were conducted to determine which first-value group means differed from each other ($p < .05$).

Maslow's framework would predict that people who value security most would also worry most about food $F(6, 489) = 2.72$, $p = .01$ shelter $F(6, 489) = 0.80$, ns, being burglarized $F(6, 489) = 2.17$, $p < .05$, and being fired $F(6, 488) = 4.32$, $p < .001$ The mean responses for the other groups should follow the hierarchy with the belongingness groups' ratings of these factors being second to the security group ratings. Although there are significant differences amongst the groups, the mean rankings do not behave in this manner (see Table 6.5). Not only did the security group not rate each of these items highest, but the two belongingness groups were separated substantially, as were the two respect-oriented value groups and the two self-actualization groups. For example, those who value a sense

Table 6.5
Summary of Values Groups Mean Responses

Measure	Value Group	Mean
Buying Food	Warm relationships	2.53
	Self-fulfillment	2.85
	Sense of accomplishment	3.24
	Self-respect	3.40
	Security	3.65
	Being well-respected	3.65
	Sense of belonging	4.11
Shelter	Self-fulfillment	4.38
	Sense of accomplishment	4.41
	Warm relationships	4.69
	Self-respect	4.76
	Security	4.86
	Being well-respected	5.00
	Sense of belonging	5.77
Being Burglarized	Warm relationships	5.66
	Self-respect	5.67
	Being well-respected	5.88
	Security	6.05
	Sense of accomplishment	6.35
	Self-fulfillment	6.37
	Sense of belonging	7.77
Being Fired	Self-fulfillment	3.25
	Warm relationships	3.47
	Self-respect	3.74
	Sense of accomplishment	3.79
	Sense of belonging	4.67
	Being well-respected	5.00
	Security	5.03
Friends	Self-fulfillment	2.48
	Warm relationships	3.22
	Self-respect	3.45
	Sense of accomplishment	3.52
	Security	4.26
	Being well-respected	4.35
	Sense of belonging	5.56
Being Popular	Sense of accomplishment	4.70
	Self-respect	4.94
	Warm relationships	4.95
	Security	4.98
	Being well-respected	5.00
	Self-fulfillment	5.05
	Sense of belonging	6.44
One's Own Achievements	Warm relationships	2.24
	Being well-respected	2.64
	Self-fulfillment	2.73
	Self-respect	2.86
	Sense of accomplishment	3.06
	Security	3.88

TABLE 6.5
(Continued)

	Sense of belonging	4.00
Competence	Self-respect	2.91
	Warm relationships	3.26
	Self-fulfillment	3.35
	Being well-respected	3.47
	Security	3.55
	Sense of accomplishment	3.62
	Sense of belonging	5.67
One's Inner Self	Warm relationships	5.10
	Self-respect	5.21
	Security	5.23
	Being well-respected	5.29
	Self-fulfillment	5.55
	Sense of accomplishment	6.11
	Sense of belonging	6.22
Being Happy With Oneself	Warm relationships	4.03
	Security	4.04
	Sense of accomplishment	4.07
	Sense of belonging	4.10
	Self-fulfillment	4.20
	Self-respect	4.23
	Being well-respected	4.35

of belonging (mean = 7.77) worry significantly more about being burglarized than those who value warm relationships with others (mean = 5.66), while also reporting similar levels of concern as those who rate self-respect most important (mean = 5.67). The security first-value group (mean = 5.03) did express the greatest concern about being fired, but this was nearly equivalent to the mean for the being well-respected group (mean = 5.00) and was significantly higher than the rating of those who value warm relationships with others (mean = 3.47). These patterns are not compatible with Maslow's hierarchy.

The sense of belonging first-value group indicated the most concern about friends (mean = 5.56) and the self-fulfillment first-value group (mean = 2.48) worried the least (as would be predicted by Maslow). But the associated belongingness group (warm relationships with others, mean = 3.22) was near the bottom of the rating spectrum $F(6, 487) = 4.12$, $p < .001$. The post hoc comparisons indicated that the mean for the sense of belonging group was significantly different than the means for the self-fulfillment and warm relationships with others groups, which were essentially equivalent. In addition, the two self-actualization groups were significantly different (means = 2.48 and 3.52 for the self-fulfillment and a sense of accomplishment groups, respectively). If the data had conformed to Maslow's hierarchy, the mean responses for the two belongingness and two self-fulfillment first-value groups would have been similar and the means for the warm relationships with others and self-fulfillment first-value groups would differ. There were no significant differences among the groups' reported concern about popularity, the second belongingness measure $F(6, 485) = 0.55$, ns. While the sense of belonging first-value group (mean = 6.44) did rate this the highest, their concern did not differ from that reported by the self-fulfillment first-value group (mean = 5.05).

Overall, the respondents reported relatively low levels of worry over personal achievements, but this concern did vary by first-value group $F(6, 485) = 3.49$, $p = .002$. Surprisingly, the highest levels of worry were among the sense of belonging (mean = 4.00) and security (mean = 3.88) first-value groups. Once more, the belongingness, respect, and self-actualization pairs were separated on the response continuum. In fact, the means of the two belongingness first-value groups anchored each end of the continuum, thereby surrounding all other group means (means = 4.00 and 2.24 for a sense of belonging and warm relationships with others, respectively). Similarly, the sense of belonging first-value group (mean = 5.67) worries significantly more about competence than people in all other first-value groups $F(6, 488) = 2.91$, $p < .01$, means ranging from 2.91 to 3.62 for the other six first-value groups. In fact, the being well-respected (mean = 3.47) and self-respect (mean = 2.91) individuals who theoretically should have been more concerned about competence in Maslow terms were at the middle and bottom ends of the response spectrum.

Accurate measurement of self-actualization affective responses may be difficult at best, as indicated by the lack of significant differences among the first-value groups for these two indicators (i.e., concern for one's inner self and being happy with oneself). The two self-actualization first-value groups do worry similarly about their inner selves $F(6, 480) = 1.17$, ns and being happy with their selves $F(6, 488) = 1.07$, ns, but contrary to Maslow's hierarchy, the highest levels of concern were stated by the sense of belonging first-value group. The general rank orderings for these two variables were not overwhelmingly in favor of Maslow's approach. While the differing mean responses for the warm relationships with others (mean = 5.10) and sense of accomplishment (mean = 6.11) first-value groups are consistent with Maslow's predictions, the marginal ($p < .10$) difference between the sense of accomplishment and self-respect (mean = 5.21) first-value groups is not. Rather, Maslow would suggest that the mean for the self-respect first-value group would resemble more closely the mean for the sense of accomplishment first-value group (difference = 0.90) compared to the mean for the warm relationships with others first-value group (difference = 0.11).

The rank ordering of the group means presented earlier (and in Table 6.5) cannot be explained in terms of Maslow's hierarchy. In some instances, predictable "clusters" are apparent, but for 4 of the 10 dependent variables, the means of the first-value groups are indicative of an external/internal continuum, not a low/high ordering. The two respect-related values do cluster in two situations, and higher order clusters are apparent, but none of the ranked mean patterns matches Maslow's lower/higher order structure. Therefore, the group comparisons offer more support for H3B versus H3A.

DISCUSSION

Maslow (1954) has provided social scientists with an approach to human values that is useful in many respects. Nevertheless, his hierarchical perspective, in which values become salient in sequential order as represented on a primitive/advanced continuum, was unable to account for a substantial number of the patterns found in this study. These results are important from both an advertising perspective and from that of theory development about value structures.

Perhaps the most interesting results in the present study were the analyses involving various affect and attitudinal judgments. The initial structural models involving attitudes did yield results that support both an external/internal and low order/high order distinction. But when constraints were imposed to test these alternative explanations directly in the affect-related models, the paths linking the values factors with affect were not stronger using a Maslow lower/higher order specification relative to an adaptation-consistent external/internal structure. The external/internal aspect of value structures is not addressed by Maslow's system.

The lack of a correlation between the higher order values construct and lower order affect is consistent with Maslow's hierarchy, but the significant relationship between internal values and low-order affect implies that Maslow's interpretation is not unique. Apparently, individuals among this sample of 577 residents in a medium-sized city in the Southwestern United States who place relatively more importance on either external or internal values are concerned with basic needs such as food and shelter. The exact nature of that concern, however, probably differs. Externally oriented persons may be concerned with food for its survival or social aspects, whereas internally oriented persons may be interested in other factors, such as nutrition.

The analyses of variance revealed that the attitudinal responses among the various first-value groups were inconsistent with Maslowian predictions. The affective responses designed directly to represent each of the five Maslow levels did not correspond to Maslow's approach. The fact that respondents who place more importance on a sense of belonging tended to worry more about each of the varied issues suggests that perhaps certain types of persons are more affectively driven and that this tendency permeates many aspects of their lives.

The notion that values become salient in a flexible, adaptive way is more consistent with the current research than is Maslow's hierarchy. The idea of an adaptive value structure fits well with current views of information processing because hierarchical processing imposes constraints that lead to inefficiency. It also frees research on individual value differences from the constraints of a predetermined value hierarchy. For example, we no longer can assume that people who primarily value warm relationships with others are satisfied with their own degree of personal safety.

The popularity of Maslow's theory may stem from its confusion of physiological and psychological processes. At the lower levels the theory is physiological, and at the higher levels it implies that the same physiological process of climbing the hierarchy also applies. Because readers accept the physiological aspects, they tend to generalize to the psychological processes, which in fact follow a far more situational and complex path to salience. But even at the physiological level the theory may fall short. In the nonorganic "failure to thrive syndrome," for example, children who have been deprived of both food and a sense of belonging (caregiver interaction) manifest physiological disruption from socioemotional factors (Goldstein & Field, 1985; Powell, Brasel, & Blizzard, 1967).

Our findings also provide implications for marketers and advertisers. Advertisers must be cautious not to assume that one's values lack situational impact. Furthermore, it is highly likely that people from very different demographic and lifestyle environments have equally strong concerns about particular needs/values. For example, while an affluent individual may be concerned with a car's ability to protect his or her children (i.e., "security"), a less privileged individual may focus on the warranty agreement because of a need to feel "secure" that any mechanical problems will be repaired cost-free for the length of the warranty. Current automobile advertising campaigns incorporate such notions. Until recently, manufacturers such as Jaguar never appealed to security, because they thought it was sufficient merely to portray a status/prestige image. In a recent Jaguar ad, the headline, "Safety is one excellent reason to buy a Jaguar," appeared after a chart comparing highway loss statistics of competing brands. Nissan has taken an alternative approach. Their campaign for the Altima promotes a reasonably priced automobile that possesses features usually associated with luxurious, expensive competitors (e.g., Lexus).

Similarly, various agencies are directing considerable advertising effort toward supporting the importance of education as a means of improving oneself. Now, all economic groups are focusing on self-improvement as a means of attaining (or maintaining) a comfortable life. No longer are self-fulfillment and self-actualization restricted to those from supportive, affluent backgrounds.

Advertisers continue to send "accomplishment-oriented" messages to people from all walks of life. Many of these messages may focus on different means of achieving goals, which may also vary, depending on the particular audience, but the underlying need/value being addressed remains the same. Perhaps the drug addict is told to seek help conquering his or her habit while the laid-off business executive is told about the necessity for retraining and development—both means of accomplishing important goals. Our results support advertisers who take a situation-specific approach when incorporating values in their strategies and campaigns and, as illustrated earlier, many seem to be doing so.

In conclusion, values do seem to influence how individuals respond to a variety of issues and objects, but the nature of that influence is more adaptive and environmentally dependent than Maslow's hierarchy implies. Which values are salient at any given time is a function of a variety of factors, and multiple values that are quite different can be important simultaneously. Maslow's (1954) theory has enhanced social science significantly, but the evidence reported here demonstrates support for a model in which values are considered adaptive rather than sequentially hierarchical.

REFERENCES

Alderfer, C. P. (1969). An empirical test of a new theory of human needs. *Organizational Behavior and Human Performance, 4,* 142–175.

Alwin, D. F., & Krosnick, J. (1985). The measurement of values in surveys: A comparison of ratings and rankings. *Public Opinion Quarterly, 49,* 535–552.

Bentler, P., & Bonett, D. G. (1980). Significance tests and goodness of fit in the analysis of covariance structures. *Psychological Bulletin, 88,* 588–606.

Carman, J. M. (1977). Values and consumption patterns: A closed loop. In H. K. Hunt (Ed.), *Advances in consumer research* (Vol. 5, pp. 403–407). Ann Arbor, MI: Association for Consumer Research.

Centers, R. (1948). Motivational aspects of occupational stratification. *Journal of Social Psychology, 28,* 187–218.

Davis, A. (1946). The motivation of the underprivileged worker. In W. F. Whyte (Ed.), *Industry and society* (pp. 84–106). New York: McGraw Hill.

Duncan, D. B. (1955). Multiple range and multiple F tests. *Biometrics, 11,* 1–42.

Goldstein, S., & Field, T. (1985). Affective behavior and weight changes among hospitalized failure-to-thrive infants. *Infant Mental Health Journal, 6,* 187–194.

Graham, W. K., & Balloun, J. (1973). An empirical test of Maslow's need hierarchy theory. *Journal of Humanistic Psychology, 13,* 97–108.

Hall, D. T., & Nougaim, K. E. (1968). An examination of Maslow's need hierarchy in an organizational setting. *Organizational Behavior and Human Performance, 3,* 12–35.

Homer, P. M., & Kahle, L. R. (1988). A structural equation test of the value-attitude-behavior hierarchy. *Journal of Personality and Social Psychology, 54,* 638–646.

Joreskog, K. G., & Sorbom, D. (1986). *LISREL VI: Analysis of linear structural relations by the method of maximum likelihood, instrumental variables, and least squares* (4th ed.). Mooresville, IN: Scientific Software, Inc.

Joreskog, K. G., & Sorbom, D. (1989). *LISREL 7: User's reference guide.* Mooresville, IN: Scientific Software, Inc.

Kahle, L. R. (1980). Stimulus condition self-selection by males in the interaction of locus of control and self-chance situations. *Journal of Personality and Social Psychology, 38,* 50–56.

Kahle, L. R. (Ed.). (1983). *Social values and social change: Adaptation to life in America.* New York: Praeger.

Kahle, L. R., Beatty, S. E., & Homer, P. M. (1986). Alternative measurement approaches to consumer values: The list of values (LOV) and values and life styles (VALS). *Journal of Consumer Research, 13,* 405–409.

Kahle, L. R., Boush, D. M., & Homer, P. M. (1989). Broken rungs in Abraham's ladder: Is Maslow's hierarchy hierarchical? In D. Schumann (Ed.), *Proceedings of Division 23, 1988 Annual Convention of the American Psychological Association* (pp. 11–16). Washington, DC: American Psychological Association.

Kahle, L. R., Kulka, R. A., & Klingel, D. M. (1980). Low adolescent self-esteem leads to multiple interpersonal problems: A test of social adaptation theory. *Journal of Personality and Social Psychology, 39,* 496–502.

Lyman, E. (1955). Occupational differences in the value attached to work. *American Journal of Sociology, 61,* 138–144.

Maslow, A. H. (1954). *Motivation and personality.* New York: Harper & Row.

Maslow, A. H. (1970). *Motivation and personality* (2nd ed.). New York: Harper & Row.

Moore, N., & Weiss, R. (1955). The functioning and meaning of work and the job. *American Sociological Review, 20,* 191–198.

Mowen, J. C. (1987). *Consumer behavior.* New York: Macmillan.

Pellegrin, R. J., & Coates, C. H. (1957). Executives and supervisors: Contrasting definitions of career success. *Administrative Science Quarterly, 1,* 506–517.

Piner, K. E., & Kahle, L. R. (1984). Adapting to the stigmatizing label of mental illness: Foregone but not forgotten. *Journal of Personality and Social Psychology, 47,* 805–811.

Powell, G. F., Brasel, J. A., & Blizzard, R. M. (1967). Emotional deprivation and growth retardation simulating idiopathic hypopituitarism. I. Clinical evaluation of the syndrome. *New England Journal of Medicine, 276,* 1271–1278.

Rokeach, M. (1973). *The nature of human values.* New York: The Free Press.

Rotter, J. B. (1966). Generalized expectancies for internal vs. external control of reinforcement. *Psychological Monographs, 80*(1, Whole No. 609).

Srull, T. K., & Wyer, R. S. (1986). The role of chronic and temporary goals in social information processing. In R. M. Sorrentino & E. T. Higgins (Eds.), *Handbook of motivation and cognition* (pp. 503–549). New York: Guilford.

Steel, R. G. D., & Torrie, J. H. (1960). *Principles and procedures of statistics, with special reference to the biological sciences.* New York: McGraw-Hill.

Trexler, J. T., & Schuh, A. J. (1971). Personality dynamics in a military training command and its relationship to Maslow's motivation hierarchy. *Journal of Vocational Behavior, 1,* 245–253.

Veroff, J., Douvan, E., & Kulka, R. A. (1981). *The inner American: A self-portrait from 1957 to 1976.* New York: Basic Books.

Vroom, V. (1964). *Work and motivation.* New York: Wiley.

Wahba, M. A., & Bridwell, L. G. (1973). Maslow reconsidered: A review of research on the need hierarchy theory. In T. B. Green & D. F. Ray (Eds.), *Proceedings of the Thirty-Third Annual Meeting of the Academy of Management* (pp. 514–520). Academy of Management: Mississippi State University.

Williams, R. M., Jr. (1979). Change and stability in values and value systems: A sociological perspective. In M. Rokeach (Ed.), *Understanding human values individual and society* (pp. 15–46). New York: The Free Press.

Part **II**

METHODOLOGICAL APPROACHES

Chapter 7

Issues Involving the Relationship Between Personal Values and Consumer Behavior: Theory, Methodology, and Application

L. J. Shrum
Rutgers University

John A. McCarty
American University

It is virtually axiomatic in the social sciences that personal values have some manner of influence on behavior. Indeed, values are often defined as such (Rokeach, 1973). Not surprisingly, a number of studies have provided supporting evidence for this notion, demonstrating that values relate to behavior in a variety of domains. With respect to consumer behavior in particular, values have been shown to relate to purchase and consumer choice behavior across several product categories (e.g., Henry, 1976; Homer & Kahle, 1988; Pitts & Woodside, 1983). Yet, supportive findings notwithstanding, the empirical evidence supporting such a relationship might also be characterized as relatively disappointing. Although researchers have produced a number of studies that demonstrate some relationship between the abstract concept of values and specific types of behavior, for the most part this body of research has been limited in several aspects. These limitations not only serve to suppress the potential contribution of personal values to a theoretical understanding of behavioral antecedents, but also limit the application of theory to real world marketing problems.

One of the limitations of past values research is that most of the studies have been at a fairly descriptive level. If one looks at the entire output of values research, especially in the domain of consumer behavior, one sees a body of work that is quite broad, but possesses relatively little depth. Most consumer values studies have been concerned with applying values theory across product categories, thereby demonstrating the breadth of the usefulness of the values construct to marketers and advertisers in a variety of situations. However, little attention has been paid to the *processes* by which these effects occur, indicating a lack of depth with respect to values investigations.

Another limitation is that values studies have tended to view the relationship between values and behavior as simple and direct. Previous studies, with only a few exceptions, have addressed simple correlations or relationships between the importance individuals place on specific values and various measures of intention, preference, or choice with respect to particular behaviors.

Focusing only on simple bivariate relationships is limiting in two respects. One, it ignores other variables, both antecedent and intervening, in the value–behavior relation. Examples of these variables include attitudes, individual difference variables, and demographics. Second, it does not address relationships *among* the values themselves, but instead treats them as individual, and often independent, entities. However, most values theorists recognize that values are not necessarily held distinctly or separately, but as part of an integrated value system (Homer & Kahle, 1988; Rokeach, 1973). Consequently, a narrow picture is painted for what is in reality a very dynamic, complex process. Although this situation may not be problematic from an applied perspective (i.e., it may still provide useful information for segmentation and targeting purposes), its contribution to theory is limited.

Another limitation of previous research concerns the strength of the relationships between values and behavior. When relationships between values and behavior have been observed, they have tended to be relatively weak. In other words, the amount of variance in the behavioral variables explained by personal values has been small. Although this lack of explanatory power may not greatly diminish the theoretical importance of the findings, the application of these findings is clearly hampered. The primary importance of personal values information to marketers lies in the use of this information to segment markets, and then tailor marketing efforts to these segments using the values information. However, if differences in product choice or use are only weakly related to personal values, then it stands to reason that the impact of values on marketing strategy will be correspondingly weak as well.

We would like to point out that our discussion of the limitations of previous studies should not be construed as harshly critical, nor should it be taken as diminishing the importance or contribution of that research. All research is of course "limited" in some respect. As a particular field or topic matures, new research is devoted to modifying, extending, replicating, and in some cases correcting, the limitations of previous efforts. Thus, almost by default, the most limited research is that done first, yet it is also some of the most important. Previous values studies have provided the groundwork for more complex theory building, more precise tests of these theories, and more varied applications of these theories to marketing problems.

Our reasons for pointing out and discussing the limitations of past research are entirely devoted to perpetuating a discussion aimed at moving values research forward. In terms of contribution to both theory and practice, we think that values research is actually at a very critical juncture, and has the opportunity to mature into an even more productive and impactful research area. When a research area is in its infancy, it is concerned with establishing a general relationship. In this regard, past values research has been successful in "proving its worth" by establishing that there is indeed something "going on," and hence worth studying. After evidence of an effect has been established, the next logical step is to understand more about the nature of the effect. Is it strong or weak? Is the effect global or situational? In short, how does the effect work?

Toward this end, we discuss findings from several studies that represent attempts at addressing some of these questions. These studies focus on three areas of inquiry: methodological issues with respect to the measurement of personal values; individual differences in value stability, value meaning and value importance; and theoretical and conceptual issues relating to the importance of both antecedent and intervening variables in the value–behavior relationship.

Our research into all three of these issues has the broader purpose of attempting to better explicate the value–behavior relationship. It is our contention that the lack of robust relationships in past research does not necessarily suggest a true weak effect. This notion is similar to that of the fallacy of "proving" the null hypothesis. We as researchers conduct studies with the goal of demonstrating that an effect is not random, and we infer that if it is not random, the effect may be attributable to the independent variable. However, null (or weak) findings do not *prove* the effect is correspondingly absent or weak; there may be many other reasons why the effect does not show up. We may not be operationalizing or measuring the independent variable properly, or, particularly in correlational studies, other variables may be suppressing the effect. Thus, lack of demonstration of strong relationships is not sufficient reason to condemn or abandon an area of research.

An analogy to attitude research may be instructive. As stated before, the idea that values guide behavior is intuitive. Similarly, the idea that attitudes guide behavior is just as face valid. Research on the attitude construct has represented an on-going investigation for the better part of the 20th century, and few would question its utility as a research area. Yet, only 25 years ago prominent psychologists were doing just that. Typical correlations between attitudes and behavior had been so inconsistent and weak that some had actually suggested that attitude research be abandoned (cf. Abelson, 1972; Wicker, 1971). However, more recent research suggests that the call to ignore attitudes in predicting behavior was premature. Contemporary attitude research has succeeded in demonstrating a stronger predictive power by articulating boundary conditions for the attitude–behavior relation. Such research has resulted in refined conceptualizations of attitudes (Fazio, 1986, 1989; Fishbein & Ajzen, 1974; Petty & Cacioppo, 1986), recognition of the role of individual differences and situation (Fenigstein, Scheier, & Buss, 1975; Snyder, 1974), and the articulation of specific conditions under which attitudes would be used as guides to behavior (Chaiken, Liberman, & Eagly, 1989; Fazio, 1989; Petty & Cacioppo, 1986).

We are proposing that values research would benefit from an approach similar to that of more contemporary attitude research. Specifically, we are suggesting that more robust value–behavior relationships may be obtained through better measurement of values, a better understanding of individual differences in value–behavior consistency, and a focus on the entire process by which values exert influence on behavior.

THE MEASUREMENT OF PERSONAL VALUES

One problem that has plagued values research is that of measurement. The primary argument in early values research concerned whether ranking or rating was the better approach. Several studies attempted to address this issue, and the results were mixed. Some studies found essentially no differences between the two methods, whereas other studies suggested that a particular method was preferred (see Alwin & Krosnick, 1985 for a discussion). Although this issue may still be important, it is apparent from more recent values studies that the trend is toward using some type of rating method (cf. Bond, 1988; Crosby, Bitner, & Gill, 1990; Homer & Kahle, 1988; Horton & Horton, 1990; McCarty & Shrum, 1993b, 1993c, 1994; Shrum & McCarty, 1992; Shrum, McCarty, & Loeffler, 1990; Triandis, McCusker, & Hui, 1990).

The primary reason for the increased use in rating methods is that the interval level data obtained via rating tasks allow the use of more sophisticated statistical analyses. In particular, rating data allow researchers to use such techniques as factor analyses, discriminant analyses and causal modeling, all of which are important in explicating relationships among a variety of variables.

Rating methods are not without their own problems, however. In particular, standard rating methods tend to yield data that show little differentiation among the values. Because the values rated are inherently positive entities, few people consider the values to be *un*important. Thus, respondents tend to "end-pile" their ratings by assigning very high ratings to all of the values. This lack of differentiation and restriction of range may serve to obscure important relationships between values and other variables. For example, correlations between values and behavior depend in part on the variability of the values measurements. Consequently, low correlations may not reflect weak relationships, but instead may result simply because the value measurements did not vary to a sufficient extent to detect their influence (cf. Wyer, Bodenhausen, & Gorman, 1985). Thus, part of our research program has been targeted toward developing and testing alternative rating techniques that address differentiation and end-piling, but still provide interval level data.

The studies we have conducted have primarily tested a "rank-then-rate" procedure and a "least–most" procedure. The rank-then-rate procedure was suggested by Munson (1984), and has been used in at least one study other than ours (Crosby et al., 1990). The procedure asks respondents to first rank the set of values in order of importance. Following the ranking task, respondents are then asked to go back and rate the values on some sort of interval scale. The goal is to have respondents compare and contrast the values in the ranking task, and with this information fresh in memory, provide interval level data in the rating procedure. This procedure would then presumably yield more differentiated value ratings than a standard rating procedure.

The least–most procedure employs the same logic. Respondents are asked to scan the list of values and pick the most important value. Next, they are asked to scan the list again and pick the least important value. Finally, respondents then rate the values on some interval level scale. The reasoning is that having the respondents pick the most and least important value will result in some sort of comparison, similar to the ranking task in the rank-then-rate procedure. However, a least–most technique overcomes the problems of time and difficulty associated with ranking. Thus, if similar differentiation results from rank-then-rate and least–most, the least–most method would generally be the preferred procedure.

Our research attempted to provide empirical tests of these underlying assumptions. In particular, we wanted to determine: (a) whether rank-then-rate or least–most do indeed provide more differentiated ratings than rate-only, (b) whether the data differ in latent structure from rate-only, (c) whether the quality of fit with respect to latent structure is better than rate-only, (d) whether least–most is equivalent to rank-then-rate on the above dimensions, and (e) whether the alternative rating measures produce more robust relationships with relevant criterion variables compared to rate-only.

Four experiments were conducted to address these issues. The studies were essentially counterbalanced with respect to sample characteristics and type of value scale used. Study 1 and Study 3 used convenience samples of college students whereas Study 2 and Study 4 used general population probability samples. Study 1 and Study 2 used the Rokeach Value Scale (RVS; see Rokeach, 1973) and Study 3 and Study 4 used Kahle's List of Values scale (LOV; see Kahle, 1983). Study 1 compared all three methods (rank-then-rate, least–most, and rate-only); the other three studies only compared least–most to rate-only.

For all of the studies, end-piling was operationalized by calculating the mean value rating across all values. The tendency to assign high ratings to all values should result in a higher mean value rating compared to those who tend to end-pile less. Thus, the higher the mean, the more end-piling. Differentiation was conceptualized as the degree to which respondents make distinctions among values. Two statistics that each tap a somewhat different aspect of differentiation were computed: (a) the within-subject standard deviation of the value ratings and (b) P_d (rho), which represents the likelihood that a particular respondent will distinguish among the values (for a more thorough discussion of this statistic, see Krosnick & Alwin, 1988; Linville, Salovey, & Fischer, 1986; McCarty & Shrum, 1993a).

Results from the four studies were very conclusive (see McCarty & Shrum, 1993a for a detailed presentation and discussion of the results). Both rank-then-rate and least–most yielded lower means than the rate-only method, suggesting that the alternative rating methods result in less end-piling. For both P_d and standard deviation, rank-then-rate and least–most resulted in significantly greater differentiation among the values being rated. Moreover, the least–most technique was essentially equivalent to rank-then-rate in terms of reducing end-piling and increasing differentiation.

Another finding of interest from these studies was that the factor structures for the most part tended to be invariant across the rating methods. In Study 2, which administered the RVS to a probability sample of the general population, and in Study 3, which administered the LOV to a student sample, the same general factor structure fit the data for each rating method. However, measures of goodness of fit (i.e., AGFI) indicated that the least–most data were a better fit than rate-only. In other words, both rating techniques yielded data that were generally consistent with each other in terms of relationships among the variables. However, least–most tended to provide better measurement of latent structure than rate-only in terms of goodness of fit, and there was less measurement error associated with least–most as well. This finding is not surprising since rate-only methods tend to yield variables that are very highly correlated with each other. Consequently, obtaining differentiated factors may be more difficult.

These results lend support to our contention that higher quality data may be obtained through a least–most (and also rank-then-rate) method compared to rate-only. However, the critical test of whether one method is preferable to the other is still to be answered. It is our contention that the lack of differentiation obtained in a rate-only may serve to suppress correlations with relevant criterion variables. To test this notion, we used the data from Study 2 (RVS, general population sample) and Study 4 (LOV, general population sample) to compute correlations between the factor scores and various criterion variables. These variables included demographics such as age and income, measures of materialism (Belk, 1985) and amount of television viewing. The results showed that in most cases, correlations between the factor scores and the other variables tended to be stronger in the case of least–most than rate-only. These results were most pronounced for demographics.

Aggregated across the four studies, the results provide empirical evidence that alternative rating procedures, in particular least–most, may provide richer and more meaningful data than the traditional rate-only method. Moreover, the better data tended to yield more robust relationships with relevant other variables. These results support our broader contention that past examples of weak effects may not necessarily be indicative of *true* weak effects. Weak effects when using *ranked* data may be the result of less powerful nonparametric analyses. In other words, the data are good but the ability to analyze them is less than optimal. On the other hand, the results of Study 2 show that rate-only data may suppress relationships for the opposite reason. The interval level data allow for more powerful parametric statistical procedures, but the quality of the data is poor. The results from these studies suggest, however, that the least–most technique may improve the quality of the data and reveal important relationships that might otherwise be obscured.

INDIVIDUAL DIFFERENCES

As stated before, that values function as guides to consumption behavior has an intuitive appeal. When confronted with a choice among alternatives that are sufficiently different, the choice that is most consistent with an individual's values would seem logical. For example, when deciding upon what type of automobile to purchase, one typically must decide among a number of category choices (sports car vs. sedan, luxury vs. economy), which differ on corresponding attributes (practical vs. whimsical, expensive vs. inexpensive). These category choices and attribute preferences may logically be driven by value priorities (excitement, fun and enjoyment, social recognition, respect, financial security, family responsibility). On the other hand, choices among brands or substitutes may have little to do with value orientations, especially for low involvement products. In other words, it may be hard to link value systems to choices between brands of soap or chewing gum. Past research tends to support this notion, suggesting that values tend to be more closely linked with choices between product classes and less with brand choice within a category (Henry, 1976; see Gutman, 1990, Reynolds & Gutman, 1988 for an alternative view.)

The foregoing example suggests that the strength of the value–behavior link may depend on the nature of the behavior. Although relatively little work has addressed the issue, we would like to suggest that the value–behavior link may also depend on the nature of the individual. It makes intuitive sense that some individuals are more aware of their internal dispositions such as motivations, attitudes, and values. Such individuals are prone to introspection, and attend to their inner feelings and states frequently. This tendency should result in these individuals being more confident of their values, and more aware of the links between internal dispositions and behavior.

Trait research has pinpointed one construct in particular that we feel captures this description, and is relevant to values research. The individual differences construct of private self-consciousness (Fenigstein et al., 1975) refers to an individual's tendency to attend to inner aspects of the self, and those high in private self-consciousness (PSC) should be "particularly conscious of their own thoughts, feelings, attitudes, motives and behavioral tendencies" (Carver & Scheier, 1981, p. 46). Given this definition, it is reasonable to think that high PSCs may differ from low PSCs on several values-related dimensions. High PSCs by definition consult their inner states and dispositions more often, and thus should have better and easier access to this internal information. Consequently, we would expect high PSCs to be more confident in reporting personal values and more sure of the role of particular values in their self-schema.

In order to test this notion, we conducted a study that considered the effect of a persuasive communication on ratings of personal values (see Shrum et al., 1990, for a full description of the study). Subjects were randomly assigned to one of three conditions. Subjects in one condition received a persuasive communication supporting the concept of social recognition, an RVS terminal value. Other subjects received a persuasive communication arguing against the concept of social recognition, and a third group (control group) received no communication. After reading the persuasive communication, subjects answered a variety of questions pertaining to the communication. Finally, ostensibly as part of a second study, all subjects completed the RVS and the Fenigstein et al. (1975) Self-Consciousness Scale.

We hypothesized that those higher on PSC would be more aware of their values and thus more certain and confident in their ratings. We further expected that this confidence would translate into a resistance to either of the persuasive communications. On the other hand, we expected low PSCs to be more affected by the external suggestions. Individuals low on PSC tend not to attend to inner aspects of the self. They are less aware of their inner thoughts, attitudes, and motives, and should be less sure in their ratings of personal values. We therefore expected an interaction between private self-consciousness and experimental condition. Those low on PSC should be influenced in the direction of the persuasive communication, whereas there should be no significant differences between any of the three conditions for high PSCs.

The results were partially supportive. We found that those high (based on a median split) on a *dimension* of private self-consciousness (self-reflectiveness[1]) were relatively unaffected by the persuasive communication, but those low on self-reflectiveness rated social recognition higher (relative to the control group) in the "For social recognition" condition and lower in the "Against social recognition" condition. The interaction between self-reflectiveness and persuasive communication condition was significant. The results are shown in Fig. 7.1.

Although encouraging, the study was only partially supportive of our underlying contention that high and low PSCs differ on values-related dimensions. In order to further explore the issue, we conducted two additional studies that approached the research question in a different manner. These two studies, both reported in Shrum and McCarty (1992), addressed the role of private self-consciousness in issues involving differentiation on a rating task. Past research has shown high PSCs to have a better articulated self-schema (Nasby, 1985, 1989), most likely due to constant monitoring and heightened importance of the self. If this is indeed the case, we reasoned that high PSCs should show greater differentiation on a values rating task (i.e., rate-only) than low PSCs. High PSCs deal with their values more often, and thus should be more aware of differences in importance. On the other hand, low PSCs by definition consult their values infrequently, and thus should be less aware of comparative importance with respect to different values.

The results of the first study indicated that, as predicted, PSC was positively associated with rating variance: The more individuals were aware of their inner feelings, the more differentiation they exhibited in their ratings of the personal values. This relationship held for both the terminal and instrumental scale of the RVS. However, given that the sample size for the

---

[1]The Fenigstein et al. (1975) scale has been shown to consist of two subscales: self-reflectiveness and internal state awareness (Burnkrant & Page, 1984; Mittal & Balasubramanian, 1987). Self-reflectiveness tends to tap the extent to which individuals examine their motives, and is more cognitive-oriented. Internal state awareness deals more with attention to feeling states and is more affective or mood-oriented. The results for the Shrum et al. (1990) study were supportive for self-reflectiveness, but findings were not significant for the full private self-consciousness scale.

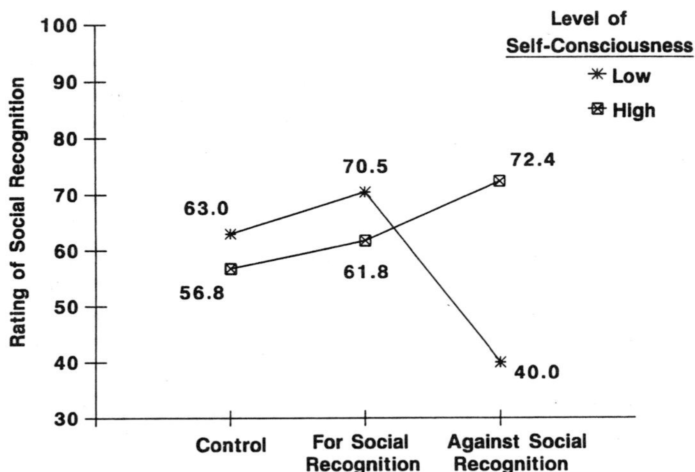

FIG. 7.1. Mean ratings of social recognition by persuasion condition and level of private self-consciousness. From "Individual differences in value stability: Are we really tapping true values?" by L. J. Shrum, J. A. McCarty, and T. L. Loeffler, in M. E. Goldberg, G. Gorn, and R. W. Pollay (Eds.), *Advances in consumer research* (Vol. 17), 1990, Provo, UT: Association for Consumer Research, p. 613. Copyright 1990 by the Association for Consumer Research. Reprinted by permission.

study was quite small ($N = 29$, student sample), a second study was conducted to replicate and extend the findings of the first study.

The second study again used the RVS with a student sample ($N = 108$). However, the administration of the value scale followed a different procedure. Instead of completing the RVS as part of a pencil and paper task, subjects rated the values on a computer screen as part of a reaction time task. Instrumental and terminal values were completely randomized, and subjects used a 10-point scale to rate the values as they appeared individually on the computer screen.

The results of the second study were consistent with those of the first study: PSC was positively correlated with rating variance. In order to understand what was driving this relationship, we divided the values into two categories: those values rated in the first half of the task and those rated in the second half. (Recall that subjects rated the values one at a time as they appeared on the computer screen. Thus, subjects had no knowledge of what values would follow, but their set of rated values in memory increased as more values were encountered and rated.) We also divided PSC into highs and lows based on a median split, and then calculated the mean rating variance for each of the four groups. The results indicated that the relationship between PSC and rating variance was due to little differentiation for low PSCs in the second half. All subjects, regardless of level of PSC, showed similar levels of differentiation in the first half, but low PSCs showed a significant drop in differentiation for the second half. High PSCs, on the other hand, maintained the same level of differentiation throughout the task. This finding suggests that the process of differentiating among the values may have been more difficult for low PSCs, and they eventually were less able or willing to make distinctions.

The results of the self-consciousness studies we have discussed point toward the conclusion that individual differences do exist in value stability and perception of values within the self-schema. These findings imply that there may also be individual differences in value–behavior consistency. Some individuals (e.g., high PSCs) may be concerned that their behavior is an accurate reflection of their inner feelings, and thus may consistently use values as guides to behavior. Others, such as low PSCs, may not be particularly interested in or concerned with their inner feelings and thus have no concern about consistency between their behavior and inner dispositions such as values, attitudes, or beliefs.

Future studies in our research program will attempt to empirically determine whether individual differences are related to consistency between values and behavior. This is an important question in that, as we discussed at the beginning of this chapter, it may help to better understand previous findings in values research. Moreover, an understanding of individual differences in value–behavior consistency should help articulate the processes involved in producing this effect.

INTERVENING AND ANTECEDENT VARIABLES

Past values research has typically viewed the effect of values on behavior as a direct one, with little regard for the role of other variables in the process. In other words, studies are conducted that seek to demonstrate simple bivariate relationships between particular values and specific behaviors. For example, one might want to show that those who place more importance on equality tend to vote for affirmative action measures, march in related demonstrations, and so forth. In terms of consumer behavior, one might seek to show that those who place greater importance on fun and enjoyment, or excitement, have a greater probability of driving a convertible, mountain climbing, or bungee jumping. These types of studies thus seek to show direct relationships between personal values and the behavior of interest.

Unfortunately, previous studies have only been moderately successful. Although a number of studies have shown direct relationships between values and behavior, considering that such research has been going on for over a decade, the absolute number of published studies is relatively small. Further, when relationships have been demonstrated, the effects are typically weak as well.

We would like to point out, however, that lack of a direct effect is not indicative of *no* effect. Both Rokeach (1973) and Kahle (1983; Homer & Kahle, 1988) have clearly pointed out that, at least in their theoretical formulations, values may *act through attitudes* in terms of influencing behavior. In other words, attitudes are expected to play a mediating role in the value–behavior relationship. Thus, while values may indeed have direct effects, one should also consider indirect effects. A complete understanding of the interrelationships among variables should provide for a more comprehensive understanding of the antecedents to behavior, and thus improve marketing techniques such as segmentation and targeting that employ psychographic information.

Another issue that has not received much attention in values research is the role of antecedent variables, in particular, demographics.[2] There have been virtually no studies that have considered the role of demographics and their influence on values and behaviors. Several studies, especially those evaluating the VALS method of measurement (Mitchell, 1983), have included demographics, along with values and lifestyle variables, in market segmentation and behavior prediction. However, these studies have not attempted to untangle the *interrelationships* among the variables, and thereby ascertain the unique contribution of each to the prediction of behavior.

In order to advance values theory, we think it is important to understand precisely what is the unique contribution of the different variables in predicting behavior. Participation in many activities, regardless of values and attitudes toward the activity, may be determined by variables such as gross income, discretionary income, age, or education. In turn, these demographic variables may be related to values and attitudes, as well as the behavior of interest. However, without considering the impact of demographics, spurious relationships may be noted between values and behavior. In other words, value–behavior relationships may be driven by demographic variables to the extent that demographics covary with both values

[2]Some may take issue with our terming certain variables, such as demographics, as antecedent variables. We use the term antecedent because we feel that demographic variables such as age, income, education, occupation (i.e., variables comprising socioeconomic status) substantially affect personal values. Most agree that values are culturally determined, and socioeconomic status is a major defining variable in subcultures within the United States. However, we are not suggesting that the influence is unidirectional. Certainly, values can also have an effect on demographic variables (e.g., income, education, occupation). However, we would contend that the major influence flows from demographics to values.

and behavior.[3] This outcome may not be overly problematic from an applied perspective, but it may serve to distort the theoretical models built to explain the relationship between values and behavior. Additionally, this covariation of other variables with both the independent variables (values) and the dependent variables (behaviors) may serve to suppress or mask value–behavior relationships.

Intervening Variables

We conducted two studies aimed at trying to better understand the complex relationships among the variables that presumably impact consumer behavior. These two studies specifically addressed the value–attitude–behavior hierarchy. Rokeach (1973) provided evidence that values are indeed related to attitudes. However, as mentioned earlier, his ordinal level of values measurement precluded any type of causal modeling that might show more clearly and precisely the interrelationships among the variables. To our knowledge, only Homer and Kahle (1988) and Horton and Horton (1990) have attempted to address the value–attitude–behavior hierarchy in a causal modeling framework. The work by Homer and Kahle (1988) was particularly impactful in that it showed that attitudes can play a mediating role in the value–behavior relationship. They found that for natural food shoppers, values were related to attitudes, and attitudes influenced buying behavior. However, there were no direct effects observed between values and behavior, suggesting that attitudes played a mediating role.

The two studies we conducted, McCarty and Shrum (1993c, 1994), attempted to address the value–attitude–behavior issue by focusing on the behavior of recycling solid wastes. One of the tentative conclusions that we reached in our review of the values literature was that in many instances significant effects of values on behavior occurred when the behavior was "principle-driven" or involved social issues. For example, values have been shown to relate to organ donation (Horton & Horton, 1990), health food shopping (Homer & Kahle, 1988), participation in civil rights activities (Rokeach, 1973), political attitudes and behavior (Almond & Verba, 1963), and cigarette smoking (Grube, Weir, Getzlaf, & Rokeach, 1984), and this list is only a subset of the whole. Thus, we chose recycling behavior because it tends to fit into the scheme of value-driven, prosocial behavior. Additionally, research has shown recycling behavior to be linked to a number

[3]It is important to note that demographic variables themselves do not "cause" anything per se, and thus are not uniquely responsible for, in this case, the value–behavior relation. Rather, correlates of demographics are the potential causal factors. However, these correlates may not be known, and thus cannot be controlled. Controlling for demographics in effect accounts for these unknown, or at least unspecified, potentially confounding variables.

of psychographic variables (Shrum, Lowrey, & McCarty, 1994, 1995, 1996; Shrum, McCarty, & Lowrey, 1995).

The first study (McCarty & Shrum, 1993c) used a student sample ($N=89$), and administered the LOV scale using a least–most rating method. Data concerning attitudes and beliefs about recycling, and level of participation in recycling activities, were also collected. Analyses using LISREL 7 (Jöreskog & Sörbom, 1988) were conducted to determine the direct and indirect effects of values on behavior. The final model is shown in Fig. 7.2.

The results of the analyses indicated that the value ratings were best explained by a three-factor model: Respect/Achievement, Enjoyment, and Security. Respect/Achievement was negatively related to beliefs about the inconvenience of recycling, which in turn were negatively related to the frequency of recycling behavior. These two direct effects equate to a *positive, indirect* effect of Respect/Achievement on recycling behavior. Both Enjoyment (positive) and Security (negative) were related to beliefs about the importance of recycling. However, importance was not related to recycling frequency. Additionally, no direct effects between the values and recycling behavior were noted, similar to Homer and Kahle (1988).

Although the results of the McCarty and Shrum (1993c) study were consistent with our theoretical reasoning, some of the paths were significant

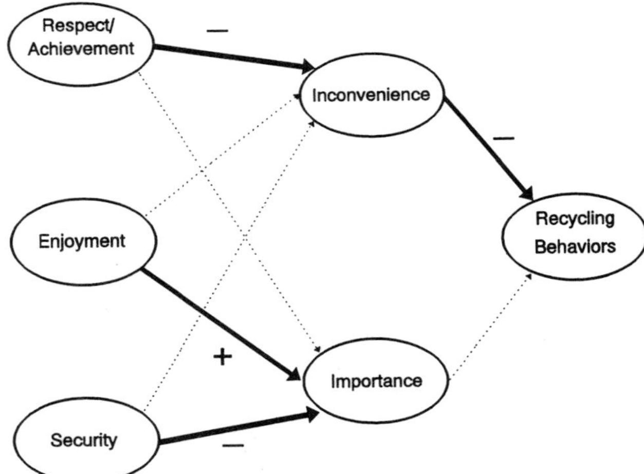

FIG. 7.2. Structural equation model showing influence of values on recycling attitudes and behavior. Solid lines represent significant paths. From "A structural equation analysis of the relationships of personal values, attitudes and beliefs about recycling, and the recycling of solid waste products" by J. A. McCarty and L. J. Shrum, in L. McAlister and M. Rothschild (Eds.), *Advances in consumer research* (Vol. 20), 1993, Provo, UT: Association for Consumer Research, p. 645. Copyright 1993 by the Association for Consumer Research. Adapted by permission.

only at the $p < .10$ level. This may have been due in part to the relatively small sample size. Therefore, a second study was conducted to replicate and extend the previous one. This second study (McCarty & Shrum, 1994) again used a student sample, but increased the sample size ($N = 134$). Following the procedure of the previous study, the LOV was administered using a least–most rating method. Additionally, three items were included that were intended to tap the value orientation of individualism–collectivism (cf. Hofstede, 1984; Kluckhohn & Strodtbeck, 1961; Triandis, 1989). Individualism–collectivism deals with the relationship of the individual to the group and how individuals relate to one another. Individualistic cultures tend to place greater emphasis on the individual, whereas collectivistic cultures tend to subordinate the individual to the group. We reasoned that this value orientation would be particularly relevant to the tradeoffs between individual needs and societal (collective) interests regarding participation in recycling programs.

LISREL was again used to analyze the data. Four value factors were found to best represent latent structure. One factor was comprised of the three items intended to tap individualism–collectivism, and we labeled this factor *Collectivism.* The other three factors, *Self-Gratification* (similar to Respect/Achievement from the previous study), *Fun/Enjoyment,* and *Security* were derived from the LOV scale, and are roughly equivalent to the value factors found in McCarty and Shrum (1993c), although the items loading on each factor were slightly different for the two studies.

The analysis indicated that Collectivism was negatively related to beliefs about the inconvenience of recycling, which in turn were negatively related to frequency of recycling behavior. Thus, Collectivism had a *positive, indirect* effect on recycling behavior. Self-Gratification was found to be negatively related to beliefs about importance of recycling, but not related to beliefs about inconvenience. This finding is somewhat different than the findings of McCarty and Shrum (1993c), where Respect/Achievement was related to inconvenience but not importance. Similar to the earlier study, Fun/Enjoyment was positively related to beliefs about the importance of recycling. However, Security showed no significant relationship with importance. Finally, as with the earlier study, no relationship was found between importance and recycling behavior, and no direct effects of values on frequency of recycling were noted.

These results provide additional insight into the findings of McCarty and Shrum (1993c). In the first study, each of the paths between values and behavior that were significant at only $p < .10$ were not significant in the second study, suggesting that these relationships may not be reliable. On the other hand, Fun/Enjoyment was shown to strongly influence beliefs about the importance of recycling for both studies. Additionally, Collectivism was shown to have a positive indirect effect on frequency of recycling.

The results of these two studies are important for both theoretical and applied reasons. They show support for indirect effects of values on behavior, and emphasize the notion that values should be viewed in the context of other variables. If attitudes had been left out of the equation, then we would have been forced to conclude that values had no effect on behavior; yet, that was clearly not the case.

From an applied perspective, the results of the two studies have important implications for strategies aimed at attitudinal and behavioral change. Using the second study (McCarty & Shrum, 1994) as an example, two avenues for increasing recycling behavior are apparent. One is to address perceptions of the inconvenience of recycling, which had a strong influence on recycling behavior. In other words, if individuals can be persuaded that recycling is really not all that difficult or inconvenient, then perhaps a behavioral change can be obtained. It could very well be that these attitudes about inconvenience are merely perceptions, and not based on experience. A second avenue towards behavioral change, and a less direct one, is to focus on the importance of recycling. As stated previously, importance did not significantly influence recycling behavior. However, this is one area where values research, and understanding the underlying dimensions of attitudes, may be important. The results of this study suggest that the more people value Fun/Enjoyment, the more they think that recycling is important. Yet, this link does not translate into recycling behavior. In order to influence behavioral change, one strategy might be to make this value–behavior link more salient, and impress upon the target that individual participation in recycling may have a very direct and immediate impact on fulfilling one's values or desired end states (for a more in-depth discussion, see Shrum et al., 1994, 1995, 1996).

The aforementioned studies provide additional evidence that attitudes function as mediating variables in the value–behavior relation. These studies suggest that it is important to look beyond simple and direct value–behavior relationships, and consider these relationships in the context of other variables.

Antecedent Variables

The previous section viewed values as antecedent variables in the context of attitudes and behavior. However, as mentioned earlier, there are also variables that themselves may act as antecedents to the value–behavior relation. In particular, demographic variables such as age, income, and education may influence both values and behavior. If this is the case, then four scenarios are possible: (a) values may exert an independent influence on behavior, (b) values may influence behavior by acting as a mediator between demographic variables and behavior, (c) the value–behavior relationship may be solely the result of shared variance between demographics and behavior, making the value–behavior relationship spurious, and (d) the covariation of demographics with values and behavior may serve to mask value–behavior relationships.

To test these possibilities, we conducted a study that attempted to address the role of demographics in the value–behavior relationship (see McCarty & Shrum, 1993b, for a complete description of the study). This study administered the RVS to a general population sample via a mail survey, and the behavioral variable was television viewing. Several studies have indicated that aspects of television viewing (e.g., total viewing, program preference) may be related to personal values (Beatty, Kahle, Homer, & Misra, 1985; Becker & Conner, 1981; Gandy, 1984). Consequently, using television viewing as the dependent variable provided us with an opportunity to test our assumptions about interrelationships among the variables, which in turn may have implications for previous findings.

The results of the study indicate that all four of the aforementioned possibilities occurred. If demographics were not entered into the model, significant relationships between particular value factors and amount of television viewed were observed. However, including demographics reduced several of these relationships to nonsignificance. On one occasion, entering demographics into the model changed the value–television viewing relationship from a significantly negative to a significantly positive one. These results suggest that failure to include demographics may indeed yield spurious relationships between values and television viewing (Scenario 3). On the other hand, other value–viewing relationships were unchanged after demographics were added, suggesting that some value dimensions do influence certain behaviors independent of demographics influences (Scenario 1). Additionally, before demographics were added, several value–television viewing relationships were nonsignificant. However, including demographics in the model revealed significant value–viewing relationships that were otherwise obscured (Scenario 4). Finally, demographics were also shown to have an indirect effect on viewing behavior, with values acting as a mediating variable (Scenario 2).

The results of the studies that considered the role of values in the context of intervening and antecedent variables suggest that if we want to understand the very complex relationship between personal values and behavior, we must consider antecedent, moderating, and mediating variables in the model. Failure to do so may in some cases obscure important relationships, and in other case render spurious correlations between values and behavior. Obviously, as more variables are entered into the model, more variance in behavior will be explained. However, there is a limit to the amount of input that can be reasonably integrated. We think that an inclusion of both demographics and attitudes can help clarify which variables are driving the value–behavior relation.

CONCLUSION

Our goal in this chapter was to initiate a discussion on the complex relationship between values and behavior. It is our contention that the role of values in consumer behavior is still an area ripe for exploration. Although the large body of work in this area has provided important direction, we think the full potential of values research has not yet been tapped.

We have proposed three areas that we believe may help accelerate values research: measurement issues, individual differences, and relationships among variables. At this stage, these issues are primarily theoretical in nature. However, we would strongly argue that they have the potential to greatly influence marketing practice, and are therefore necessary and important precursors to the application of values theory.

We have presented some of our own studies that have addressed issues in these three areas. The results have been encouraging. In some cases, we have tried to follow up on the seminal work of others, in particular the work of Homer and Kahle (1988), which addressed the intervening role of attitudes in the value–behavior relation, and the work of Munson (1984), which discussed the issue of alternative measurement methods. At other times, we have tried to break new ground, such as our work on individual differences and their relationship to values.

As we pointed out earlier, our overriding goal is to better explicate the value–behavior relation. To date, our work has been primarily concerned with testing *assumptions* necessary to move toward value–behavior explanations, but the critical behavioral questions still remain to be studied. Future work will attempt to apply the knowledge gained from these initial studies in order to better understand the role of personal values in guiding consumer behavior.

Author Note

Our contributions to this chapter were equal; order of authorship was determined by coin flip.

ACKNOWLEDGMENTS

We would like to thank Dr. Tina M. Lowrey of Rider University for her helpful comments on this manuscript, and acknowledge her contributions to the various projects described in this chapter. We would also like to acknowledge the financial support provided by the Rutgers University Research Council to the first author, and by the James Webb Young Fund, Department of Advertising, University of Illinois at Urbana–Champaign, to the second author.

REFERENCES

Abelson, R. (1972). Are attitudes necessary? in B. T. King & E. McGinnies (Eds.), *Attitudes, conflict, and social change.* New York: Academic Press.

Almond, G. A., & Verba, S. (1963). *The civic culture.* Princeton, NJ: Princeton University Press.

Alwin, D. F., & Krosnick, J. A. (1985). The measurement of values in surveys: A comparison of ratings and rankings. *Public Opinion Quarterly, 49,* 535–552.

Beatty, S. E., Kahle, L. R., Homer, P. M., & Misra S. (1985). Alternative measurement approaches to consumer values: The list of values and the Rokeach Value Survey. *Psychology and Marketing, 2,* 181–200.

Becker, B. W., & Conner, P. E. (1981). Personal values of the heavy user of mass media. *Journal of Advertising Research, 21,* 37–43.

Belk, R. (1985). Materialism: Trait aspects of living in the material world. *Journal of Consumer Research, 12,* 265–280.

Bond, M. H. (1988). Finding universal dimensions of individual variation in multicultural studies of values: The Rokeach and Chinese value surveys. *Journal of Personality and Social Psychology, 55,* 1009–1015.

Burnkrant, R. C., & Page, T. J. (1984). A modification of the Fenigstein, Scheier, and Buss self-consciousness scales. *Journal of Personality Assessment, 40,* 620–637.

Carver, C. S., & Scheier, M. F. (1981). *Attention and self-regulation: A control-theory approach to human behavior.* New York: Springer-Verlag.

Chaiken, S., Liberman, A., & Eagly, A. H. (1989). Heuristic and systematic processing within and beyond the persuasion context. In J. S. Uleman & J. A. Bargh (Eds.), *Unintended thought* (pp. 212–252). New York: Guilford Press.

Crosby, L. A., Bitner, M. J., & Gill, J. D. (1990). Organizational structure of values. *Journal of Business Research, 20,* 123–134.

Fazio, R. H. (1986). How do attitudes guide behavior? In R. M. Sorrentino & E. T. Higgins (Eds.), *The handbook of motivation and cognition: Foundations of social behavior* (pp. 204–243). New York: Guilford.

Fazio, R. H. (1989). On the power and functionality of attitudes: The role of attitude accessibility. In A. R. Pratkanis et al. (Eds.), *Attitude structure and function* (pp. 153–179). Hillsdale, NJ: Lawrence Erlbaum Associates.

Fenigstein, A., Scheier, M. F., & Buss, A. H. (1975). Public and private self-consciousness: Assessment and theory. *Journal of Consulting and Clinical Psychology, 43,* 522–527.

Fishbein, M., & Ajzen, I. (1974). Attitudes towards objects as predictors of single and multiple behavioral criteria. *Psychological Review, 81,* 59–74.

Gandy, O. H. (1984). Is that all there is to love?: Values and program preference. In S. Thomas (Ed.), *Studies in mass communication and technology* (pp. 207–219). Norwood, NJ: Ablex.

Grube, J. W., Weir, I. L., Getzlaf, S., & Rokeach, M. (1984). Own value system, value images, and cigarette smoking. *Personality and Social Psychology Bulletin, 10,* 306–313.

Gutman, J. (1990). Adding meaning to values by directly assessing value–benefit relationships. *Journal of Business Research, 20,* 153–160.

Henry, W. A. (1976). Cultural values do correlate with consumer behavior. *Journal of Marketing Research, 13,* 121–127.

Hofstede, G. (1984). *Culture's consequences.* Beverly Hills: Sage.

Homer, P. M., & Kahle, L. R. (1988). A structural equation test of the values–attitude–behavior hierarchy. *Journal of Personality and Social Psychology, 54,* 638–646.

Horton, R. L., & Horton, P. J. (1990). Organ donation and values: Identifying potential organ donors. In M. P. Gardner (Ed.), *Proceedings of the society for consumer psychology* (pp. 55–59). Washington, DC: American Psychological Association.

Jöreskog, K. G., & Sörbom, D. (1988). *LISREL 7: A guide to the program and applications.* Chicago: SPSS Inc.

Kahle, L. R. (Ed.). (1983). *Social values and social change: Adaptation to life in America.* New York: Praeger.

Kluckhohn, F. R., & Strodtbeck, F. L. (1961). *Variations in value orientations.* Evanston, IL: Row, Peterson.

Krosnick, J. A., & Alwin, D. F. (1988). A test of the form-resistant correlation hypothesis. *Public Opinion Quarterly, 52,* 526–538.

Linville, P. W., Salovey, P., & Fischer, G. W. (1986). Stereotyping and perceived distributions of social characteristics: An application to ingroup–outgroup perception. In J. F. Dovidio & S. L. Gaertner (Eds.), *Prejudice, discrimination, and racism.* New York: Academic Press.

McCarty, J. A., & Shrum, L. J. (1993a). *Developing alternative methods for measuring personal values: A test of three measurement procedures.* Unpublished manuscript.

McCarty, J. A., & Shrum, L. J. (1993b). The role of personal values and demographics in predicting television viewing behavior: Implications for theory and application. *Journal of Advertising, 22*(4), 77–101.

McCarty, J. A., & Shrum, L. J. (1993c). A structural equation analysis of the relationships of personal values, attitudes and beliefs about recycling, and the recycling of solid waste products. In L. McAlister & M. Rothschild (Eds.), *Advances in consumer research* (Vol. 20, pp. 641–646). Provo, UT: Association for Consumer Research.

McCarty, J. A., & Shrum, L. J. (1994). The recycling of solid wastes: Personal and cultural values and attitudes about recycling as antecedents of recycling behavior. *Journal of Business Research, 30,* 53–62.

Mitchell, A. (1983). *The nine American lifestyles.* New York: Warren.

Mittal, B., & Balasubramanian, S. K. (1987). Testing the dimensionality of the self-consciousness scales. *Journal of Personality Assessment, 51,* 53–68.

Munson, J. M. (1984). Personal values: Considerations on their measurement and application to five areas of research inquiry. In R. E. Pitts & A. G. Woodside (Eds.), *Personal values & consumer psychology* (pp. 169–185). Lexington, MA: D. C. Heath.

Nasby, W. (1985). Private self-consciousness, articulation of the self-schema, and recognition memory of trait adjectives. *Journal of Personality and Social Psychology, 49,* 704–709.

Nasby, W. (1989). Private and public self-consciousness and articulation of the self-schema. *Journal of Personality and Social Psychology, 56,* 117–123.

Petty, R. E., & Cacioppo, J. T. (1986). *Communication and persuasion: Central and peripheral routes to attitude change.* New York: Springer-Verlag.

Pitts, R. E., & Woodside, A. G. (1983). Personal value influences on consumer product class and brand preferences. *The Journal of Social Psychology, 119,* 37–53.

Reynolds, T. J., & Gutman, J. (1988). Laddering theory, method, analysis and interpretation. *Journal of Advertising Research, 28,* 11–34.

Rokeach, M. (1973). *The nature of human values.* New York: The Free Press.

Shrum, L. J., Lowrey, T. M., & McCarty, J. A. (1994). Recycling as a marketing problem: A framework for strategy development. *Psychology & Marketing, 11,* 393–416.

Shrum, L. J., Lowrey, T. M., & McCarty, J. A. (1995). Applying social and traditional marketing principles to the reduction of household waste: Turning research into action. *American Behavioral Scientist, 38,* 646–657.

Shrum, L. J., Lowrey, T. M., & McCarty, J. A. (1996). Using marketing and advertising principles to encourage pro-environmental behaviors. In R. P. Hill (Ed.), *Marketing and consumer behavior in the public interest* (pp. 197–216). Beverly Hills: Sage.

Shrum, L. J., & McCarty, J. A. (1992). Individual differences in differentiation in the rating of personal values: The role of private self-consciousness. *Personality and Social Psychology Bulletin, 18,* 223–230.

Shrum, L. J., McCarty, J. A., & Loeffler, T. L. (1990). Individual differences in value stability: Are we really tapping true values? In M. E. Goldberg, G. Gorn, & R. W. Pollay (Eds.), *Advances in consumer research* (Vol. 17, pp. 609–615). Provo, UT: Association for Consumer Research.

Shrum, L. J., McCarty, J. A., & Lowrey, T. M. (1995). Understanding the buyer characteristics of the green consumer: Implications for advertising strategy. *Journal of Advertising, 24*, 71–82.

Snyder, M. (1974). Self-monitoring of expressive behavior. *Journal of Personality and Social Psychology, 30*, 526–537.

Triandis, H. C. (1989). The self and social behavior in differing cultural contexts. *Psychological Review, 96*, 506–520.

Triandis, H. C., McCusker, C., & Hui, H. (1990). Multimethod probes of individualism and collectivism. *Journal of Personality and Social Psychology*, 59, 1006–1020.

Wicker, A. (1971). An examination of the 'other variables' explanation of attitude–behavior inconsistency. *Journal of Personality and Social Psychology, 19*, 18–30.

Wyer, R. S., Bodenhausen, G. V., & Gorman, T. F. (1985). Cognitive mediators of reactions to rape. *Journal of Personality and Social Psychology, 48*, 324–338.

Chapter 8

"Seeing With the Mind's Eye": On the Use of Pictorial Stimuli in Values and Lifestyle Research

Suzanne C. Grunert-Beckmann
Copenhagen Business School, Denmark

Søren Askegaard
Odense University, Denmark

PICTORIAL STIMULI IN ADVERTISING AND CONSUMER BEHAVIOR RESEARCH

Although there are many unanswered questions concerning how our visual system functions and how an image is formed within our minds, anatomical, psycho-physiological, and psychological research has progressed impressingly within the last few decades. Within the theory about how physical stimuli are represented in the brain and thus turned into a recognizable pattern, feature and prototype models have replaced the rather primitive template models, the *Gestalt* principles of organization are becoming more and more developed, and there have been fruitful discussions concerning the nature and function of the human imagination system, indicating that it requires a complementary system for labeling the imagery, for example, an interpretative system (for an overview, see Spoehr & Lehmkuhle, 1982).

Advertising research has always been the natural domain for an extensive use of pictorial stimuli such as portraits of consumer and consumption situation stereotypes, advertisement layouts, animatics, and the like. The manifold copy-testing approaches and techniques witness to the profound interest in consumers' perception of verbal, visual, and pictorial stimuli, or, semiotically speaking, to the signifiers and signifieds in an advertising context.

The use of pictorial stimuli in consumer behavior research has traditionally been limited to qualitative research methods where they have proven their suitability particularly in the context of projective techniques. Within quantitative research, however, they have not been used very extensively, presumably to the fact that, at first glance, the meanings expressed in and connotations associated with pictorial stimuli seem difficult to assess and analyze quantitatively. Only a few studies within an information processing context have employed pictorial stimuli. Most of these studies have referred to theories and research on the existence of different hemispheric information processing styles and consumer behavior implications hereof (Hansen, 1981), supporting the proposition that the processing and comprehension of pictorial stimuli predominantly takes place in the right hemisphere, thus leading to a qualitatively different information processing style than is the case when confronting the respondent with verbal stimuli.

One of the first studies of the effect of pictorial variables and their role compared to verbal stimuli in consumers' judgments of product attributes and designs was conducted by Holbrook and Moore (1981). They summed up the findings of cognitive psychology concerning the distinctive features of verbal and visual information processing as follows: "task input—words versus pictures; code—verbal system versus imagery system; cerebral hemisphere—left versus right; mode—sequential versus simultaneous; and response output—few versus many main and interaction effects" (p. 105). However, they explicitly stated that such a dichotomous view represented an oversimplified presentation of reality and that they would at best express tendencies.

Several of these assumptions have since then, not surprisingly, been questioned. Domzal and Unger (1985) replicated the study of Holbrook and Moore, using what they themselves considered a "more functional product," wristwatches, as stimuli instead of the sweater designs used in the original study. They concluded by questioning the assumption that verbal input activates verbal information processing and visual input activates the imagery system, and suggested instead that the distinction should be made rather along a dividing line of abstract versus concrete stimuli, such as that more concrete stimuli excite more visual imagery and more abstract stimuli excite verbal information processing. The suggestion that pictorial stimuli generate more main effects and feature interactions was also challenged by this study, which led to exactly opposite results. Domzal and Unger explained this by differences in the samples of the two studies.

In addition to these critical points of view, Meyers-Levy (1989) suggested that a sharp distinction line between the two hemispheric information processing types is a predominantly male phenomenon, with women having a more balanced information processing style regardless of the type of input.

Childers and Houston (1984) examined the efficiency of visualized variables in generating a higher level of memorization of brand names. They found such visual messages superior to verbal messages in generating memorization of brand names especially under conditions of low involvement or relatively short exposure time, and concluded: "Visual ads were superior to verbal ads in certain conditions in this study, and in no conditions were they inferior" (p. 653). Thus encouraged, these authors continued to evaluate various methods for measuring individual differences in information processing styles (Childers, Houston, & Heckler, 1985).

We feel confident too that the use of pictorial stimuli, if these are carefully selected and tested, could be a useful tool for solving one major problem within cross-cultural value research, namely what has been referred to as "the problem of culture-specific connotations of the value verbalizations [. . .] a one-word stimulus, provided out of context, can lead to a wide variety of response modes, which can themselves be culturally specific" (Grunert, Grunert, & Beatty, 1989, p. 37).

Needless to say that pictures also evoke culturally specific connotations. But there are many more additional cues in a picture to provide the context that may help the respondent in her or his interpretation process of the picture. And even though it is probably not possible to conceive of a universal pictorial value measurement tool, we take our point of departure in the idea that it should be possible to generate an instrument with a certain cross-cultural validity, that is, within, for example, Western Europe. Hence, the conclusion "that both academic and practical researchers should seriously consider the benefits of visual stimulus presentations in terms of realism and accuracy" (Louviere, Schroeder, Louviere, & Woodworth, 1987, p. 81) stimulated our search for further evidence of the usefulness of pictorial variables within the specific realm of values research.

PICTORIAL STIMULI IN VALUES AND LIFESTYLE RESEARCH

One of the problems facing value research is the semantic ambiguity inherent in the abstractness of value constructs and how they usually are presented, unrelated to any context, thus threatening the comparability of data. The use of pictorial stimuli may solve this problem, because they present the value construct in a context and give additional cues to its interpretation. In quantitative values and lifestyle research, however, pictorial stimuli have played a minor role so far. To our knowledge, only the Centre de Communication Avancé (CCA) research agency in Paris has made extensive use of pictorial stimuli in their lifestyle questionnaires. CCA has used pictorial variables to assess respondents' aesthetic tastes concerning designs and colors of different consumption objects: Clothes, cars, type of ideal home, interior decoration, bottle designs, types of in-store displays or other kinds of merchandizing, and the like. This latter type of variable leads to the other main group of pictorial variables used by the CCA, namely for expressing different communicative styles. This does not only mean responses to different types of advertising but also to other types of graphic or photographic illustrations, magazine covers, record covers, font types, or logotypes (Cathelat, 1990). Hence, in this framework, the prime function of illustrations in the context of values and lifestyle research is the realism they convey. Many of these variables would be impossible to express other than by a pictorial presentation.

CCA has also used pictorial variables to represent an abstract concept, like a value or a general idea. For example, in a study in the United States as well as in a pan-European study, pictorial variables were used to express several conceptualizations of the cultures' past and future, internal and external relations, rituals, stereotypical people, social leaders, and cultural emblems, that is, symbols expressing the quintessence of the cultural unity. All of these dimensions are rooted in a specific model of cultural identity (cf. Askegaard, 1991). Unfortunately, however, these data can, for commercial reasons, not be submitted to scientific scrutiny.

In general, CCA uses four types of pictorial stimuli: (a) *Objective* pictorial questions where an item is represented as an iconic drawing or photo, in general without verbal cues about how to interpret the item; (b) *symbolic* pictorial questions, where an item is presented by a drawing or a photo evoking the concept, the feeling or the idea that the item is to represent, these may or may not be supported by verbal stimuli; (c) *illustrated* questions, where a verbal item (monosemic or polysemic) is supported by an explicative drawing; and (d) *schematic* questions, where the response choices in their totality come in the form of a drawing, on which the respondent has to indicate her or his response(s) (Cathelat, 1990, p. 276).

Much more common with value and lifestyle research, however, is the use of quantitative techniques with standardized measurement instruments, such as inventories like the Rokeach Value Survey (Rokeach, 1973), Values and Lifestyles VALS (Mitchell, 1983), the List of Values LOV (Kahle, Beatty, & Homer, 1986), or the Schwartz Value Indicator SVI (Schwartz & Bilsky, 1990). Given the abstractness of the values and lifestyle concepts, it seems promising to develop an assessment procedure that combines the advantages of both qualitative and quantitative research techniques by helping the respondents to better understand the requested task. This approach may also overcome some of the difficulties found in cross-cultural values and lifestyle research with regard to semantic versus content differences (cf. Grunert & Scherhorn, 1990).

Theoretical Background

A cognitive–emotive view toward values is employed here, that is, human behavior is regarded as being determined by cognitive–emotive structures and processes. According to this view, culture is expressed in collectively shared cognitive–emotive structures which direct behavior mainly via automatic cognitive–emotive processes (Grunert, Grunert, & Kristensen, 1992). Cognitive–emotive structures are the organization of knowledge and experience in memory—values and lifestyles are an important part of this knowledge and experience, and can thus be interpreted as rather abstract cognitive–emotive categories.

Values are commonly regarded as the point of intersection between the individual and society because they help to know and understand the interpersonal world and guide the individual's adaptation to the surrounding conditions. A convenient definition of values outlines their five main features: Values are (a) concepts or beliefs (b) about desirable end states or behaviors (c) that transcend specific situations, (d) guide the selection or evaluation of behavior and events, and (e) are ordered by relative importance (Schwartz & Bilsky, 1987). This definition tries to capture most of the value features emphasized by different research approaches within social sciences.

Both values and lifestyle concepts have been extensively used in consumer behavior research, but neither value inventories nor lifestyle typologies have been proven very efficient in predicting specific consumer behavior. The problems encountered are not so much related to the theoretical conceptualization of values and lifestyle itself, but rather to the difficulty of modeling the relationship between these highly abstract cognitive–emotive categories and the organization of everyday life as well as assessing this relationship.

One of the main problems recognized by many researchers, but rarely dealt with in practice, is the question of whether and how values, lifestyle, and their influence on behavior can be verbalized and thus made accessible for measurement. A general model of the measurement process is shown in Fig. 8.1 (cf. Grunert, Grunert, & Beatty, 1989): On the one side are the people whose value systems are to be measured. On the other side is the researcher who usually starts with some theoretical basis, some catalogue of values, or any other a priori notion about values, thus having a value hypothesis. In trying to operationalize her or his value hypothesis, the researcher develops a set of value indicators. The respondents, on the other hand, express their value systems in some way in their behavior, which also includes their speech behavior, that is, their language. The core of the measurement process is trying to match respondents' behavior and the researcher's value indicators.

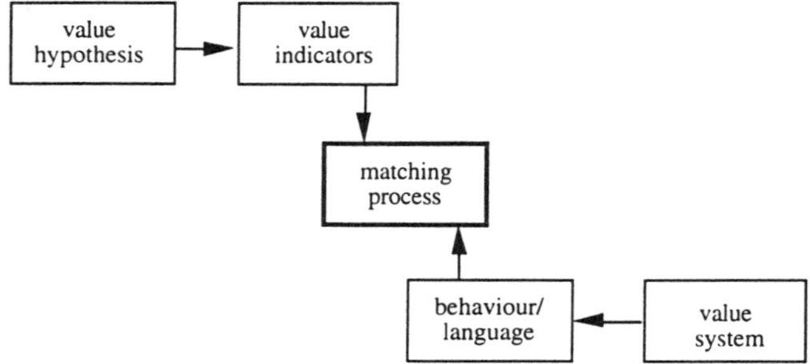

FIG. 8.1. A general model of value measurement.

The researcher's value indicators have, as mentioned before, usually been verbal inventories within the framework of quantitative techniques where respondents rank or rate values according to their relative importance in their daily life. Using pictorial stimuli to investigate consumers' values and lifestyle would enlarge this approach by a qualitative aspect, that is, designing the inventories as "communication catalogues." Such an approach would turn them into indicators of consumers' perception toward communicational strategies and specific forms of expressions in, for example, advertisements, thus increasing their potential for predicting consumer behavior and reactions to different communication styles.

The view of culture, and the role of values and lifestyle within and between cultures, explained earlier, has measurement implications. When using an inventory, the data obtained will be the result of both automatic and strategic cognitive–emotive processes acting on the respondents' cognitive–emotive structures. In order to rank or rate the items, the respondent has to recognize the word sequence and relate it to an existing cognitive–emotive category. If that category is not immediately associated with a strong evaluation, then the task of expressing an evaluation in terms of ranking or rating will be solved by trying to relate the item to some other, usually more abstract, cognitive–emotive categories, which carry such an evaluation with them. Up to this point, the process is mostly automatic. Only if the item appears very unfamiliar, or if there are no strong associations to categories which carry an evaluation, will strategic processes be invoked. Finally, there may be some strategic control on whether the spontaneously, that is, automatically, formed evaluation will be expressed or not. In most cases, the obtained answer will depend heavily on automatic processes and the underlying cognitive–emotive structure, with strategic processes having a much lesser importance. It is suggested that the use of pictorial stimuli will increase the activation of automatic processes due to an easier and quicker understanding of the item presented, which in its verbal form rather often appears as a very abstract term difficult to handle by respondents. In the remainder of this chapter we focus exclusively on values, as this concept was the central research subject of our exploratory study.

VALUES AND MOTIVATIONAL DOMAINS: SOME THEORY

Values can be conceptualized as criteria used by individuals to select and justify their actions, thus representing motivations. These criteria are assumed to differ in content as well as in the structural relations among these. This assumption hinges on the meaningful content of values, which is defined as cognitive representations of three types of universal human requirements: Biologically based needs of the organism; social interactional claims for interpersonal coordination; and social institutional demands for group welfare and survival (cf. Kluckhohn, 1951; Maslow, 1959; Rokeach, 1973). Values thus serve both individualistic and collectivist interests as well as a mixture of these (cf. Hofstede & Bond, 1984; Triandis, McCusker, & Hui, 1990).

Using a facet theory approach which provides a metatheoretical framework for empirical research (cf. Borg, 1986; Canter, 1985), values can formally be defined by the mapping sentence shown in Fig. 8.2. Eleven motivational domains of values are described by the value theory of Schwartz and Bilsky (1987, 1990; Schwartz, 1992), which at the same time postulates that these domains are culturally universal in their content and structure. These domains consist of both instrumental and terminal values that belong to either the individualistic interest dimension, or the collectivist, or both. They were derived from the work of a number of researchers in social sciences (e.g., Bandura, 1988; Berlyne, 1967; Deci & Ryan, 1985; Kluckhohn, 1951; Maslow, 1959; Scitovsky, 1976). The content of these different value types is briefly described in Table 8.1.

It is suggested that these 11 motivational domains are structured in a circular arrangement of regions emanating from a common origin with

A value is an individual's concept of a transituational GOAL (F1) that expresses INTERESTS (F2) concerned with a MOTIVATIONAL DOMAIN (F3) and evaluated on a RANGE OF IMPORTANCE (R) as a guiding principle in her/his life.

with

F1: terminal or instrumental
F2: individualistic, collectivist, or both
F3: ten to eleven different universal domains
R: very important to very unimportant

FIG. 8.2. Mapping sentence to define values formally.

TABLE 8.1
The Motivational Content of Eleven Value Types

Self-direction (SDI, individualistic domain):
The motivation for this value type is independent thought and action, derived from the organismic need for mastery and control through choosing, creating, and exploring, and interactional requirements of autonomy and independence. It means to be unconstrained by externally imposed limits.

Stimulation (STI, individualistic domain):
Stimulation values are related to the need for variety in order to maintain an optimal level of activation and their motivational goals are excitement, novelty, and challenge in life.

Hedonism (HED, individualistic domain):
Closely related to stimulation, this value type is described as representing pleasure and sensuous gratification for oneself.

Achievement (ACH, individualistic domain):
This domain is defined by the goal of personal success through demonstrating competence according to social standards and thereby obtaining social approval.

Power (POW, individualistic domain):
The central goal of power values is the attainment of social status and prestige, control or dominance over people and resources.

Security (SEC, individualistic and collectivist domain):
This motivational domain derives from basic individual and group requirements and represents the goal of safety, harmony, and stability of society, of relationships, and of self.

Conformity (CON, collectivist domain):
Restraint of actions, inclinations, and impulses likely to upset or harm others and violate social expectations and norms, this is the defining goal of this value type.

Tradition (TRA, collectivist domain):
The motivational goal of tradition values consists of respect, commitment, and acceptance of the customs and ideas that one's culture or religion impose on the individual.

Spirituality (SPI, collectivist domain):
This domain should encompass all those values that represent the attainment of meaning in life and inner harmony through transcending everyday reality.

Benevolence (BEN, collectivist domain):
Benevolence values are motivated by the goal to preserve and enhance the welfare of those people with whom one is in frequent personal contact.

Universalism (UNI, individualistic and collectivist domain):
This domains' motivational goal consists of the understanding, appreciation, tolerance, and protection for the welfare of all people and nature.

each region containing values from only one motivational domain. This is called a polar facet (Shye, 1985), graphically represented in a two-dimensional space as a circumplex structure (Borg, 1981), which is predicted when two or more of several elements in a qualitative facet are in conceptual opposition or compatibility, respectively, to each other.

Figure 8.3 shows the hypothesized structural relations among the 11 value domains. The figure illustrates that adjacent value types are most compatible, whereas an increasing distance around the circular order indicates a decreas-

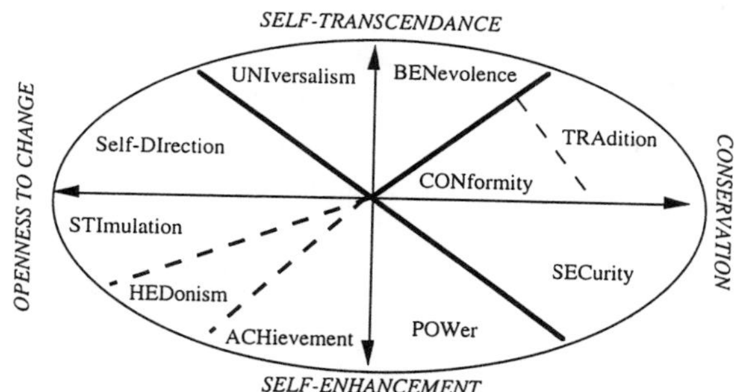

FIG. 8.3. Value domains and the structural relations among them.

ing compatibility and therefore an increasing conflict. Value types that emerge in opposing directions from the origin should be in greatest conflict. The 11 motivational domains are furthermore related to four higher-order value dimensions, namely *self-transcendence, conservation, self-enhancement,* and *openness to change.* These dimensions are similar to the MDS-dimensions found in a study using the LOV instrument: *love, comfort/constancy, achievement,* and *pleasure/change,* (Grunert & Scherhorn, 1990).

RESEARCH DESIGN AND DATA COLLECTION

Given the exploratory nature of the study and its emphasis on methodological issues, a convenient way of sampling was chosen. The samples consisted of graduate business students who attended a course in applied marketing research at Odense University, Denmark, and students attending a seminar in European Life Style Studies at the Strasbourg Business School, France. This latter sample included both French and exchange students from seven European countries and Québec, Canada. For the Danish sample, students were briefly introduced to the study's objectives and promised to be kept informed continously about it's progress and results. Collection of data for this sample occurred in three steps, while the international sample only completed the task of the last step.

The first part of the study consisted of an association task. Fourty-four Danish students participated. They were shown one value after the other of the Schwartz Value Indicator (SVI) written on transparencies. They were asked to write down the first three associations that came to mind. The idea was to derive at semantic connotations that could be used in selecting pictorial stimuli for the third step of the study.

In the second part of the study, students were asked to fill in a questionnaire that contained six sections: The SVI in verbal form, attitudinal statements on environmental problems, multiple-choice questions about environmental knowledge, and questions concerning self-reported sustainable consumption behavior (Grunert & Juhl, 1995), Kahle's List of Values LOV (Kahle, Beatty, & Homer, 1986), and the demographic variables sex and age. The students were asked to use a letter-code only they would be able to recognize in order to allow comparisons between the data of part two and part three. Fourty-one students returned a questionnaire. The data should serve as an empirical test on Schwartz's theory with regard to value structure and content—the 56 values and their 11 motivational domains are shown in Table 8.2. Combining the SVI with both environmental concern variables and LOV had two main objectives: a replication of a previous study on the relationships between values and environmental concern (Grunert & Juhl, 1995), and a test of the compatibility between SVI and LOV. These aspects will, however, not be addressed here.

TABLE 8.2
Values and Motivational Domains of the SVI

Terminal Values			*Instrumental Values*		
1	equality	UNI	31	independent	SDI
2	inner harmony	SPI, UNI, SEC	32	moderate	SEC, TRA
3	social power	POW	33	loyal	BEN, CON
4	pleasure	HED	34	ambitious	ACH
5	freedom	SDI	35	broadminded	UNI
6	a spiritual life	SPI	36	humble	TRA, CON
7	sense of belonging	SEC	37	daring	STI
8	social order	SEC	38	protecting the environment	UNI
9	an exciting life	STI	39	influential	ACH, POW
10	meaning in life	SPI, UNI	40	honoring of parents/elders	CON, TRA
11	politeness	CON	41	choosing own goals	SDI
12	wealth	POW	42	healthy	SEC, HED
13	national security	SEC	43	capable	ACH
14	self-respect	ACH, SDI	44	accept my portion in life	TRA, SPI
15	reciprocation of favors	SEC	45	honest	BEN
16	creativity	SDI	46	preserve my public image	POW, SEC
17	a world at peace	UNI	47	obedient	CON
18	respect for traditions	TRA	48	intelligent	ACH, SDI
19	mature love	BEN, UNI	49	helpful	BEN
20	self-discipline	CON	50	enjoying life	HED
21	detachment	SPI	51	devout	TRA, SPI
22	family security	SEC	52	responsible	BEN, CON
23	social recognition	POW, ACH, SEC	53	curious	SDI, STI
24	unity with nature	UNI, SPI	54	forgiving	BEN
25	a varied life	STI	55	successful	ACH
26	wisdom	UNI	56	clean	SEC, CON
27	authority	POW			
28	true friendship	BEN			
29	a world of beauty	UNI			
30	social justice	UNI			

Note. The motivational domains ACH, POW, HED, STI, and SDI are representing individualistic values, whereas CON, TRA, BEN, and SPI contain collectivist values, and SEC and UNI values that serve both collectivist and individualistic interests.

The SVI part of the questionnaire was identical with the one used in a cross-cultural research project initiated and organized by Shalom Schwartz (1992; and Schwartz & Bilsky, 1987, 1990). The original English version of the questionnaire was translated simultaneously, but independently into Danish by a student and a trained translator. The two versions were then compared with each other. If the proposals were identical, the translation was retained. In case of discrepancies, decisions were made by discussing the connotative meanings of the terms. The revised version was then checked by two Danish senior researchers and Shalom Schwartz together with a Danish collaborator, thus leading to the final version employed in the survey.

Respondents were asked to rate the importance of 56 values as "a guiding principle in my life," using the following 9-point scale: 7 = of supreme importance, 6 = very important, 5, 4 (unlabeled), 3 = important, 2, 1 (unlabeled), 0 = not important, and −1 = opposed to my values. In order to minimize shifts in scale use, an anchoring technique, also called the least-most method, was used by requesting respondents first to determine the value that is of utmost importance to them, then the one that is definitely opposed to their values, and finally to rate the remaining values.

The third part of the study was the pictorial stimuli test. Twenty-four color transparencies of pictures selected from 40 magazines such as geographical, lifestyle, business, fashion, and inflight magazines were presented to the Danish and international students (N=51 and N=88). Pictures were selected by the authors on the basis of students' associations in the first part of the study. Most of the pictures were meant to represent those values found to discriminate between environmental concern and nonconcern in the study by Grunert and Juhl (1995). Students were consecutively shown the 24 pictures and asked to associate a value with the picture; rate their association/value on a 9-point scale of importance; and after being told what the picture was meant to represent, to indicate the degree to which their associated value and the intended (verbal) value were compatible.

RESULTS

Step One

For illustrative purposes, Figs. 8.4a to 8.4c show the Danish students' associations with 3 of the 56 SVI values. In the case of "creativity," the students' associations emphasize art and culture in a somewhat broader sense than the motivational domain SDI of this value suggests. "Unity with nature" is mainly related to societal aspects of environmental issues and personal experiences in natural environments, thus being in accordance with the meaning of this value's motivational domain UNI. Associations with

CREATIVITY (uniqueness, imagination)

inventiveness - ability to play football - creative art - develop ideas - self development - sewing (5) - cooking (2) - creative powers (3) - internal resources - strength - ability to express oneself (2) - brightness (very important) - imagination (7) - colours (2) - happiness - pictures (2) - art (5) - hippies - members of the Danish Socialist People's Party - knitting (2) - painting (6) - alternative/different thinking (7) - daring - drawing (3) - always open to new ideas - new impulses - acting - be spontaneous (3) - predicting things - one side of the brain governing us - faculties (3) - advertising - artistic (2) - "creative bookkeeping" - positive (2) - films - books - paintings (3) - thinking - intelligence - singing - dancing - ability to create new things - use oneself - teaching - raising your child - inventing (2) - dreaming - freedom of thinking - opening new borders - possibilities - research - theatre - innovation - music (3) - synergy effect - clay - patchwork - to be able to see further than your own nose - culture (3) - development within your own opportunities (2) - cannot be developed after the age of 30 - important ability (2) - progress - collage - arts and crafts - handicraft - visions - day dreams - spirituality - artist (2) - ornaments - watercolour painting - shapes - exhibitions - develop something from your imagination - life quality - hobbies - making life rich - very few people - a pleasure to have this power- writing - making poetry - identity - self esteem - acceptance - creating something unique - adding a new dimension to life - the ability to do a lot at very low costs - emotional expression

FIG. 8.4a. Danish students' associations with the value "creativity."

UNITY WITH NATURE (fitting into nature)

Eskimos and other primitive people (2) - environmentally conscious behaviour (10) -hermits (2) - being one with nature - go back to your roots (2) - canoeing (in Sweden) (2) - fresh air - you cannot eat money - liberty (2) - long life - safety - grandchildren - joy (2) - buildings - bridges - roads - summer colours - green (5) - brown - environmental problems - forests (4) - green fields - horseback riding - mother Nature - beach (2) - living without violating nature (3) - let nature take its course - run along the stream with nobody else around - being in places where nobody else has set foot - environmental policy - adaptation of production - aboriginals - fishing - hunting - camping (2) - wilderness (2) - Plato - being part of an ecological unity - difficult to combine with modern life in a modern society - bare feet in the sand - let go of your emotions - the green - ecological (3) - refuse dumps - left wing - flower power children - picnics - environment (3) - natural disasters - pollution (3) - (jungle) indians (3) - wild tribes - Socialist - social workers and teachers - primitive man - ancient times - other parts of the world - desirable, but unthinkable - a set of values developed in recent years by many people - basis for our existence - unpolluted environment - walking in nature (3) - fresh water - less pollution - Music Festival at Skanderborg - green waste - the North Sea in November - outdoor life - a lost society - mountains - hiking - enjoying nature - harmony - the seasons of the year - good sense of loneliness - the ultimate freedom - Europe's future - nature worship - traditional societies - culture - primitive

FIG. 8.4b. Danish students' associations with the value "unity with nature."

SOCIAL RECOGNITION (respect, approval by others)

the "little" man - understanding of foreigners - education (4) - money (3) - position (2) - snobbishness - important to be accepted (5) - joy (3) - strength - enterprise - status (3) - job (3) - leader of a firm - minister - accepting other ways of living, not think that one's own way it the most correct (2) - performances - powers - social integration - being respected (2) - praise and criticism (3) - a pat on your back (2) -recognition for what ? - motivation - extra effort - groups (2) - being brought up to be good boys/girls - self-concept - family - power (2) mind - personality - intelligence (2) - grades/marks - yes-men - accepted in spite of different opinions (2) - self-respect (2) - pride (2) - being a kind and helpful person - surpassing others or achieving the same level - sports star - success - happiness - sports - well-founded criticism - help from others to solve problems - being admired - envy (2) - friends (2) - pleasant (2) - desirable - popular - human characters - arrogance - important (2) - you are what other people think you are - behaviour often determined by other people's reactions - love - somebody to fall back on and being there for others to fall back on - authority - oppression - too much respect - Hans Christian Andersen - Henrik Pontoppidan - proper car - living at the proper address - freedom of expression - getting along - funny - witty - results

FIG. 8.4c. Danish students' associations with the value "social recognition."

"social recognition" stress both personal success and the attainment of status and prestige as it is predicted by the motivational domains ACH and POW this value is intended to cover. The associations with the other 21 values revealed similarly satisfying—by the face-validity criterion—accordance with theory.

Step Two

The value data were analyzed on the basis of a Pearson correlation matrix derived from the importance ratings of the 56 values by using a nonmetric multidimensional scaling technique, that is, smallest space analysis SSA with the Guttman-algorithm, which is appropriate for the structural analysis of similarity data (Davison, 1983).

The emerging picture is interpreted by using a so-called configurational verification approach (Borg, 1981; Lingoes, 1981), that is, by interpreting the configurations of substantively related points that emerge to form regions and the arrangement of these regions in space relative to each other. The content universe is conceived as a geometrical space in which the specific values are but a sample of all conceivable values comprising the total space with points everywhere, whereas the axes are not assumed to have substantive meaning as they are arbitrary. This implies that one might find some values at the edge of one region correlating less with other values of the same region than with certain values on the edge of a neighboring region. Partition lines denoting regions may be straight or curved, as long as they yield regions having continuous boundaries that do not intersect with the boundaries of other regions. The center is central in terms of content, not in terms of some abstract mathematical notion. The facet plays a polarizing role, thus defining different directions in space.

It is assumed that the motivational content of values is the most powerful principle in the organization of individuals' value preferences, thus the organizing effects of motivational content may be evident even in the projection of value points obtained with a two-dimensional solution. The first analysis step therefore examined whether the points filling the two-dimensional space could be partitioned into distinct regions that reflect the a priori eleven motivational domains. At the same time, it can be checked whether the regions obtained form the suggested circumplex structure of compatible and conflicting value domains.

The results are shown in Table 8.3 and Fig. 8.5. Table 8.3 lists the 56 values contained in the questionnaire, the motivational domain they theoretically belong to, and the domain deviations found. In addition, significant gender differences found through t tests on mean value ratings are mentioned. Figure 8.5 displays the results of a two-dimensional SSA-solution (*alienation*: 0.318, *stress*: 0.317), representing the hypothesized moti-

TABLE 8.3
Values, Motivational Domains, and Sex Differences

Item	*Expected Domain*	*Deviation Found*	*Higher for . . .*
1 equality	UNI		
2 inner harmony	SPI, UNI, SEC		
3 social power	POW		men
4 pleasure	HED		
5 freedom	SDI		
6 a spiritual life	SPI	SDI	
7 sense of belonging	SEC		women
8 social order	SEC	UNI & BEN	
9 an exciting life	STI		
10 meaning in life	SPI, UNI		
11 politeness	CON	SDI	
12 wealth	POW		
13 national security	SEC		
14 self-respect	ATH, SDI		
15 reciprocation of favors	SEC		
16 creativity	SDI	UNI & BEN	
17 a world at peace	UNI		women
18 respect for traditions	TRA	SDI	
19 mature love	BEN, UNI		
20 self-discipline	CON		
21 detachment	SPI	SDI	
22 family security	SEC	SDI	
23 social recognition	POW, ACH, SEC		
24 unity with nature	UNI, SPI		
25 a varied life	STI		
26 wisdom	UNI	SDI	
27 authority	POW		
28 true friendship	BEN		
29 a world of beauty	UNI		
30 social justice	UNI		
31 independent	SDI		women
32 moderate	SEC, TRA		
33 loyal	BEN, CON		women
34 ambitious	ACH		
35 broadminded	UNI		
36 humble	TRA, CON		
37 daring	STI		
38 protecting the environment	UNI		
39 influential	ACH, POW		
40 honoring of parents and elders	CON, TRA	UNI & BEN	
41 choosing own goals	SDI	STI & HED	
42 healthy	SEC, HED		
43 capable	ACH	STI & HED	
44 accepting my portion in life	TRA, SPI		women
45 honest	BEN		women
46 preserving my public image	POW, SEC		
47 obedient	CON		
48 intelligent	ACH, SDI, UNI		
49 helpful	BEN	SEC	
50 enjoying life	HED	STI	
51 devout	TRA, SPI		
52 responsible	BEN, CON		
53 curious	SDI, STI	UNI & BEN	
54 forgiving	BEN		
55 successful	ACH		
56 clean	SEC, CON		

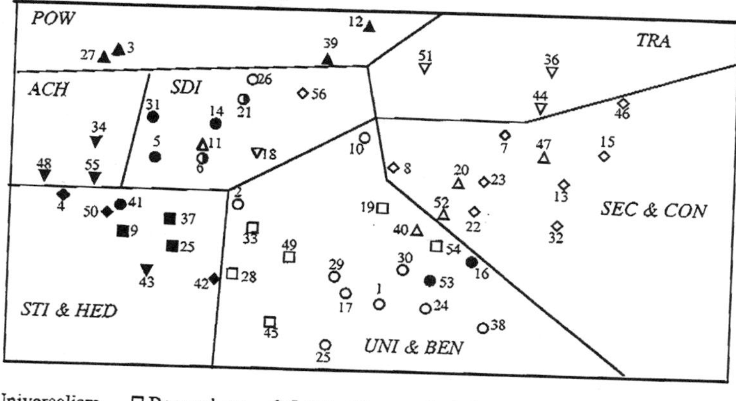

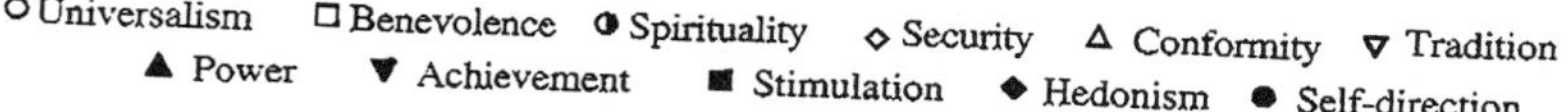

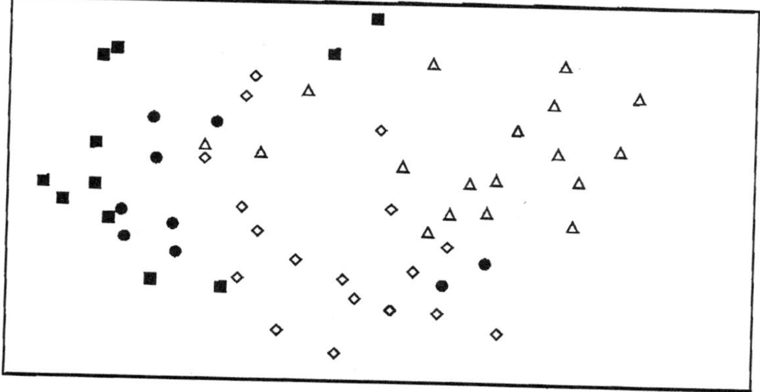

FIG. 8.5. Smallest space analysis of SVS.

vational domains of the 56 values, and, at the same time, the distinction between interests served by these values (filled for individualistic, opaque for collectivistic values). The second picture in Fig. 8.5 illustrates the second-order value dimensions.

The results should, however, be interpreted with care. The low number of cases (41 respondents) considerably reduces the chances to find the expected value structure and content. Nonetheless, both structure and content were partially confirmed. One motivational domain in particular did not appear distinctively by forming its own region, namely spiritualism. This phenomenon has been observed in other studies, too (e.g., Grunert & Juhl, 1995, Schwartz, 1992). No clear distinct regions emerged for several other value types, but its values were intermixed with those of a type postulated to be adjacent. This holds for universalism and benevolence, security and conformity, as well as hedonism and stimulation. The two motivational domains, power and achievement, do not reach the center, thus indicating respondents' low involvement with the values belonging to these.

Although the structure found does not separate the 11 regions as well as hypothesized, the order of the types around the circle and the basic oppositions and compatibilities, expressed in the higher-order dimensions of self-transcendence vs. self-enhancement (UNI, BEN vs. ACH, POW) and openness to change vs. conservation (STI, SDI vs. SEC, CON, TRA), are in good accordance with theory. This finding implies, at the same time, that the hypothesized distinction between individualistic, collectivist, and mixed interests of values is approved.

The facet of terminal vs. instrumental values could, however, not be found, thus supporting the results of other studies (e.g., Montgomery & Johansson, 1988) and hence casting further doubt on this distinction proposed by Rokeach (1973). It seems that individuals, at least in surveys, do not distinguish sharply between goals and end states.

Step Three

Danish and international students' evaluation of compatibility between their associated value and the intended value are given in Tables 8.4 and 8.5 where figures are in percentages. Overall, Danish students were slightly better in understanding the pictorial stimuli than the students in the international sample. One explanation may be that the Danish students had been through all three steps of the study, thus facilitating their understanding of the general value concept. Both groups had in common that they had less difficulties in grasping pictorial stimuli that were meant to represent condition (or terminal) values than those conveying behavioral (or instrumental) values: Accordance scores are generally better for the first 12 value items than for the last 12. Students in both groups also reacted in a similar way when a stimulus was more difficult to understand: Instead of associating more abstract values they switched over to a descriptive interpretation of the cue. This, however, made it difficult for them to decide on the degree of compatibility which, in turn, is partially responsible for the high figures in the "none" and "somewhat" columns.

The tables also contain a revised version of compatibility degree computed on the basis of the authors' evaluations. These were done by checking students' associations with the motivational domain meanings explained earlier (see Tables 8.1 and 8.2). This revision was deemed necessary as it turned out that many students seemed rather uncapable of understanding the abstract value concepts and relate them to their own associations. This

TABLE 8.4
Danish Students' and Authors' Evaluation of Compatibility Degree

Values	*Students*			*Authors*		
	None	*Some*	*Good*	*None*	*Some*	*Good*
Social power	8.6	48.6	42.9	16.2	5.4	78.4
Sense of belonging	5.6	63.9	30.6	10.5	52.6	36.8
An exciting life	65.7	25.7	8.6	21.6	71.0	5.4
Wealth	16.7	25.0	58.3	5.1	30.8	64.1
National Security	62.9	25.7	11.4	64.9	10.8	24.3
Creativity	17.1	25.7	57.1	13.6	35.1	51.3
Respect for traditions	79.4	11.8	8.8	77.8	19.4	2.8
Family security	5.6	19.4	75.0	10.5	42.1	47.4
Social recognition	55.9	29.4	14.7	61.2	19.4	19.4
Authority	41.7	25.0	33.3	42.1	39.5	18.4
A world of beauty	44.4	27.8	27.8	26.3	47.4	26.3
Social justice	25.7	42.9	31.4	65.8	13.2	21.0
Independent	79.4	17.6	2.9	77.8	11.1	11.1
Loyal	75.0	18.8	6.3	47.1	50.0	2.9
Ambitious	73.5	26.5	0.0	72.2	27.8	0.0
Broadminded	61.8	32.4	5.9	77.8	19.4	2.8
Daring	17.6	44.1	38.2	13.5	24.3	62.2
Protecting the environment	50.0	28.1	21.9	44.1	35.3	20.6
Choosing own goals	70.6	20.6	8.8	62.2	18.9	18.9
Capable	68.6	31.4	0.0	62.2	35.1	2.7
Obedient	50.0	5.9	44.1	56.8	13.5	29.7
Intelligent	53.1	28.1	18.8	42.9	25.7	31.4
Curious	88.9	5.6	5.6	78.9	15.8	5.3
Successful	29.0	51.6	19.4	32.4	35.2	32.4

could be corrected by our revision and resulted in sometimes very different accordance figures.

Part of the low compatibility degree with some value items was due to a more systematic "misunderstanding," that is, most of the students interpreted a certain pictorial stimulus in the same way but different from the intended meaning—sometimes exactly reversed. In the Danish sample, for example, the picture meant to represent "social recognition" showed travelers in the historic Orient-Express train socializing in fashionable clothes, but was very often associated with "wealth." Another example: The picture meant to illustrate "national security" showed a young woman in a combat suit and was often interpreted by Danish students as "war," "danger," and "aggression" or as "game" and "point-ball," while some respondents of the international sample associated "women's lib." The pictorial stimuli for the value "independent," showing a young career woman, was mainly associated with "beauty" and "sexuality." And the value "intelligent," which we tried to illustrate with a man sitting at his desk surrounded by working paraphernalia probably representing the advertising business, was often

TABLE 8.5
International Students' and Authors' Evaluation of Compatibility Degree

Values	*Students*			*Authors*		
	None	*Some*	*Good*	*None*	*Some*	*Good*
Social power	29.5	23.9	46.6	30.7	13.6	55.7
Sense of belonging	27.3	45.5	27.3	19.3	52.3	28.4
An exciting life	71.6	21.6	6.8	64.8	30.7	4.5
Wealth	27.3	30.7	42.0	11.4	40.9	47.7
National Security	79.5	18.2	2.3	90.9	6.8	2.3
Creativity	28.4	33.0	38.6	21.6	32.9	45.5
Respect for traditions	42.0	5.7	52.3	42.0	6.8	51.1
Family security	9.1	34.1	56.8	12.5	8.0	79.5
Social recognition	48.9	33.0	18.2	43.2	45.5	11.4
Authority	69.0	23.0	8.0	60.2	28.4	11.4
A world of beauty	42.0	51.1	6.8	34.1	61.4	4.5
Social justice	59.8	24.1	16.1	73.5	20.7	5.8
Independent	66.3	20.9	12.8	65.9	20.5	13.6
Loyal	67.8	21.8	10.3	53.4	26.1	20.5
Ambitious	65.9	27.3	6.8	71.6	20.4	8.0
Broadminded	65.5	27.6	6.9	71.6	22.7	5.7
Daring	17.0	36.4	46.6	20.4	43.2	36.4
Protecting the environment	72.4	14.9	12.6	61.7	30.7	8.0
Choosing own goals	72.4	19.5	8.0	68.2	23.8	8.0
Capable	63.5	31.8	4.7	73.9	21.6	4.5
Obedient	53.4	34.1	12.5	78.4	9.1	12.5
Intelligent	39.1	32.2	28.7	46.6	22.7	30.7
Curious	58.0	26.1	15.9	56.8	39.8	3.4
Successful	47.7	40.7	11.6	51.1	40.9	8.0

associated with "diligent" and "hard-working." The picture representing the value "capable" was almost unanimously by both groups interpreted as "creativity." The international sample showed some of the same, but also other systematic misinterpretations. For example, the pictorial stimulus for "a world of beauty," showing a beautiful tropical landscape, was interpreted by many as expressing "peace" and "tranquility." On the other hand, the international (primarily Central European) sample was much better at recognizing the value "respect for traditions" in a picture of two Germans in *Lederhosen* at a *Schützenfest.*

DISCUSSION AND CONCLUDING REMARKS

The results of Step One, where respondents were asked to list their main associations with the verbal expressions of SVI, revealed exactly the problem that inspired our methodological exploration in the first place, namely the semantic multitude of sometimes very different associations that a verbal value stimulus may evoke. Hence, this part of the study confirmed the suggested need for another approach than those hitherto employed to measure consumer values.

The results of Step Two confirmed that the SVI is a valid instrument for value research, since the expected dimensions and groupings were found even within our small convenience sample. This is especially true for the underlying dimensions and the level of the motivational domains. This outcome indicates that semantic problems are more severe at the single value level than at the value domain level. This makes intuitive sense, because a respondent is more likely to grasp the underlying motivational domain of a value than the specific intended meaning of a single value. Moreover, this finding is compatible with the earlier definition of culture as collectively shared cognitive–emotive structures, not single concepts. Given that the SVI has proven its cross-cultural validity in some 45 countries by now (Schwartz, 1992), we felt confident in choosing the SVI as basis for both the association task and the selection of pictorial stimuli.

When confronted with the pictorial stimuli in Step Three, however, the respondents often expressed a similar amount of difference in the interpretation of the stimulus. In general, the results indicate that we have operated with three types of pictorial stimuli. First, pictures that express the intended value relatively good, that is, where the value association is identical, almost similar, or somewhat similar, by which we mean pertaining to the same motivational domain as the intended value. Second, pictorial stimuli that reveal a systematic bias, that is, the respondents more or less agree with what the stimulus represents, however, what they agree upon is not the originally intended meaning. And third, pictures that are unclear and ambiguous, thus evoking very different value associations across respondents. In other words, we had selected appropriate pictorial stimuli that are right, appropriate pictorial stimuli that are wrong, and inappropriate pictorial stimuli.

Given the exploratory nature of this study, the findings are not at all discomforting. The main problem encountered was the quality of the selected pictorial stimuli. However, there is good reason to believe that with an improved, more controlled selection process it should be possible to construct a survey instrument that contains only pictorial stimuli of the first category. There are several possibilities to achieve this objective. For example, both focus group interviews and the laddering technique may be used as a means of evaluating pictorial stimuli before employing them in the main survey. Another way of reducing stimulus ambiguity would be to have a professional artist or photographer create "custom-made" stimuli in order to avoid dependence on already published material. These two possibilities may, of course, be combined.

Although we are rather positive about the possibility of solving the stimulus quality problem within a given cultural context, the results do not provide a clear indication as to whether it is possible to generate cross-culturally valid pictorial stimuli. The fact that the differences between the international and the Danish sample were negligible indicates that cross-culturally valid stimuli may be developed. However, the sample size does not allow any firm statement about this. Hence, a profound evaluation procedure in each of the cultural areas included in a future study is required. If the problem should remain unsolved, interpretations and comparisons of international samples will have to be delimited to higher-order value domains and dimensions.

REFERENCES

Askegaard, S. (1991). Toward a semiotic structure of cultural identity. In H. H. Larsen, D. G. Mick, & C. Alsted (Eds.), *Marketing and semiotics. Selected papers from the Copenhagen symposium* (pp. 11–30). Copenhagen: Handelshøjskolens Forlag.

Bandura, A. (1988). Self-regulation of motivation and action through goal systems. In V. Hamilton, G. H. Bower, & N. H. Frijda (Eds.), *Cognitive perspectives on emotion and motivation* (pp. 37–61). Dordrecht: Kluwer Academic.

Berlyne, D. E. (1967). Arousal and reinforcement. In D. Levine (Ed.), *Nebraska symposium on motivation* (Vol. 15, pp. 1–110). Lincoln: University of Nebraska Press.

Borg, I. (1981). *Anwendungsorientierte multidimensionale skalierung* [Applied multidimensional scaling]. Berlin: Springer.

Borg, I. (1986). Facettentheorie. Prinzipien und beispiele [Facet theory. Principles and examples]. *Psychologische Rundschau, 37,* 121–137.

Canter, D. (Ed.). (1985). *Facet theory.* New York: Springer.

Cathelat, B. (1990). *Socio-Styles-Système.* Paris: Editions d'organisation.

Childers, T. L., & Houston, M. J. (1984). Conditions for a picture-superiority effect on consumer memory. *Journal of Consumer Research, 11,* 643–654.

Childers, T. L., Houston, M. J., & Heckler, S. E. (1985). Measurement of individual differences in visual versus verbal information processing. *Journal of Consumer Research, 12,* 125–134.

Davison, M. (1983). *Multidimensional scaling.* New York: Wiley.

Deci, E. L., & Ryan, R. M. (1985). *Intrinsic motivation and self-determination in human behavior.* New York and London: Plenum.

Domzal, T. J., & Unger, L. S. (1985). Judgments of verbal versus pictorial presentations of a product with functional and aesthetic features. In E. C. Hirschman & M. B. Holbrook (Eds.), *Advances in consumer research* (Vol. 12, pp. 268–272). Provo, UT: Association for Consumer Research.

Grunert, K. G., Grunert, S. C., & Beatty, S. E. (1989). Cross-cultural research on consumer values. *Marketing and Research Today, 17,* 30–39.

Grunert, S. C., & Juhl, H. J. (1995). Values, environmental attitudes, and buying of organic foods. *Journal of Economic Psychology, 16,* 39–62.

Grunert, S. C., & Scherhorn, G. (1990). Consumer values in West Germany: Underlying dimensions and cross-cultural comparison with North America. *Journal of Business Research, 20,* 97–107.

Grunert, S. C., Grunert, K. G., & Kristensen, K. (1992). The cross-cultural validity of the list of values LOV: A comparison of nine samples from five countries. In J. J. G. Schmeets,

M. E. P. Odekerken, & F. J. R. van de Pol (Eds.), *Developments and applications in structural equation modelling* (pp. 89–99). Amsterdam: Sociometric Research Foundation.

Hansen, F. (1981). Hemispheral lateralization: Implications for understanding consumer behavior. *Journal of Consumer Research, 8,* 23–36.

Hofstede, G., & Bond, M. H. (1984). Hofstede's culture dimensions: An independent validation using Rokeach's value survey. *Journal of Cross-Cultural Psychology, 15,* 417–433.

Holbrook, M. B., & Moore, W. L. (1981). Feature interactions in consumer judgments of verbal versus pictorial presentations. *Journal of Consumer Research, 8,* 103–113.

Kahle, L. R., Beatty, S. E., & Homer, P. M. (1986). Alternative measurement approaches to consumer values: The list of values (LOV) and values and lifestyles (VALS). *Journal of Consumer Research, 13,* 405–409.

Kluckhohn, C. (1951). Values and value-orientations in the theory of action: An exploration in definition and classification. In T. Parsons & E. A. Shils (Eds.), *Toward a general theory of action* (pp. 388–433). New York: Harper and Row.

Lingoes, J. C. (1981). Testing regional hypotheses in multidimensional scaling. In I. Borg (Ed.), *Multidimensional data representations: When and why* (pp. 280–310). Ann Arbor, MI: Mathesis.

Louviere, J. J., Schroeder, H., Louviere, C. H., & Woodworth, G. C. (1987). Do the parameters of choice models depend on differences in stimulus presentation: Visual versus verbal presentation? In M. Wallendorf & P. Anderson (Eds.), *Advances in consumer research* (Vol. 14, pp. 79–82). Provo, UT: Association for Consumer Research.

Maslow, A. H. (Ed.). (1959). *New knowledge in human values.* New York: Harper.

Meyers-Levy, J. (1989). Priming effects on product judgments: A hemisperic interpretation. *Journal of Consumer Research, 16,* 76–86.

Mitchell, A. (1983). *Nine American lifestyles: Who we are and where we are going.* New York: Macmillan.

Montgomery, H., & Johansson, U. (1988). Life values: Their structure and relation to life situation. In S. Maital (Ed.), *Applied behavioral economics* (Vol. 1, pp. 420–437). Brighton: Wheatsheaf.

Rokeach, M. J. (1973). *The nature of human values.* New York: The Free Press.

Schwartz, S. H., & Bilsky, W. (1987). Toward a universal psychological structure of human values. *Journal of Personality and Social Psychology, 53,* 550–562.

Schwartz, S. H. (1992). Universals in the content and structure of values: Theoretical advance and empirical tests in 20 countries. In M. Zanna (Ed.), *Advances in experimental social psychology* (Vol. 25, pp. 1–65). Orlando, FL: Academic Press.

Schwartz, S. H., & Bilsky, W. (1990). Toward a theory of universal content and structure of values: Extensions and cross-cultural replications. *Journal of Personality and Social Psychology, 58,* 878–891.

Scitovsky, T. (1976). *The joyless economy.* An inquiry into human satisfaction and consumer dissatisfaction. Oxford, England: Oxford University Press.

Shye, S. (1985). Nonmetric multivariate models for behavioral action systems. In D. Canter (Ed.), *The facet approach to social research* (pp. 97–148). New York: Springer.

Spoehr, K. T., & Lehmkuhle, S. W. (1982). *Visual information processing.* San Francisco: W. H. Freeman.

Triandis, H. C., McCusker, C., & Hui, C. H. (1990). Multimethod probes of individualism and collectivism. *Journal of Personality and Social Psychology, 59,* 1006–1020.

Chapter 9

Developing Useful and Accurate Customer Profiles

Brian Wansink
University of Illinois, Champaign–Urbana

Demographic data have their limits in helping us generate insights (Haley, 1984, 1985). And so do most psychographic data. Not only do psychographic data frequently lack objectivity, but they are costly to assemble and limited in how easily they can be interpreted (Wells, 1974). This chapter introduces a technique called "customer profiling," which uses a laddering procedure to describe a very specific member of a target subsegment in detail. The assumption is that the insights obtained from describing and analyzing this individual can frequently be generalized across a broader segment. It is quick, inexpensive, and easily interpretable.

Customer profiling is useful for generating hypotheses about customers that can be further examined in focus groups with questionnaires. It can also, however, be an effective starting point for developing a marketing communication program. After the customer profiling technique is described, we test how effectively managers can use it by determining how accurately they can predict which of 261 adults are most likely to be members of a public radio station. The accuracy of these predictions are then contrasted with the accuracy of predictions generated from conventional segmentation methods. These results are discussed, and additional applications of this robust technique are described.

BACKGROUND

Knowing Your Best Customer

Mentally visualizing a prototypical member of a market segment is critically important (Wansink 1994). Mentally "walking in the customer's shoes" helps a marketer understand what unarticulated needs this person might have, and how to communicate most effectively to the segment the customer represents (Weinstein, 1987). It has been claimed that "the fifth 'P' of marketing is Personalization" (Schultz, 1991). That is, the classic four Ps of marketing—product, price, place (distribution), and promotion—are effective only to the extent that they are used to make a "personal" connection with the customer. "Every sale is a personal sale," although not new (Carnegie, 1937), that is not well understood by most marketers.

Many marketing decisions are instead driven more by data bases than by a personal understanding of the customer. When told the importance of "really knowing your customer," many marketers and advertisers would claim they already know their customer:

> Our primary target customers for frozen pie crusts are women 35 to 60 with a high school education living in the Midwest and Southeast, making $20,000 to $35,000 per year and with 3.2 children who no longer live at home but who visit 2 times per month.

They may even say that they know their target customer "so well" that they can say . . .

> Forty-three percent of category purchasers use our brand; 32% are Brand B users, and 25% are Brand C users. Forty percent of our market are heavy category users, and 85% are loyal. Only 60% of the nonusers are brand loyal, and we draw more switchers from Brand C than Brand B when we advertise heavily. When we price promote, we draw from both brands equally.

Suppose we could find 100 women who fit this general description, then ask them to write down 10 characteristics that they might use to describe themselves. It is doubtful that even one of these 100 would say:

> Hi, my name's Susan, and I'm a 30 to 60 year old with a high school plus eduction and 3.2 kids who no longer live at home but who visit 2 times per month. I also like to think of myself as a heavy user of pie crusts compared to people who live in the northeast or people or who live in large cities. Although I'm pretty brand loyal when I shop for pie crusts, I guess I would shop around if I had a really big coupon. You could say I'm more a switcher when it comes to laundry detergent than with frozen pie crusts, and I'm definitely a variety seeker when it comes to breakfast cereals. Well, I guess that about covers it.

No consumer sees herself or himself as a bundle of mere statistics. As Fortini-Campbell (1990) writes, "Statistics alone do as much good describing people as a ruler does measuring a beach ball." It does not wrap around the ball, and it says nothing of when and where it is used. Nor does the ruler tell us anything about what people feel or think when they are playing with the ball. Yet when attempting to identify target markets, marketers often make no attempt to move "past the data" and use any method other than the ruler (Haley, 1968; Plummer, 1984; Wells & Tigert, 1971).

No matter how much a marketer, advertiser, or consultant knows about marketing and advertising, he or she will never know as much about the bagged concrete industry, or about the accounting profession, or about retail meat channels as the people in these industries. Such industries are less burdened by computer printouts of demographic and sales data than the packaged goods markets. How can they possibly know their customers? Consider Ronnie, the marketing manager for a company that produces bagged concrete. If we were to ask him to describe some of his best customers, he would probably name a specific person and proceed to describe the person in detail.

Consider, however, that the specific person Ronnie mentions probably represents (with small variations) a generalizable and much larger segment of his company's market. That is, if Ronnie describes "Tony Bower at Siouxland Industries," Tony is probably representative of a much larger segment of customers (or potential customers). As a result, the more that Ronnie talks about Tony—his motivations and aspirations, what he does in his free time, who he wants to impress, where he wants to be in 10 years, why he buys Ronnie's bagged concrete, and so on—the more insights we begin to gain about this basic segment of which Tony unknowingly is a part.

Of course, developing this "customer profile" of Tony accounts for only one segment of the market. That is, if Ronnie is asked, "What other types of good customers do you have?" we would be off onto another segment.

Limitations

The value of profiling lies in attempting to disclose the basic needs and wants of a particular segment of consumers. This customer profiling process provides an opportunity to exercise one's creativity in an effort to generate hypotheses about the motivations and behaviors of individual customers. Although the focus is on individual customers, the marketing-related insights that can follow from this are invariably relevant to large segments of customers. The customer profiling technique can focus on an "ideal customer," or on "the kind of customer who is a great word-of-mouth champion," or "the kind of customer who is a heavy user," or the "nonuser." It has also proven useful when profiling the type of customers who can most easily be encouraged to increase their usage rates of a mature brand (Wansink, 1996; Wansink, Ray, & Batra, 1994; Wansink & Ray, 1996).

Is there a risk of this approach being too narrow? Possibly. But just as conventional segmentation methods often simplify a market by generalizing across too many different types of segments, the customer profiling approach makes our thinking more specific. When the continuum ranges from "Everyone-to-Someone," we do better by looking at a number of very specific, but very richly profiled "Someone" segments than we do looking at "Everyone" segments that are too general. In an ideal situation, any intuitive insights one generates should be followed up with a quantifiable research plan that can either confirm or disconfirm these insights.

The Basic Process and Technique

Developing a rich customer profile is one way to segment very specific psychographic market segments. The value of the customer profiling process is directly related to how vividly one can visualize the person, and how accurately and creatively one can describe him or her. The basic process is as follows:

1. Recall (or imagine) an ideal customer (or decision maker). Name him or her.
2. Describe him or her in "recognizable" detail, such as:
   Why does the person use the product/service he or she uses?
   How does this person "see" himself or herself?
   How would this person's neighbors describe him or her?
   What is important to this person?
   Whom does this person want to most impress?
3. Recall another type of model customer (and describe)
4. Repeat the process until the profiles start to overlap
5. Generalize into highest-potential yield target markets and highlight important details.
6. Use the relevant insights to inform marketing activities

This technique is called "laddering." In effect, by constantly asking "why," one keeps "going down rungs" until arriving at basic values that may be important in motivating this person in this context (Haskins & Kendrick, 1989). The emphasis in such an approach is on creativity. The more we can intuit about our customers, the more effective our efforts at reaching and satisfying them.

The critical test of this approach, however, is how well it can answer three questions:

1. How do customer profiling insights compare with insights generated from more general methods of segmentation analysis?

2. How accurate and valid are customer profiling insights?
3. How useful are customer profiling insights in providing implementation guidance for a marketing communication program?

These questions are examined in each of the next three sections.

HOW DO CUSTOMER PROFILING INSIGHTS COMPARE WITH SEGMENTATION ANALYSIS INSIGHTS?

Methodology

The objective of this study is to determine how accurately the segments obtained through a customer profiling technique describe a broader base of customers. To evaluate the accuracy of the customer profiling technique, the relevant comparison is with target market segments generated through the more general forms of segmentation analysis. Although the methodology of segmentation analysis certainly varies from manager to manager, a number of managers were asked to articulate their approach, and the similarities were notable.

Thirty-two managers were asked to take part in a mail survey to identify and specify target markets. Twenty-three of these individuals responded (72% response) in a timely enough manner to be included in the study. Nineteen of the 23 individuals were either brand managers or account managers; salaries ranged from $62,000 to $107,000 per year. All were recent MBA graduates of the Amos Tuck School of Business at Dartmouth College, with the average age of 31. As MBA students, all had taken a course in Marketing Communication.

One intent was to determine the accuracy and validity of segmentation efforts, so it was necessary to use a product or service with which all respondents would be equally familiar. It was assumed (and subsequently verified) that they would be familiar with the local public radio station that had been broadcasting while they were students (Vermont Public Radio—WVPR). All 23 managers were asked to identify three segments of people who were most likely to be members of WVPR (at $25 per year). None of these managers had any specific information about membership or listenership. The only information included in the mailing was a copy of the station's monthly programming guide.

The only portion of the mailings that differed was the instructions on how the managers were to go about determining these three target markets. Half of the subjects were asked to identify the target markets using whatever segmentation analysis method they would normally use to approach such a problem. After defining these target markets, these managers were asked to articulate the basic procedure they used. The other half of these managers were asked to use the customer profiling technique that was outlined earlier. After defining three target markets, these managers were also asked to articulate—in their own words—the basic procedure they used, including any modifications they made on the guidelines they had been given.

All subjects then returned their questionnaire through the mail. Of the 23 questionnaires returned, 13 were from the managers who had been asked to use their own segmentation analysis procedure; the other 10 were from managers who had been asked to use the customer profiling technique.

Comparing the Two Approaches

It appeared that the managers using segmentation analysis tended to use a four-step procedure. Although this exact procedure was not used across all 13 managers, it fairly represents the general approach they articulated. Broadly speaking, these managers first thought about the target market in terms of demographic variables (such as age, income, education, profession, and so on). They next made inferences about the related interests or affiliations of these different segments (e.g., belongs to other arts organizations, subscribes to many magazines). Third, these managers considered why such segments might become a member of WVPR, and used these inferences to better describe these segments. Last, a determination was made as to which three of these segments best described portions of the WVPR membership. This general procedure is outlined in Table 9.1.

In contrast, the managers using the customer profiling technique were instructed to think about a specific individual they considered as an "ideal" WVPR member. Although these managers also described this person in terms of demographic variables, related interests or affiliations, and inferences as to why the person joined, their descriptions tended to be richer and to contain more detail than those descriptions generated from those using segmentation analysis. Part of this happened because the managers asked and tried to answer difficult, speculative, and personal questions about their customer. The modified customer profiling procedure they used and some of these questions they asked are also outlined in Table 9.1.

Comparing the Results of the Two Approaches

In general, those managers using the customer profiling technique generated an average of 11.4 thoughts about each of the three profiles they described compared to the 6.8 thoughts generated by those managers using segmentation analysis. This difference was significant ($t = 3.9$; $p <$

TABLE 9.1
Customer Profiling Versus Segmentation Analysis: The Process of Insight Generation

A General Approach to Customer Profiling *(n = 10)*	*A General Approach to Segmentation Analysis* *(n = 13)*
1. Imagine a specific person in the target segment.	1. Define by standard demographic variables . . . • Education • Profession • Age • Income • Gender • Family size • Geography
2. Define him or her in vivid detail. For example . . . • Why does the person use the product/service he or she uses? • How does this person "see" himself or herself? • How would this person's neighbors describe him or her? • What is important to this person? • What are his or her goals and ambitions? • Describe this person's "perfect" day off? • Who does this person most want to impress?	2. Infer related interests or affiliations.
3. Recall another person in this segment (and describe).	3. Infer reasons they might buy.
4. Repeat the process until the profiles start to overlap.	4. Split into the highest-potential yield target markets.
5. Split into the highest-potential yield target markets.	
6. Use the relevant insights to inform marketing activities.	

.01), and was driven by the difference in thoughts related to psychographic criteria. Managers using the customer profiling technique generated many more psychographic dimensions ($\overline{X} = 8.3$) than those using segmentation analysis [$\overline{X} = 3.1$ ($t = 4.2$; $p < .01$)].

Although numerous different market segments were alluded to by both sets of managers, four segments were mentioned with notable frequency by both groups. These segments of WVPR members were commonly defined as the "yuppies," "establishment-types," "intelligentsias," and "granolas." The most frequently described segments were the first two. Some typical comments managers chose to describe these segments appear in Table 9.2.

Three points about Table 9.2 are especially revealing. First, it is notable that both groups of managers identified similar segments with high frequency. Second, the level of detail provided by the managers using the customer profiling technique was much more specific than that given by the managers who used segmentation analysis. Some descriptions of an individual from the yuppies segment, for instance, include: "Likes to impress others; not loyal to institutions; more of a spender than a saver; can be self-righteous."

The last feature in Table 9.2 that is notable can be seen in the descriptions given by those who used segmentation analysis. There is lack of clear psychographic distinction between their descriptions of the yuppie segment and the establishment segment. With the exception of the members' age and the ages of their children, there is no significant difference between the two segments. The descriptions given by those using the customer profiling technique, in contrast, provide much more clear delineation between the two segments.

It is important to note that the approach itself (customer profiling versus segmentation analysis) had little impact on whether a particular target group would be identified and described. The primary difference between the approaches is illustrated in the extent to which the segments can be defined in distinct detail—detail that will eventually be useful in helping generate important marketing communication applications.

HOW ACCURATE ARE CUSTOMER PROFILING INSIGHTS?

Although the differences illustrated in Table 9.2 are provocative, the important question is whether they are of value in actually predicting membership in WVPR. To the extent that the customer profiling technique provides a better understanding of current membership, it should help station management learn how to appeal more effectively to similar individuals in the segment who have not yet joined WVPR's membership ranks.

TABLE 9.2

Customer Profiling Versus Segmentation Analysis: Their Insights About Two Segments of Public Radio Supporters

		Two Frequently Defined Segments	
		Yuppies	*Establishment Types*
SAMPLE	*Segmentation Analysis Approach*	• Highly educated • White-collar professional • High income • Appreciates the "finer things" • Cultured • 30-50 years of age • Young children	• Highly educated • White-collar professional • High income • Appreciates the "finer things" • Cultured and sophisticated • 50-60 years of age • Children are grown
INSIGHTS	*Customer Profiling Technique*	• Likes to impress others, can tend to "snobbishness" • Not too loyal to institutions • More "spender" than "saver" • Sees knowledge as a tool; reads to learn; learns to do/say • Sees children as either investments or showpieces • Sometimes self-righteous	• Community-oriented • Wants to be mentor-like • More benevolent than in past • Getting socially overcommitted • Developing strong tastes (art, music, etc.) --less concerned about the crowd --sees no need to justify preferences • Comfortable with life and with friends • A definite pattern to their schedule • Sometimes wishes life would be a bit more exciting • Wishes they would have spent more time with their children when they were younger

Methodology

To examine the accuracy of the two groups of managers, 261 adults were contacted to provide the demographic and psychographic information that would be necessary for a comparative validation. These subjects were recruited through eight PTA (Parent–Teacher Association) groups in small New England towns, with $6 donated to the respective organization for each member who participated in the study. Ninety-one percent of the subjects were between the ages of 30 and 70. Their educational background was heterogeneous.

Subjects were met in groups of 6 to 30 at the school where the PTA met. Upon arriving, they were asked to take every-other seat, and were given a closed packet of materials, that contained a cover sheet of instructions and a number of consecutively labeled booklets. One of the booklets asked if the respondent was a member of WVPR; the respondent then answered over 80 questions related to characteristics earlier identified in the segmentation and customer profiling descriptions of the 23 managers. Some questions, for instance, were generally related to the types of information noted in Table 9.2. That is, some of these questions were demographic, while others were descreetly worded psychographic questions. Although every subject was asked the identical questions, the order of the questions was randomized to avoid a bias due to fatigue. Of the 261 individuals involved in the study, 93 (36%) were members of WVPR.

Analysis and Results

Recall that each of the 23 managers involved in the study described three distinct market segments they believed would currently constitute WVPR membership. Because we are comparing the accuracy of two different approaches (customer profiling vs. segmentation analysis), the prediction accuracy of these managers reflects one dimension of the relative value of the two approaches. Given a description of a segment, accuracy is defined as that percentage of people who fit that description *and* who are members. For instance, a description of a particular segment would be absolutely accurate to the extent that 100% of the people who meet that description do indeed happen to be WVPR members. Regardless of whether the defined group is large or small, the higher the percentage of membership, the more accurate the description is considered.

For *each* market segment described by each manager, two numbers were recorded: The total number of people in the sample (out of a possible 261) who fit that general description, and the number of those who were WVPR members. To develop a composite measure of effectiveness for each manager, the results from these three segments were added together to form a cumulative measure of effectiveness. (It is assumed the three segments are mutually exclusive.) The rank-ordering of the results (based on their accuracy) is shown in Table 9.3.

The managers using segmentation analysis tended to describe target markets that are much larger than those described by managers using the customer profiling technique. Their "hit rate" (number of members/total segment membership), however, is much lower. This attests to the accuracy of a more focused approach such as customer profiling. The six most accurate managers in the study are those who used some version of customer profiling. The other four managers using this technique are not as accurate in their profiling, but they are no less accurate than those who used segmentation analysis. Taking a manager's hit rate as the dependent variable, we find those using the customer profiling technique to be significantly more accurate in identifying and describing current member segments than those using segmentation analysis ($t = 5.5$; $p > .01$).

HOW USEFUL ARE CUSTOMER PROFILING INSIGHTS?

We have suggested that a quick, inexpensive first step in any attempt at qualitative research is to use the data we have been collecting all our lives—data about human nature—to begin drawing a customer profile of specific target markets. Such an approach has been empirically shown to deliver deep and accurate insights about current customers, thus enabling a researcher either to conduct more focused research or to build on these insights to think of more effective marketing applications.

But how useful are these customer profiling insights? These profiles help to make customer segments vivid. That is, knowing the age and the switching patterns of a customer segment is not equivalent to visualizing that segment. Being able to visualize this segment enables one to form hypotheses that can either be used as a basis for further research or as a basis for developing a marketing communication plan. Examples of each follow.

Example 1: Using Customer Profiling to Develop Insights for Additional Research

Take the example of a large consumer packaged goods company. Customer profiling can be used here to generate working hypotheses about various customer segments within the target market. Depending on how confident the researcher or manager is about these hypotheses, and depending on what is at stake, he or she can use customer profiling to brainstorm prior to focus group research, or use it as a first step toward survey research.

TABLE 9.3
Customer Profiling Versus Segmentation Analysis: Their Accuracy in Predicting WVPR Membership

(Number in Defined Segment who are WPVR Members)/(Total Number in the Defined Segment)

Technique Used	*Manager$_x$*	*Cumulative Performance*	*%*	*Segment$_1$ Performance*	*Segment$_2$ Performance*	*Segment$_3$ Performance*
Target Profiling	Manager $_1$	13/17	(76%)	4/5*	6/0	3/3
Target Profiling	Manager $_2$	11/15	(73%)	4/5	5/8	2/2
Target Profiling	Manager $_3$	8/11	(73%)	5/6	1/2	2/3
Target Profiling	Manager $_4$	12/18	(67%)	7/10	5/7	0/1
Target Profiling	Manager $_5$	6/9	(67%)	1/2	4/5	1/2
Target Profiling	Manager $_6$	12/19	(63%)	3/3	3/5	6/11
Segmentation Analysis	Manager $_7$	20/32	(62%)	4/9	11/17	5/9
Segmentation Analysis	Manager $_8$	18/29	(62%)	6/11	5/9	7/9
Target Profiling	Manager $_9$	10/17	(59%)	5/9	3/3	2/5
Segmentation Analysis	Manager $_{10}$	40/68	(59%)	19/33	4/11	17/24
Segmentation Analysis	Manager $_{11}$	32/56	(57%)	29/44	0/3	3/9
Segmentation Analysis	Manager $_{12}$	23/43	(53%)	0/1	15/29	8/13
Target Profiling	Manager $_{13}$	3/6	(50%)	2/3	1/1	0/2
Segmentation Analysis	Manager $_{14}$	26/56	(46%)	13/22	10/26	3/8
Segmentation Analysis	Manager $_{15}$	41/90	(46%)	29/53	12/33	0/4
Segmentation Analysis	Manager $_{16}$	7/17	(41%)	6/11	0/2	1/4
Target Profiling	Manager $_{17}$	2/5	(40%)	0/0	0/0	2/5
Segmentation Analysis	Manager $_{18}$	28/90	(31%)	14/59	2/10	12/21
Segmentation Analysis	Manager $_{19}$	29/90	(30%)	4/15	23/65	0/10
Target Profiling	Manager $_{20}$	5/23	(22%)	1/5	1/9	3/9
Segmentation Analysis	Manager $_{21}$	28/143	(20%)	14/79	0/12	14/52
Segmentation Analysis	Manager $_{22}$	31/163	(19%)	15/88	16/72	0/3
Segmentation Analysis	Manager $_{23}$	23/122	(19%)	6/50	14/41	3/31

Note. Of the 4 respondents who fit the manager's description, 4 were WVPR members.

A recent meeting with a consumer packaged goods company, for example, was focused on increasing usage among the medium- and light-user segments of a particular baking product. The marketing plan included a heavy drop of free standing inserts that was to be supported with one of five different advertising campaigns. The product group manager, the brand manager, and the assistant brand manager all knew the customer well from a demographic standpoint. When they were asked to describe someone they personally knew who is a member of one of these medium- or low-user segments, however, only one of the three managers could name a specific person she knew who actually used the product.

Walking through this customer profiling process, it became clear that perhaps couponing and price-sensitivity did not drive the usage patterns of medium- and light-users, but that such usage was driven instead by situation-related needs, such as special occasions. Given the infrequent use of the product, and because of the special nature of its use, price and couponing were now hypothesized to play less of a role in usage than other aspects such as situation-related needs, brand familiarity, and the extent to which "easy usage ideas" might be included on or in the packaging.

In this instance, the insights generated from the customer profiling technique were viewed as hypotheses to be tested. They were then examined in focus groups, and a questionnaire was used to examine the validity of these insights further.

Example 2: Using Customer Profiling to Develop a More Effective Marketing Communication Plan

If little or no time and research money are available, insights from customer profiling can be used as a starting point for developing a marketing communication plan. One such example involves a company that manufactures outdoor Christmas lights. Although there was little research budget for this product, it was critical that the marketing communication budget be highly leveraged. The company had thought about allocating most of this budget to in-store signage, cooperative advertising, and POP displays.

The customer profile technique was then used to describe ideal customers. Initially, too much time was spent trying to profile the heavy user of Christmas lights . . . the homeowner whose household lighting pageantry is the neighborhood's bane and the power company's delight. Although interesting psychographic profiles were developed for this segment, customer profiling determined that the larger markets would consist of homeowners in the Midwestern snowbelt who have a modest display of lights but who are witnessing a gradual escalation of lighting in their neighborhoods. To the extent that use is spreading, there is implicit pressure on neighbors either to "stay ahead" or to simply "keep up"—in either case to escape the Scrooge stigma.

Although these profiles consisted merely of a set of hypotheses, customer profiling led to a marketing communication plan focused on encouraging newspapers to sponsor "neighborhood lighting contests." The plan included story ideas, logistical recommendations, and judging suggestions that the newspaper could use to encourage contests. This press packet was included in a small box of Christmas lights and mailed to features editors at targeted newspapers throughout the snowbelt.

In this instance, the insights generated by customer profiling were not tested, because the company did not wish to go through the time and expense of conducting formal research. Nevertheless, the technique provided insights for a distinctive marketing alternative to cooperative advertising and signs that would have been lost in a retail sea of red and green.

FINAL SUGGESTIONS AND IMPLEMENTATION ISSUES

Any effort at customer profiling is valuable, insofar as it makes us look beyond the superficial demographic information typically used. The most effective marketing applications, however, tend to be associated with the most detailed customer profiles. These profiling efforts have two characteristics in common: They take "psychological license" in describing what motivates the person, and they always ask, and try to answer, the question "why?" For instance:

> Keith listens to WVPR for news programming.
> WHY?
> Because he likes to be well-informed.
> WHY?
> Because he likes to be seen as a valuable person to talk to, or because he likes to feel in control of his environment, or because he believes it is what "smart" people do, and so on.

Is it valid to speculate this way? We must remember that the value of customer profiling lies in trying to uncover some basic needs that *might* motivate a customer, and such a discovery is not likely to be found in demographic data or in scanner data. Obtaining these insights is critical whether we are analyzing consumers of baking products or consumers of Christmas lights. Furthermore, these profiles can be sliced in a number of ways: heavy users, nonusers, ex-users, high potential users, Word-of-Mouth prone users, and so on.

A last advantage of customer profiling is that no one needs to know you do it. In its most public use, customer profiling can be a stimulus for brainstorming on a entire creative team. In its most private use, it is part of one's own creative black box.

The insights generated can either serve as a departure point for further research and hypothesis testing, or they can be used to develop a more effective marketing communication program. Generating these insights is a form of research. Implementing them is marketing.

REFERENCES

Carnegie, D. (1937). *How to win friends and influence people.* New York: Simon and Schuster.

Fortini-Cambell, L. (1990). *The customer insight book.* Chicago: The Copy Workshop.

Haley, R. I. (1968). Benefit segmentation: A decision-oriented research tool. *Journal of Marketing, 32*(3), 30–35.

Haley, R. I. (1984). Benefit segments: Backwards and forwards. *Journal of Advertising Research, 28*(3), 19–25.

Haley, R. I. (1985). *Developing effective communications strategy: A benefit segmentation approach.* New York: Wiley.

Haskins, J., & Kendrik, A. (1989). *Successful advertising research methods.* Lincolnwood, IL: NTC Business Books.

Plummer, J. T. (1984). How personality makes a difference. *Journal of Advertising Research, 28*(4), 27–31.

Schultz, D. (1991). *Integrated marketing communications.* Homewood, IL: Irwin.

Smith, W. R. (1956). Product differentiation and market segmentation as alternative marketing strategies. *Journal of Marketing, 20*(3), 3–8.

Wansink, B. (1994a). Developing and validating useful consumer prototypes. *Journal of Targeting, Measurement and Analysis for Marketing, 3*(1), 18–30.

Wansink, B. (1994b). Antecedents and mediators of eating bouts. *Family and Consumer Sciences Research Journal, 23*(2), 166–182.

Wansink, B. (1996). Can package size accelerate usage volume? *Journal of Marketing, 60*(3), 1–14.

Wansink, B., & Ray, M. L. (1996). Advertising strategies to increase usage frequency. *Journal of Marketing, 60*(1), 31–46.

Wansink, B., Ray, M. L., & Batra, R. (1994). Increasing cognitive response sensitivity. *Journal of Advertising, 23*(2), 62–74.

Wells, W. D. (1974). *Lifestyle and psychographics.* Chicago: American Marketing Association.

Wells, W. D., & Tigert, D. J. (1971). Activities, interests, and opinions. *Journal of Advertising Research, 11*, 27–35.

Weinstein, A. (1987). *Market segmentation.* Chicago: Probus.

Chapter 10

A Causal Analysis of Means-End Hierarchies: Implications in Advertising Strategies

Pierre Valette-Florence
Ecole Supérieure des Affaires, Grenoble, France

Means-end analysis has greatly developed in recent years, notably under the influence of the work of Reynolds and Gutman (1988) in the United States, and the researches of Valette-Florence and his colleagues in France (Aurifeille & Valette-Florence, 1992, 1995; Roehrich & Valette-Florence, 1991, 1992a, 1992b; Valette-Florence & Rapacchi, 1989a, 1990, 1991a, 1991b). These recent studies have paid particular attention to the proposition of methodological improvements in the obtaining of resultant chains from the synthesis of individual ladders. In this connection, methods using multiple correspondence analysis and graph theory (Valette-Florence & Rapacchi, 1991a, 1991b) have ceded to more pertinent analyses, based on constrained clustering of chains (Aurifeille, 1991; Aurifeille & Valette-Florence, 1992, 1995). These newer methods involve the seeking of those chains which best synthesize the different ladders evoked by individuals.

In this research, we propose an additional approach in order to define *latent chains* with a structural equations model based on the method of partial least squares (PLS) performed on categorical variables. Based on an empirical study related to cigarette consumption, this work describes the different methods currently used, and particularly emphasizes the proposed methodology; presents the data collection procedure used; and finally explores the various results of the analysis and puts the stress on the related implications in advertising strategies. Future research perspectives are outlined in the conclusion.

RECALL OF METHODOLOGY

Means-end chain analysis leads to the identification of *Attributes → Consequences → Values* sequences involved in the purchase of a given product. In reality, these sequences do not conform to classical theory, which considers values to be the main antecedents of behavior (Homer & Kahle, 1988). These sequences can only be justified in connection with the data collection method used to determine the individual ladders. It would therefore seem judicious to consider a network of relations more in keeping with the theory: *Values → Consequences → Attributes.* Due to the discrete nature of the measuring variables (choice or nonchoice of various elements), it would be advisable to opt for a statistical method capable of apprehending the type of causal relations involved. In this work, our aim is not so much to test diverse conceivable theoretical alternatives (which could be done in a future work), but rather to propose a new method of causal analysis. This method would be capable of testing the validity of the theoretical relationships, which come into play during the obtaining of the diverse individual means-end hierarchies.

To date, several methods have been put forward for the analysis of ladders collected by means of a *laddering* technique. These methods are reviewed first. Then, we present in detail our proposed analysis which employs a structural equations model applied to categorical measurement variables.

Previous Methods

Following an article published by Reynolds and Gutman in 1988, it became rapidly apparent that their approach suffered greatly from the lack of a method, automatic and reliable, which would permit rapid treatment of information and, above all, the easy construction of resulting hierarchical value maps (HVM). For this reason, Valette-Florence and Rapacchi (1990, 1991a, 1991b), proposed a method founded jointly on *graph theory* and *multiple correspondence analysis,* making these authors the first to evoke the interest of a multidimensional approach permitting the *segmentation* of individuals having widely differing *ladders.* Nonetheless, a certain number of problems have rapidly emerged in connection with the authors' procedure, which fails to take properly into account the indirect relations in the corresponding hierarchical value maps. Consequently, Roehrich and Valette-Florence (1991, 1992b) have proposed an extension of graph theory in order to better understand direct and especially indirect relations, as well as their importance for the *semantic coherence* of resultant chains.

A second research theme has developed around the work of Aurifeille (1991), and Aurifeille and Valette-Florence (1995). Their methodology advocates *constrained clustering of chains* in order to seek *virtual chains* (i.e., those which may or may not have been mentioned by any individual), which best synthesize the ladders actually evoked by interviewed subjects. This technique enables, through the use of *nonmetric multidimensional analysis,* to evaluate the *semantic coherence* of proposed chains as well as *the number of persons* that one can assign to the chains. This innovative procedure, which avoids as it were, the tedious construction of hierarchical value maps, has further been automated with a software package designed by Aurifeille (1992). However, in its actual formulation, this approach does not permit the determination of an optimal solution. It still requires the investigation of a bicriterion curve representing number and coherence of the different possible solutions.

Furthermore, neither of the two previous methods incorporates nor tests the *causal relations* prevalent in studies centered on values and their influence on consumer behavior. It is interesting to note that chain construction always commences from the *attribute → consequences → values relations,* whereas the usual theory in consumer behavior inverts these relations to study the effect of values on behavior or attitudes. In this sense, it would be appropriate to invert the relations and therefore to study the *values → consequences → attributes sequences.* In reality, none of the existing methods permit the comprehension of the nature of the causal relations considered to be prevalent during the act of purchasing a given product. It appears advisable to study further the nature of these relations by extending previous procedures to the definition of *latent chains.* This extension would use an original methodology initially proposed by Valette-Florence and Rapacchi (1989b). To this effect, we suggest the utilization of a new method which, to our knowledge, has never been used in the study of means-end hierarchies, namely an extension of *general canonical analysis*[1] to *categorical variables* by means of a structural equations model based on partial least squares (PLS).

Presentation of the Structural Equations Model for Categorical Variables

The structural equations models were introduced into marketing by Bagozzi during the 1980s. Currently, two principal methods exist: the first, based on the analysis of covariance structures, is better known by the name of one of its programs, LISREL; the second uses partial least squares analysis and there currently exists only one program, that of Lhomöller (1985). In the approximate totality of present studies, the analyses are carried out with continuous variables. However, PLS has the advantage of being able to handle categorical variables and, even better, mixed sets of categorical and continuous[2]

[1]For a detailed presentation of general canonical analysis and for a description of connections between various methods see Tenenhaus and Young (1985).

[2]LISREL can also be applied to the analysis of discrete variables. Nevertheless, a sample of important size (> 200) proves to be necessary (Lee, Poon, & Bentler, 1992). Furthermore, results obtained do not appear very reliable, regardless of estimation methods employed (Rigdon & Ferguson, 1991).

variables. This latter facility, often unknown, was essentially developed by Wold and Bertholet (1981), and Lhomöller and Wold (1982). We shall briefly present the transformations necessary for the application of PLS to categorical variables.

As we have emphasized earlier few researchers have shown in *explicit* fashion the use of PLS in the study of *contingency tables* (Wold & Bertholet, 1981; Bertholet & Wold, 1983), and even fewer have shown the relevance of PLS to the *conjoint* analysis of *categorical and continuous variables* (Lhomöller & Wold, 1982). In practice, the analysis is made possible by the fact that any categorical variable with k states can be decomposed into k boolean variables x, which assume uniquely values 0 and 1, such that:

$$\Pr(x = 1) = 1 - \Pr(x = 0) = \mu \quad (\mu \text{ is the frequency})$$

$$E(x) = \sum_i \Pr(x = i).i = \mu.1 + (1 - \mu).0 = \mu$$

$$E(x^2) = \sum_i \Pr(x = i).i^2 = \mu.1^2 + (1 - \mu).0^2 = \mu$$

$$\ldots\ldots$$

$$E(x^r) = \sum_i \Pr(x = i).i^r = \mu.1^r + (1 - \mu).0^r = \mu$$

$$\sigma^2(x) = \mu(1 - \mu) = \mu - \mu^2$$

Such properties permit the simple calculation of covariance matrices $S = (s_{ke})$, correlation matrices $R = (r_{ke})$, normalized moment matrices $Q = (q_{ke})$, and normalized and centered moment matrices $D = (d_{ke})$. These latter matrices D are used in canonical correlation analysis applied to categorical variables. Table 10.1 lists values corresponding to the elements of these different matrices for the case of a product of two dichotomous variables and the case of a product of a dichotomous variable with a continuous variable.

As several authors have indicated (cf. Giffi, 1990), canonical correlation analysis applied to matrices S, R, and D gives identical results, even though these matrices are not of full rank. In their article, Lhomöller and Wold (1982) have shown that a PLS model applied to a D-matrix is in fact equivalent to a *canonical correlation analysis with categorical variables.* As indicated in the PLS user's manual, a general canonical analysis applied to categorical and continuous variables can easily be conducted in *reflective mode,* provided that the analysis bears on a D-matrix (centered and normalized moments). The results obtained are interpreted in identical manner to those coming from a classical PLS model.

Finally, as was emphasized by Bertholet and Wold (1983), the extraction of additional dimensions (as in a classical canonical or factor analysis) is done through repetition of the process with the residual covariances obtained after extraction of the first dimension. One should also note, to

TABLE 10.1
Values of Different Moments of A Dichotomous Variable

Variable x_k	*Product of Two Dichotomous Variables*	*Product of a Dichotomous Variable and a Continuous Standardized Variable*
Boolean		
$x_k \in \{0, 1\}$	m_{ke}	$m_{kz} = m_k \bar{z}_k$
Normalized		
$x_k \in \left\{0, \frac{1}{\sqrt{m_k}}\right\}$	$q_{ke} = \frac{m_{ke}}{\sqrt{m_k m_e}}$	$q_{kz} = m_{kz} / \sqrt{m_k}$
Centered		
$x_k \in \{-m_k, 1-m_k\}$	$s_{ke} = m_{ke} - m_k m_e$	$s_{kz} = m_{kz}$
Normalized and centered		
$x_k \in \left\{\frac{-m_k}{\sqrt{m_k}}, \frac{1-m_k}{\sqrt{m_k}}\right\}$	$d_{ke} = \frac{m_{ke} - m_k m_e}{\sqrt{m_k m_e}}$	$d_{kz} = m_{kz} / \sqrt{m_k} = q_{k2}$
Standardized		
$x_k \in \left\{\frac{-m_k}{\sqrt{m_k - m_k^2}}, \frac{1-m_k}{\sqrt{m_k - m}}\right.$	$r_{ke} = \frac{m_{ke} - m_k m_e}{\sqrt{(m_k - m_k^2)(m_e - m_e^2)}}$	$r_{kz} = \frac{m_{kz}}{\sqrt{m_k - m_k^2}}$

Note. From Lhomoller (1985). *Program manual: Latent variables path analysis with partial least squares estimation.* Zentralarchiv Fur Empirische Sozialforshung, Universität zu Köln.

conclude this presentation, that the PLS model as used here belongs to the same family as the models recently diffused in the scientific community, which are based on optimal data transformation methods (Alternative Least Squares Optimal Scaling: ALSOS; Giffi, 1990).

RESEARCH PROCEDURES

We now expose the product that was retained for this work, as well as sample characteristics. As a preamble, we recall that this data has already been used by Aurifeille and Valette-Florence (1992) to illustrate their method of constrained clustering, and to compare the obtained results with those from a more traditional approach based on a cluster analysis of Kahle's values.

Choice of the Product

The choice of cigarettes seems to quite suite a procedure based on the study of *means-end chains.* As noted by Moschis (1989), cigarette consumption leads to important social consequences for the individual. Strong connections between the act of smoking and the self-concept have been put forward by several researchers (Chassin, Presson, Sherman, Corty, & Olshavsky, 1981; Sheth, Newman, & Gross, 1991). Furthermore, cigarettes have often been associated with brand choice (Chapman & Fitzgerald, 1982) and with important behavioral consequences (Grube, Weir, Getzlaf, & Rokeach, 1984). Finally, one might note that people who smoke often have the habit of questioning themselves about the significance of their act, as for example in the following: *"Could I stop smoking if I wanted to? Does this help me to be more confident? Does this bother others? Is smoking dangerous for my health? Are light cigarettes really less harmful?"*, etc. This remark should act to limit the possibility that the cognitive processes involved might artificially be amplified by the data collection method (Grunert & Grunert, 1991).

Sample

The subjects were 65 students selected by convenience sampling. Everyone volunteered for an individual interview of approximately 1 hour. The interview protocol detailed by Reynolds and Gutman (1988) was carefully followed. The list of obtained items is shown in Table 10.2. All in all, 138 ladders were collected, which corresponds to an average of 2.12 scales per person (a figure consistent with that of Reynolds and Gutman). In addition, we note that the data collection also measured the quantity of cigarettes smoked daily as well as first and second most favored brands out of a total list of 14 cigarette brands (cf. Table 10.3). Lastly, the respondents had to fill out an extended version of Kahle's scale. This scale will not be used for the present work, but see Aurifeille and Valette-Florence (1992).

ANALYSIS AND RESULTS

Before exposing in greater detail the main results of this work, some principles of the analysis are specified. Indeed, traditional causal analyses directly test the intended conceptual relations without worrying about possible effects that might exist if one were to extract dimensions of higher order (i.e., from residual matrices). This strategy, justifiable for analyses with continuous variables (extracted variance being in general superior to 50%), is much less suitable for discrete variables (inertia reproduced by the first axes being weak). As in conventional *correspondence analysis,* it is desirable to

TABLE 10.2
List of Items Obtained for the Consumption of Cigarettes

ATTRIBUTES			
A1	Low nicotine	A5	Mild tobacco
A2	Strong taste	A6	Natural aspect (little alteration of taste or composition)
A3	Low tar		
A4	Moderate price		
CONSÉQUENCES			
C1	Physical appearance	C4	Prestige, charm
C2	Health	C5	Self-confidence
C3	Stimulation	C6	Identity
		C7	Communication
INSTRUMENTAL VALUES		*TERMINAL VALUES*	
VI1	Broadmindedness	VT1	An exciting life
VI2	Cheerfull	VT2	Happiness
VI3	Independent	VT3	Self-fulfillment
VI4	Dynamic	VT4	A sense of belonging
VI5	Intellectual	VT5	To be well-respected
VI6	Capable	VT6	Wisdom
VI7	Self-control	VT7	Warm relations with others

extract several axes successively in order to have a more complete and more accurate understanding of the examined phenomenon.

Analysis Principles

In this research, we have also used a procedure which, to our knowledge, has not previously been used and which involves the extraction of higher-order dimensions. This technique corresponds in fact to the successive extraction of axes as in principal components factor analysis or general factor analysis. Therefore, to each axis corresponds a decreasing amount of inertia with, as a corollary, an increase in total inertia reproduced by the axes. We recall, in

TABLE 10.3
Purchased Brands

CODE	*BRAND NAMES*	*CODE*	*BRAND NAME*
M1	Benson	M8	Malboro
M2	Camel	M9	Pall Mall
M3	Chesterfield	M10	Peter Stuyvesant
M4	Craven	M11	Philip Morris
M5	Dunhill	M12	Rothman
M6	Gauloise	M13	Royale
M7	Lucky Strike	M14	Winston

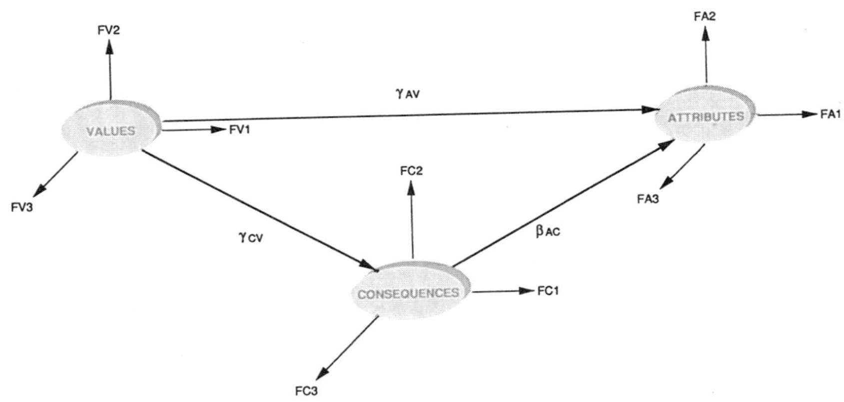

FIG. 10.1. Categorical structural equations modeling approach.

this connection, that the maximum number of extractable axes is in fact equal to the maximum number of variables contributing to the measure of a latent concept (Valette-Florence & Rapacchi, 1989b).

Generally, the model tested corresponds to that of Fig. 10.1 where we have represented three axes for each concept (values/consequences/attributes), although additional dimensions might eventually be obtained. Given the different elements that were generated during the interviews (cf. Table 10.2), we decided to consider only *four*[3] successive levels: *Terminal Values/Instrumental Values/Consequences/Attributes.* In addition, the results presented in Table 10.4 concern solely, for the sake of simplicity, the first three axes obtained (total reproduced inertia 45%), whereas we extracted a total of four axes (total reproduced inertia 52%). Finally, the last section of Table 10.4 corresponds to the universe of brands purchased as first and second choices. In short, the complete model to be succinctly discussed corresponds to the diagram in Fig. 10.2, where also represented is the quantity of cigarettes smoked daily (analysis to follow). We also note that Table 10.4 presents the weights corresponding to the *categorical scaling* of the measurement variables, whereas for a conventional analysis with continuous variables, one interprets and uses the factor loadings.

Rather than naming each axis, we prefer to make an interpretation that would be both simpler and closer to the general philosophy of means-end chains by locating the *associations* (*latent chains*) that emerge through the four levels retained for analysis. We note, beforehand, that a Jackknife analysis will allow the testing of the statistical validity of presented results (T-tests > 2). This point is particularly important not just in the context of small samples, as in our case, but also in the event of sensitivity of the

[3]Complementary analyses using more levels and finer distinctions such as psychosociological consequences/functional consequences do not improve the quality of the results.

TABLE 10.4
Categorical Weights Obtained for Three Dimensions (PLS)

Items	*Dimension 1*	*Dimension 2*	*Dimension 3*
An exciting life	-0,222	**1,185**	*-0,739*
Happiness	0,019	**0,559**	*-1,817*
Self-fulfillment	*-1,344*	**0,934**	*1,106*
A sense of belonging	**1,038**	0,297	-0,172
To be well-respected	**0,391**	*-0,638*	**0,903**
Wisdom	*-0,519*	*-2,000*	**1,095**
Warm Relations with others	**1,064**	**0,757**	**1,563**
Broadmindedness	**1,436**	*-0,792*	*-0,446*
Cheerfull	**0,700**	**0,370**	**2,176**
Independent	*-0,525*	0,162	-0,204
Dynamic	**0,337**	**0,965**	**0,951**
Intellectual	*-0,890*	**0,431**	**0,694**
Capable	-0,080	0,105	*-0,602*
Self control	*-0,559*	*-1,616*	**1,543**
Physical appearance	**0,317**	-0,021	0,266
Health	**1,119**	*-1,037*	*-0,525*
Stimulation	*-0,613*	**1,028**	*-1,259*
Prestige, charm	**0,408**	-0,043	**0,467**
Self-confidence	**0,354**	**0,632**	*-1,809*
Identity	*-0,959*	*-1,060*	*-0,739*
Communication	0,230	**0,446**	**0,499**
Low nicotine	**1,646**	-0,213	*-0,529*
Strong taste	*-0,432*	**1,477**	**0,984**
Low tar	**0,512**	0,055	**1,957**
Moderate price	-0,236	**0,254**	*-1,556*
Mild tobacco	*-0,307*	*-1,696*	0,277
Natural aspect (little alteration of taste or composition)	*-1,128*	0,055	*-1,159*
Benson	*-0,279*	*-0,246*	*-0,502*
Camel	0,119	**1,319**	*-1,313*
Chesterfield	**0,223**	*-0,324*	0,138
Craven	-0,105	0,014	0,102
Dunhill	*-1,235*	*-0,644*	*-0,269*
Gauloise	-0,164	0,028	0,074
Lucky Strike	-0,057	**0,790**	**0,631**
Malboro	**0,910**	**0,669**	**1,077**
Pall Mall	-0,039	0,078	**0,218**
Peter Stuyvesant	**1,073**	*-0,977*	**0,681**
Philip Morris	**1,078**	*-0,216*	*-1,294*
Rothman	**0,238**	0,084	*-0,482*
Royale	*-1,082*	0,014	**0,534**
Winston	*-0,195*	0,017	*-0,254*

Note. Characters in bold type refer to important positive weights, whereas characters in italics refer to important negative weights (*T* tests > 2).

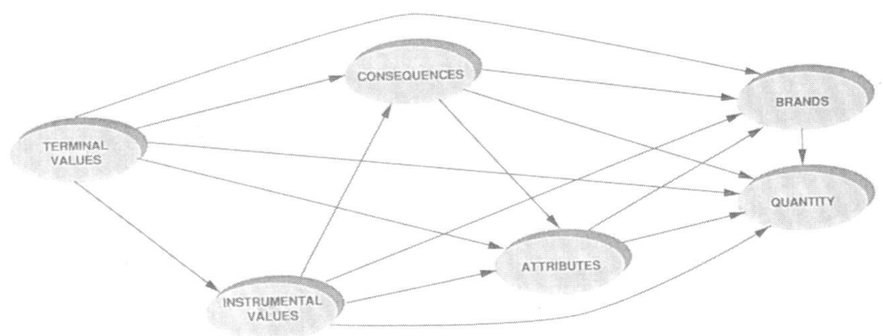

FIG. 10.2. Full model (PLS): Cigarettes.

proposed solutions to those elements with low frequencies (especially true for multiple correspondence analysis).

Detailed Results

Reading the *categorical weights* obtained for each of the variables composing the four conceptual levels previously defined (Table 10.4) allows us to better understand how cigarette consumption is structured. Actually, each *latent concept* is evaluated in *dual fashion* (as in multiple correspondence analysis) by the opposition between elements having *positive weights* and those having *negative weights.* Without entering into the details of the results presented in Table 10.4, one can nevertheless select certain elements for inspection. For example, the quest for *warm relations with others* (*VT7*) and for a *sense of belonging* (*VT4*) affect *broadmindedness* (*VI1*), *cheerfulness* (*VI2*), *health preservation* (*C2*), and the demand for *low nicotine* (*A1*) and *low tar* (*A3*). *Philip Morris* (*M11*) and *Peter Stuyvesant* (*M10*) are naturally associated with this *latent chain,* as is also, to a lesser degree, *Marlboro* (*M8*). With regard to negative weights, one makes out the following *latent chain* (only taking into account the most important elements): *self-fulfillment* (*VT3*) → *intellectual* (*VI5*) → *sense of identity* (*C6*) → *natural aspect* (*A6*), with which one can associate *Dunhill* (*M5*), as the principal brand. The interested reader can, by applying the same approach to the second and third dimensions, bring to light equally interesting relations such as for example the search for an *exciting life* (*VT1*) → *dynamism* (*VI4*) → *stimulation* (*C3*) → *strong taste* (*A2*) and the fact of liking to smoke *Camel* (*M2*), *Marlboro* (*M8*), or *Lucky Strike* (*M7*).

In addition, Table 10.5, presenting the nature of the structural relations, indicates for each of the dimensions which are the dominant levels. Thus, for the second dimension, it is the *consequences* that best explain desired attributes ($\beta = 0.515$), whereas for the first dimension, the *terminal values* ($\beta = 0.243$) and the *consequences* ($\beta = 0.294$) have the same influence on

TABLE 10.5
Path* Coefficients for the 3 Dimensions (PLS)

		Terminal values	*Instrumental values*	*Conse-quences*	*Attributes*	*Brands*	R^{-2} (%)
DIMENSION 1	Instrumental values	0,619					38,4
	Consequences	0,456	0,099				27,4
	Attributes	0,243	NS**	0,294			24,0
	Brands	0,279	0,129	0,466	0,202		43,3
	Quantity	-0,090	-0,110	NS**	0,126	0,095	4,8
DIMENSION 2	Instrumental values	0,550					30,2
	Consequences	0,198	0,322				21,3
	Attributes	-0,080	0,142	0,515			31,2
	Brands	NS**	-0,068***	0,267	0,302		22,9
	Quantity	0,216	-0,110	NS**	0,181	0,084	10,4
DIMENSION 3	Instrumental values	0,280					7,8
	Consequences	NS***	-0,346				12,1
	Attributes	0,163	0,122	-0,369			23,3
	Brands	0,438	0,124	0,323	NS**		28,5
	Quantity	-0,162	-0,129	-0,152	0,188	0,095	10,1

* Interpreted vertically
** Jackknife test ($T < 2$)
*** Significant at $P < 0.10$

the attributes. For each latent concept, the researcher is therefore better able to comprehend the causal relations involved. Furthermore, in similar manner to the approach proposed by Reynolds and Sutrick (1986), albeit with greater simplicity, one can directly determine the level with greatest influence on brand choice or smoked quantity. Overall, *consequences* have the greatest influence on brand choice ($\beta_1 = 0.466$; $\beta_2 = 0.267$; $\beta_3 = 0.323$; respectively for dimensions 1, 2, and 3), whereas *terminal values* ($\beta_1 = 0.279$; $\beta_3 = 0.438$) and *attributes* ($\beta_1 = 0.202$; $\beta_2 = 0.302$) arrive in second place. Generally speaking, the effect of the explanatory power of each dimension on brand choice space, which decreases for each dimension extracted (respectively 43.3%, 22.9%, and 28.5%), is relatively important (on average 31.6%) and even superior to that obtained (19.6%) by Aurifeille and Valette-Florence (1992). These authors had used a different methodology (*multinomial logit* model) to predict real brands (unlike the choice universe used here). Finally, one will note that smoked quantity is less well-explained (respectively 4.8%, 10.4%, 10.1% for dimensions 1, 2, and 3), as is the case for the previously cited study (Aurifeille & Valette-Florence, 1992). This result confirms that the choice of a brand is more conditioned by considerations of psychosociological nature than is the case for the quantity smoked. The quantity smoked is no doubt more connected with external considerations (circumstances) or personal characteristics (age, gender, etc.), which have not been taken into account in this work.

Implication in Advertising Strategies

In the absence of the ability to predict the quantitative aspects of cigarette consumption, a parameter over which marketing people have little control anyway in the present legislative context, it is nonetheless possible to distinguish the qualitative characteristics or the psychosociological domains associated with cigarettes and consequently those characteristics associated with chosen brands. The investigation of consumption styles (Roehrich & Valette-Florence, 1992a) associated with the previously defined latent chains is a rich provider of information from a managerial point of view:

1. This allows the definition of the main latent chains as well as their respective importance (the factors restitute a decreasing amount of inertia) and the main brands associated to them (Fig. 10.3);

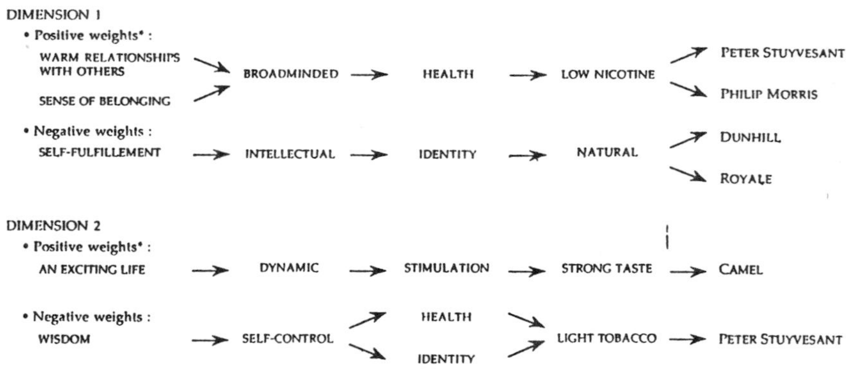

FIG. 10.3. Latent chains for dimensions 1 and 2 and associated brands.

2. The direct effect of latent chains on brand choice makes possible the location, for each latent chain, of the determining element (values/consequences/attributes) which should be emphasized during the making of advertising communication (e.g.: consequences for dimension 1);

3. The present approach permits not only the definition of key elements of sensitivity to brands (i.e., values/consequences/attributes), but also the identification of possible polysemy of the nature of the brands studied. Thus, *Marlboro,* the leading brand on the market, is associated with *all* consumption styles and this reinforces the strong polymorphous nature of its identity. On the other hand, *Dunhill* or *Royale* are mainly associated with a single (monosemy) consumption practice.

Clearly, future complementary researches should allow refinement of these illustrations. Nonetheless, we believe our analysis brings new insights for a better understanding of product positionings and the definition of advertising strategies. This is further illustrated through the use of *cognitive mappings,* which can easily be built by projection of the *component loadings*[4] of the diverse A/C/V elements. Assume, for instance, we want to design an advertising strategy for *Marlboro.* Figure 10.4 gives the corresponding picture portraying the relations of *Marlboro* with the main elements picked up by respondents. Hence, *warm relationships with others, self-confidence,* and to a lesser extent *dynamic* or *cheerful* represent the main points to be stressed in the building up of an advertising message.

Our analysis also helps the researcher to identify which brands are in connection with specific elements (values/consequences/attributes) it might be willing to use. Figure 10.5 gives such an illustration for the consequences which, as we recall, have the greatest influence on brand choice. In this example, it appears that *Marlboro* is mainly associated with *self-confidence* (as previously stressed), whereas *Peter Stuyvesant* seems to be in close connection with *health.*

Finally, a full picture of the market is illustrated by Fig. 10.6. Notice that the diverse brands under study are obviously not associated with the same means-end elements. For instance, *Royale* is mainly associated with a *natural aspect,* whereas *Lucky Strike* or *Camel* are mainly associated with *stimulation* and an *exciting life.* Of course, due to the convenience nature of our sample, these results cannot be taken as granted. Indeed, replications with fully representative samples are deemed necessary. However, we believe that our methodology already brings new opportunities for a clever design of related advertising campaigns.

---

[4]Component loadings represent the correlations of the original variables with the latent factor scores.

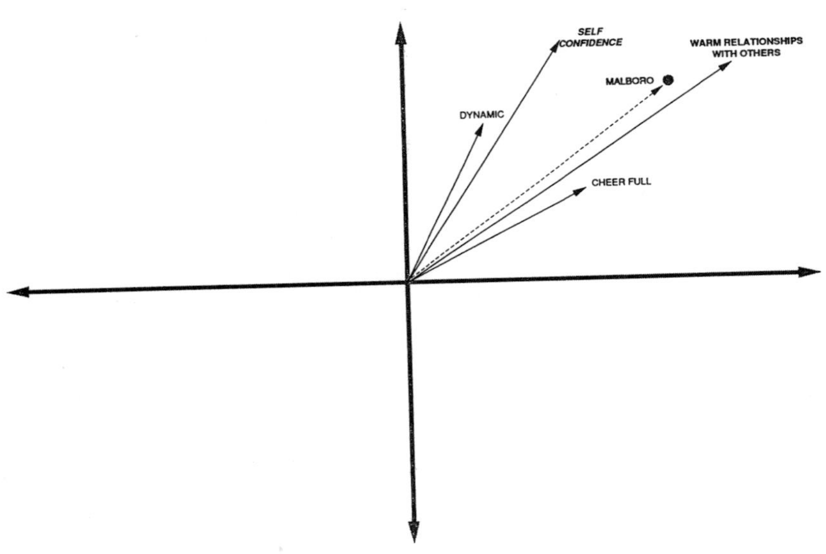

FIG. 10.4. Cognitive mapping: Marlboro.

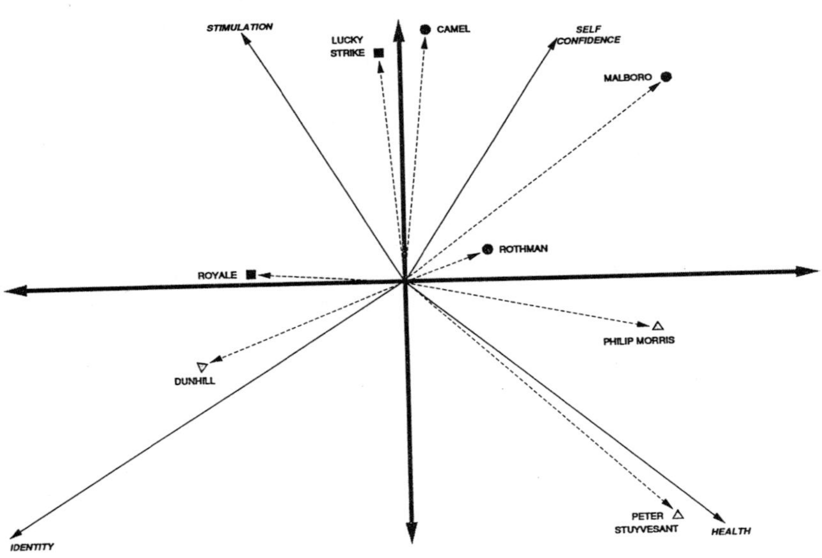

FIG. 10.5. Cognitive mapping: Consequences space.

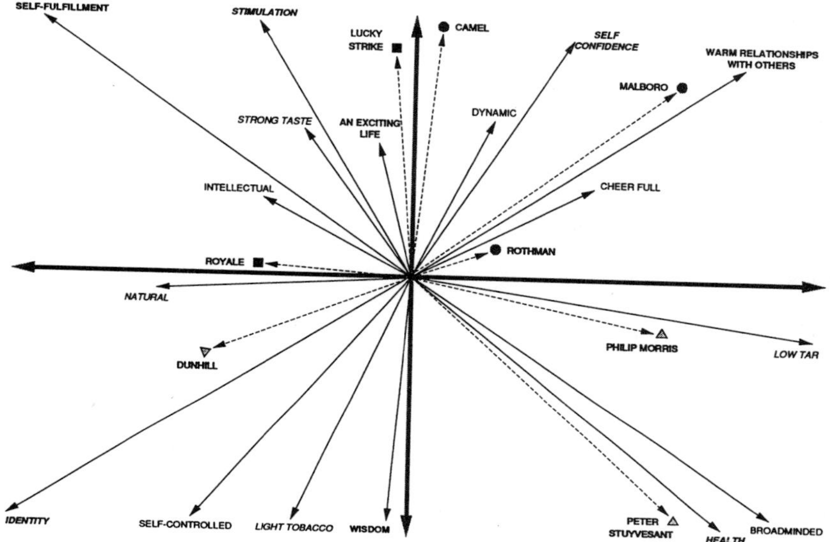

FIG. 10.6. Full mapping.

CONCLUSION

This research has illustrated the analysis of means-end chains, applied here to cigarette consumption, in the context of the application of a structural equations model to categorical variables. The retained estimation model, based on partial least squares (PLS), puts forward the feasibility of the proposed method and, especially, its potential for the characterization of specific consumption styles.

Although several implications, managerial as well as theoretical, can now be underlined, several improvements are still possible. The first evidently concerns the sample which was limited in size and restricted to a student population. Extended to a representative sample of the real universe of cigarette consumption, the results obtained in this work would no doubt have more relief and range. Furthermore, the analysis presented here adheres to the methodological paradigm which considers that categorical observed variables are in fact the expression of continuous underlying latent variables. Resorting to latent classes (an extension of log-linear models) would allow the extension of the analysis to also include categorical latent variables; the latter being perhaps more representative of the studied phenomenon. Finally, the use of more powerful—if less flexible methods—should permit statistical testing of the number and nature of dimensions brought to light in this work. Thus, recent structural equations models proposed by Muthén (1987, LISCOMP program) or Lee et al. (1992) should provide some elements of response in this direction.

Often termed *soft* modeling, the PLS approach used here, though less rigorous from a strictly statistical point of view, still provides several interesting elements of response to researchers as well as practitioners. Therefore, the results proposed here belong to the line of causal analyses that have always prevailed in consumer behavior. In particular, these results emphasize not only the preeminence of consequences, thus confirming the work of Reynolds and Sutrick (1986), but also to a lesser extent the use of values to explain the choice of brands. Above all, they enable the marketing manager or product manager to better identify the *consumption styles* (to use the expression of Roehrich & Valette-Florence, 1992a) that allow the depiction of specific brand choices. In that respect, implications in terms of positioning as well as definition of communication strategies seem evident.

In closing, we emphasize the contribution of the proposed methodology to the classification of respondents in terms of *evoked ladders*. One of the particularly interesting properties of PLS, when applied to categorical variables, is that an obtained *factor score* is directly equal to the *categorical weight* of the chosen modality (i.e., value/consequence/or attribute evoked; or equal to the sum of *categorical weights* of the selected modalities). Thus, a cluster analysis of factor scores performs automatically and without distortion a clustering of *ladders* evoked by respondents. Comparison of this analysis with the results that would be obtained by applying the methodology of Aurifeille and Valette-Florence (1992, 1995) would also illustrate the complementarity of these two approaches. In addition, analysis with PLS not being subject to item *order*, the problem of codification, so frequently encountered during data collection, is automatically solved. This also permits the extension of the analysis to the study of "*cognitive structures*," which might be a more convenient way to represent in a global sequence all the elements picked up by the respondents (as suggested by Grunert & Grunert, 1991). Lastly, one could perform the analysis by concentrating on the number of evoked elements per ladders, rather than on the different concepts (values/consequences/attributes) to be comprehended. Consequently, certain individuals having shorter ladders than others are more inclined to purchase certain brands than others who evoke longer and more complex ladders. An analysis of this kind would make it possible to discern whether certain brands refer more often to cognitive than to affective elements or vice versa. Generally, we think that the proposed model (PLS) prefigures a number of pertinent applications from a theoretical point of view as well as from a perspective of applied research. The interest of the marketing community in the study of means-end chains should be refreshed from this, as should its interest in research done in this field.

REFERENCES

Aurifeille, J. M. (1991, October). Contribution of "instrumental values" to means-end chain analysis and to advertising conceptualization. *Workshop on Value and Lifestyle Research in Marketing*. Brussels, European Institute for Advanced Studies in Management.

Aurifeille, J. M. (1992). *M3C: Means-end chain constrained clustering*. Logiciel de typologie contrainte des chaînages, version 1.0ß, Macintosh.

Aurifeille, J. M., & Valette-Florence, P. (1992, May). An empirical investigation of the predictive validity of micro versus macro approaches in consumer value research. In K. Grunert (Ed.), *Marketing for Europe—Marketing for the future*. European Marketing Annual Conference, Aarhus, pp. 65–81.

Aurifeille, J. M., & Valette-Florence, P. (1995). Determination of the dominant means-end chains: A constrained clustering approach. *International Journal of Research in Marketing, 12*, 267–268.

Bertholet, J. L., & Wold, H. (1983). Recent developments on categorical data analysis by PLS. *NATO Advanced Workshop on Analysis of Qualitative Spatial Analysis*, Amsterdam.

Chapman, S., & Fitzgerald, R. (1982). Brand preference and advertising recall in adolescent smokers: Some implications for health promotion. *American Journal of Public Health, 82*, 491–494.

Chassin, L., Presson, C., Sherman, S. J., Corty, E., & Olshavsky, R. W. (1981). Self images and cigarette smoking in adolescents. *Personality and Social Psychology Bulletin, 7*, 670–676.

Giffi, A. (1990). *Nonlinear multivariate analysis*. New York: Wiley.

Grube, J., Weir, I., Getzlaf, S., & Rokeach, M. (1984). Own value system, value images and cigarette smoking. *Personality and Social Psychology Bulletin, 10*, 306–313.

Grunert, K. G., & Grunert, S. C. (1991, October). Measuring subjective meaning structures by the laddering method: Theoretical considerations and methodological problems. *Workshop on Value and Lifestyle Research in Marketing*, Brussels, European Institute for Advanced Studies in Management.

Homer, P., & Kahle, L. (1988). A structural equation test of the value-attitude-behavior hierarchy. *Journal of Personality and Social Psychology, 54*, 638–646.

Lee, S., Poon, W. Y., & Bentler, P. M. (1992). Structural equation models with continuous and polytomous variables. *Psychometrika, 57*, 89–105.

Lhomöller, J. B. (1985). *LVPLS 1.7 Program manual: Latent variables path analysis with partial least squares estimation*. Zentralarchiv Für Empirische Sozialforshung, Universität Köln.

Lhomöller, J. B., & Wold, H. (1982). Path models for latent-variables indirectly observed by categorical and interval-scaled variables: An extension of partial least-squares (PLS) soft modeling. *Symposium on Cultural Indicators for the Comparative Study of Culture*, Vienna.

Moschis, G. P. (1989). Point of view: Cigarette advertising and young smokers. *Journal of Advertising Research, 29*, 51–60.

Muthén, G. (1987). LISCOMP: *Analysis of linear structural equations using a comprehensive measurement model*. Chicago: Scientific Software.

Reynolds, T., & Gutman, J. (1988). Laddering theory, method, analysis and interpretation. *Journal of Advertising Research, 28*, 11–31.

Reynolds, T., & Sutrick, K. (1986). Assessing the correspondence of one or more vectors to symmetric matrix using ordinal regression. *Psychometrika, 51*, 101–112.

Rigdon, E., & Ferguson, C. (1991). The performance of the polychoric correlation coefficient and selected fitting functions in confirmatory factor analysis with ordinal data. *Journal of Marketing Research, 28*, 491–497.

Roehrich, G., & Valette-Florence, P. (1991, October). A weighted cluster-based analysis of direct and indirect connections in means-end analysis: An application to lingerie retail.

Workshop on Value and Lifestyle Research in Marketing, Brussels, European Institute for Advanced Studies in Management.

Roehrich, G., & Valette-Florence, P. (1992a, May). Apport des chaînages cognitifs à la segmentation des marchés. *Actes du 8ème Colloque International de l'Association Française du Marketing,* pp. 479–498.

Roehrich, G., & Valette-Florence, P. (1992b, July). Creation of a valid hierarchical value map in means-end chain analysis. *Marketing Science Conference,* London.

Sheth, J. N., Newman, B., & Gross, B. (1991). Why we buy what we buy: A theory of consumption values. *Journal of Business Research, 22,* 159–170.

Tenenhaus, M., & Young, F. W. (1985). An analysis and synthesis of multiple correspondence analysis, optimal scaling, dual scaling, homogeneity analysis and other methods for quantifying categorical multivariate data. *Psychometrika, 50,* 91–120.

Valette-Florence, P., & Rapacchi, B. (1989a, May). Value analysis by linear representation and appropriate positioning: An extension of laddering methodology. *European Marketing Annual Conference,* Athènes, pp. 969–989.

Valette-Florence, P., & Rapacchi, B. (1989b, September). Note méthodologique sur l'utilisation de PLS appliqué à des variables catégorielles: Une illustration portant sur les chaînes moyens-fins. *Communication au Séminaire Exploration et Analyse de Données,* Carcassone.

Valette-Florence, P., & Rapacchi, B. (1990, May). Application et extension de la théorie des graphes à l'analyse des chaînages cognitifs: Une illustration pour l'achat de parfums et eaux de toilette. *Actes du 6ème Colloque de l'Association Française de Marketing,* pp. 485–511.

Valette-Florence, P., & Rapacchi, B. (1991a). Improving means-end chain analysis using graph theory and correspondence analysis. *Journal of Advertising Research, 31,* 30–45.

Valette-Florence, P., & Rapacchi, B. (1991b, December). A cross-cultural means-end chain analysis of perfume purchases. *Proceedings of the Third Symposium on Cross-Cultural Consumer Behavior and Business Studies,* Hawaii, pp. 161–173.

Wold, H., & Bertholet, J. L. (1981). The pls (partial least squares) approach to multidimensional contingency tables. In A. Rizzi (Ed.), *Special Issues of Metron: Transactions of International Meeting on Multidimensional Contingency Tables,* Rome.

Chapter 11

The Use of Psychographics by Advertising Agencies: An Issue of Value and Knowledge

Stephen J. Gould
Baruch College, The City University of New York

From the inception of their use, psychographics have remained a controversial subject in terms of their validity and utility. Thus, most research on them has concerned issues of validity (Kinnear & Taylor, 1976; Lastovicka, 1982; Lastovicka, Murray, & Joachimsthaler, 1990; Wells, 1975). However, given such factors in advertising research as the costs of psychographic research, their relative effectiveness or lack of it when placed head to head with other variables such as demographics, and the generally small percentage of variance explained by psychographic predictors (similar to personality variables)—10% or less (Kassarjian & Sheffet, 1991), an equally important although by no means unrelated issue concerns the perceived utility of psychographics to the research people who generate and/or buy them within advertising agencies. This chapter examines this issue by reporting on a survey of advertising research directors in large and medium size agencies.

A key framing theoretical concept for investigating psychographic utility is knowledge use which has been widely studied in the marketing area (Deshpande & Zaltman, 1982, 1984, 1987; Menon & Varadarajan, 1992). Market intelligence has been said to play a critical role in the development and maintenance of a market orientation by a firm (Kohli & Jaworski, 1990). For advertisers, psychographics are but one form of market intelligence among others (e.g., demographics, attitude measures, behavioral use measures) and thus may be seen as competitors for scarce research dollars. Similarly, various forms of psychographic research are also competitive with each other (e.g., syndicated versus customized psychographics; one syndicated service vs. another; various forms of measures vs. others, such as the List of Values versus Values and Lifestyles [Kahle, Beatty, & Homer, 1986] and the Drinking-Driving segmentation scheme also versus VALS [Lastovicka et al., 1990]).

The knowledge-based use of psychographics may be framed in such terms as what is used (content), who uses it, and the type of use. What is used may be seen in terms of various forms of measures that are designed to gain psychological insight into the consumer (Wells, 1975). Who uses them in the advertising setting consists of researchers who obtain the information from consumers and feed it to creatives to help them create advertising. It should be added that psychographic information thus translated into actual advertisements in turn influences consumers. As consumers are researched again, a continuing cycle of lifestyle evolution is evidenced (cf. Englis & Solomon, chap. 2, this volume). The type of knowledge-based use of psychographics may be framed in terms of three possibilities: *action-oriented use* (changes in activities, practices, and policies directly linked to research studies); *knowledge-enhancing use* (acquiring of new knowledge); and *affective use* (using information to feel satisfied, confident and good about decisions [Menon & Varadarajan, 1992]).

Based on these three aspects of use (i.e., content, users, and type of use), this chapter examines the perceived credibility and validity of psychographics information, its perceived usefulness, and its perceived cost relative to benefit (John & Martin, 1984; Menon & Varadarajan, 1992).

METHOD

A survey was conducted of research directors in the largest U.S. advertising agencies (i.e., with billings of $100 million or more as given in the 1992 issue of the Standard Directory of Advertising Agencies)—the range of billings in the sample was from $125 million to $1 billion dollars. Respondents were guaranteed anonymity. In this regard, not even the size of the agency nor the individual titles of the respondents will be given when they are quoted to protect their confidentiality. It can be said that the respondents were individually listed in the *Standard Directory* and held positions listed at the vice-presidential or executive vice-presidential level. [Note: One eligible advertising agency research head, namely one of the co-chairs of the Advertising & Consumer Psychology Conference was omitted from the sample in order to avoid conflicts of interest]. They were given a preaddressed, postage-paid envelope, plus the opportunity to receive copies of the results if they requested it. Seventeen surveys were returned out of

73, for a return rate of 23.2%, which is in line with other surveys of top advertising professionals (cf. Hunt & Chonko, 1987).

The focus of the survey was on an open-ended question that asked the research directors "to describe in your own words your experience with using psychographics." Some additional guide questions were included within the text of this question to provide some direction to the answers while still allowing plenty of room for the respondents to go where they wanted with the question (e.g., "What do you find are their strengths and weaknesses?"). Other questions asked involved scale-type items and were drawn up to reflect some of the dimensions of knowledge use considered in related marketing articles. These included: the percentage of research spent on psychographics; the perceived usefulness of psychographics in creating advertising copy (Menon & Varadarajan, 1992); the perceived usefulness of psychographics in targeting consumers (Menon & Varadarajan, 1992); the amount actually spent on psychographic research; the amount actually spent on all advertising research; the perceived cost/benefit relationship of psychographics (Menon & Varadarajan, 1992); the perceived validity/credibility of psychographics (cf. John & Martin, 1984); a listing of the syndicated psychographics used, such as VALS used; the exact job title of the respondent; and the billings of the agency (see Appendix for the questionnaire).

RESULTS

The results of both the quantitative and qualitative questions are reported in this section. The means for a number of the quantitative questions (based on a 5-point scale with "1" representing a *low score* and "5" a *high score*—2, 3, and 4 are intermediate scores) are reported in Table 11.1.

Attitudes Toward Psychographics

Perceived Usefulness of Psychographics in Creating Advertising Copy. More respondents in our survey found psychographics to be not very useful or somewhat useful (10 of them) while only 3 thought them to be quite or very useful.

TABLE 11.1
Means for Questions on Perceived Usefulness

	M
Usefulness in targeting consumers	2.43
Usefulness in creating advertising	2.50
Cost/Benefit of psychographics	2.38
Validity/Credibility of Psychographics	3.13

Perceived Usefulness of Psychographics in Targeting the Consumer. Similar results were found for the usefulness of psychographics in targeting consumers as were found for their usefulness in creating advertising copy. While 10 respondents found them to be not very useful or somewhat useful, only 3 found them to be quite or very useful.

Perceived Benefits of Psychographics Relative to Their Cost. Eleven of our respondents found that psychographics were either extremely costly or somewhat costly relative to their benefit while only 3 thought they were extremely beneficial.

Perceived Validity/Credibility of Psychographic Research. Our sample split fairly evenly on the issue of the validity of psychographic research. On the negative side, 7 thought they were either extremely invalid or somewhat invalid while on the positive side, 7 thought they were somewhat valid or extremely valid. The mean was a little higher for this item than for the others indicating a slightly better (though by no means approving) attitude toward the validity of psychographics as opposed to their usefulness.

Percentage of Research Expenditures on Psychographics in Relation to Total Advertising Research Expenditures. With respect to the percentage of all advertising research expenditures devoted to psychographics, most reported a low percentage—see Table 11.2. This is something we would expect in that psychographics are generally regarded as only "one piece of the puzzle" as one of our respondents put it in his or her open-ended response. However, some differences in reporting, especially in terms of the one respondent who reported a very high percentage (i.e., 81%–100%), may be due to the different definitions people apply to the term psychographics.

Reported Use of Syndicated Psychographics

More respondents reported that they used syndicated psychographics and related services than reported they did not (10 to 7). Of the 10, one indicated that his or her agency did not use any on a regular basis but would look at available research. Another reported that his or her agency had its own "VALS-type" proprietary approach. Of the 8 remaining, 4 reported using VALS, 2 MRI, and 1 each for PRIZM, Roper Influentials Survey, and Yankelovich Monitor—note the numbers add to 9 because one respondent reported using both VALS and MRI. One respondent who reported using a syndicated service nonetheless found syndicated psychographics to be of limited value relative to customized psychographics of specific segments (e.g., coffee drinkers, mascara users) although the latter are expensive to gather. Thus, there appears to be some direct competition

TABLE 11.2
Psychographic Research Expenditures in Relation to Total Advertising Research Expenditures

	Number
0-20.90%	10
21-40.99%	3
41-60.99%	2
61-80.99%	0
81-100%	1

for research dollars between syndicated and customized services, which quite likely extends to competition between syndicated services although no one mentioned this in their answers. With respect to knowledge use, we may suspect that customized psychographic research is more likely to lead to direct actionable use whereas syndicated services, to the degree that they are perceived as too general, might serve more in the role of knowledge enhancement (cf. Menon & Varadarajan, 1992).

Open-Ended Responses

As our close-ended responses indicate, most of the directors in our study found there to be major problems with psychographics. Only a few reported them to be in one of the two top boxes as being quite or very useful. However, even one of these respondents reported that the account people in his or her agency were skeptical about psychographics. The more general attitude seemed to be reflected in the following quote from another respondent who in response to the close-ended questions had found psychographics to be not very useful either in targeting consumers or in creating advertising:

> I've used both syndicated and custom psychographics in the past, but try to avoid using them today because of extremely disappointing results.

In order to explore these problems further, we examined and content-analyzed for thematic content the texts of the open-ended responses. The following themes emerged:

1. For some respondents, there was confusion as to what psychographics even mean or are. For example, one respondent asked:

> What do you mean by "psychographics"? This term is ill-defined and can be interpreted in a number of ways.

Another respondent interpreted them in a broad ranging way from:

> Quantitative research—it ranges from "sociological studies" (e.g., examining the garbage of luxury car owners to focus groups).

2. The segments obtained from the research have nothing to do with the category being advertised. This seemed to be a problem with general and syndicated psychographics and reflected the competition between syndicated and customized psychographics discussed above. One respondent who found psychographics to be not very useful either for creating copy or targeting the consumer noted:

> General psychographics don't take into account that the same person may have a very different mindset when buying different categories of product.

3. Psychographics are ineffective with respect to the media as three respondents noted and the segments they provide are hard to reach efficiently through the media. As one respondent noted who found psychographics only somewhat useful in general:

> However, for the most part, [psychographics are] difficult to translate to actual media selections.

4. Although psychographics are seen as more helpful to creatives than others in providing with them with what one respondent describes as "psychological proximity" between the advertiser and the target consumer, even for them, psychographics may only play a small part. As the research head for one agency put it:

> [Their] most effective use is to help creatives better understand target market segments. To feel their needs and desires. It is only a small part of their learning process, however.

Moreover, creatives may have problems making use and sense of psychographics. As the research head of one agency states in pointedly criticizing psychographics:

> You can tell when an ad has been written for a psychographic target, because it doesn't seem to be talking to a living, breathing person.

This latter criticism is particularly intriguing in light of the fact that psychographics are often said to be the very thing that brings the consumer alive to creatives, as noted earlier.

5. Different situational or role factors may intervene. As one respondent notes:

> For example, a consumer may be a "belonger" when buying beer and an "experiential" when buying ice cream, etc.

6. Psychographics may be useful for small numbers of consumers but too restrictive for larger markets. One survey respondent stated:

> Our attitude toward psychographics is simple when dealing with a mass market or packaged goods product. Psychographics is too limiting. It becomes restrictive by its very definition. We need to target large numbers not small groups. It is most effective when your target is small, clearly defined, and somewhat isolated in terms of type of used base.

7. Psychographics are wasteful and simply restate what should be obvious from the demographics. One respondent cited a major syndicated service in this regard and noted:

> Psychographics often simply restate (in an unnecessarily complicated and expensive way) what should be obvious from demographics.

8. Other consumer response measures are more useful. For example, the research head of one agency noted that:

> Selective perception is the most important force in message delivery.

DISCUSSION AND IMPLICATIONS

The results of this study serve to mirror to advertising agency research directors a sample of views across their profession. They indicate, at least in the eyes of many of them, that psychographics have for the most part a limited utility, although there are individual differences in that assessment. Framing our results in terms of knowledge use while acknowledging the limitations of this study in terms of its provisional character and limited sample and response rate (those who did not respond to the survey might differ from those who did although we were unable to detect any systematic difference), we nonetheless can reach two conclusions of note: First, some people such as creatives may be more positive about psychographic use, but even they have some problems with them and perhaps as often as not tend to rely on their own intuitive insights. Second, psychographics seem to be more knowledge-enhancing than action-oriented, thus resulting in low affectivity in terms of overall satisfaction for those advertising agency people who use them.

At this time, I offer some suggestions for future research, based on the respondents' statements, which can help to determine whether psychographics can provide greater utility or not in terms of advertising effectiveness.

1. One respondent cited simple attitudinal measures related to a product's purchase as being helpful and another cited selective perception. Future research might examine what sorts of attitude measures are seen as most useful to advertising people.

2. The idea of situational psychographics (i.e., people engage in different lifestyle roles as suggested by one respondent) suggests some directions in situational and role-playing that might be pursued.

3. In relation to the first two points, we might investigate the relative effectiveness of other measures of describing a market target, its response to advertising, and its product purchase and use behavior. Examining these might lead to psychographics that are more product category specific and therefore potentially useful to advertisers.

4. Psychographic research might also be improved by the use of interpretive methodologies in two possible ways: (a) applying various quantitative psychographic and value measures and then doing in-depth interviewing and observation (e.g., ethnographic, phenomenological, open-ended questions) to see how the measures play out in ways meaningful to researchers, if at all (Gould, 1991; Lastovicka et al., 1990), and (b) developing ways to assess values and psychographics on a totally interpretive basis (Gould, 1991).

5. We might explore the uses of demographics in the same terms as explored here and also in terms of their relationships with other consumer profile measures including psychographics and behavioral data.

6. With knowledge use frameworks in mind, we might explore why some research directors were more satisfied with psychographics than others. For instance, might it be organizational culture (Menon & Varadarajan, 1992), organizational structure (Deshpande, 1982; Deshpande & Zaltman, 1982; John & Martin, 1984; Menon & Varadarajan, 1992), or better research methodology that causes these individual differences? Do researchers attitudes toward psychographics change and evolve over time based on their career position and/or experience with psychographics and other forms of advertising and consumer research? Do different research styles possibly account for these differences (cf. Hirschman, 1985)? Can we form a model of research styles and agency research cultures that are analogous to creative styles and cultures in agencies (e.g., hard vs. soft-sell creative styles; Wells, Burnett, & Moriarty, 1992).

7. We need also to account for the different views of various participants in the psychographic use/research process. In this regard, future studies should be made of the attitudes toward psychographics of others concerned (e.g., creatives, account people, the advertiser), because their different aims and career experiences and trajectories might produce somewhat different views and perspectives (Hirschman, 1989; Perkins & Rao, 1990). Thus, we might also look at the relationship between researchers and users of research to see how trust and other factors enter into the various parties' attitudes toward psychographic data (Moorman, Deshpande, & Zaltman, 1993). Agency relationship theory which considers the effects of one party (i.e., the advertising agency creative; the advertising agency; the advertiser) in depending on another (i.e., the advertising agency research director; the outside research vendor; the advertising agency, respectively) should also be explored as a tool for assessing the perceived effectiveness of psychographics across interested and relevant parties (Bergen, Dutta, & Walker, 1992).

8. Closely related to the fifth and sixth points, we need to investigate the research and research use processes themselves to see how research is created, used, marketed internally by agency people and externally by market research vendors to agencies. Qualitative methodologies, such as case studies and in-depth interviewing would be of particular interest here, since we are interested in developing detailed models and insights into the nature of the process.

9. Finally, as the focus of this chapter has been on researchers and their relationships with consumers and others, we might consider some exercises (Gould, 1993, 1995) that can sharpen our understanding of those relationships. By analogy to the countertransference in psychoanalysis where analysts investigate their own feelings toward their clients in order to better understand them, researchers can include their own feelings toward the consumers they are profiling. Wansink (chap. 9, this volume) suggests an excellent visualization technique in which the researcher is to recall or visualize an ideal or model consumer and describe him or her in abundant and "recognizable" detail. Within this exercise, the researcher might also include his or her feelings toward that consumer (e.g., "I (dis)like this consumer"; "I feel this consumer and I could be friends who enjoy some of the same things"). Such exercises as Wansink demonstrates might help to improve the validity and usefulness of psychographic research.

Another set of exercises could involve researchers looking at their feelings about creatives, as well as creatives about researchers (e.g., "When I present creatives with this research they are (un)grateful) and (un)interested"). These feelings can be explored in depth to see how psychographic research functions in facilitating the creative process, if at all. Our research reported here indicates a breakdown in this process that such exercises might shed light on.

CONCLUSION

Our results although very tentative and exploratory, nonetheless raise some very grave concerns about the perceived usefulness of psychographics. Thus, all future research suggested here is based on the perceived problematic nature of psychographic use as it presently stands. Indeed, the very idea of focusing this year's Advertising & Consumer Psychology Conference on "Values, Lifestyles, and Psychographics" implies that we need to know a great deal more about them. In many respects, psychographic research could use some of the suggestions made by Wells (1993), especially his idea of investigating a small area and trying to stay within the bounds of the real. Replication and longitudinal investigations might prove to be particularly useful in this regard but only if the measures are valid to begin with. Thus, future research should not so much attempt to resurrect current psychographics or their use patterns if they offer so little as our survey respondents indicate, but instead, should focus on new avenues of use and new more "market-valid" measures of psychographics that can be useful, effective, and valuable.

REFERENCES

Bergen, M., Dutta, S., & Walker, O. C., Jr. (1992). Agency relationships in marketing: A review of the implications and applications of agency and related theories. *Journal of Marketing, 56*, 1–24.

Deshpande, R. (1982). The organizational context of market research use. *Journal of Marketing, 46*, 91–101.

Deshpande, R., & Zaltman, G. (1982). Factors affecting the use of market research information: A path analysis. *Journal of Marketing Research, 19*, 14–31.

Deshpande, R., & Zaltman, G. (1984). A comparison of factors affecting researcher and manager perceptions of market research use. *Journal of Marketing Research, 21*, 32–38.

Deshpande, R., & Zaltman, G. (1987). A comparison of factors affecting use of marketing information in consumer and industrial firms. *Journal of Marketing Research, 24*, 114–118.

Gould, S. J. (1991). Jungian analysis and psychological types: An interpretive approach to consumer choice behavior. In R. H. Holman & M. R. Solomon (Eds.), *Advances in consumer research* (Vol. 18, pp. 743–748). Provo, UT: Association for Consumer Research.

Gould, S. J. (1993), Introspective versus extrospective perspectives in consumer research: A matter of focus. In R. Varadarajan & B. Jaworski (Eds.), *Marketing theory and applications* (Vol. 4, pp. 199–200). Chicago: American Marketing Association.

Gould, S. J. (1995), Researcher introspection as a method in consumer research: Applications, issues, and implications. *Journal of Consumer Research, 21*, 719–722.

Hirschman, E. C. (1985). Scientific style and the conduct of consumer research. *Journal of Consumer Research, 12*, 225–239.

Hirschman, E. C. (1989). Role-based models of advertising creation and production. *Journal of Advertising, 18*, 42–53.

Hunt, S. D., & Chonko, L. B. (1987). Ethical problems of advertising agency executives. *Journal of Advertising, 16*, 16–24.

John, G., & Martin, J. (1984). Effects of organizational structure of marketing planning on credibility and utilization of plan output. *Journal of Marketing Research, 21*, 170–183.

Kahle, L. R., Beatty, S. E., & Homer, P. (1986). Alternative measurement approaches to consumer values: The List of Values (LOV) and Values and Life Style (VALS). *Journal of Consumer Research, 13*, 405–409.

Kassarjian, H. H., & Sheffet, M. J. (1991). Personality and consumer behavior: An update. In H. H. Kassarjian & T. S. Robertson (Eds.), *Perspectives in consumer behavior* (3rd ed., pp. 281–303). Englewood Cliffs, NJ: Prentice-Hall.

Kinnear, T. C., & Taylor, J. R. (1976). Psychographics: Some selected findings. *Journal of Marketing Research, 19*, 422–425.

Kohli, A., & Jaworski, B. (1990). Market orientation: The construct, research propositions, and managerial implications. *Journal of Marketing, 54*, 1–18.

Lastovicka, J. L. (1982). On the validation of lifestyle traits: A review and illustration. *Journal of Marketing Research, 19*, 126–138.

Lastovicka, J. L., Murray, J. P., Jr., & Joachimsthaler, E. (1990). Evaluating the measurement validity of lifestyle typologies with qualitative measures and multiplicative factoring. *Journal of Marketing Research, 27*, 11–23.

Menon, A., & Vardarajan, P. R. (1992). A model of marketing knowledge use within firms. *Journal of Marketing, 56*, 53–71.

Moorman, C., Deshpande, R., & Zaltman, G. (1993). Factors affecting trust in market research relationships. *Journal of Marketing, 57*, 81–101.

Perkins, W. S., & Rao, R. C. (1990). The role of experience in information use and decision making by marketing managers. *Journal of Marketing Research, 27*, 1–10.

Wells, W. D. (1975). Psychographics: A critical review. *Journal of Marketing Research, 12*, 196–213.

Wells, W. D. (1993). Discovery-oriented consumer research. *Journal of Consumer Research, 19*, 489–504.

Wells, W. D., Burnett, J., & Moriarty, S. (1992). *Advertising: Principles and practice* (2nd ed.). Englewood Cliffs, NJ: Prentice-Hall.

APPENDIX

Survey

Please answer the following questions by checking the appropriate response:

1. About what percentage of your agency's advertising-related research involves psychographics in some direct way?

0-20.99%	21-40.99%	41-60.99%	61-80.99%	81-100%
________	________	________	________	________

2. How useful do you find psychographics in creating your advertising copy?

Not very useful	Somewhat useful	About as useful as not	Quite useful	Very useful
________	________	________	________	________

3. How useful do you find psychographics in targeting your consumer?

Not very useful	Somewhat useful	About as useful as not	Quite useful	Very useful
________	________	________	________	________

4. How much would you estimate your agency spends on psychographic research?
$____________

5. How much would you estimate your agency spends on all advertising research, including psychographics?
$____________

6. How beneficial would you say psychographics are relative to the cost of doing the research on them?

Extremely costly	Somewhat costly	Even in benefit/ cost	Somewhat beneficial	Extremely beneficial
________	________	________	________	________

7. How valid/credible would you say psychographic research is?

Extremely invalid	Somewhat invalid	About 50% valid	Somewhat valid	Extremely valid
________	________	________	________	________

8. What syndicated psychographics (e.g., VALS) and related services do you use if any?

1. ____________________
2. ____________________
3. ____________________
4. ____________________

9. The following questions are asked for classification purposes only:

A. What is your job title? ____________________

B. What is the approximate size of your agency in terms of billings?
$____________

10. Finally and perhaps most importantly for our understanding of psychographics in relation to advertising research and copy, we would like you to describe in your own words your experience with using psychographics. What do you find are their strengths and weaknesses? How has their use enhanced or not enhanced your agency's ability to deliver a strong creative message? Also you might discuss how you have measured the, how meaningful, valid, and credible you find these measures and their applications are, how you have used them, and what direction your agency might go in the future in using them. Finally, you might assess whether there are different attitudes within your agency regarding the use of psychographics. For instance, do researchers differ in their attitudes toward them from creatives?

You may take as many sheets of paper as you feel necessary to answer these questions. THANKS VERY MUCH FOR YOUR RESPONSE.

Chapter 12

Using Attitudinal Segmentation to Target the Consumer

Irma J. O'Connor
Bozell, Inc.

In recent years Bozell Advertising has conducted several large scale attitudinal segmentation studies for its clients. In an environment of shrinking research budgets, how did we convince clients to embark on such major research? By convincing them that such research would help target the right consumer with the right message with the right product. Advertisers need to target, and attitudinal segmentation *is* a targeted approach to marketing. No one would dispute that marketers have to concentrate on the people they really want to attract. Increasing population diversity, product proliferation, and media saturation require this more targeted approach to marketing.

This chapter offers a strong case for segmenting by attitudes by showing how important attitudes and emotions are in understanding one's customers and their relationship to one's brand. Since the Bozell data are proprietary, the fashion and apparel industry has been chosen for hypothetical illustrations throughout and for the hypothetical case study. I chose it because the apparel industry is an image-driven category where attitudes are so important but where little research is done.

HISTORICAL PERSPECTIVE

First, some historical perspective. Back in the 1950s there were two separate avenues of market research: one quantitative, represented by Alfred Politz and his polling studies, and the other motivational research, typified by Ernest Dichter. Dichter, from Austria, was reared in a Freudian atmosphere with emphasis on unconscious motivations. It may seem humorous now to think that baking a cake may be an unconscious metaphor for giving birth as Dichter maintained, but he was on the right track.

Some of our recent qualitative research on baking does indicate a wealth of emotions in the process of baking—feelings of control, being organized, feeling peaceful, loving, and loved when abundantly praised by family and friends for the baked goodies. So Dichter was right in probing below the conscious rational level. Importantly, using projective techniques was the process used by Dichter to obtain these unconscious motivations.

Then came the 1960s—the decade of benefit segmentation associated with Russ Haley. Segmenting consumers was done on rational product benefits, the assumption being that products and brands were differentiated by rational product benefits sought by different segments of consumers. The segments were then run by different psychographic measures such as lifestyle, activities, interest, values, and pen and pencil standardized personality inventories to describe the benefit segments psychographically. However, attitudes were not an integral part of the segmentation process itself.

After the 1960s came the 1970s, the decade of segmenting consumers on more abstract values and lifestyle factors. American adults were grouped solely by general personalty or value constructs. The original VALS, based on Maslow's needs hierarchy, was a typology of the American population defined by values and demos. Not tied to any product or brand behavior, VALS could measure value shifts and lifestyle changes over time. Furthermore, the Yankelovich Monitor began measuring social trends in the 1970s and segmenting Americans into groups based on the social trend data. PRIZM and other geographic segmentation systems came into existence as well during this decade.

By the end of the 1980s, however, VALS was considered by some to be simplistic and too general and theoretical to be applicable to consumer behavior (see Gates, 1989). VALS II was SRI's answer to these criticisms, but today there is a trend to return to some of the principles and methods of the 1950s and 1960s, as shown in Fig. 12.1:

> First, an emphasis on emotions and using projective techniques to uncover feelings not on the conscious rational level. Projective techniques are used today, not to uncover the unconscious as Dichter did in the 1950s with his emphasis on Freudian principles, but to delve below the surface to the layer between the conscious and unconscious—the subconscious. Many agencies today have developed techniques to uncover the subconscious feelings and emotions that drive category use, brand choice, and brand loyalty.
>
> Second, the need to segment on product-related needs and desires. Today there is a return to a focus on attitudes toward the category and brand rather than more general abstract attitudes, lifestyles, and values.

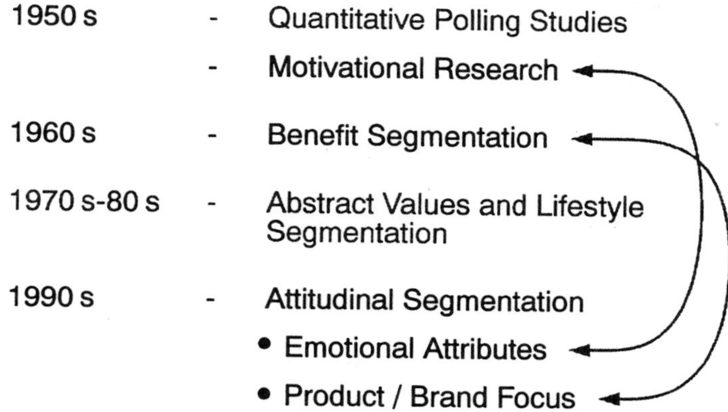

FIG. 12.1. Historical perspective.

REQUISITES FOR ATTITUDINAL SEGMENTATION

Attitudes Anchored to Specific/Category Brand

To conduct an attitudinal segmentation study, one must first uncover the emotions and attitudes operating in category use and brand selection. An extensive series of one-on-one, in-depth interviews using projective techniques—pictures, words, stories—can be used to generate a rich array of emotions and attitudes. Importantly, these attitudes are expressed *within* the context of the particular category/brand being discussed in the interview. If a woman says she feels confident when she wears a particular outfit or a certain piece of lingerie, it doesn't mean she necessarily feels confident in all other aspects of her life choices. The point is that the confidence engendered by particular choices of clothing or lingerie may or may not be consistent with her general self-esteem overall as measured by a psychological test.

For this reason, attitudes must be anchored to a *specific* category and brand. The less abstract and more personal the data, the more relevant and discriminating is the segmentation, and the more powerful and motivating is the resulting advertising strategy. There may be different emotions and needs for products within the same category. Would you not expect lingerie choices to express different emotional and rational needs than suit or dress choices? Even within the lingerie category, different pieces of lingerie may each involve different emotional and rational needs (see Fig. 12.2).

In sum, there may be underlying personality dimensions and values one lives by, but the more focused and specific the attitudes and emotions, the more powerful the analysis, and the more targeted is the message.

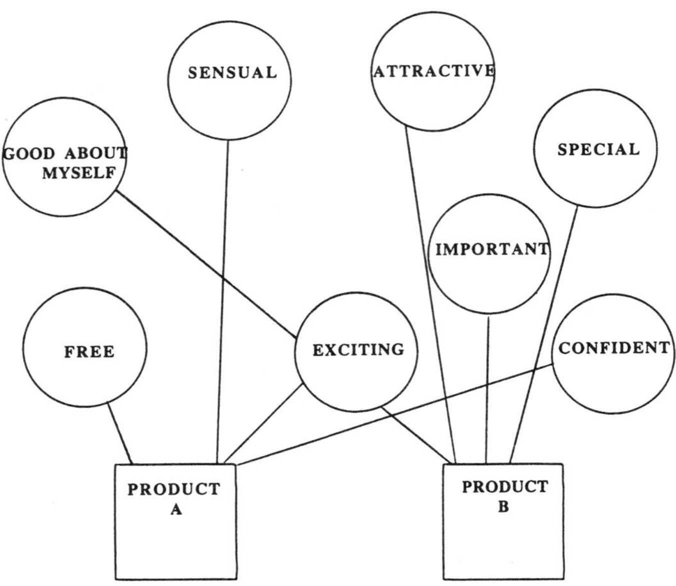

FIG. 12.2. Attitudes are anchored to a specific category and brand.

The Emotional Components of Brand Image

These qualitative data are then used to develop the quantitative questionnaire. In the quantitative study, respondents are asked to rate the importance of 80+ product and emotional attributes generated by the qualitative research.

Brand images of many brands are measured by the same list. By rating the brands on the emotional as well as the rational attributes, a measure of emotional interaction may be constructed between the brand and the respondent—a concept discussed by Blackston (1962) in the *Journal of Advertising Research* to further refine brand image. The article suggested that we ask not only what you think of the brand but what you think the brand thinks of you. If a consumer, for example, rates a brand high on status and quality but believes that the brand does not find her worthy of that status, then she won't feel good about the brand and won't feel that she belongs (e.g., see Fig. 12.3).

The key concept is emotional interaction between the brand/product and the consumer—the relationship between them. Consumers are not blank slates. Everything must relate back to the consumer's interpretation. For example, specific feelings might influence one's particular choice of lingerie to wear for a special occasion. The story doesn't end there, however. The lingerie, in turn, influences how one feels about oneself during the occasion and the wearing of the lingerie.

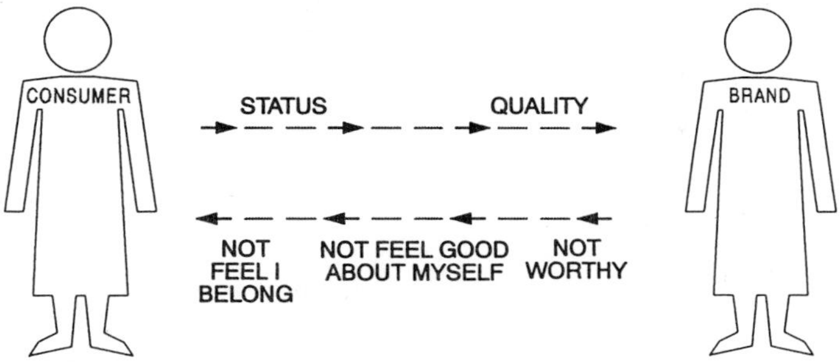

FIG. 12.3. The relationship between status and quality.

User Versus Nonuser Imagery

Brand image is also measured in our studies by user imagery, but with an additional twist—a user versus nonuser comparison. The respondent's self-image is compared with her image of the "other group" (i.e., user rating a non user or vice versa). This is a dynamic and discriminating indicator of how one really feels about the brand and its users and nonusers. This technique is better than self-description alone, which is seldom very illuminating.

From a study conducted by Bozell, note how nonusers of a particular product perceive themselves to be much more fun-loving, caring, bright, and energetic than they perceive users to be. These data dramatically illustrate nonusers' brand image of that product and its users (see Table 12.1).

Other Important Elements

Another important element in the quantitative study is information that can provide guidance to future product/service development, gleaned from both the attribute list of product benefits and from fairly specific questions about needs and product preferences in the category. For ex-

TABLE 12.1
Perception Gaps

		Nonusers' Perception of	
	Self %	*Users* %	*Difference* %
Fun-loving	67	25	-42
Caring	78	56	-22
Bright	51	22	-29
Independent	61	28	-33
Feel good about myself	60	35	-25
Active, Energetic	51	20	-31

ample, pictures could be shown of different apparel styles and fashions, to obtain preferences and likes and dislikes.

Other areas of inquiry are those typically included: activities, usage occasions, interests, media data, and, of course, marketing data on brand and category use and awareness, and so on. It would be useless to segment a national sample and not know which segment represented your current strongest franchise.

The sample should be a national probability sample, with a few broad parameters relevant to the category such as 18 to 60 or earning $20,000+. Only with a national probability sample can one get a total view of the marketplace. If one studies only users, one will never know the potential of different nonuser segments or totally understand why users use one's product.

WHY SEGMENT BY ATTITUDES

Is Demographics Enough?

Now let's address the question: *Why segment by attitudes?* An important question. Demographics are often the primary determinant of targeting. But demographics don't tell the whole story: Even day-old babies can be segmented by their personality differences.

Of course, demographics—or the more current concept of life stages—are important. Teens, for example, differ from adults in life situation and needs. Note in Table 12.2 how the emotional needs of teens differ from adults. However, *within* each age group there are certainly attitudinal differences that are major determinants of category and brand use.

An *American Demographics* article by Wolfe (1992) argued that older consumers should not be segmented attitudinally because each older consumer is a "segment of one." The author described the older consumer

TABLE 12.2
Emotional Needs of Teens

	Percentage Differences *Teens - Adult*
Get noticecd	+29
Look good in frontof friends	+26
Feel I belong	+19
Feel I have good taste	+26

as becoming more highly "individuated," that is, less egocentric and materialistic and more motivated by inner values. However, segments reflecting similar attitudes toward fashion most certainly will include older as well as younger women in each. To deny that is to have an underlying, rather antiquated bias of what aging means in contemporary life.

Product Benefits No Longer Discriminate

But there's even more to the argument of why segment by attitudes. Broader manufacturing expertise has resulted in a proliferation of products competing for the same dollar and many of these products are indistinguishable from one another. Products can no longer be sold on product features and innovation; they must differentiate themselves by tapping into the emotional needs and benefits people are looking for. One research study by an advertising agency determined that consumers were more likely to find brand differences in categories that rely on emotional appeals rather than rational (see Biel, 1992).

Consumers Seek Products to Fulfill Emotional Needs

On the other side of the communication equation, consumers are also changing. They are becoming more sophisticated, educated, and self-reliant. Consumers no longer respond to mass market appeals; they have more individual tastes and they are searching for a more individual style. When faced with similar products, they may choose the brand toward which they feel emotional bonds and which fulfills their emotional needs (see Piirto, 1991).

Of course, attitudinal segmentation is more relevant for some categories than others; for example, in image categories compared to low-involvement packaged goods categories which are more rational. Image categories include those not only where brand image is a determining factor of purchase but also where a person is more emotionally involved in the purchase. The more one's ego plays a part, the more intense is that emotional involvement.

A CASE STUDY: THE APPAREL INDUSTRY

To show how attitudinal segmentation is used in targeting, I describe a hypothetical case study in fashion and apparel—an image industry that does not rely on research. Research often means tracking what sells and what doesn't. Many reasons are volunteered by the trade for this absence of research in the apparel industry:

- Apparel trends change too fast, say some.

- Others say "we lead," we do not follow fashion. When you lead fashion, you can't research where you are going. People can't tell you what they don't know.
- And yet others say: We focus on aspirations, not on people "just like me." Aspirations reflect ideal standards of beauty and researchers cannot define this ideal beauty. Apparel manufacturers may believe they are the best judges of what women aspire to.
- Lastly, some designers feel that research will inhibit their creativity.

To quote from a 1993 interview with the CEO of a major apparel company: "using focus groups . . . borders on revolutionary in apparel where fashion prima donnas traditionally make million dollar decisions on divine guidance ego and instinct" (see Underwood, 1993).

The following case study focuses on this image-driven apparel industry. Let's imagine the company is a small but successful business in accessories and in lingerie, including sleepwear. Their primary distribution is to department stores but they have also opened up their own shops in a few upscale malls in large urban areas. Their prices are high end, and they have always thought of their target as upscale professional women. Now they want to enter the women's apparel business, and decide to do a national attitudinal segmentation study to evaluate their opportunities and guide their targeting decisions.

The Segments

The study shown in Fig. 12.4 results in 6 segments. The first three seek emotional fulfillment in the clothes they choose to buy and wear.

The Status Seeker. This woman buys well-known brands, most of which she has bought before. She buys good quality clothing that is classic, plain, and simple in its style. She wants something pretty. Buying brand names is not only a way for her to reward herself, but it also gives her confidence in her choices. She chooses brands and clothing that help her feel special and that she belongs. As such, she is into designer and other recognizable logos.

Demographically, she is in her mid to late 30s and 40s. She is married and is more likely than other groups to be a homemaker. Her household income is about $50,000. Her activities include: housework/yardwork, gourmet cooking, entertaining guests, and playing tennis. Her fabric preferences are soft, natural/synthetic blends. She prefers conservative colors. She shops in department stores and designer outlet stores (see Fig. 12.5).

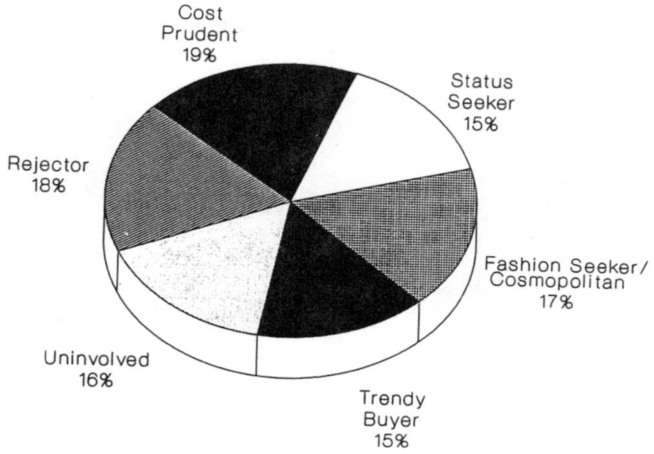

FIG. 12.4. The attitude segments.

The Cosmopolitan Fashion Seeker. The Cosmopolitan Fashion seeker is more striking in her appearance (see Fig. 12.6). She wears expensive clothes which are both stylish and elegant and enhance her attractive figure. She is proud of her body and wants to show it off in her clothes. She buys what looks good and doesn't need the reassurance of a brand name. She gets noticed for her style. The Cosmopolitan Fashion woman wants clothes that help her feel elegant and sophisticated, as well as feminine. She loves to get dressed up for special occasions, being outgoing and self-expressive. She uses clothes to her advantage.

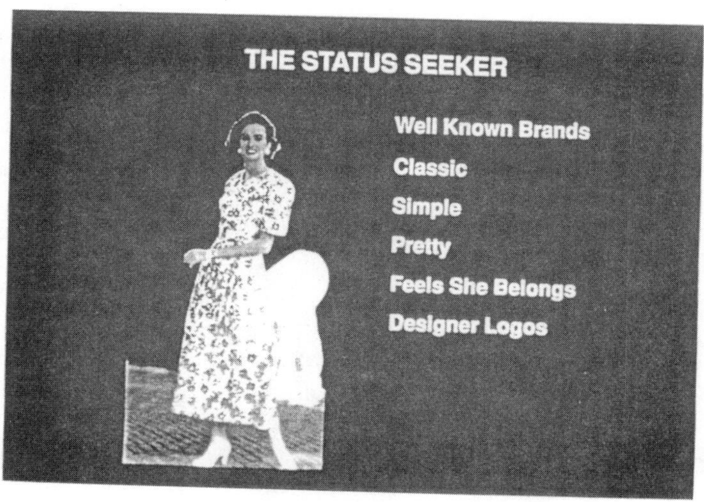

FIG. 12.5. The status seeker.

FIG. 12.6. The cosmopolitan status seeker.

She is in her mid 30s; she is a married, college graduate with a white collar job and a household income of $60,000. She is very social: She attends cultural events, goes to formal dinner parties, travels, and exercises for her health. Looks are more important than fabrics, brand, cost, being machine washable, or any other practical reason. She shops in women's specialty and department stores.

The Trendy Buyer. The last group seeking emotional fulfillment and gratification from clothes is the Trendy Buyer. This woman is very self-involved and seems to be constantly aware of how she feels and looks. She puts a lot of time and effort into shopping and choosing clothes (see Fig. 12.7).

The Trendy Buyer wears apparel that is stylish and cutting edge—showing off her body and clothes and getting noticed. She wants her clothes to fit closely and hug her body. She buys by brand and wants something her man would like. The Trendy woman wants clothes that help her feel sexy, outgoing, active, and help her express herself and feel good about herself. Clothes are an important part of her self-image. She wants stylish colors as well as young, bright, vibrant colors. The Trendy woman is young, in her late 20s and early 30s, and single. She is employed with a household income of at least $30,000. Activities focus on appearance, either working to enhance it (exercising for physical fitness, dieting, sunbathing, shopping), or for socializing (dancing, parties, vacations). She shops in department stores.

The next three groups seek less emotional fulfillment through their clothes because they are unconcerned and not too interested in clothes

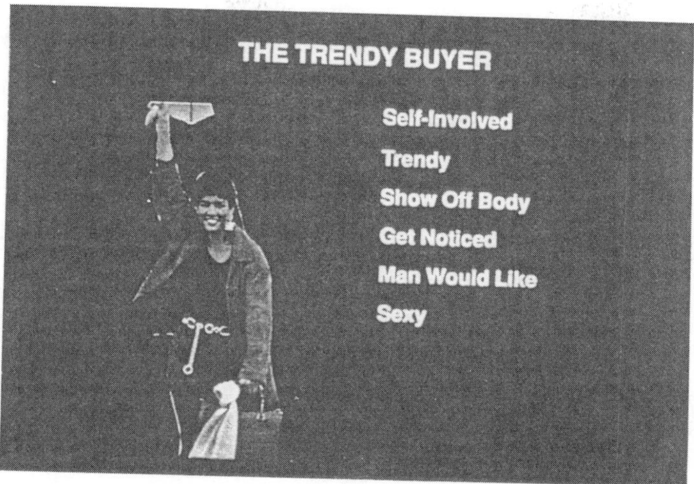

FIG. 12.7. The trendy buyer.

and/or they are not as involved with looks and feelings and how clothes can influence how one feels.

The Uninvolved. The Uninvolved also purchases quality clothing as does the Status Seeker, but she is looking for a good value—not because she can't afford what she wants, but because she wants to get the most for her money. She buys relatively plain casual clothing, that fits well, and is easy to care for. She is very practical in her choice of clothes and doesn't understand why others feel that clothes are so important. She says proudly that her esteem comes from within and from relationships with her family. She feels that clothes should not influence how others react to her, and she is very casual in her attitude toward clothes.

She is a well-educated, busy woman who is confident in her life choices. Demographically, she is in her late 30s, well-educated, and married with kids. She works part-time and has a household income of $50,000+. Her activities tend to focus around her family and community: PTA, school meetings, volunteer work, BBQ's, and informal parties. Athletics are important to her. For hobbies she reads, gardens, and plays a musical instrument. She shops in J.C.-Penney and Sears. Brand and fashion are relatively not important to her (see Fig. 12.8).

The Rejector. The Rejector is more than disinterested: She almost rejects style, only looking for loose-fitting clothing that she doesn't have to tuck in to hide her figure flaws and to feel comfortable. She buys clothes that are machine washable.

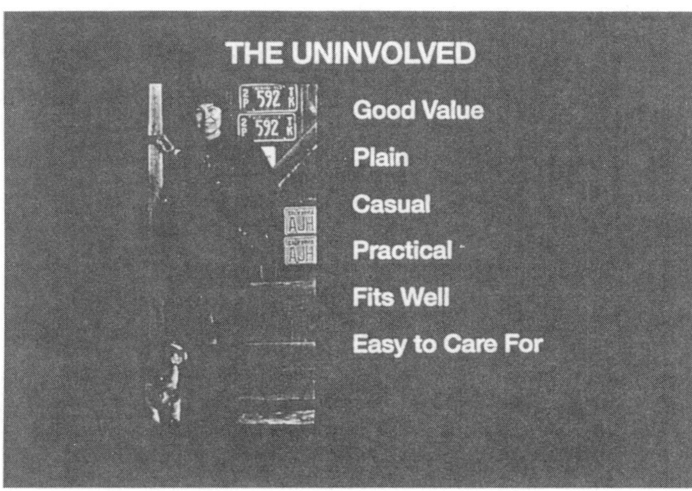

FIG. 12.8. The uninvolved.

The Rejector tends to be a little older, late 30s and married. She is high school educated and has a household income of under $40,000. She does housework, runs errands, visits family and friends, watches TV at home, and participates in community groups such as church. She shops in factory outlets, K Mart, and WalMart (see Fig. 12.9).

The Cost Prudent. Value to the Cost Prudent is determined solely by cost. Unlike the Uninvolved, she does not have a great deal of discretionary income and does not want to spend her money on clothes. She'll buy on sale but not especially to get good value but to buy something inexpensive. She also looks for items that are machine washable and won't shrink.

Demographically, she is in her late 20s/early 30s and married. She has a high school education and a household income of under $35,000. Her activities are casual: entertaining family and friends, renting videos, going to the beach, playing the lottery. She loves to travel. She also shops in K Mart and WalMart and looks for bargains in women's specialty shops (see Fig. 12.10).

Targeting With Attitudinal Segmentation

The Analysis. How do we use these attitudinal segments to target? We segment to:

- Identify and describe the target group.
- Develop a targeted advertising strategy. Creatives then know to whom to direct their words and images and which messages most likely will appeal in order to persuade and interest consumers to act.

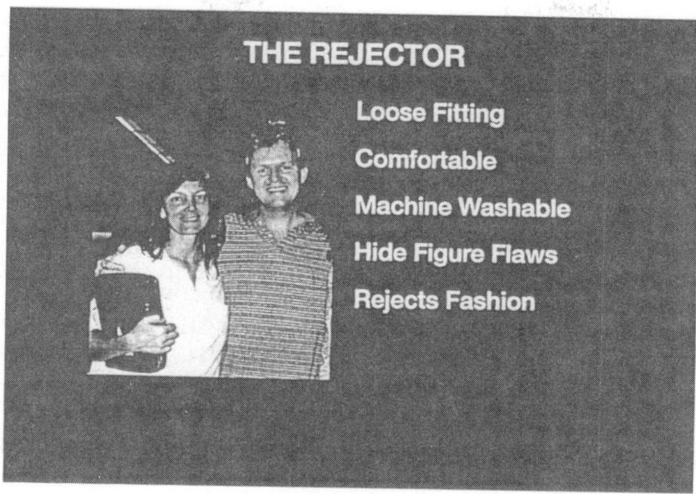

FIG. 12.9. The rejector.

- Target new product/service development. Once you know your consumers and their preferences and tastes, you'll have some good ideas about what to develop for them.

With these three objectives in mind, let's return to the hypothetical case study. Whom should the company target and what should the advertising strategy be to communicate with that target. Here are some questions, among many, the analyst and the company must ask: Who is the current

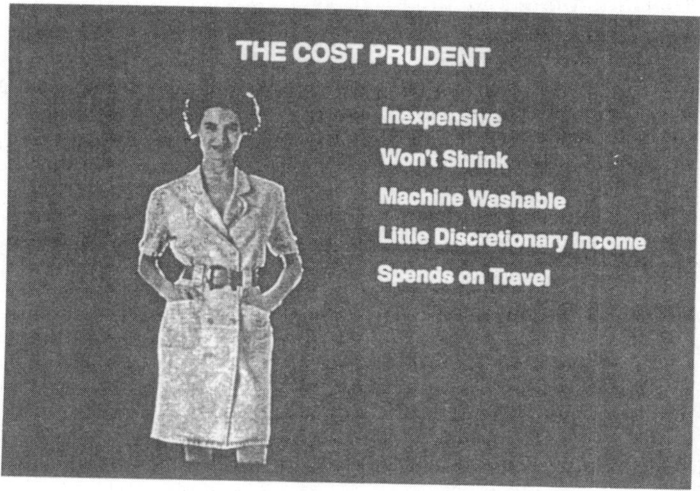

FIG. 12.10. The cost prudent.

customer? What segment fits best with the company's current image? What segment has the most potential in size, frequency of purchase, and emotional involvement in the category? What brands comprise the competitive set—are some segments totally loyal to one brand? Where do they shop? One must understand the reasons why each segment does or does not use the category/brand. The target group identified may be your current franchise or it may be a prospective target group for future marketing efforts. The variables are many, and all the data must be synthesized, analyzed, and agonized over to make the right decision. There is no one right way to proceed because everyone's marketing situation is different.

Choosing the Target Group. The company decides to target the Cosmopolitan Fashion Seeker for its new apparel line. Although many factors and a thorough understanding of the data will influence this decision, the following are illustrations of possible important factors in the choice:

1. Because this group does not depend on the security of choosing apparel by brand or designer name, they will try new brands of clothing that appeal to them.
2. The Cosmopolitan Fashion Seeker is very committed to buying and wearing clothes that fit her needs. As such, she is willing to spend both time and money. These women spend more money on clothing than any other segment and are the most frequent shoppers of apparel.
3. The Cosmopolitan Fashion Seekers are heavily involved in the category and have many emotional needs which are met by their apparel choices. They buy clothes that are stylish, elegant, and sophisticated and that show off and enhance their figures.
4. The company's current image from its lingerie and accessories lines is compatible with the emotional and product benefits sought by this segment. The upscale lifestyle and demographics of this segment coincide with the demographics of the company's current customers. This segment is more aware of the company than other segments and is more likely to have purchased the company's products.
5. These women shop more than other segments in department and specialty stores, which fit the lines of distribution available to the company through its current products.

The Creative Strategy. The recommended creative strategy expressed as the single most important consumer benefit to be communicated by the advertising is: *Wear this company's clothes to enhance and show off your body to look your most elegant and sophisticated best.*

To support this creative strategy, the research can offer many suggestions for tone, setting, etc. For example, the Cosmopolitan Fashion Seeker loves to get dressed up for special occasions, such as cultural events and dinner parties. She is very social and outgoing, and one might consider showing a social event with friends and family.

Targeting the Product. New product development should support the elegant and sophisticated positioning with fashionable clothes in stylish colors and prints that look elegant and sophisticated. The clothes should be youthful and look up to date but not especially trendy. One should keep in mind that "showing off her body" is an important benefit to this group. Materials might be soft and silky but not at the expense of projecting elegance and sophistication. The study can offer more specific fashion guidelines on fabrics, colors, styles, and so on.

Targeting the Media. Until now we've targeted the segment, the advertising message, and new product development. How about targeting media, which some might call a limitation of attitudinal segmentation. For apparel, media targeting is easier than many industries because print is the primary media vehicle. More targeted niche advertising can be accomplished in print advertising than in broadcast. Women's magazines are grouped by editorial content and environment—such as fashion, high fashion, women's lifestyle, or women's service magazines. The editorial "correctness" is emphasized not only because it reaches the correct target group but also because of compatibility with the creative, acceptance by the trade, and competitive presence. Further, we will have included some media questions in the custom study to provide further guidance.

Using syndicated data such as that provided by Simmons and MRI, a "surrogate measure" for the Cosmopolitan Fashion segment could be defined. This surrogate measure would include about 25+ variables such as product data and demographics, plus many indicators of the group's psychographics. In sum, this surrogate measure, data from the custom study, and knowing the editorial content and environment would all guide media selection.

In our actual experience with other image-driven categories, emotional attributes are generally more discriminating predictors of segment and brand image than are rational benefits, which are often the price of entry. Quality, for example, the important word for the 1990s, is often very important, but is also the price of entry in the category.

CONCLUSION

This chapter has argued for using attitudinal segmentation to define one's advertising message in image-driven categories. The essential components of an attitudinal segmentation study have been identified, stressing the importance of understanding the relevant attitudes and emotions operating in the category. The need to anchor these emotional benefits to specific product categories and brands was discussed. Further, measuring user brand imagery through users rating nonusers and vice versa was presented. Finally, using the apparel industry as a hypothetical case study, six attitudinal segments were defined and analyzed to illustrate the process of effectively targeting the right group with the right message and with the right product using attitudinal segmentation.

REFERENCES

Biel, A. L. (1992, November/December). How brand image drives brand equity. *Journal of Advertising Research.*

Blackston, M. (1982, May/June). Observations: Building brand equity by managing the brand's relationships. *Journal of Advertising Research,* 78–83.

Gates, M. (1989, June). VALS changes with the times. *Incentive,* 27–30.

Piirto, R. (1991). *Beyond mind games: The marketing power of psychographics.* American Demographics Press.

Underwood, E. (1993, February 8). A high-tech marketer in disguise. *Brandweek,* 14–17.

Wolfe, D. B. (1992, September). Business mid-life. *American Demographics,* 40–44.

Woods, R. (1993, February 2). Why has advertising gone blank? *Brandweek,* 14–17.

Part III

SOCIAL TRENDS

Chapter **13**

Gender Role Changes in the United States

Patricia Cafferata
Young and Rubicam

Martin I. Horn
DDB Needham

William D. Wells
University of Minnesota

On June 18, 1983, Sally Ride became the first woman to fly on a U.S. "manned" space mission. Almost exactly 10 years later, Les Aspin, the Secretary of Defense, gave women the green light to fly combat missions. A double-edged achievement, to be sure!

On the ground, "women's" jobs are slowly being infiltrated by members of the opposite sex. Male secretaries' share-of-occupation increased 11% between 1972 and 1990. Male nurses' share-of-occupation more than doubled during that period of time (U.S. Department of Labor, 1991).

What is going on? Are gender differences disappearing, or are these stories isolated, minor, faddish examples of journalistic "hype?" Are gender roles transforming, or are male and female roles essentially unchanged?

This chapter reviews changes in gender-role attitudes and behaviors over the past 20 years. Its main source of trend information is the DDB Needham Life Style Study, an annual mail panel survey that has been conducted every year since 1975. The sample of 2,000 male and 2,000 female heads-of-household is matched to the U.S. population on age, income, and area of residence. Response rates have varied slightly from year to year, but have averaged around 80%.

The Life Style questionnaire contains more than 500 questions covering diverse activities, interests, attitudes and opinions, many of which pertain to gender roles. This chapter focuses on the gender-role responses that have changed the most—and, for contrast, on some gender-role responses that have not changed very much. Data from the U.S. Census and from other sources such as the Harris Poll and Mediamark Research also are provided as important cross-checks and to help fill in details not covered by Life Style.

WORK

Many of the significant gender role changes have taken place in the workplace. These changes have, in turn, affected attitudes and opinions about roles at home.

Despite occasional news stories to the contrary, gender role changes in the workplace seem to be going quite peacefully. Men and women are reshaping their thinking along similar lines. For instance, the belief that "The Women's Liberation Movement is a good thing" has been growing among both sexes at roughly the same rate (Fig. 13.1). Further, although it should be no surprise that fewer and fewer women are ready to agree that "a woman's place is in the home," it may not be entirely obvious that men's responses to that sentiment are changing almost as fast. In the most recent responses, males and females are nearly identical in their views (Fig. 13.2). It's a good thing that both sexes feel this way, because women are moving—albeit slowly—into jobs that have been traditional bastions of the male. For example, the proportion of females who are physicians doubled between 1970 and 1991. Law and accounting also show dramatic increases (U.S. Bureau of the Census, 1986, 1992). See Figs. 13.3, 13.4, 13.5, and 13.6.

A less known, but important, trend is educational composition of the labor force (Fig. 13.6). Figure 13.7 shows the percentage of women and men in the labor force who have at least 4 years of college within each of six age groups. Among workers 35 and over, more men have college degrees

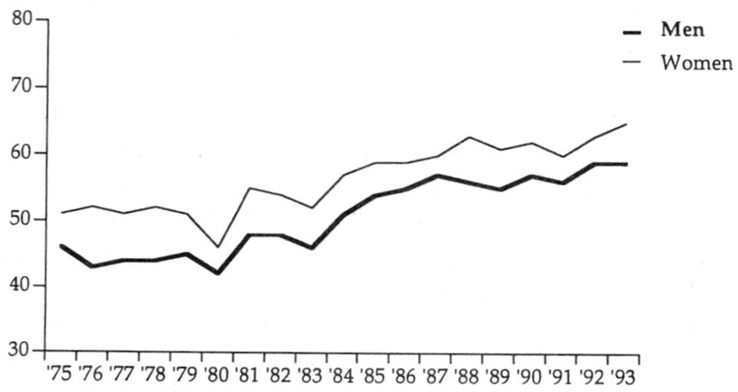

FIG. 13.1. "I think the women's liberation movement is a good thing." From DDB Needham Life Style Study (1993).

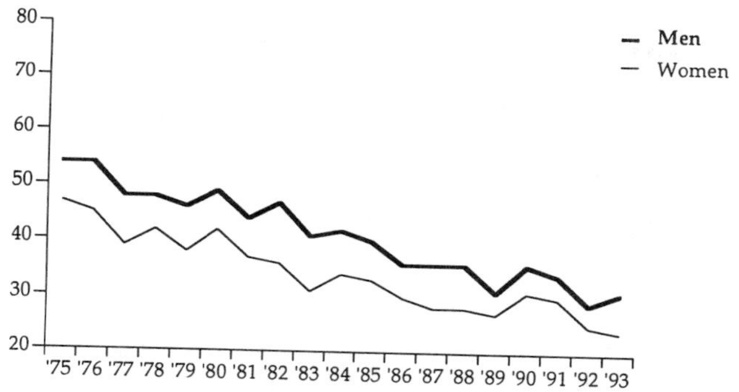

FIG. 13.2. "A woman's place is in the home." From DDB Needham Life Style Study (1993).

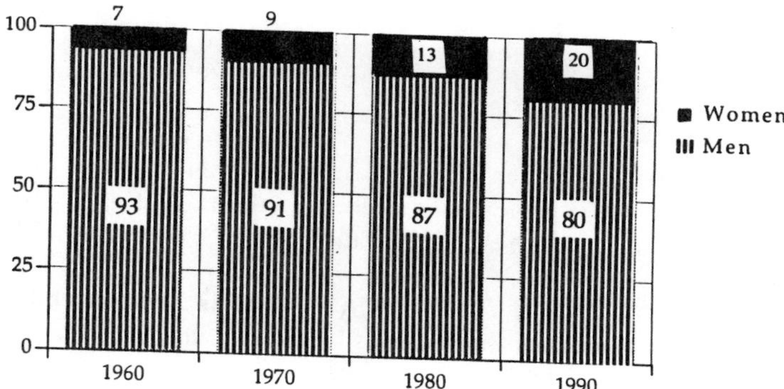

FIG. 13.3. "Physicians." From U.S. Bureau of the Census (1986). *Statistical Abstract of the United States* (106th ed., Table 677, pp. 400–401), and U.S. Bureau of the Census (1992). *Statistical Abstract of the United States* (112th ed., Table 629, pp. 392–394). Washington, DC: U.S. Government Printing Office.

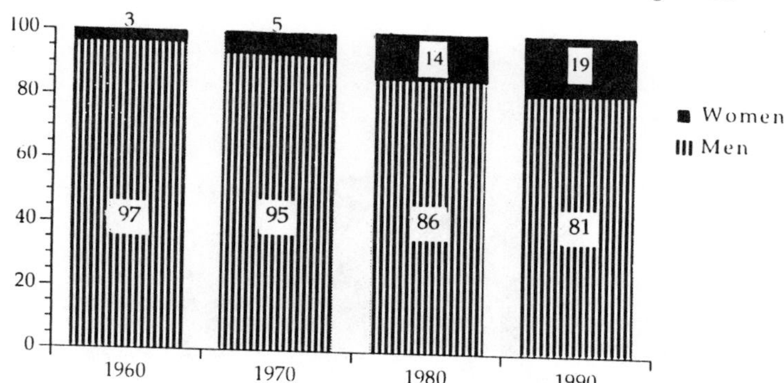

FIG. 13.4. "Lawyers." From U.S. Bureau of the Census (1986). *Statistical Abstract of the United States* (106th ed., Table 677, pp. 400–401), and U.S. Bureau of the Census (1992). *Statistical Abstract of the United States* (112th ed., Table 629, pp. 392–394). Washington, DC: U.S. Government Printing Office.

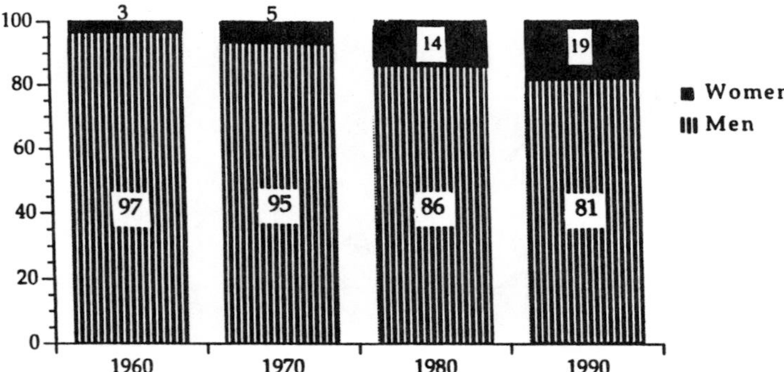

FIG. 13.5. "Accountants and auditors." From U.S. Bureau of the Census (1986). *Statistical Abstract of the United States* (106th ed., Table 677, pp. 400–401), and U.S. Bureau of the Census (1992). *Statistical Abstract of the United States* (112th ed., Table 629, pp. 392–394). Washington, DC: U.S. Government Printing Office.

than do women. However, among workers under the age of 35—those who will eventually replace older workers in the labor force—the opposite is true (U.S. Bureau of the Census, Educational Attainment in the United States, 1992).

Assuming that many of these women will remain in the workforce during their child-bearing years, this trend is likely to have profound effects. College education is now and always has been the entrée to higher professional and managerial rank. With more and more women in the work force, the steady increase in college-educated working women predicts that women will more often be someone's boss.

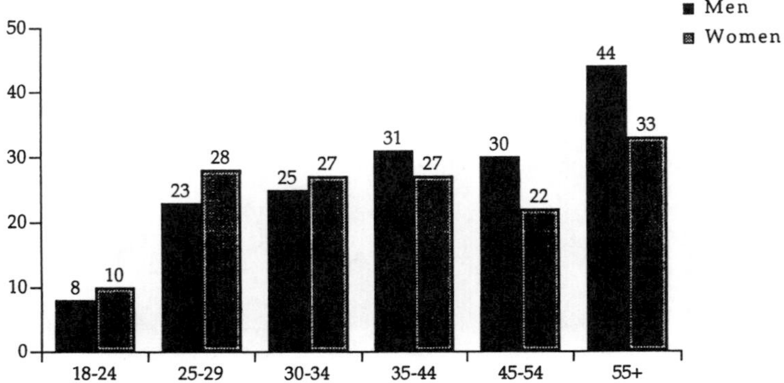

FIG. 13.6. "College educated workers." From U.S. Bureau of the Census, Current Population Reports (1992). *Educational Attainment in the United States: March 1991 and 1990* (Series P-20, #462, Table 6, p. 430).

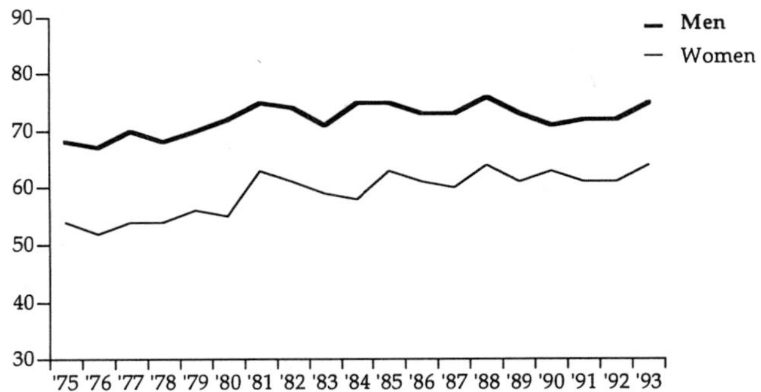

FIG. 13.7. "I like to be considered a leader." From DDB Needham Life Style Study (1993).

How do people feel about an increased leadership role for females? The most recent Life Style survey shows that nearly 2 out of 3 women (compared with 3 out of 4 men) agree that they "like to be considered a leader"—the highest level of agreement among women we have seen on this item (Fig. 13.7). As would be expected, this response is considerably higher among women who work outside the home than it is among full-time homemakers, 68% versus 54%, respectively. On the other hand, 43% of men assert that "men are naturally better leaders than women" (Fig. 13.8). In our view, that's not too bad; it means that the majority of men dismiss this outdated and inaccurate idea. Nevertheless, only 17% of women hold this view—so there is still a fairly large schism between the sexes even today.

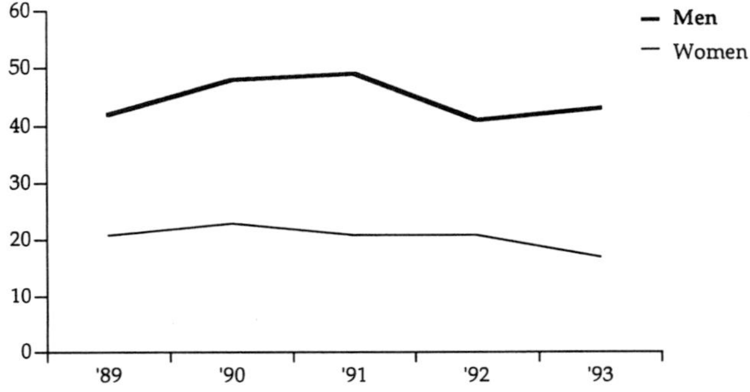

FIG. 13.8. "Men are naturally better leaders than women." From DDB Needham Life Style Study (1993).

How about having a female boss? The Life Style data suggest that men are coming to grips, while women are much more comfortable—though not entirely—with the idea (Fig. 13.9).

Although the item, "I wouldn't want my next boss to be a women," has not been tracked as long as many of the other Life Style items, the most recent data suggest a converging trend. In the 1993 survey, only 37% of men and 25% of women have an aversion to a female boss. It is interesting to ask: Which is more indicative—the finding that only 37% of men say they wouldn't want a female boss, or the finding that as many as 25% of women say the same thing?

Before leaving the workplace, it is important to emphasize that women are still a long way from taking over the managerial ranks. According to Mediamark Research, only 16% of "management"—individuals who hold senior rank in a company and earn at least $35,000 a year—are women, a level roughly one-fifth that of men (Mediamark Research, 1992). And though, as mentioned earlier, the percentage of male secretaries increased 11 percentage points and the percentage of male nurses nearly doubled between 1972 and 1990, only 1% of secretaries and only 5½ percent of nurses are now males (U.S. Department of Labor, 1991). As everyone knows, secretaries and nurses are still a lot more likely to be women; doctors and lawyers are still a lot more likely to be men.

Despite the inroads women are making in the workplace, they do not earn as much as men (Fig. 13.10). The pay disparity is largely due to women dominating clerical, support, and lower-paying white- and blue-collar positions, while men dominate the higher white- and blue-collar ranks.

What if that pay disparity suddenly disappeared? What if women made as much as—or more than—men? What if a wife made more than her husband? What would people think? The Life Style data suggest that neither men nor women would be especially upset (Fig. 13.11). Insofar as survey

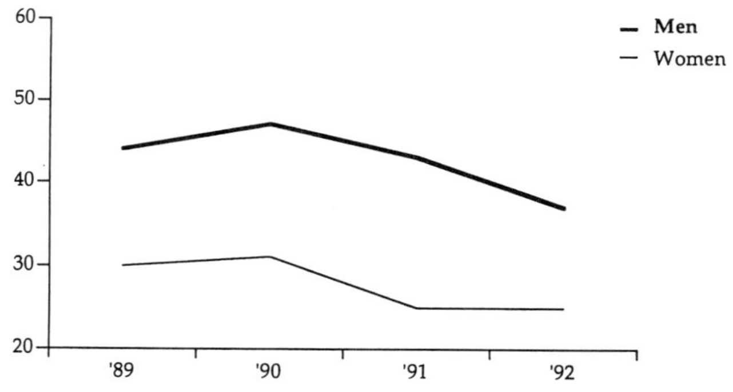

FIG. 13.9. "I wouldn't want my next boss to be a woman." From DDB Needham Life Style Study (1993).

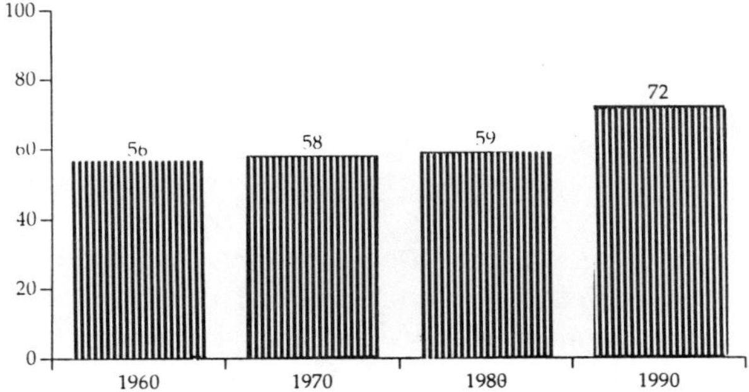

FIG. 13.10. "Full-time female workers pay as share of men's pay." From U.S. Department of Labor, Bureau of Labor Statistics (August 1991, Bulletin 2385). *Working Women: A Chartbook,* p. 21.

responses can predict, attitudes about men's traditional breadwinner role do not seem unbreakable.

Before going on, let's take stock. Thus far we have seen that the workplace is undergoing changes, and those changes are important. However, change is exceedingly slow. The powerful female CEO and the efficient, dutiful male secretary are indeed realities, but they are far from the norm. Roles are converging slowly in a world where large divergences still exist.

This observation is important because advertising and marketing executives (and other observers in academia and in the popular press) have tended to assume that the convergence they have heard so much about, and in some cases have even seen around them, is the norm. In constructing advertising messages and marketing programs, it is important to avoid exaggeration and wishful (or fearful) prognostication. It is important to

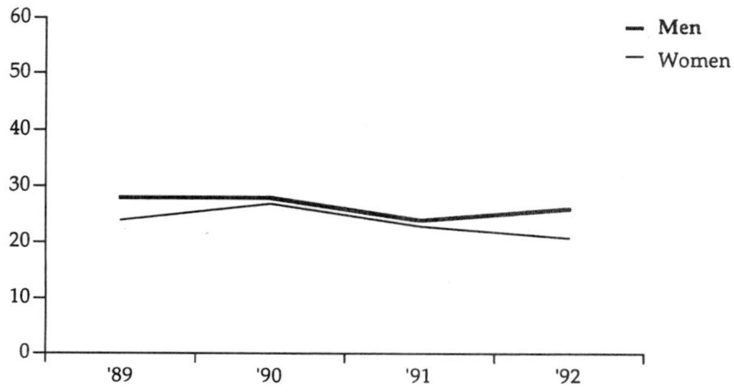

FIG. 13.11. "I would be uncomfortable if (I/my wife) earned more than my (husband/I did)." From DDB Needham Life Style Study (1993).

understand the attitudes and opinions of typical consumers, and not to act under the mistaken impression that trends have gone farther and faster than they have.

HOME

As the workplace slowly transforms itself, and as women slowly adopt work roles traditionally occupied by men, conventional wisdom suggests the men must be assuming homemaking chores once the sole preserve of women: cooking, cleaning, grocery shopping, changing diapers, and so on.

What do the Life Style data show? Once again, we see a convergence and divergence of attitudes and behaviors. On one hand, even during the so-called "Me Generation," similar and increasing majorities of both men and women agree that "when making important family decisions, consideration of the children should come first" (Fig. 13.12). Also, the Life Style data, and other surveys, indicate that more married men and more married women now prefer a marriage in which both husband and wife work and share household responsibilities (Fig. 13.13).

But what is actually happening at home? Although a majority of husbands say they help out around the house from time to time, a more stringent test of their domestication is the chores they *routinely do.* Figure 13.14 shows the housework married men in the Life Style sample say they "usually" do. At face value, the numbers indicate that some men do indeed bear the brunt of what is unaffectionately referred to as "women's work." Furthermore, the percentage of men who say they do that has grown. However, Fig. 13.14 also makes it obvious that the percentage of husbands who *usually* vacuum or dust, do the laundry, wash dishes, or go grocery shopping is relatively small. (Incidentally, even male baby boomers have

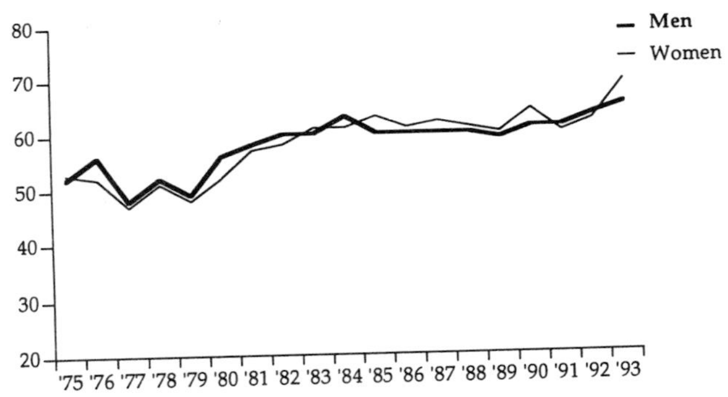

FIG. 13.12. "When making important family decisions, consideration of the children should come first." From DDB Needham Life Style Study (1993).

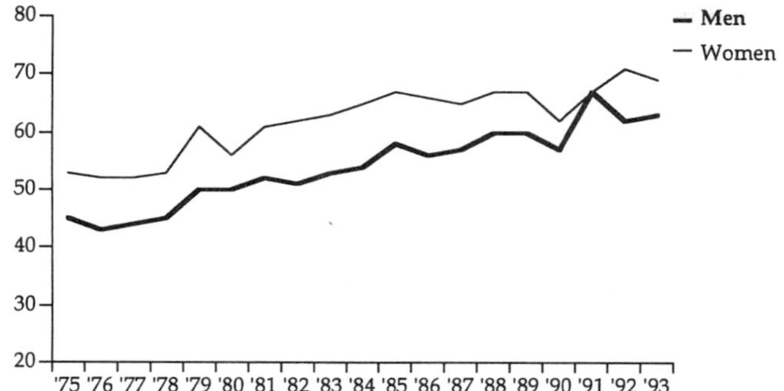

FIG. 13.13. "Prefer a marriage where husband and wife both work, share household responsibilities." From DDB Needham Life Style Study (1993).

not taken over the household chores. Retired men often are substantially more likely to wear the apron strings than are their younger counterparts.)

Figure 13.14 indicates that the chores women and men do around the house are pretty much what they have always been. Women cook and clean, while men putter around fixing things—and take out the garbage, as is their rite.

Some trend watchers suggest that grocery marketers ought to pay special attention to the "nontraditional male," on the premise that this "exploding segment" is now or is becoming the prime target for detergent, scouring powder, tub and tile cleaner, Roll-O-Matics, cake mix, and the like. Figure 13.15, and other Life Style data, indicate that following such counsel may not be in the marketer's best interests. Although some men—single men, for instance—are good candidates for many household products, the number of men who purchase and use these products are relatively small. Even

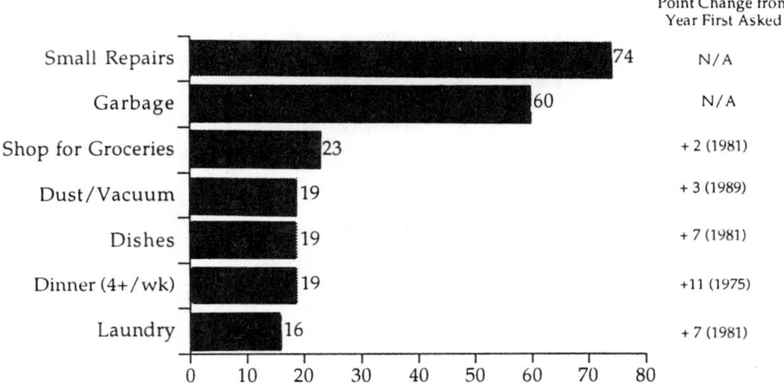

FIG. 13.14. "Household work usually done by married men." From DDB Needham Life Style Study (1993).

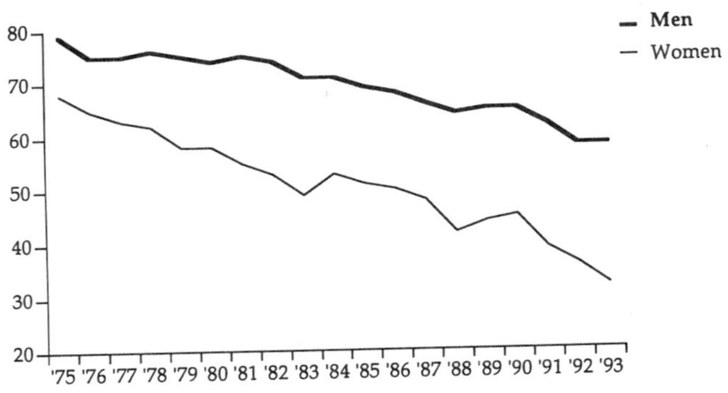

FIG. 13.15. "The father should be the boss in the house." From DDB Needham Life Style Study (1993).

where the numbers are growing, they are growing slowly, and they do not yet approach the critical mass most household products marketers must have.

Other domestic prejudices die hard as well. For instance, although the belief that "the father should be the boss in the house" has declined among both men and women, it has declined much faster among women than among men (Fig. 13.15). In 1975, the disparity between the sexes on this item was 11 percentage points. By 1993, the gap had increased to 26 points!

So, while some of the traditional "masculine" roles and attitudes toward housework and homework are being relaxed, the trend is far from uniform, and it is far from "explosive." Some of the alleged transformations at work and at home are actually occurring, and some are not. Even among the transformations that are occurring, the pace of change is surprisingly slow.

Furthermore, the transformations that are occurring are unbalanced: Women are adding new facets to their lives, and men are not taking up the slack. This "lopsided" transformation of duties and obligations has increased the pressure women are feeling to the point where women and men now share a perverse equality (Fig. 13.16).

Of the gender-related trends in the Life Style data, increased agreement among females with "I feel I am under a great deal of pressure most of the time" is among the most dramatic. Although both stay-at-home women and working women feel the pressure of unreciprocated duties and obligations, those duties and obligations bear most heavily on working women, as Fig. 13.17 reveals.

So, both at work and at home, the picture of gender roles is painted in shades of gray. On some gender-related issues, men and women see eye-to-eye, as they always have. On others, they remain miles apart. On still others, attitudes and behaviors contradict each other. On still others, attitudes and behaviors slowly converge.

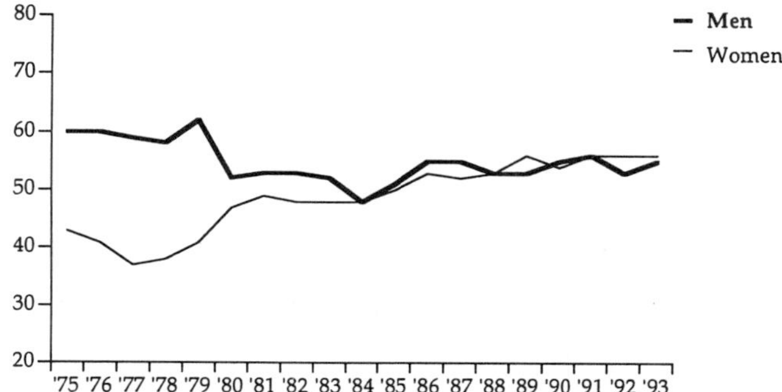

FIG. 13.16. "I feel I am under a great deal of pressure most of the time." From DDB Needham Life Style Study (1993).

In constructing marketing programs and advertising messages, it is important to know and to understand the specifics of these convergences and divergences, and to appreciate the glacial nature of what is going on.

The glacial nature of gender-role transformations also liberates advertisers and marketers to acknowledge the ways in which men and women remain distinctly different. For instance, men and women still fear different things (Harris Poll, 1992; Table 13.1). Women are more apt to enjoy baking than are men (Fig. 13.18). Men have been, and continue to be, more likely to agree that "I would do better than average in a fist fight" (Fig. 13.19).

According to a survey sponsored by *Sports Illustrated* (1991), men and women differ markedly in the types of professions over which they fantasize. Men's "fantasy professions" lean toward those of "power" while women's preferences run toward the "creative" (Table 13.2).

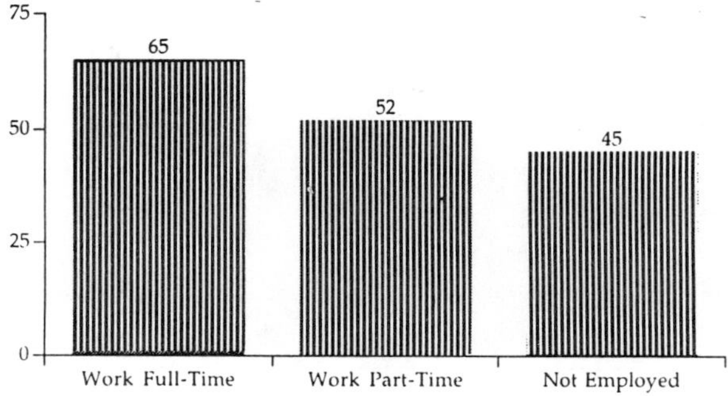

FIG. 13.17. "I feel I am under a great deal of pressure most of the time" (working vs. nonworking women). From DDB Needham Life Style Study (1993).

TABLE 13.1
Fears

	Men %	*Women* %
Snakes	22	57
Alone in a forest	5	37
Insects	7	25
Mice	1	20
Flying on a plane	6	14
Leaving home at night	1	12

Source: *The Harris Poll* (1993).

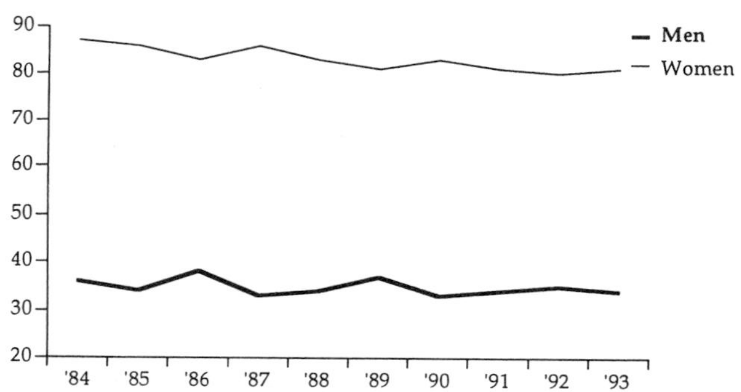

FIG. 13.18. "I like to bake." From DDB Needham Life Style Study (1993).

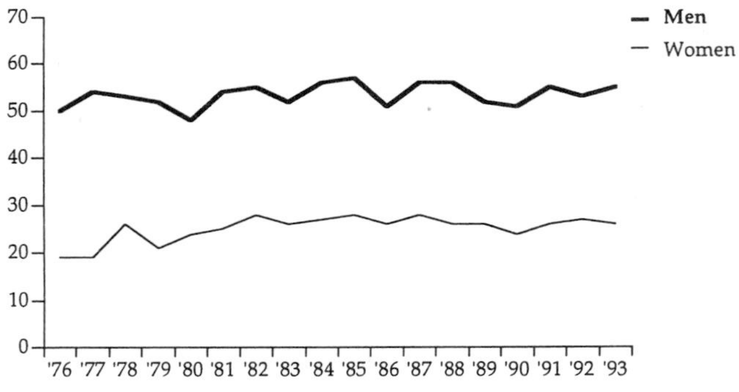

FIG. 13.19. "I would do better than average in a fist fight." From DDB Needham Life Style Study (1993).

TABLE 13.2
Fantasy Professions

	Men %	*Women* %
Athlete	48	13
Business leader	38	27
Movie star	24	19
Singer	23	35
Scientist	20	11
Doctor	19	29
Author	15	31
Leader	13	7
Chef	12	25
Artist	9	22

Source. *Sports Illustrated* "The American Male '91"/ The Time Inc. Magazine Company (1991).

It is just as important that advertisers and marketers understand and appreciate the specifics of these large and continuing differences as it is that they understand the complex specifics of the changes that are taking place. In this province, oversimplification is easy. Simplistic slogans abound. But when it comes to making marketing and advertising decisions, a careful, patient, fact-based scrutiny of the details of how consumers are feeling, thinking, and behaving—and an equally careful, patient, fact-based scrutiny of how those feelings, thoughts and behaviors are and are not changing—is essential to rational solutions in every case.

REFERENCES

DDB Needham Worldwide, Inc. (1993). *The DDB Needham Life Style Study.* Unpublished survey data.

Harris Poll. (1992, December). *Our fears.* Available from Louis Harris & Associates, 630 Fifth Avenue, New York, New York 10111.

Mediamark Research, Inc. (1992). *Doublebase, 1992.* Unpublished survey data.

Sports Illustrated. (1991). *The American Male '91.* The Time Inc. Magazine Company.

U.S. Bureau of the Census, Current Population Reports. (1992). *Educational attainment in the United States: March 1991 and 1990* (Series P-21, No. 462). Washington, DC: U.S. Government Printing Office.

U.S. Bureau of the Census. (1986). *Statistical Abstract of the United States: 1986* (106th ed.). Washington, DC: U.S. Government Printing Office.

U.S. Bureau of the Census. (1992). *Statistical Abstract of the United States: 1992* (112th ed.). Washington, DC: U.S. Government Printing Office.

U.S. Department of Labor, Bureau of Labor Statistics. (1991). *Working women: A chartbook* (Bulletin 2385). Washington, DC: U.S. Government Printing Office.

Chapter 14

The New Materialists

Larry Chiagouris
Brand Marketing Services

Leeann E. Mitchell
Backer Spielvogel Bates, Inc.

There has long been an implicit concept that consumers can be defined in terms of either the products they acquire or use, or in terms of the meanings products have for them or their attitudes toward products.

Materialism is the foundation of an inherently competitive humanity. A philosophy ingrained in the history of the United States of America and the capitalist society we hold so dear. We strive to accumulate goods, products, things that carry with them the external status symbolism that fosters perceived power and influence. It is the core of consumer behavior that has, throughout time, evolved through numerous phases of development.

The dawn of the 1990s has been termed the "Age of Frugality." Stringent economic times and the aging of the national community have shifted values to reflect negatively on the concept of materialism. The excessive concentration of wealth, spending, and accumulation in recent decades has created a backlash that leads many to believe that, in today's world, materialism is dead. The reality of consumer behavior proves otherwise.

A detailed examination of the psychology of materialism traced its roots that remained tied to today's consumer. The discovery . . . materialism is alive and well, but it has undergone a basic change in the way that it is expressed.

WHAT IS MATERIALISM?

A great or excessive concern with material as opposed to spiritual or intellectual things.
—Webster's Dictionary

A tendency to prefer material possessions and physical comfort to spiritual values.
—Oxford Dictionary

Though varied, the central focus of the definitions of materialism is, as Belk (1984) phrased it, "happiness-seeking via consumption." We want things that allow us a measurable value of self-worth and identity. The materialist believes that this value and identity are the basis of a happiness and pleasure that is achieved through accumulation of absolute goods.

The psychology of materialism is multifold. Its being is essentially grounded in the ideal that: "Possessions are valued because they give a certain status and are instrumental in projecting a desired self-image." The materialist is constantly in search of self-worth and the perception is that it may be discovered in holding material good. In reality, this goal is never fully satisfied and accumulation continues to extraordinary proportions.

Fournier and Richins (1991) suggest that materialism is even further based in the foundation of external application. There is an increased emphasis on the desire to "show-off" one's valued possessions and accumulation with the intense need for acceptance of peers and society at large. The definition of the self is completed by the recognition of others. Materialism is a function of observation. Possessions convey social information to others that directly relates to the satisfaction of the materialist. Thus, behavior extends beyond simple ownership.

> Behaviors most frequently associated with materialism involve conspicuous consumption, in which audience reaction is very significant and provides product satisfaction, compulsive consumption and the value of credit. (Fournier & Richins, 1991)

Often, the consumption behavior of the materialist is "performance" focused and, therefore, extremely conspicuous. The social identity that is so desired is directly responsible to a set of impressions that may be the result of specific acts of consumption. The behavior, in many instances, becomes compulsive and reliance upon "fronts," those defining impressions for the sake of others, may be the materialists' primary value and concern. Obsessive manipulation of the possessions one surrounds oneself with are used to make reliable personality inferences. Clothing, cars, home furnishings, and other appearance-related items are all among the possessions used to relate such messages. This self-presentation model goes beyond personal perception theories in its suggestion that, in addition to behavior, the physical context surrounding the behavior provides substantial social information for the observer. As society is increasingly involved in the consideration of these messages, there is an evident centralization of a "consumer culture" in which goods consumption is the central goal.

The "culture of consumption" is the foundation of a capitalist society. "Our economic system is largely predicated on the assumption that having more money and goods leads to greater satisfaction." Why, then, is materialism associated with negative connotations? Perhaps it is grounded in the personality traits common to materialistic tendencies. Belk (1985) investigated the traits of materialistic behavior and isolated three tendencies of particular strength and recurrence: possessiveness, nongenerosity, and envy. Each of these characteristics is viewed in negative social terms. Fromm (1976) further describes materialists as excessively competitive in spirit and in need of superiority, thus often antagonistic and insecure. Power, for the materialist, is gained through compulsive selfishness.

Overall, materialists are consumed by the "psychology of more." They seek worth and identity through the social impression that may be marked by possession of particular goods. Satisfaction is the unattainable goal.

HOW DID MATERIALISM BEGIN?

Our team of anthropologists determined that materialism has a history of change that is marked by three distinct periods: the "Culture of Consumption," "Great Prosperity," and "The Time of Greed." Each phase was born of the last and parallels the environmental aspects of timely culture and society.

The late 19th century introduced the culture of consumption with the birth of corporate capitalism. The shift from small scale entrepreneurial economics to a broad based industrial society had intense societal effects. Increased urbanization, coupled with increased technology and communication allowed for more efficient industry and big business. Cheap labor was provided by the influx of immigrants and the exploitation of the working classes. The middle classes increased in size and discovered the pleasures and opportunities of disposable income. In accordance with this newfound surplus of wealth, leisure time had increased importance and new desires introduced the need for product creation and a focus on material luxuries. The 1920s typified the culture of consumption as spending increased and external appearance was a common concern.

If depression and war stalled the materialist development for a brief period in history, economic recovery and victory reinstated it tenfold. In the period following World War II, the era of "great prosperity" took hold.

The baby boom turned society's interest to youth and the explosion of the suburbs reinforced family values and focused on the home. The development of Levittowns established a standard of living, before unstated. There was a huge demand for children's, home, and family oriented products. By the middle 1960s, most homes had televisions and by the 1970s the glitz of the disco era had a very evident impact on fashion and leisure spending.

The third phase of materialism reached its climax in the 1980s. While the late 1970s had rejected the presidency of Jimmy Carter, as he attempted to display a common man image (known for carrying his own suit bag and walking to his own inauguration), the 1980s invited Ronald Reagan into the White House. The wealthy republican actor introduced Reaganomics to intentionally spur on national spending. The result was extraordinary and we moved into what is often referred to as "A Time of Greed." As the baby boomers entered the workforce in large force, they were increasingly involved in the spending independence generated by high income levels. Yuppies were the heros of the age and their BMWs, Ralph Lauren clothes and housewares, and Tiffany jewels made them stand out as such. Donald Trump personified the monetary emphasis of the age and Madonna, the "Material Girl," integrated it into pop culture.

HAS MATERIALISM ENDED?

> *Materialism has dwindled. The Back to Basics movement is real and will continue after the recession lifts. Aggressive shopping is outdated and frugality is en vogue. The 1990's are considered a backlash against the flaunting of the 1980's.*
>
> —John Naisbitt (1984)

In 1987, the stock market crashed over 500 points. For many, this marked the fall of materialism as it was once known. Ivan Boskey and Leona Helmsley were jailed, and Donald Trump had experienced financial difficulty. There are no longer heroes of conspicuous consumption. Perceived recession has slowed spending and real estate and employment are troubled markets.

The aging baby boomers are understanding the costs of family and home life in a time of uncertain economic stability. Their values have shifted to more conservative spending and increased home and family concern. With them, society has adopted the "politically correct" manner of behavior more fitting for a sluggish economy. Extravagance, for its own sake, and conspicuous consumption cannot be rationalized in an age of homelessness and unemployment, urban riots, and health problems.

The global community has, too, shifted so dramatically in recent years as to warrant uncertainty. Polarity in international relations has subsided and many are unsure as to its full effect. And, the health of the planet is uncertain. Material goods are sometimes disruptive to the environmental plea of the late 1980s and 1990s. The population has been struck by the AIDS epidemic and more people die each year. The total increase in social ills and global concerns has caused the median generation, in particular, to stop and take stock of their value system. Social responsibility has shifted a central focus of values from the "Me Decade" to the "We Decade" and more people are concerned with the well-being of the world around them. Life seems out of control and, in reaction, we desperately seek to grasp the reigns by returning to a more simple way of life. This priority is not, however, limited to the baby boomers, but spans generations old and young.

> Excess has been replaced by "small indulgences." These are small wants as opposed to limitless luxuries. They are affordable, small, material rewards in contrast to financial over-extending to buy luxuries seen during the 80's. (Faith Popcorn, 1992)

Excessive luxury spending does not seem in tune with the tone of the present age. Critics are quick, therefore, to assume that materialism has died completely in order to give way to the practical requirements of the day. It is often said that the time we live in is the payment of the extraordinary costs that we built up in the 1980s "Time of Greed." If this is so, will we be so apt to re-engage in our old ways once the bills are paid? Is materialism really dead, or has it merely been placed on the "back burner" for the time being? Or better still, is materialism alive and well, disguised in a new form of *inconspicuous* consumption?

Qualitative research and analysis reports that materialism is, in fact, alive and well. In pursuit of greater understanding, consumer interviews were conducted. The subjects of these 100 30-minute interviews conducted in February 1993 claim that materialism is a fact of our lives and will not fade away so quickly and painlessly.

> We're still materialistic, but we can't afford things now, so it's suppressed.
>
> [Materialism]'s not dead, just on the back burner for now. We'll be materialists again.
>
> I like nice things, I'll always want them. I can't always have them, but I'll always want them.

These consumers were adamant about the existence of materialism, even in today's world. They described materialism as a core part of the

American Dream and discussed that it would not be easily released. In this time, it may not be at the forefront, but there is no doubt that materialism is fully ingrained in our tastes and in our culture.

But, if materialism is so alive, how is it that we are so convinced that it is a thing of the past? The psychology of materialism has not faltered, rather, the behavior associated with the philosophy of accumulation, has been altered so as to become less obvious, more limited, and reflective of the practical nature of the 1990s. The observer function of possession remains a strong determinant of value, but the observer is seeking out new things. In conjunction with this new approach, the materialists themselves have taken new form.

WHO ARE THE NEW MATERIALISTS?

As a method for understanding the composition of the new breed of materialists, Backer Spielvogel Bates, Inc. tuned into its proprietary database of lifestyle, attitude, and behavior segmentation.

GLOBAL SCAN™ is the largest and most comprehensive attitude and lifestyle segmentation study, conducted by an advertising agency, in the world to date. Comprised of a sample spanning 19 countries and 14 languages, GLOBAL SCAN is conducted annually with a sample size of 3,000 respondents over the age of 18 years in Australia and the United States, and 1,000 respondents over the age of 18 years in other nations throughout Europe and the Far East. To date, the total sample size is over 60,000. Investigation of values, opinions, attitudes, psychographics, and lifestyle segmentations, allows GLOBAL SCAN to serve as a source of application in terms of targeting, competitive frame analysis, trending, and projections. Analyses are conducted on the basis of attitude clusters, lifestyle typologies, brand user profiles, opinion leadership, media behavior, and demographic groupings.

We began to investigate the new materialists in terms of a *materialism construct* based on two key GLOBAL SCAN attitudes. The two statements captured different and equally important aspects of the philosophy rooted in materialism.

> I like owning things others don't have.
>
> It's important to me to make a lot of money.

The first statement focuses on the value of possessions, a pure definition of success for the traditional materialist, and captures the social perspective of comparison and competitiveness . . . the drive to have more than others. This statement is further connected to the observer function as it is a means to outer-directed impression and status. Belk's subscale of envy focuses on this aspect of others' possessions and perceived achievement through impression. This statement defines the strength of the philosophy of materialism as it determines and targets those to whom ownership is essential and possessions are interrelated to self-worth and identity.

The second statement is overtly related to the materialists' drive to acquire and the importance focused on the means with which to do so. Monetary value is the prerequisite to consumption and, therefore, is always a necessity. Richins and Dawson (1992) found materialists to value financial security more highly than the nonmaterialists and associated monetary security as a success measure. In many instances, it was discovered that the materialists emphasized financial security and freedom as related to a sense of accomplishment and self-fulfillment, more than other life goals, including family and career life.

A materialist is defined as one who was in agreement with both statements (top two boxes on a 5-point *agree/disagree* scale) and nonmaterialist as those who were in disagreement with both statements (bottom two box agreement). In another measure, the "Near Materialists" were those who agreed with one of the two statements and not necessarily in disagreement with either of the statements.

To better understand the motivations driving materialistic behavior, comparisons were made between the materialists and the nonmaterialists. Analysis of these groupings at two separate points in time (1988 and 1992), clearly identified how materialism has trended. The composition of the new materialists was, then, investigated in terms of demographic measures and groupings and psychographic attitudinal measures, thus allowing a view of the composition of the grouping that may have changed over time. Demographic variables included: gender, age, occupation, income, education, marital status, presence of children, census region, county size, and MSA. Psychographic measures ranged from local and global attitudes about a variety of topics. The conclusion . . . materialism is, in fact, alive and well, and the so-called materialists are changing in composition.

The number of materialists in 1992 is, on the whole, a stable figure in comparison with the data obtained for 1988 (Table 14.1). Though the percentage of materialists has declined 3% from 21% to 18%, the difference is negligible. The percentage variation is small. In addition, to factor in today's more socially undesirable connotations of agreement with the two statements makes the decrease of minute effect. Furthermore, the definition used to classify a consumer as a materialist is narrow in that it excludes those individuals who want to own things that others DO have.

Nonmaterialists remain steady at between one fifth and one fourth of the population, about the same as the materialist segment. The slight increase in so-called nonmaterialists is explained by the weak economy

TABLE 14.1
Comparison of Stability of Materialists

	1988	*1992*	*Change % Points*
Materialists	21	18	-3
Near Materialists	57	46	-11
Non-Materialists	18	25	+7
Neutrals	4	11	+7

and lack of capability as real income is on the decline (Fig. 14.1). Naturally, under such circumstances, the nonmaterialists would increase slightly, but they have not, as seen before, effected the standing of the population of materialists. Instead, this portion of nonmaterialists has drawn its increase from the near materialists who have decreased, from 57% in 1988 to 46% in 1992. Likewise, the growth in the neutral grouping draws upon the decrease of near-materialists.

Overall, changes in the association of figures are minor with the exception of the largest group, the near-materialists. While suffering the greatest decrease, this group of peripheral materialists maintains the bulk of society. The near-materialists have a tendency toward materialism while not necessarily concentrating on its actuality compulsively.

The materialists of today are of a different composition demographically than in 1988, although rooted in familiar psychopathology. The New Materialists are more strongly defined, demographically, than in the 1980s. Perhaps, the practicality of the 1990s and the perception of economic

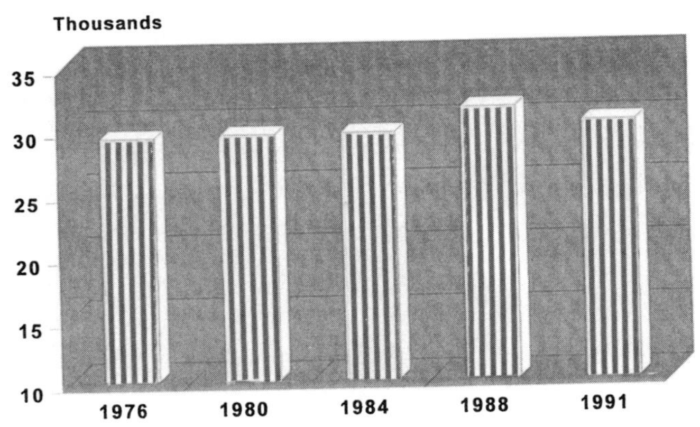

FIG. 14.1. Median household income (1991 CPI-U-X-I $) *Source:* Current Populations Reports Bureau of the Census.

TABLE 14.2
Comparison of Materialists by Age

	1992
	%
Males	*60*
Females	*40*
20-29	36
29-49	36
50+	21
Under $20,000	32
$20,000 - $39,999	25
$40,000 +	43
Single	42
Married	44
Married with children	21

recession weeded out the "transient materialists" leaving behind a sample composed of a sharply focused typology.

Today's materialists compared to 1988 have evolved to a grouping comprised of more males, twentysomethings, and singles (Tables 14.2 and 14.3). The grouping is younger than in years past and their income is more bimodal, skewing more toward the high and low end.

TABLE 14.3
Materialism Index to Total Population

	1988	*1992*
Males	***106***	***125***
Females	*94*	*77*
20-29	**106**	**125**
29-49	97	60
50+	74	60
Under $20,000	**100**	**119**
$20,000 - $39,999	117	78
$40,000 +	**83**	**105**
Single	**129**	**191**
Married	93	73
Married with children	130	70

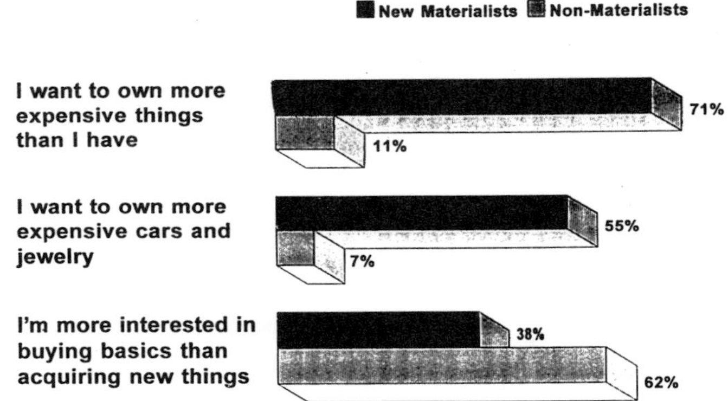

FIG. 14.2. Possessions and more possessions. *Source:* BSB Global Scan™.

The youthful materialists referred to as the "New Materialists" are financially independent for the first time. They have recently acquired "spending ability" and have a compulsion toward its exercise. As the children of the decade of greed, they have grown accustomed to immediate gratification and the "rite of passage" that materialism has become in our society. The New Materialists, as compared to materialists of the past, are less likely to have the responsibilities of home, family, and education that are hindering their parents and they are not conscious of the ethics of saving. In short, they want to consume as much as they can while they can, even if it is sometimes beyond their means. Possession is the central concern of proving one's independence and success (Fig. 14.2) and identifiable brands are of great concern and interest.

"New Materialists" view themselves as opinion leaders and trendsetters (Fig. 14.3). It is ingrained in their quest to make an impression in society.

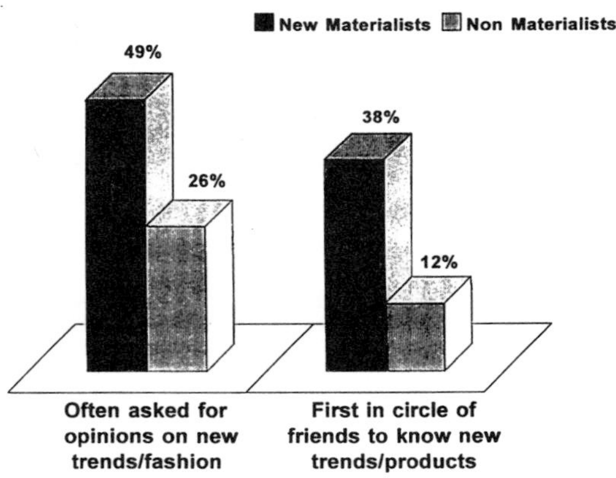

FIG. 14.3. View selves as opinion leaders. *Source:* BSB Global Scan™.

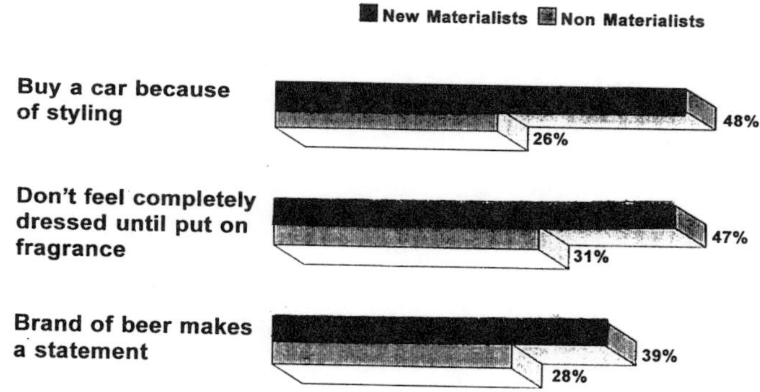

FIG. 14.4. Also in their behavior. *Source:* BSB Global Scan™.

They have an unbridled desire to be the first to discover, purchase, and possess the newest in material goods. The "New Materialists" strive to define themselves through perception. And, 43% of them truly enjoy being the center of attention. They consider themselves sophisticated trendsetters, and yet 61% of them "when doing something, wonder what others will think of them." They are, in effect, in frequent conflict between initiating trends and wondering whether their initiation meets with the approval of others.

It is rather ironic that these self-proclaimed leaders seek belonging through material behavior as they admit that certain material goods comprise a central and defining part of their identity. The same leadership and individuality of possession of products that others do not or cannot have is, in contrast, that which allows the materialist to feel like an accepted part of society's "in-group." In a sense, the materialist must feel like an individual in order to feel like an accepted member of the "group." Cars, clothing, and even the right beer are conscious choices (Fig. 14.4) that may be a symbol of a person's being and worth, in this capacity, as long as the status associated is evident to observers and accepted as belonging to the "correct" social measures or, at the very least, recognizable traits that may be personally definitive. The focus of purchase behavior is captured in the intense desire to style oneself according to preestablished standards.

The New Materialists are Sensation Seekers who enjoy taking risks and are satisfied with immediate gratification factors. They tend to seek out and enjoy new experiences and look for stimulation in action (Table 14.4). They are not a lazy bunch and spend their limited leisure time pursuing activity to fulfill their active desires. New Materialists frequent night clubs and bars, sporting events, and generally social settings where they might be recognized for their high involvement level (Table 14.5).

It is important to note that the New Materialists, like their predecessors of the 1980s, never really find contentment and satisfaction in their des-

TABLE 14.4
New Materialists as Risk Takers

	New Materialists %	*Non-Materialists* %	*New Versus Non-Materialists* %
Taking risks makes me feel more alive.	66	24	+24
I'll try anything once.	73	51	+22
Like to try foreign foods.	73	54	+19

perate search. Theirs is a philosophy that is discontenting because it is never fulfilled. And, yet they never stop trying to gain happiness through consumption. In many cases, the New Materialists find themselves entangled in a web of sacrifice as they search desperately for the never-ending "more." Impressed with their newfound relative wealth and greater independent discretionary spending capability, they have a tendency to become engrossed in their work not as a means to furthering career goals, but in the simple quest to make money. They make wealth accumulation and work, for that sake, a primary goal, often abandoning family and friends. As a result, frustration targets money worries and, although spending does not decrease, the New Materialists feel that they can never be financially comfortable, in terms of their expectations (Fig. 14.5).

The compulsion for monetary success leads to increased pressure for this group and their time is increasingly valuable. They are constantly under the pressure of limited time and excessive duty to their goals. Thus, convenience services play a major role in the New Materialists' lives. They are concerned with immediate gratification in all aspects of their lives and incorporate simplicity through convenience with the availability of services from fast food restaurants to automatic banking and high technology in general (Fig. 14.6).

TABLE 14.5
New Materialists as Sensation Seekers

	New Materialists %	*Non-Materialists* %	*New Versus Non-Materialists* %
Bars / Night clubs	35	18	+17
Rather enjoy attending sporting events	59	47	+12
Rather spend an evening at home	69	80	-11

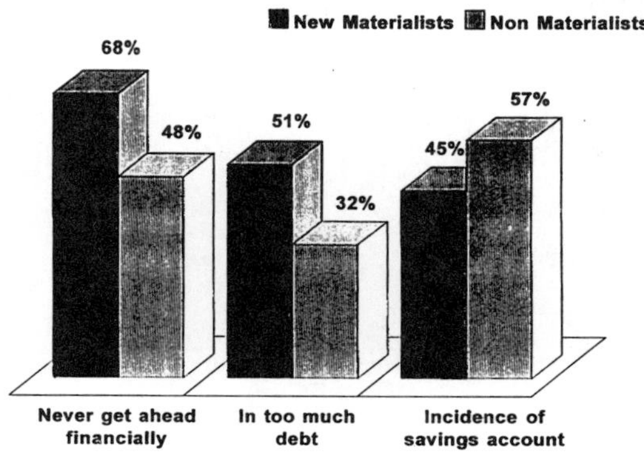

FIG. 14.5. Quest to acquire makes for money worries. *Source:* BSB Global Scan™.

An overwhelming 57% of New Materialists feel that their life is out of control and 35% feel that "Others get more out of life" than they do. It is evident, therefore, that the philosophy of materialism as a means to happiness is unrewarding overall. Pleasure becomes available only through escape and the New Materialists are often found daydreaming about being someone else in order to live out unfulfilled goals (Fig. 14.7). In accordance with the attempt to escape reality, the New Materialists seek out new experiences or simply simulate the experiences as they have a greater incidence of beer usage and seek to compensate their empty lives through fantasy and heightened social lives, when time permits (Fig. 14.8).

The life of the New Materialist is disconcerting as they seek to find happiness and discover only the pressure they inflict upon themselves and the lack of true value in life goals unmet. Even in their unhappiness, they are young and impressed with the novel capabilities of their inde-

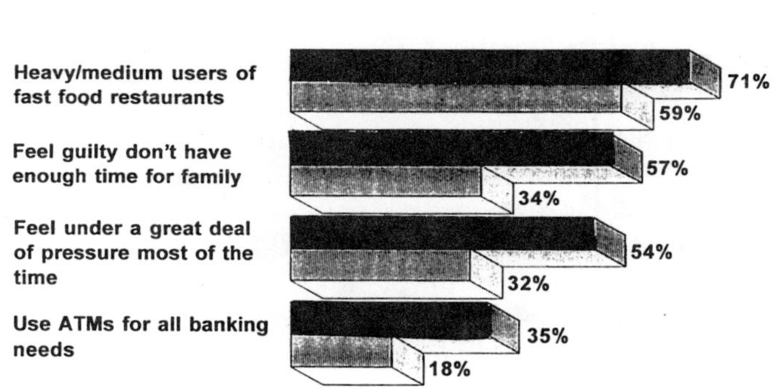

FIG. 14.6. Time pressured. *Source:* BSB Global Scan™.

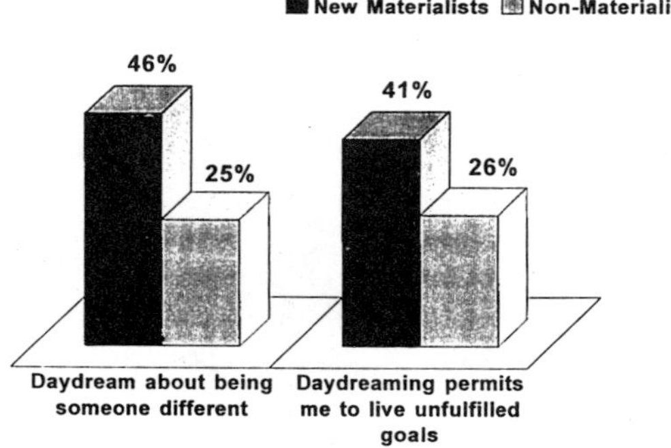

FIG. 14.7. So, must escape. *Source:* BSB Global Scan™.

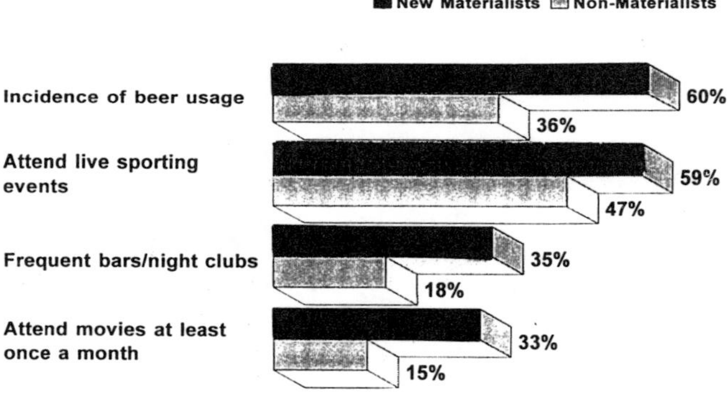

FIG. 14.8. And, escape through . . . *Source:* BSB Global Scan™.

pendence and seem to become victim to the reality of their own philosophical standards.

WHY WILL MATERIALISM THRIVE?

The single most important aspect of possession and consumption for the New Materialists is the association of goods with brand name recognition. As outer-directed status recognition is a key foundation of the materialist base, brand names are a characteristic of the definition of status. New Materialists are highly sensitive to branding and are willing to pay more to rely on the emotional value of well-known brand names (Fig. 14.9). The immeasurable value of the abstract emotional associations of brand names with public and personal reactions further expounds the existence of a culture grounded in materialist psychology.

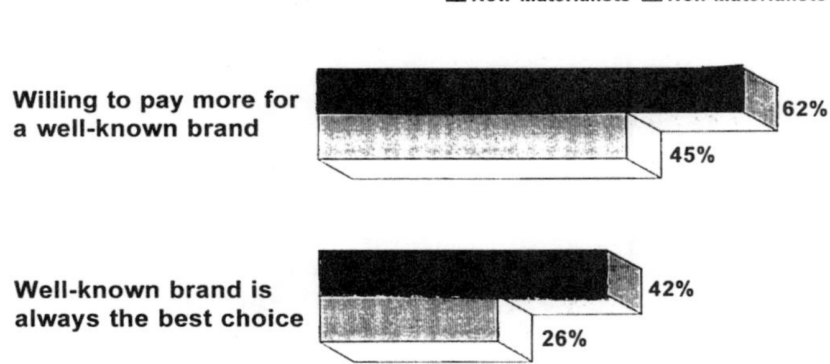

FIG. 14.9. Importance of brand names. *Source:* BSB Global Scan™.

Even as children, consumption socialization teaches us the "values" and rewards of good behavior, hard work, and dedication to success. Money is the foundation for this understanding and its central role in the American Dream is a constant message received by people of all ages. In recent years, children, in particular, have been more greatly empowered as consumers by doubling their personal income and they form a new, targetable market that, too, is sensitive to the benefits of material possession on a personal and societal plane (Fig. 14.10).

The methods of consumption socialization are becoming increasingly varied as technology and innovation create media sources never before tapped. Even the most obvious forum for advertising integration, television, has assumed renewed impact as the amount of commercial messages is on the rise (Fig. 14.11). Coupled with the new media fragmentation, the messages of materialism are virtually inescapable. The message is clear . . . the standards of measurable success define one's standing in the community. Even in these times of new economic realities, materialism is the underpinning of the drive for success.

Capitalism has proven itself as the stronghold economic system in the world today. Thus, even in these times of perceived financial trouble and

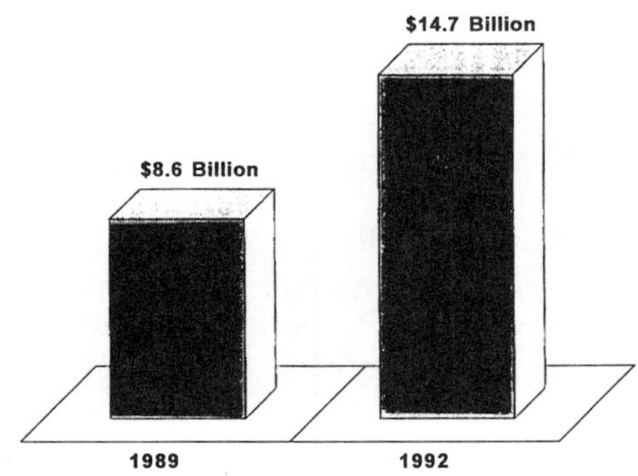

FIG. 14.10. Children 4–12 total income. *Source:* U.S. Census; American Demographics, 1992.

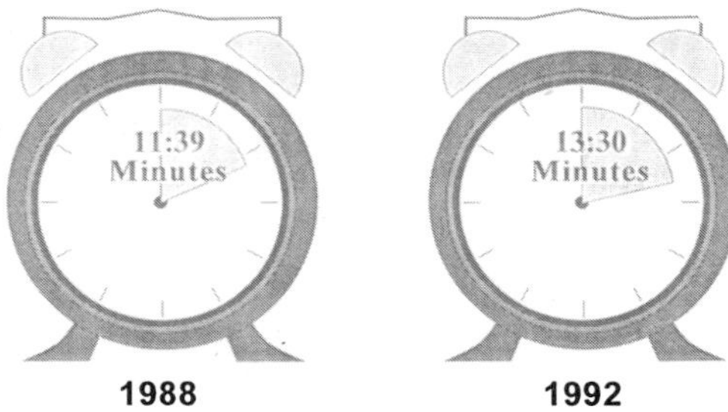

FIG. 14.11. There's an average of 13½minutes of advertising in an hour of television . . . an increase of 1:51 since 1988. *Source:* AAAA Television Commercial Monitoring Report (average is based on the three networks).

social disaster, the hope of the American Dream continues to flourish. There is optimism in the idea that our world economic situation will recover and that the opportunity for renewed achievement and success, as identifiable in outward measure, will be a reality. In effect, we find hope in the idea that we may, in the future, be materialists again. Why, then, do well-intended observers discuss the philosophy as if it was extinct? The answer is twofold.

One must keep sight of the negative social connotations of raw materialism. Because of its association with selfishness, as Belk (1985) suggests, and the envy it incurs, materialism, on the whole, has an undesirable connectedness to society. Many observers would like to see the fall of materialism. There exist those observers who believe that the definition of person/of society through material worth is false representation of humanity and denies the core being of soul and individuality. To become subject to our environment, self-inflicted or otherwise, is a concept we seek to escape. Humanity is, for the thoughtful, indefinite. If its central worth can be purchased, it is no longer worth anything. Thus, materialism is denounced as dehumanizing and demeaning and many wish to witness its demise.

In today's world, it is easy to discuss materialism in its desirable passing while it assumes the new role of inconspicuous consumption. Materialism has been reshaped to exist in accordance with the economic realities of the day. Although it has not disappeared completely, it is no longer a luxurious and excessive demonstration. Rather, the impact defines itself in terms less obvious . . . *materialism is in disguise.* Critics choose to ignore the character behind the disguise, while the New Materialists foster its role in everyday life. Materialism is hidden in our homes and cars, and on ourselves as we turn to the exploitation of material goods' functional capabilities. Materialism in the 1990s is Functional Materialism.

WHAT IS FUNCTIONAL MATERIALISM?

Evian mineral water is no longer the choice of Yuppies, but has evolved to become "Something good for your body" . . . an all natural health drink that is consumed by the physically concerned. Mastercard is no longer just another credit card, rather it is "Smart Money" that the financially savvy use as a means to managing their spending. Mercedes Benz is a safety machine. And, Miller Genuine Draft is a cold filtered beer. In reality, these brands are no different today than they were in 1987.

Functional Materialism is a rationalization and understanding of the new focus of materialism that promotes purchase behavior and accumulation on the basis of product capabilities. And, these capabilities are often either far in excess of what is needed or, in most cases, what will or can be used. It provides an explanation for why thousands of four-wheel drives are sold in Florida and Southern California each year when there is very little need for four-wheel drive capability in those areas. Functional materialism supports the continued proliferation of consumer electronics "gadgets" that provide features that frequently go unused and remain essential purchase influencers. Badge seeking for the sake of badge seeking is a thing of the past. Today's materialists are seeking out specific badges on the basis of what they claim to do or be in a functional and practical manner. Quality is a standard among the brands that attract materialistic attention, but it is no longer enough.

The "Back to Basics" movement has certainly had its impact on materialism, but it has not killed it. As more and more people turn to their families and homes, their focus of accumulation is centered on those same factors. Ikea discount home furnishings, for example, has reported that their customers are spending more than in recent years, showing a trend toward materialism in home purchase. The public recognizes the practicality of goods as beneficial first and foremost and showers respect on those who are of the functional class of materialists.

Functional Materialism is a means to social status through perceived knowledge and consideration. To be functional in purchase behavior, even excessively so, is to be a smart shopper—you get more for your money. Those who are involved in the trend are, therefore, the wisest among shoppers. They are able to rationalize extraordinary purchases on the basis of capability. It is insignificant if these capabilities are beyond what is required or even considered in their product usage. In a time of economic disabilities, spending for the sake of spending is frowned upon. If, however, one may justify spending on behalf of value, function, or benefit pricing, purchase behavior is acceptable. Often, the same brands are being purchased for the same relative price that was marked in the midst of the supermaterialism of the 1980s, but the benefit has shifted and the purchase is accepted by the norm. Extravagant purchases are not merely status symbols, but intelligence symbols as well. Materialists today are marked by their knowledge and reasonability.

New Materialists are respondents to trends and fashion, regardless of their self-proclaimed opinion leadership. They are among the first, therefore, to alter their tastes to whichever trend will grant the most response by others. Today, they are as involved in the functional materialism movement as any other grouping and generally more so. They are less concerned with spending great amounts of money for the sake of spending and focus their energies on the impractical practical. Thus, they are recognized, by those around them, as smart consumers and not merely excessive consumers.

The Functional Materialism movement will keep materialism alive through the challenging economic times and maintain the strength of materialist influence on society. While it is a well-disguised, inconspicuous form of materialist behavior, the core philosophy remains the same. People will continue to look to accumulation of material goods in their quest for happiness and acceptance and they will still receive the same external confirmation of their actions. In effect, this new phase of materialism may strengthen its philosophical hold on the people of capitalist societies. Not only do the benefits of materialist behavior remain, but they may now be rationalized in a flattering and socially acceptable manner. Excessive spending in this recession has a cause, so aren't we really getting our money's worth? Materialism is here to stay, in whatever form it may be hidden.

IMPLICATIONS

The New Materialists and their concentration on the functionalism of their spending has caused many marketers and advertisers to take notice. Evian, MasterCard, Mercedes Benz, and Miller Genuine Draft are among the first products to recognize this trend and attentively reposition their products to address New Materialist concerns and wants. For others, there are extensive marketing implications that cannot be ignored in today's marketplace.

Branding takes on renewed importance as the New Materialists are highly sensitive to the recognizable and reliable. As in the past, the materialists of today seek to gain "bragging rights" associated with purchase behavior and do so easily when there is an identifiable brand name connection. But this benefit, in and of itself, is not enough. Marketers must learn to consciously position their products to enhance the functional, as well as emotional, attributes. As a means for rationalization, materialists look for the functional benefits of particular brands, even if they are falsely represented, as practical.

Service is greatly sought after by the New Materialists. In line with the functionality of products is the consideration of extraordinary service, but there is even greater emphasis on this aspect of product promotion and marketing because it takes the consumer pressures and concerns into consideration. The high pressure lifestyle of the New Materialists demands convenience and quality service to make the most of their precious time. They do not have the time or desire to wait for services or goods, rather they want prompt attention and special benefits that allow them to feel as though the money that they spend is worth it. The end result is the feeling of satisfaction with a purchase that encourages repeat purchase combined with the emotional satisfaction of "belonging" to an elite group who are handled with extra care.

Trendsetting is a continual conflict for the New and functional Materialist. While they desire to be the first to discover new trends and fashions and are self-proclaimed decision makers, they are constantly worried about the acceptance of their discoveries. A marketer capable of resolving this conflict would be satisfying an essential psychological need for the New Materialists. Perhaps better use of idolized spokespersons or the endorsement of a reputable third party would enable the materialist mentality to take the risks of independent decision making. In doing so, the marketer would fulfill the emotional gap between innovativeness and recognizable branding.

Truth in Advertising is perhaps the most important aspect of message delivery to the New Materialists. In order to reach this target, there is a definite need to promote products legitimately. The New Materialists are not a happy group and are, therefore, inclined to search for possessions that will bring them satisfaction in their everyday lives. They are likely to rely heavily on these products and will be devastated if promises are left unmet. Although they are highly susceptible to the charm of a known brand name, their brand loyalty is shallow and will be abandoned quickly if expectations, practical or fantastic, are unsatisfied. Furthermore, like their counterparts, the nonmaterialists, New Materialists are "smart shoppers" who are concerned with price and are willing to pay only for what they receive. The successful marketer will use only advertising and promotion that, while carefully molded to enhance certain product aspects, is grounded in reality to appeal to this group in order to legitimately fulfill their psychological need for rationalization of purchase.

REFERENCES

Belk, R. (1984). Cultural and historical differences in concepts of sell and their effects on attitudes toward having and giving. *Advances in Consumer Research, 11*, 753–760.

Belk, R. (1985). Materialism: Trait aspects of living in the material world. *Journal of Consumer Research, 12*, 265–280.

Bilello, S. (1992). Outlet fever. *Newsday*, August 10, p. 23.

Burroughs, W. J., Drews, D., & Hallman, W. (1991). In F. W. Rudmin (Ed.), To have possessions: A handbook on ownership and property. *Journal of Social Behavior and Personality* (Special Issue), Vol. 6.

Cushman, P. (1990). *American Psychologist, 45*, 599–611.

Fournier, S., & Richins, M. L. (1991). In F. W. Rudmin (Ed.), To have possessions: A handbook on ownership and property. *Journal of Social Behavior and Personality* (Special Issue), Vol. 6.

Fox, R. W., & Lears, T. J. J. (1983). *The culture of consumption: Critical essays in American history, 1880–1980.* New York: Pantheon.

Fromm, E. (1976). *To have or to be.* New York: Harper & Row.

Naisbitt, J. (1984). *Megatrends.* New York: Warner Books.

Popcorn, F. (1992). *The Popcorn Report.* New York: Harper & Row.

Chapter 15

Change Leaders and New Media

Bruce MacEvoy
Affinicast

Today I want to share with you some thoughts about advertising and new media from the perspective of my research into social change and new communications technologies. The approach I describe evolved as part of a $2.1 million project I led for the Values and Lifestyles (VALS™) Program at SRI International, in collaboration with the Research Institute for System Science of NTT Data & Communications Corp., to understand social change in Japan. A primary outcome of this research was the idea of change leaders—individuals who are earliest to adopt product and service innovations. I will examine change leaders in the context of advertising and the information available through rapidly developing new media, such as the Internet and interactive television.

The combination of these two elements—a specific communication and information resource called "new media" and a specific consumer group called change leaders—makes possible new markets and consumer communications, with particular relevance to the assumptions shaping customer relations and advertising (see Fig. 15.1).

NEW MEDIA

First, what is intended by the label "new media"? An eclectic summary of the new media likely to have the greatest future impact is:

- Targeted direct mail, including catalog shopping to niche demographic or consumer segments (via customer database marketing or purchased lists)

- Credit card and banking data networks, and retail scanner data networks used in merchandising, inventory ordering and distribution, and couponing
- A broader array of consumer telephone services, including call forwarding, pagers, centralized voicemail systems, car phones and pocket-sized cellular phones, and 1-800 or 1-900 numbers
- Cable "narrowcast" programming through current cable feeds (with a near-term ceiling of a few hundred channels), which can be enhanced by television sets or VCR computer chips to read programming codes and select or record programs that the viewer finds interesting—or block programs with codes the viewer deems objectionable
- "Infomercials" or home shopping channels, combined with product orders placed by telephone using EFT or credit transactions, and relying on a rapid and flexible distribution and delivery infrastructure
- Targeted magazine and newspaper editorial and advertising content, at present targeted regionally through customized free-standing inserts (FSIs) and run-of-press (ROP) advertising, and within urban areas targeted to individual households through newspaper precision home delivery systems
- Multimedia computer and video programs via CD-ROM or networks, including interactive education programs, retail informational or purchasing kiosks, and online purchasing via computer simulations of products and retail selections (some already in use for market research applications)
- Electronic publishing or information services such as Nexus or Dialog

FIG. 15.1 Change leaders and new media.

- Interactive video entertainment and information, including pay-per-view (already used in many sporting events) and video-on-demand (coming in perhaps 3 to 5 years)
- Home-based financial services transacted from home computers (online banking and brokerage)
- The global Internet, accessed through educational or corporate LANs (for personal purposes), online services such as America Online or Prodigy (many now with their own national networks), or dialup bulletin boards such as ECHO or the WELL, Internet service providers, home ISDN lines, or (coming in a few years) cable modems

Some applications (such as video-on-demand or personal communications networks) will only play a significant economic role in the next century—if at all. Some already exist and are doing very well (direct mail, home shopping channels, and electronic couponing); while others are not performing as well as expected (online computer shopping and home banking). Still others are just starting but maturing quickly: new joint ventures between cable, telephone, and "content provider" broadcast or entertainment companies to create new forms of interactive entertainment are announced almost monthly. The number of communications nodes on the Internet is doubling annually and seems likely to continue growing rapidly through the end of this decade. All these forms of media and communications can create enormous and highly detailed transaction databases, grist for the parallel-processing computers of consumer "data mining" services—nearly all of them subsidiaries of existing communications or financial conglomerates.

These developments are a continuation and acceleration of the trends that sociologist James Beniger (1984) called *The control society*—a cybernetic system of bureaucratic and computational information processing that modulates the manufacture of products in response to consumer market demand for those products. New media, along with new types of automated manufacturing, inventorying, and distribution, increase the immediacy and clarity of market feedback. As a result, companies are evolving "customer driven" strategies to capitalize on the wealth of individual customer information available to them. Consumers in turn are able to make increasingly idiosyncratic requests for personalized products and services in areas such as automotives, fashion, home furnishings, foods, and consumer durables. In addition, new media and home delivery make it possible for manufacturers to bypass retailers and the chokehold of shelf space and deal directly with the customer—not just as a consumer of specific goods, but as a primary source of design, quantity, and delivery instructions within the cybernetic system. The result is a more dynamic and responsive relationship among consumers, manufacturers, and retailers than had been possible before.

New media increase the power of consumers to choose the information, entertainment, and product offerings they will see or not see, and thereby increase the competitive pressure on businesses to understand and anticipate each consumer's individual or household patterns of consumption. Consumer businesses, seeing information as a competitive resource and customers as a strategic advantage, act to accelerate the development of these new technologies. Reduced business costs, new business alliances, and increased consumer transactions and advertising revenues all help to pay the way.

CHANGE LEADERS

Realizing the opportunities created by new media will require a clear idea of the target consumer as an individual. But there are also generic attributes that many new media audiences share, attributes that can help us to generalize about audience expectations in the future. I have developed a definition of people who are most likely to adopt new products or services—social change leaders. The attributes of change leaders reveal the consumer traits that businesses will encounter in markets created by new media.

If we hypothesize a segment of people who act as change leaders in society, then a definition follows logically. A change leader must first of all pursue activities or buy products before most other people do, so these activities must have a low base rate in the population. However, change leaders must pursue many of these unusual activities, across many different areas of life, if we expect them to influence the behavior of other consumers. Thus, pursuit of low base rate behaviors and a high level of activity represent the core attributes of the change leader segment of society.

To identify individuals corresponding to this definition in survey data, I create a broad list of reactional activity, media use, product consumption, and service use indicators—usually 250 or more in total. I weight each item according to how infrequently it is chosen in the total population—products with a low base rate (few people in the population own or buy them) receive a large weight, products with high base rates get a small weight. I then sum for each survey respondent the weighted indicators the respondent has chosen. In mathematical notation, for p number of consumer indicators, the change leader score for respondent i is:

$$CL_i = \sum_{j=1}^{p} (c_{ij}) (1 - \beta_j)$$

where β_j is the base rate of product j, and c_{ij} is the probability that consumer i uses product j. For most data sets, this probability is 1 if there is a record of consumer purchase, and 0 if not.

According to this definition, change leaders are individuals who try many infrequent activities—whatever they may be. The intriguing feature of this score is that it does not require us to judge whether the individual choices actually are "innovative" or not. Nor does the definition discriminate in principle between socially "acceptable" and "unacceptable" behavior—many deviant or unacceptable behaviors also have low base rates. Yet these apparent failings in the specificity of the activity indicators do not seem to detract from the power of this change leader score. The essential point is to choose consumer indicators across a sufficiently wide range of consumer activities and product base rates.

I have explored the correlates of change leader scores in national consumer surveys of 1,500 to 5,500 adult consumers in the United States, Canada, Japan, and Europe, and the type of person that emerges as a change leader is remarkably consistent across cultures. Table 15.1, for instance, shows the 24 attitude items that correlate highest with change leaders scores defined in a 1991 survey in Japan and a 1989 survey in the United States. I invite you to guess which group of items was quite large—over 300 items. The content of items was drawn from a broad spectrum of personality constructs, including self-monitoring, extraversion, inner- and outer-directedness, a variety of political and social values, achievement orientation, and over two dozen others. The consistency of the results across cultures is not, therefore, an artifact of a "change leader" item pool. (The items labeled Culture A are from the Japan survey; Culture B is the United States.)

If I perform a factor or cluster analysis on the 50 or so items correlating highest with this change leader measure, six homogeneous and robust personality attributes emerge as characteristic of change leaders across all the cultures I have surveyed:

- *Novelty Seeking.* "I like to try things that are new and different." Curiosity, adventurousness, attraction to the new and unusual.
- *Stimulation Seeking.* "I often crave excitement." Desire for physical and emotional stimulation for its own sake, risk-taking and sometimes even thrill seeking.
- *Information Seeking.* "I like to learn about art, culture, and history." Attraction to learning, information, culture.
- *Self-Confidence (or Leadership).* "I can make things I want happen if I really try." Feelings of mastery, control, and expectations of positive outcomes; in Japan this dimension emerges as expressions of leadership, in the United States it appears as self-confidence.

TABLE 15.1
Item Loadings on Change Leader Scores in Two Different Cultures

	Correlation With CL Score	*Item*
Culture A	0.37	I like to try unknown things
	0.34	I have many hobbies
	0.32	I like being in charge of a group
	0.32	I want to be a trend setter
	0.31	I tend to be a leader
	0.30	I would like to spend a year in a foreign country
	0.30	I like to host parties for friends
	0.30	Other people often ask me for advice
	0.28	I want to be a leader in many areas of life
	0.26	I like outrageous people and things
	0.26	I like studying many different things
	0.26	I exercise regularly
	0.26	I like trying new things
	0.26	I often read books on culture and art
	0.25	I like a lot of variety in my life
	0.24	I can make happen whatever I really want
	0.24	I like to show off
	0.24	I like to go to concerts and museums
	0.24	I am sensitive to fashion trends
	0.24	I am always looking for a new thrill
	0.23	I like to live differently from others
	0.23	I consider myself an intellectual
	0.23	I would rather create a trend than follow one
	0.23	I like to buy unique things
Culture B	0.25	I am often interested in theories
	0.24	I like being in charge of a group
	0.24	I like doing things that are new and different
	0.23	I have many hobbies
	0.22	I would like to spend a year in a foreign country
	0.22	I consider myself an intellectual
	0.22	I like taking chances
	0.21	I like trying new things
	0.21	I like a lot of variety in my life
	0.20	I express my individuality whenever I can
	0.19	I like dangerous activities
	0.19	I like a lot of excitement in my life
	0.18	I often crave excitement
	0.18	If someone else cooked, I'd eat a rattlesnake
	0.18	I would like to know more about how the universe works
	0.17	I would enjoy traveling by myself
	0.17	I would love a two-week trip in the mountains
	0.17	I often do things for the heck of it
	0.17	I like meeting new people
	0.16	I like outrageous people and things
	0.16	I like to learn about things
	0.16	I like telling other what to do
	0.16	I am a talkative person
	0.16	I am always looking for a new thrill

- *Sociability.* "I like an active social life." Desire for social communication, friendship, companionship.
- *Fashion Awareness.* "I dress more fashionably than most people." Awareness of what's in and what's out, in dress but also in terms of specific lifestyle areas, entertainment, and social trends.

The association between these attributes and the change leader score is statistically very strong. Using these six scales and five demographic items (sex, age, education, income, home ownership), I can predict an individual's change leader score with an R-squared of about 0.40 (between 0.38 and 0.46 in the survey samples I have used).

These attributes form a syndrome in the sense that they are mutually reinforcing: leadership or self-confidence arises from information and many social contacts; stimulation seeking enhances novelty seeking, fashion trends and novelty go together, and so on. As a result, the behaviors associated with a high change leader score reflect these psychological tendencies. The characteristic activities include frequent socializing and occupational communication, wide range social contacts (friends in many different occupational fields or social groups), frequent recreational activities (especially activities in groups, such as hiking, electronic games, competitive or team sports), heavy use of a wide range of media (including niche media and entertainment or informational services), frequent travel (especially to foreign nations), and above average physical vigor (suggested by the sheer range of choices and the frequency of outdoor sports or regular exercise).

The SRI International 1992 Leading Edge survey of 1,500 upscale households (annual income of $50,000 or more) allowed me to look in particular at the technology use of change leaders, and I found that they are more likely than the general population to use computers (at home and at work), computer networks, computer games, videogames, industry media, professional training seminars, cable television, and the elements of what will become personal communication networks (PCNs and email)—such as laptop computers and cellular or car phones. In the SRI International Digital Video project, using product-based definitions of future video application audiences and markets, our analyses also indicated that these change leader consumers were the most likely early adopters and most frequent users of new video services. So, other lines of inquiry converge to suggest that change leaders will be highly active in emerging new media.

Demographically, change leaders span age cohorts from the 20s to the 50s. All tend to be slightly more affluent and better educated for their age group, but these differences are usually small. In some surveys, two clusters of people seem to appear within the age spectrum (Fig. 15.2): a young, active group that is highest in fashion awareness, stimulation seeking, and

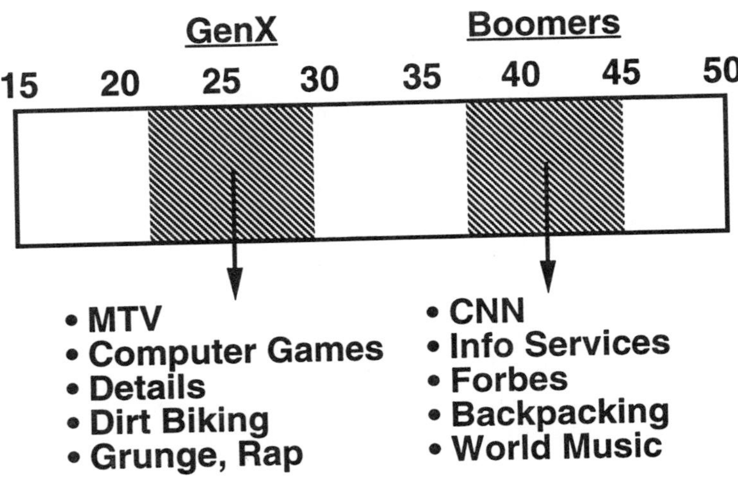

FIG. 15.2. Generational differences in change leaders.

sociability; and a middle-aged, professionally mature group that is highest in self-confidence and information seeking. (Both groups are high in novelty seeking, which is logically and empirically the core trait of the change leader personality.) This underlies the fact that social change is occurring in many different social groups exposed to the new media, suggesting that new media audiences as a whole may appear fragmented and complex. Indeed, there are other groups of consumers—teens and preteens—that also exert a major impact on consumer markets, which new media will be able to reach directly with dramatic results.

Though diverse in some respects, change leaders share an approach to life that emphasizes the new, the different, the informative, the stimulating, the sociable, the fashionable, and the challenging. All seem to have a unique, well-developed sense of self. These attributes—which make change leaders so attractive as a consumer group—also mean they will be demanding and sophisticated users of the media channels advertisers now use and the new media that advertisers must learn to master.

CHANGE LEADERS AND THE NEW MEDIA

Just those distinctive communications features that new media can offer are the same benefits that change leaders seek in their consumer choices (Table 15.2). These parallels suggest some of the issues facing advertisers as they attempt to communicate with change leaders in new media contexts.

Novelty Seeking and Stimulation Seeking. These related change leader attributes are best served by new media diversity and interactivity. For those interested in novelty, new media promise to open access to many new types

TABLE 15.2
Functional Fit Between Attributes of Change Leaders and New Media

Change Leader Attributes	*New Media Attributes*
Novelty Seeking	Great content diversity
Stimulation Seeking	Interactivity
Information Seeking	Wide archive, service access
Self-Confidence	Personalized, user-controlled
Sociable	Connectivity, networking
Fashionable	Timely, lifestyle focus

of content—local and niche cable channels, large archives of historical and rare foreign films, special-interest or ethnic programming. For stimulation, new media will offer erotic, exotic, and highly charged action programming, interpersonal electronic games (like two-player arcade videogames, but between geographically distant players), private bulletin board conferences on intimate topics, and online chat.

Information Seeking. Change leaders are heavy users of a wide range of information media: in today's world, information and knowledge connote power and status. They strongly gravitate to professional or "expertise" media (titles in narrow categories such as video or photography, audio equipment, computers, specific sports, automotives); news media (especially with an international focus—*Newsweek* in Japan, the *Economist* in the United States); fashion magazines with a lifestyle and new products focus; and a broad range of eclectic niche media, such as *Utne Reader* or *Wired.* The involvement of change leaders in computer networks and other telecommunications media is an extension of their interest in timely information. They enjoy hearing different points of view, personal insights, and detailed expert discussions; lively debate is a characteristic recreation. New media will amplify several times the ability of individuals to access international information archives, commentary and documentary programs, niche text, and broadcast information.

Leadership (or Self-Confidence). Self-confidence denotes consumers who place high value on control, rational decisions, and individual recognition. Each of these is significantly enhanced by new media. Online services and targeted print media can provide consumers with greater personal control of banking, investing, purchases, and travel reservations and accommodations; real-time information about stocks, bonds, and other markets; individually addressed services and solicitations; and professional advice or analysis services.

Sociability. Change leaders strongly associate new media with personal social networks—both professional and personal or recreational. Change leaders seem especially high in what sociologists call weak ties—acquaintances in different social groups, locales, occupations, and lifestyles. These ties are dispersed, but are neither frequent nor central to the person's life (in the way family and friendship ties usually are). However, with these ties change leaders get and give unusual and sometimes valuable information. The ties serve to inform, to create an individual identity, and to link the individual to valued communities of interest. New media form an essential component of these weak tie networks. For instance, most niche media define communities of interest through special columnists, letters to the editor, knowledgeable reviews, reader classifieds, manufacturer special offers, product information cards, and community event announcements. They link together communities of interest by providing a common forum or venue for weak tie relationships to develop. I see no justification to say that new media create entirely new kinds of communities, but new media do vastly increase the cohesion of real world communities of interest that are geographically dispersed, numerically small, or socially deviant.

Fashion-Consciousness. Finally, by providing access to lifestyle programming and entertainment, online shopping for very specific clothes and accessories, and interactive information within specific user communities, new media enhance the ability of consumers to identify and associate with the new ideas and consumer purchases that signal a specific lifestyle or fashion choice. Accelerating the process of market feedback in the control society, and enhancing the cohesion of small or deviant lifestyle groups, new media allow an even greater diversity of fashions to appear in ever smaller cycles of innovation.

IMPLICATIONS FOR ADVERTISING

With the attributes of new media and change leaders as background, I want to address some of the implications these hold for advertising and marketing. I can summarize these implications as a contrast between the practices of traditional "mass" advertising and new media (Table 15.3):

- Mass media traditionally targeted a mass audience—millions of people. Narrowcasting has already created niche audiences of a few thousand; new media push this targeting capability down to individual people or households.
- Because mass media target markets were so large, mass media typically were targeted by location—the places (stores, neighborhoods, chan-

TABLE 15.3
Functional Contrast Between Attributes of Mass Media and New Media

Mass Media	*New Media*
Mass audience	Individual audience
Targeted by location (this place and time)	Targeted by name (Mr. John Doe)
Public, passive audience	Private, interactive audience
Standardized, repetitive messages	Tailored, on-demand messages
Consolidates audience	Fragments audience

nels) and times (dayparts) where large numbers of the target audiences congregated their attention. New media can target individuals; with personal addressability (via computer, bank and credit accounts, home addresses, and PCNs), this targeting can occur at the consumer's convenience—anyplace, anytime.

- Mass targeting was consistent with a homogeneous society because it was not economical to serve small markets. Because the new media rely, in one way or another, on computerized databases, communications, manufacturing systems, and delivery networks, they can be used to accurately identify and serve even very small groups of specialized consumer tastes—and thereby facilitate cultural fragmentation.
- Mass advertising has developed a rhetoric of images and presentation that suits communications in public contexts to largely inattentive and passive audiences. New media can deliver messages in a private setting that are tailored to the purchase or transaction histories of individual consumers, and that invite the recipient to interact with the supplier of information rather than just "sit and look."
- Because of limitations in the channels (including outdoor spaces) used for advertising, mass media have had to standardize and repeat messages, and to rely on slogans and trademarks that can be used in a variety of contexts. New media can use highly tailored, on-demand messages (in many cases created by computers linked to the switching networks that deliver the messages), so that content, visuals, and even product offers can be varied to suit the preferences of the end user—adding greatly to the array of persuasive tools.
- The standardization of advertising content furthered a generic stereotyping and simplification in mass media—of the target audience, of social issues, of product benefits. Simplification is an essential component of communications that must be standardized, brief, and repetitive. In new media, the emphasis on interactive connections among individuals permits information to be shaped and expanded as the

communication relationship evolves; consumers can gradually learn more detail about products and services presented from their individual point of view.

To understand better how advertising might negotiate these shifts in media contexts—how it must rework or abandon old assumptions, and create new strategies—we should consider the new "customer code" that relationships created by new media must adopt. Among the most salient themes:

- Communications can be on a first-name basis, and potentially rich background information can be developed on individual consumers. As a result, advertising appeals will need to be individually "tuned" to signal a personal relationship—in effect, to let the recipient know that "I know you as an individual."
- Communications at this level mean that privacy and intimacy are essential. Mutual trust therefore becomes the highest priority value shaping the consumer-business relationship. In a subtle but pervasive way, the functions of advertising (to create public awareness) and selling (to close a transaction) will merge.
- Because they create personalized communications in relationships based on trust, new media inject consumer businesses as members of a customer community. Business must work toward the best interests of the community as a whole, and in some cases look out for individuals' interests. Any perception that a business or advertiser is out to exploit consumers will be fatal to its credibility and future market access.
- As members of a community, businesses will eventually be drawn into a variety of stratifying strategies. Privileged customer clubs, frequently purchaser couponing or rebating, limited access product offers, and special affiliations will seek to reward long term and high profit customers for their patronage. As a result, media will increasingly feature the audience as part of the programming, and will act to orchestrate and respond to customer interest in new products and services.
- Freedom from many of the traditional infrastructure contexts and constraints (clutter, scheduling conflicts, anonymity of audience) means that consumers' tolerance of traditional advertising interruptions will decline. As advertising becomes more addressable, consumers become more aware of the advertiser's choice to intrude on their time. As a result, advertising will increasingly occupy "marginal" spaces in customer interactions—the "natural dead areas" along the edges of a computer screen, in the blank leader on videotapes, or in the time between requesting and routing long-distance calls or ATM transactions.

TABLE 15.4
Change Themes for Advertiser Techniques

	Mass Media	*New Media*
Form of Audience	Crowd	Individual
Status of Source	Domenant	Slightly Submissive
Claim of Message	"Listen to me"	"Want to play?"
Implied Relationship	Solidarity Authority	Intimacy
Impact of Message	Emotional Arousal Imagery Associations Memorization	Information Formed Relationship Increased Intention
Structure of Message	Standardized Stereotyped Generalized	Variable Personalized Specific
Goal of Message	New Purchase	Further Interaction

These considerations can be summarized as some transition themes for advertisers in the future (Table 15.4). New media will not be the standardized message from a dominant source addressed to a crowd as an incentive to purchase, but the personalized information from a submissive source addressed to individuals as an incentive to play with alternatives and new possibilities. The feeling tone of advertising changes from a distant, status-driven relationship to an intimate, playful one.

Advertising will fill "natural dead areas" in dramatic content (a character, a scene, or a story) by acting as a prop in the entertainment content or by expanding the licensing of characters or trademarks. To create the illusion of personal relationships, informational media can mix image and copy in a conversational, elocutionary way, addressing the audience as a member of the user community. Advertising will seek to deliver what users already get from their other weak tie relationships—valuable information, opportunities for further communication, access to experts and product innovators. Even the language of advertising will communicate community membership through slang, icons, and abbreviated evaluations. When effective at this "subgroup membership," advertising would actually exclude or turn off some members of the audience who are not part of the community, just as a community tends to discriminate against outsiders through its speech and dress.

In the longer term, advertising will likely move toward a professional service or sales model, justifying its persuasion attempts by the explicit opportunity to enhance the individual's quality of life. As professional entertainment, advertising will merge with the script, visuals, and franchising of entertainment, and in the specific comparisons discussed in informational media. Advertising will become as database driven as retailing, and will shift from "selling the product whatever it may be" to "informing only those who really want to know." Today the real economic and personal value of information very often derives from its scarcity, novelty, and personal relevance to the individual informed. To survive, advertisers must learn how to better target messages, and to do so in contexts that will be defined both by information scarcity and personal addressability.

Privacy is an area of potential difficulty. Imagine for a moment what is entailed in doing telemarketing if everyone is plugged into a personal communications network, in which individual people, not telephones, have addressable numbers and can be reached wherever they are at any time. At present, telemarketing is based on the admittedly slim premise that a household telephone is a public utility that any company can, if they choose, use as a communications medium. With a personal communications network, the phone number genuinely represents an individual, and the "public utility" interpretation is no longer tenable.

Even more pointedly, consider the advertisement for a free T-shirt that went out over a pay cable channel carrying the recent Evander Holyfield title fight. As reported in *Newsweek*, the advertisement was technically altered so that it was received only by households illegally tapping into the cable broadcast. Everyone who sent in a request for the shirt received a short form letter offering to settle the cable violation for $2,000 (rather than the court settlement of $10,000 or more that is usual in such cases). The implications of such actions for how narrowcast advertising is perceived are chilling. It underlines the vulnerability that electronic media users may feel about the eavesdropping and data snooping by providers into users' program choices, transactions, and usage times. And it points up the confused and sometimes Orwellian legal situations—in customer information files, in secure or private transmissions—that new media will certainly create.

CONCLUSION

Two issues bear special emphasis in any discussion of consumers, advertisers, and new media.

The first concerns current social and legal norms regarding individual control of privacy and personal access. These are issues on which even informed speculation widely disagrees. For businesses, the paramount issue is likely to be the security and proprietary use of customer data. Reselling customer information, or allowing third-party vendors to use proprietary channels, in ways that violate consumer expectations of privacy and community responsibility may drastically erode customer confidence in the businesses involved. For consumers, the paramount issue is likely to be protection from fraud, entrapment, and harmful hacking (security violations). New media may greatly increase the responsibility for privacy and security that customers impute to businesses, whether or not businesses can or should be held responsible. Gone forever is the comfortable distance between customers and businesses imposed by the mass media model of communications.

The second caveat concerns market acceptance and social feasibility. How fast will new media be integrated into the American economy? How fast will businesses take competitive advantage of the new customer relationships that new media make possible? How many households will actively use the new media channels available to them? Analyses at SRI International suggest that many of the growth projections for new media applications in entertainment and information services have been greatly inflated. I believe that by the year 2000 there will probably be around 5 to 30 million households (depending on the specific application) using the currently most innovative new media channels or services. (Note that database targeted direct mail and computer network services are already addressing audiences in that range.) However, in several respects, cultural expectations are now overtaking technological capabilities; the *image* of new media is sufficient to define a possible new way of life.

The most important cultural fact is the close fit between the benefits that new media provide and the benefits desired by change leader consumers. Even if the audience for new media remains smaller than expected (because consumers as a whole are reluctant to embrace new electronic technologies, or businesses do not exploit the channels aggressively), change leaders will be disproportionately represented in these audiences. Even if new media are accepted by the mass of the population, change leaders will be disproportionately more active, more skilled, and more adventurous in using new media. In either the high- or low-growth technology scenarios, then, new media appear likely to accelerate the age, ethnic, and occupational segregation of American society; to enhance consumer expectations for personalization, interactivity, tailored appeals, and freedom from unwanted information; and to do so in a way that will reinforce the social networking activities of change leader groups.

The message for advertisers, then, is to begin thinking of new media as a reality and new opportunity to be seized—even if these media have a long road yet to travel—because consumer expectations and American culture are already moving in that direction.

Although we have a while to go until we live in a society entirely connected through PCNs, change leaders will be among the first to enter that new world and the largest segment in its early development. Until the time that new media become old hat, change leaders will support and be most receptive to any approximation of new media that reinforces their basic drive to build diverse and individualistic social networks. Start practicing now the skills you will need to address them, because you can use those skills even today to reach a highly valuable segment of consumers.

REFERENCE

Beniger, J. (1984). *The control society*. Cambridge, MA: Harvard University Press.

Chapter 16

The Benevolent Society: Value and Lifestyle Changes Among Middle-Aged Baby Boomers

Thomas E. Muller
Griffith University–Gold Coast, Queensland, Australia

During the years 1946–1964, post-World War II America experienced relatively high annual birth rates (number of births per thousand total population). Demographers have demarcated Americans born in that 19-year period as members of the postwar baby-boom cohort—commonly dubbed baby boomers. The baby-boomer generation, presently aged between 33 and 51, numbers 76 million—almost a third of the American population and the largest birth cohort in United States history.

What impact will such a numerous generation have on American society in the years ahead? By the middle of the first decade in the 21st century, all baby boomers will be firmly in midlife (aged 41–59). Clearly, any long-term change in the value priorities of maturing baby boomers would result in a major shift in societal attitudes and lifestyles.

This chapter argues that significant value changes can be expected among baby boomers and predicts some of the implications of these shifts for American society. These ideas are presented in two parts. The first half of the chapter highlights the chief environmental forces that will reshape the value systems of baby boomers, as they experience middle age and continue to endure the generational competition that has ruled their fortunes throughout their lives. The second half lays out the implications of this realignment in boomers' value priorities and predicts the types of attitudes and behaviors that will become commonplace among baby boomers. These represent lifestyle patterns that should surface as trends in American society during the first two decades of the 21st century.

Several compelling questions introduce the key issues we address here. What factors can cause an important shift in boomers' value priorities? Two value-shaping forces are identified: the degree of competitive pressure on personal welfare, stemming from the sheer size of a birth cohort; the process of maturation (growing older), with a focus on personality change and ego development, as people experience middle age.

What specific values will be liberated by the psychological metamorphosis transpiring within aging boomers? The predictions developed here point to values which embody: a spirit of cooperation, an appreciation of the complex nature of reality, a commitment to the solution of societal problems, a community-minded ethos, a reliance on spiritual values, a philosophy of feeling and caring, a reliance on intuition, a desire for self-discovery, and a widening of one's horizons by moving beyond self-absorbed roles and interests.

What will be the lifestyle consequences of such a change in boomers' value orientations? What activities, interests, and opinions can we anticipate from middle-aged boomers if they redefine the values by which they find meaning in life and self-fulfillment? The cumulative future behavior of individual baby boomers will likely surface as trends, eight of which are advanced in this discourse: voluntarism, commitment to grandchildren, spirituality, nostalgia, entrepreneurship, political activism, learning for self-fulfillment, and discovery tourism. Though these lifestyle scenarios are necessarily speculative, they offer an insight into the types of phenomena that should become commonplace among middle-aged boomers in the first and second decades of the 21st century.

SOCIAL FACTORS AS ANTECEDENTS OF VALUES

Values, as abstract principles (e.g., *self-respect, a sense of accomplishment, security, self-fulfillment, warm relationships with others, fun and enjoyment in life*), guide a person's behavior and their relative importance determine what goals that person will strive for in life—what is worth achieving, fostering, protecting, acquiring, or consuming. Each person attaches varying degrees of importance or priority to specific values and this leads to a hierarchy of values within a personal value system. Typically, a person's one or two most important values will largely determine what activities, interests, and opinions that person will cherish. "Individuals choose their primary value as part of their self-definition and selectively perceive their situations and themselves in this light" (Eisert & Kahle, 1983, p. 224).

The concept of values as antecedents of consumption behavior has been well established empirically. However, much less consumer research has been devoted to the *antecedents of values*—factors in the consumer's environment that form and reshape personal values. The antecedents of *values* are of critical importance in understanding the future behavior of baby boomers.

Milton Rokeach viewed values as cognitive representations of various human needs, tempered by societal demands (Rokeach, 1979, p. 48). Thus, values are needs which have been mitigated and seasoned by numerous environmental conditions—social, political, cultural, and economic. Munson (1984, p. 18) has suggested two categories of variables that contribute to the acquisition or realignment of consumers' value priorities: *microindividual* (e.g., status in lifecycle, age, education, sex, IQ, job performance, perceived success, personal experience) and *macrosocial* (e.g., economic conditions, culture, subculture, social class, race, religion, reference groups, family influence).

In particular, *value change* in a person—namely the reordering of value priorities within a person's organized system of values—will often come about as a result of the constantly shifting microindividual and macrosocial influences. As Crosby, Gill, and Lee (1984) point out, a knowledge of the antecedents of values is important because forecasts of the future course of demand can be made more precise by taking such antecedents into account. This exercise is pivotal when making long-term predictions about the nature of a society, based on anticipated value changes among members of the large baby-boomer cohort.

Focusing only on variables related to aging, for example, Crosby et al. (1984) observed differences in value priorities across four age groups and across 12 life-status categories (defined by marital and workforce status, and existence of dependent children). Similarly, Muller (1989) detected that the relative importance of certain values varied across 12 age groups ranging in age between 18–22 and 70–85. However, age-group differences in such cross-sectional studies probably confound the results of two effects on values: a maturational effect, that is, a restructuring of values as a person ages; and a cohort-historical effect, that is, differences in socialization values due to the historical period (with its unique conditions and events) when a cohort was born and bred.

Notably absent from consumer research are studies examining how (a) general economic conditions and (b) the relative size of a birth cohort have impacted the value systems of cohort members. Of these two factors, probably general economic conditions has received more attention from social scientists interpreting the effect of historical conditions and events on the value orientations of various birth cohorts—Great Depression babies, War Babies, Early-Boomers, Late-Boomers, Baby Busters, and so on (see Crosby et al., 1984). But, with few exceptions (Easterlin, 1987; Muller & Kahle, 1991; Muller, Kahle, & Chéron, 1992), intracohort competition due to the numerical size of a generation has not received much attention as an antecedent of cohort members' value priorities. We turn to this issue, next.

INTRACOHORT COMPETITION AND ECONOMIC WELFARE

Though baby boomers represent about 30% of the United States population, the oldest and youngest boomers are only 18 years apart. Thus, all boomers are roughly in the same stage of their lives, competing for the same finite economic resources, and wanting to succeed in a society that has trouble accommodating the demands and lifecycle needs of such large numbers all at once. In this sense, the law of supply and demand has worked against baby boomers: Their wages and salaries have been depressed by the sheer supply of labor, and career progress has required greater sacrifices, intensity of work, and dedication to job than members of smaller generations experience. For example, the economic reality facing the smaller generation of Americans born in the 1930s was one of many jobs and relatively plentiful opportunities for career advancement, progress in life, social recognition, self-fulfillment, and material rewards.

Easterlin (1987) has cogently argued how the relative size of a generation affects its chances in life: The quality of life among cohort members is affected by the size of the birth cohort—the larger the cohort, the more intracohort competition is generated and the less fortunate are its members.

He notes that "The entry of the baby boom generation into the labor market over the last decade or so has led to a deterioration in their wage and unemployment rates relative to older adults, and probably to comparatively slower upward job mobility as well" (Easterlin, 1987, p. 180). Therefore, in response to the deterioration in their relative labor market position during young adulthood, and in order to maintain their income and economic status relative to older adults (their parents), baby boomers have had to make a number of personal adjustments. These have included shunning or deferring marriage and family life at unprecedented rates, reduced childbearing, and the increased labor force participation of young baby-boomer women.

In other words, baby boomers' apparent economic prosperity in young adulthood (ages 20–40) has been purchased at the expense of family life. Traditional sex roles and family norms have been abandoned, and these decisions have led to psychological stress. "For those who do have a family, the problem of conflicting responsibilities arises. Parents wonder if they are spending enough time with children—or if they are, they may feel guilty that they are not working hard enough to get ahead on the job. A damaged self-image may result from failure to come up to society's and one's own expectations" (Easterlin, 1987, p. 98).

Easterlin (1987) has also documented the behavioral symptoms of this stress: divorce, illegitimacy, and family breakdown; resentment toward others—blaming employers, "politicians," or society generally; a decline in happiness; crime and suicide; and political alienation: "When young adults find it easier to achieve their life-style aspirations, they are more likely to identify with the society in which they live; when they find it difficult, they are more likely to feel rebellious and alienated. Hence, one would expect that changes in generation size would be correlated with feelings of alienation. And this too turns out to be true" (p. 108). In short, there is empirical evidence that the struggle to achieve economic prosperity has sapped boomers' attention and devotion to other domains of life—marriage, family, community, and society.

Looking ahead, the economic struggle is unlikely to abate for baby boomers. As several observers have noted, the competition among boomers in the labor market is expected to linger and it is probable that boomers will continue to mature through a period that remains similar, in important respects, to their economic environment at earlier stages of their lives (Ehrlich, 1989; Greenwald, 1989; Thomas, 1986; Thurow, 1981; Yankelovich, 1981). In Easterlin's (1987) terms, contrasted with small cohorts, numerically large generations will continue to be at a significant economic disadvantage throughout their lives: "But the effect of generation size, good or bad, persists throughout the life cycle. Every generation follows the pattern of below-average earnings in early working life and above-average earnings later. But the earnings pattern of a small generation is more favorable throughout its career than that of a large generation . . ." (pp. 29–30).

In such an environment, the achievement of material and financial aspirations is likely to remain a struggle; to many baby boomers, the traditional workplace will not be a source of self-fulfillment and personal pride ("Boomers Gloomy," 1990; Muller et al., 1992).

Because of this relatively high intracohort competition, some sociologists argue that many crucial aspects of baby boomers' past and future behaviors can be understood most clearly in terms of economic rather than some other macrosocial variables (see Rosenfeld & Stark, 1987). This is probably true in a narrow sense. However, the purely economic approach to comprehending boomers is unlikely to yield a complete picture. A more appropriate route to fathoming this generation and predicting its future behaviors is to assess the consequences of intracohort competition—due to generation size—on value orientations. Thus, the key question becomes: What have crowding, competition, and the struggle to maintain economic status relative to their parents done to boomers' personal values? We turn to some answers, next.

THE EFFECTS OF COMPETITION ON BOOMERS' VALUE PRIORITIES

Let us briefly examine what has happened to the value priorities of baby boomers in recent years, following a young adulthood marked by economic struggle due to crowding and competition. The evidence comes from values data collected in two, large-scale, nationally representative U.S. surveys taken 10 years apart (Kahle, Poulos, & Sukhdial, 1988; Veroff, Douvan, & Kulka, 1981) and reanalyzed by Muller and Kahle (1991). In 1976, and again in 1986, American adults were asked to reveal their single most important value from a list of nine terminal values developed at the University of Michigan Survey Research Center (Kahle, 1983), and based partly on Maslow's (1954) hierarchy of human needs. The nine values (listed here in hierarchical order to correspond with Maslow's need categories) are *excitement, fun and enjoyment in life* (values expressive of physiological needs), *security* (safety needs), *a sense of belonging, warm relationships with others* (belongingness and love needs), *self-respect, being well respected* (esteem needs), *a sense of accomplishment,* and *self-fulfillment* (self-actualization needs).

Figure 16.1 isolates the data for two baby-boom cohorts: early-boomers (birthyear 1947 to 1955) and late-boomers (1957 to 1964), and shows what percentage of each cohort chose a particular value as most important. The 1976 survey included early-boomers, then aged under 30, but missed late-boomers who were still teenagers. Ten years later, late-boomers (aged 22–29) appeared in the 1986 sample, and early-boomers were by then 30–39. This cross-sequential study design shows what happened to the value priorities of early-boomers as they aged by 10 years (compare black vs. gray bars), and contrasts early- and late-boomers, when both were in their 20s (compare black vs. white bars). The data for *fun and enjoyment in life* and *excitement* (both hedonistic values) were pooled for this analysis.

Although the percentage fluctuations in Fig. 16.1 suggest shifts in the acceptance of many of these primary values, only four of these contrasts are statistically significant (chi-square tests of choice frequencies) and merit closer attention. Two changes in value priorities occurred among early-boomers between 1976 and 1986. As they aged by 10 years, the acceptance of *self-respect* as a primary value almost doubled among members of this cohort. Whereas 14% espoused it in 1976, 25% chose it in 1986; in 10 years, its rank in popularity among values rose from fifth to definite favorite. Meanwhile, the proportion adopting *self-fulfillment* as a value of top-most importance swung in the opposite direction: from 18.7% in 1976 to 10.8% by 1986.

Differences between early- and late-boomers—when members of both cohorts were in their 20s—surface for two values. In 1976, 18.7% of

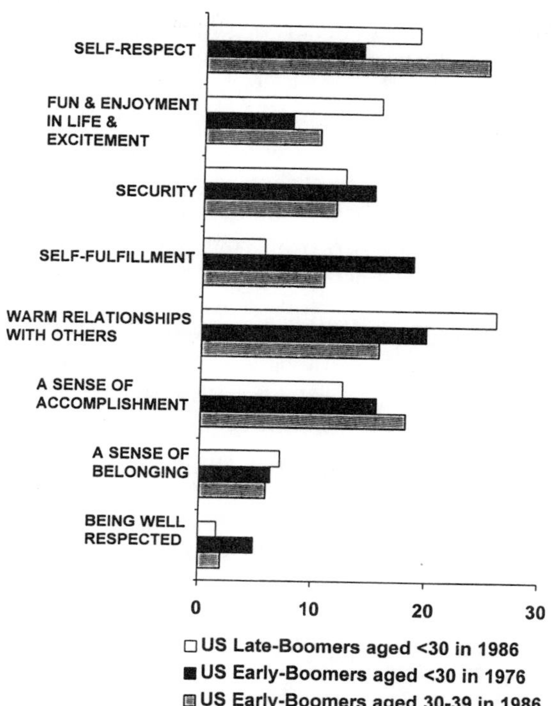

FIG. 16.1. Percentage of early-boomers and late-boomers choosing each value as most important, 1976 and 1986. From Muller and Kahle (1991).

early-boomers chose *self-fulfillment* as a primary value. It was the second most frequently adopted value (after *warm relationships with others*). Ten years later, among late-boomers, self-fulfillment was essentially shunned as a primary value; 5.5% adopted it as their leading guiding principle in life, making it next to last in acceptance among eight values. The second biggest difference in acceptance between early- and late-boomers shows up with *fun and enjoyment/excitement* as a primary value. Twice as many late-boomers in their 20s chose it as their primary value (15.7%) compared to early-boomers in their 20s (7.8%). In 1976, fun and enjoyment/excitement was the sixth most commonly chosen early-boomer value; by 1986, it ranked third in popularity among their younger generational peers, the late-boomers.

These have been the shifts in value priorities among early-boomers, following a decade of relatively severe generational competition. And among late-boomers, this economic rivalry had already registered its effects on their value priorities during early socialization. By 1986, dominated by their struggle for economic progress, occupational achievement, and material contentment, many boomers had given up on self-fulfillment as an attainable goal. Self-fulfillment, as a value, had become a need gratification that severe intracohort competition had temporarily made infeasible—even impractical. They had shifted their value priorities in a direction corresponding to a downward movement in Maslow's hierarchy of needs—away from values expressive of "self-actualization" needs and toward values expressing "esteem" needs, and even "physiological" needs.

Moreover, it is likely that this swing away from self-fulfillment and the wider acceptance of self-respect as a primary value has taken place while boomers are still interpreting happiness and value fulfillment in terms of material and financial success. Yet, even as they continue to equate the attainment of respect and esteem with economic success, the "American Dream" of relatively easy material prosperity that they had observed in their parents will, in the eyes of many boomers, continue to elude them.

A central prediction of this chapter can now be stated. As struggling boomers continue to confront the unrelenting economic hardship of severe competition, they will be increasingly predisposed to search for self-fulfillment and meaning in life in other, noneconomic domains of their lives. That is to say, the economically induced psychological stresses they are experiencing will cause them to realign their value priorities to reflect nonmaterial, nonfinancial measures of achievement and sources of satisfaction and happiness.

Put another way, their current materialistic interpretation of value fulfillment will gradually give way to nonmaterialistic means for expressing need-driven values. Economically hard-pressed baby boomers have for many years ignored other sources of fulfillment in their headlong struggle to achieve material prosperity and maintain their economic status relative to older adults. As a group, throughout this stage of their lives, they have largely neglected their communities, ignored their politicians, dodged their burden as citizens, bridled their concerns with societal problems, and postponed their commitment to others. To many boomers, economic success and prosperity attained at these costs may well appear hollow. They will increasingly realize that self-fulfillment and a satisfying, meaningful life can be achieved with other, more easily attainable, more pleasurable, less materialistic agendas.

In short, as boomers mature through middle age and approach late adulthood, they will be prone to seek out self-fulfillment and meaning in life in noneconomic spheres of their lives. In the process, baby boomers will realign their value priorities to reflect nonmaterial, nonfinancial measures of success and fountains of happiness and satisfaction with life.

What form will this realignment of value structures take? What shifts in value priorities and consequent activities and sources of happiness can one anticipate among maturing, middle-aged boomers? Research on human aging and life-span development can be helpful in our quest for futuristic scenarios.

MIDDLE AGE AND SHIFTING VALUE PRIORITIES

Bernice Neugarten's programmatic studies of aging and personality change, across the adult life span, furnish an impression of the mentally healthy, well-adjusted middle-aged adult. Salient characteristics of middle adulthood include the perception that one is in control of one's life and actively involved in the world, and entering a period in which latent talents and capacities can be put to use in new directions. In-depth interviews confirm "that middle age is a period of heightened sensitivity to one's position within a complex social environment; and that reassessment of the self is a prevailing theme . . . middle adulthood is the period of maximum capacity and ability to handle a highly complex environment and a highly differentiated self" (Neugarten, 1968, pp. 93, 97). Also, the perception of greater maturity and a better grasp of realities is a major source of reassurance to middle-aged people. Other striking qualities observed in middle-aged persons are a keener self-understanding, a preoccupation with self-utilization (How can I make the best use of my "self," my experience, my skills?), and reflection on life and one's contribution to it:

> . . . the stock-taking, the heightened introspection, and above all, the structuring and restructuring of experience—that is, the conscious processing of new information in the light of what one has already learned; and turning one's proficiency to the achievement of desired ends. (p. 98)

As a pioneer of the stage theory of ego development—which encompassed the effects of maturation, experience, and social institutions on the developing individual—Erikson (1963) characterized middle adulthood as a stage when individuals (if they are to successfully adapt to both inner- and outer-world demands and develop a positive evaluation of self) need to give of themselves by teaching and guiding the next generation. There needs to be an expansion of ego interests and a sense of having contributed to the future. The challenge for the middle-aged person in this stage of life is to care for oneself, but also to care for others and for the world as a whole; there is a concern for the "maintenance of the world" and with passing the culture on to coming generations (Erikson, 1976, pp. 15, 27).

Peck (1968) expanded on Erikson's notions about the adjustments facing a person in middle and later life. Moreover, Peck's model integrates the concept of a realignment in value priorities as a person matures during middle age and old age. This model of psychological development seems to lend itself well to predictions of value orientation changes among aging baby boomers. Peck (1968, pp. 89–90) describes seven kinds of psychological adjustments at different stages in the latter half of life, and five of these appear to be relevant to baby boomers in middle age:

1. *Valuing Wisdom vs. Valuing Physical Powers.* People who age successfully in this stage are those who "switch from physique-based values to wisdom-based—or mental-based—values, in their self-definition" and as their main resource for solving life's problems.

2. *Socializing vs. Sexualizing in Human Relationships.* This transition consists of "redefining men and women as individuals and as companions, with the sexual element decreasingly significant," and implies that interpersonal relations can now operate on a depth of understanding which was more difficult to attain with the earlier, somewhat egocentric sex drive.

3. *Emotional Flexibility vs. Emotional Impoverishment.* Those who adjust well in middle age have the capacity to shift emotional investments from one person or activity to another. In middle age, many people attain their greatest range in potential objects of emotional investment: They achieve the widest circle of acquaintances and contacts in their community and job-related worlds; others, both young and old, actively turn to them as "mature" or "experienced" people. Moreover, many opportunities for shifting emotional investments arise: Children grow up and leave home; parents, relatives, and friends die; grandchildren are born.

4. *Mental Flexibility vs. Mental Rigidity.* As a part of adaptation in middle age, the challenge is to avoid being closed minded to new ideas and set in one's ways. Those who are mentally flexible during the middle years "learn to master their experiences, achieve a degree of detached perspective on them, and make use of them as *provisional* guides to the solution of new issues."

5. *Ego Differentiation vs. Work-Role Preoccupation.* This transition in value priorities is a way of reappraising and redefining one's worth, following either retirement, semi-retirement, temporary retirement, or the decision to shift emphasis away from one's vocation to other domains in life. It allows men and women to take satisfaction in a broader range of role activities than just their long-time specific work role. Successful adaptation in this stage of life requires that the person find "a varied set of valued activities and valued self-attributes, so that any one of several alternatives can be pursued with a sense of satisfaction and worthwhileness."

What implications do the transitions marked by these five stages in midlife have for middle-aged baby boomers? If we combine Peck's model of aging with the observations of Neugarten and Erikson, we are likely to witness at least a partial realignment of boomers' value structures along the dimensions shown next.

FROM		TO
Valuing physical powers	→	Valuing wisdom
Sexualizing	→	Socializing in human relationships
Emotional impoverishment	→	Emotional flexibility
Mental rigidity	→	Mental flexibility
Work-role preoccupation	→	Ego differentiation

A variation on the general nature of the value transitions characterized here comes from biologist Jonas Salk (Hampden-Turner, 1981, pp. 160–161; Salk, 1973). Salk was addressing the types of human values—and shift in value orientation—needed to ensure the survival of humanity and a balanced ecosystem. Though he did not refer to changes in value priorities as people aged, the general type of change predicted for baby boomers as they experience middle age is neatly captured by Salk's value dichotomy:

EGO VALUES	BEING VALUES
Intellect	Intuition
Reason	Feeling
Objective	Subjective
Morality	Reality
Differences	Differentiation
Competition	Cooperation
Power	Influence
Win-Lose	Win-Win

One writer (Wolfe, 1990, pp. 166–167) has drawn the analogy between this type of value dichotomy and the differences between the hemispheric specializations of the brain: "Ego values" are similar in character to the functions of the left brain (logic, abstraction, reasoning, objectivity), while "being values" tend to parallel right-brain operations (intuition, feeling, holistic thinking, subjectivity). Thus, the shift from "ego values" to "being values" would be analogous to a shift in cognitive pattern from left-brain to right-brain ways of thinking about the world.

To summarize, values of the following kind are predicted to govern the restructured value systems of a large proportion of middle-aged baby boomers: a spirit of cooperation, an appreciation of the complex nature of reality, a commitment to the solution of societal problems, a community-minded ethos, a reliance on spiritual values, a philosophy of feeling and caring, a reliance on intuition, a desire for self-discovery, and a widening of one's horizons by moving beyond self-centered roles and interests.

Yet, even before large numbers of boomers have reached middle age, there is already some evidence of a shift to community-oriented values, altruistic behavior, and political involvement among members of this cohort. Public opinion pollsters report that boomers have to some extent shifted their orientations away from the workplace and toward family and spiritual concerns, are turning out to vote, caring about the neighborhood, and widening their network of friends (Edmondson, 1991, 1992, 1993).

MODELING THE ANTECEDENTS AND CONSEQUENCES OF MIDDLE-AGED BOOMER VALUES

The major themes discussed, thus far, may now be integrated into a conceptual model so that the strategic planning implications of boomers' shifting value priorities can be offered in the final part of this chapter. Figure 16.2 charts the hypothesized relationships among *antecedents* of baby-boomer values, their *values* in middle age, the predicted *behavioral consequences* of value-system realignment, and the *social consequences* of baby boomers' collective behaviors.

Acting as one antecedent of values, is *maturation* during middle age. As was apparent from the review of studies on aging, the psychological adjustments occurring in middle adulthood, the change in roles and statuses, and the changing perspective on life brought on by experience all have a tendency to restructure value priorities.

Adding impetus to the maturation process is a second antecedent, *economically induced stresses*, described earlier. Easterlin (1987) has documented some of the mental stresses that have resulted as baby boomers have struggled to maintain their economic status vis-à-vis their expectations: societal

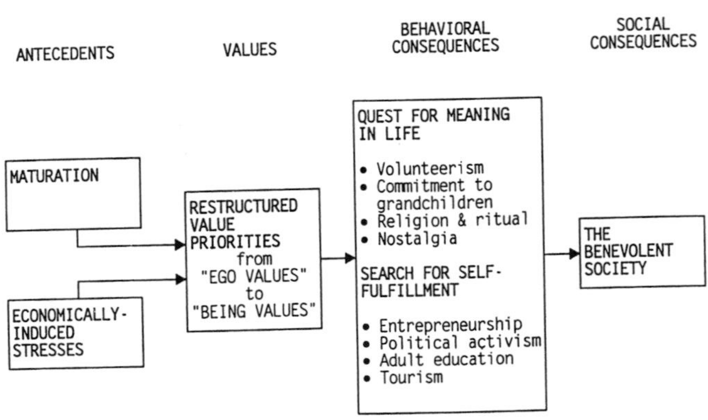

FIG. 16.2. A model of the antecedents and consequences of baby-boomer values in middle age.

alienation, conflicting obligations to family and job, postponement of family formation, feelings of inadequacy, self-doubt, hopelessness, despair, resentment, bitterness. "Mental stress increases because large generation size weakens the economic underpinning of personal life. . . . The economic difficulties encountered when working age is reached are just one more confirmation that life is tough, but it is a crucial one because economic success is so fundamental to the attainment of most aspirations" (p. 99). But, for boomers, the struggle to maintain economic status is continual and requires huge sacrifices in other domains of life. Therefore, boomers would be prone to search for self-fulfillment and meaning in life in noneconomic domains. Their stressful experiences would lead them to realign their value priorities to reflect nonmaterial measures of success and sources of happiness and satisfaction with life.

Hence, maturation in middle age and the desire to lessen economically induced stresses, together, should amplify their separate impressions on boomers' value systems—redefining or prescribing what in middle-aged life is worth shouldering, committing to, undertaking, protecting, achieving, acquiring, and consuming. And, given the foregoing discussion on values in middle age, the *restructured value priorities* in the model are predicted to be reflections of Salk's "being values."

The implications of baby boomers' new system of values in middle age are shown under "Behavioral Consequences." The model predicts two interrelated and somewhat overlapping sets of consequences: behaviors that would represent boomers' *quest for meaning in life,* and behaviors that would reflect the *search for self-fulfillment.* As shown, these two genres of behaviors surface as eight modes of expression—outlets for boomers' values that are likely to turn into societal trends. These trends are presented in the next section. Finally, the model includes the social consequences of baby boomers' collective behaviors and attitudes, namely, what I have chosen to call a *Benevolent Society*—an America that benefits from the actions of many millions of baby boomers whose lifestyles in the period, say, 2005 to 2015 reflect the importance of "being values."

CONSEQUENCES OF BOOMERS' VALUE PRIORITIES IN THE 21st CENTURY

In the year 2005, all of America's baby boomers will be in their 40s and 50s—an age bracket that places them inside the conventional designation for middle age. Early-boomers will have been in middle age for many years, and undoubtedly will have set the tone for the realigned value structure that is predicted to occur. Their sway will probably accelerate the realignment to middle-age values among late-boomers. The behavioral consequences of these prevailing value priorities could be divided into two classes: attitudes and acts that embody a quest for meaning in life; and a mind-set and behaviors that signify a search for the self-fulfillment that was largely postponed in young adulthood.

In this concluding section, are offered some predictions on specific consumption behaviors within these two broad classes of value consequences. These hypothesized future behaviors of baby boomers are presented as eight trends to watch for. They represent scenarios of attitudes and behaviors in eight major domains of private and public life, and therefore components of baby boomers' future lifestyles. The hypothesized trends are interpretations of some of the long-term consequences of middle-age values as presented earlier and are, in keeping with the arguments made, less materialistic expressions of those value priorities. Strategic planners in the business, labor, government, education, and nonprofit sectors of the economy need to be sensitive to the marketing implications of these and similar trends, since they will be fueled by a massive cohort in the population.

The eight trends are: voluntarism, commitment to grandchildren, spirituality, nostalgia, entrepreneurship, political activism, learning for self-fulfillment, and discovery tourism. These trends acknowledge that middle-aged baby boomers will probably strive to achieve self-fulfillment and a satisfying, meaningful lifestyle through less materialistic, *and more attainable*, activities than the previously revered economic formula.

The scenarios are necessarily speculative, but they offer some insight into the types of phenomena that should become commonplace among middle-aged boomers in the first and second decades of the 21st century. For brevity, they are presented in point form in Table 16.1.

THE BENEVOLENT SOCIETY

As the very first decade of the third millennium advances, American society is surmised to undergo a subtle but ubiquitous shift in moral and psychological orientation. Aging baby boomers, a generation of 76 million Americans locked together in a crowded chase for contentment and achievement, are now approaching midlife. In early adulthood, boomers—as a cohort with very high expectations of life—were largely self-absorbed, socially uncommitted, and intensely competing but economically troubled and vocationally enervated citizens. Frustrated by a perceived lack of progress in the workplace and the struggle to find self-fulfillment in a competitive economic environment, many maturing boomers are now poised for a reversal of spirit.

In middle age, the heretofore nascent social conscience of baby boomers is expected to awaken, if not blossom. We should witness a boomer outlook

TABLE 16.1

Eight Hypothesized Trends Among Baby Boomers in Middle Age

I. THE QUEST FOR MEANING IN LIFE

---

1. VOLUNTARISM. *Doing meaningful things for others:*

- Social connectedness, altruism, community spirit are important goals
- Involvement in neighborhood
- Volunteering their time
- Are good sources of advice; good counselors (have broad, wisdom-giving experiences)
- Serving as mature teachers in schools, colleges, community centers
- Serving as volunteer mentors to school kids with problems
- Teaching a younger generation the values of patience, wisdom, and tolerance
- They favor companies involved in good works

2. COMMITMENT TO GRANDCHILDREN. *Erik Erikson's "generativity" in effect—teaching or guiding their grandchildren:*

- As grandparents, they have resources (inheritances, time) to endow grandchildren with

    Care
    Entertainment
    Opportunities for growing and learning
    Money and possessions

- Fertility and family size in baby boomlet cohort (boomers' children) will be higher
- Becoming adoptive grandparents if children have no offspring
- Attitudes toward youth will be more positive
- Want to leave a legacy for the future
- Passing the culture on to grandchildren

3. SPIRITUALITY. *Looking for answers in a communal setting:*

- The search for peace of mind, certainty, simplicity
- The turn toward spirituality will be to traditional faiths and churches
- But some will find answers in

    Nontraditional forms of worship
    Nonmainstream, unconventional religions
    Nondenominational churches

- Traditional holidays take on a less commercial, more spiritual tone
- Practicing spirituality through charitable work

4. NOSTALGIA. *Keeping a continuity with the past:*

- Attached to familiar objects of their past
- Possessions give a sense of comfort/continuity
- Pets, scrapbooks, diaries, letters, photo albums, keepsakes are treasured
- Will reminisce and dwell in the past—the *life review* (Butler, 1975, pp. 412-414)
- Nostalgia and mild regret are key emotions
- A nostalgia industry needed to meet the demand for

    Reunions and searching for "lost" friends
    Writing or tape-recording their *autobiographies* (Birren, 1987)
    Searching out their genealogies
    Making pilgrimages to places imbued with memories
    Movies, remakes, music of 1950s-1970s era

TABLE 16.1
(Continued)

II. THE SEARCH FOR SELF-FULFILLMENT

5. ENTREPRENEURSHIP. *Wanting to remain productive:*

- Well-educated, maturing boomers will have fitness, vitality, mental acuity
- Facing a restructured economy offering many project-oriented opportunities
- Facing a looser, less compressed timetable–*the fluid life cycle* (Neugarten & Neugarten, 1986, p. 36)
- Small businesses (pre- and postretirement)
- Working from the home
- Married couples forming entrepreneurial partnerships
- Flexible hours
- Working for many clients
- Renting-my-brains-to-others philosophy

6. POLITICAL ACTIVISM. *Bernice Neugarten's "complexity" in effect--feeling actively involved in the world:*

- A well-educated and savvy cohort
- Taking on community responsibility
- Likely to be dependable voters
- Supporting causes
- Lobbying
- Taking legal action when wronged, or when others are wronged

7. ADULT EDUCATION. *Striving for personal growth:*

- A means of reaching intellectual potential
- Mature boomers will be the disciples of adult education
- Exploring new fields of inquiry
- Taking courses for fun
- Developing serious avocations
- Wanting retirement-planning workshops and guidance
- Group tours of plants and museum tours
- Educational expeditions
- Shadowing the lives of professionals to see how they live and work

8. DISCOVERY TOURISM. *Discovering another world and finding fun and enjoyment:*

- "Safe" travel to exotic destinations
- Scaled-down adventure travel
- Guided tours to sites loaded with culture
- Slow boats to china
- Luxury train travel
- Cruises to popular destinations
- Retreats at resort hotels
- Visits to shrines, religious sites, health spas, national parks
- Visits to ancestral homes and origins

that has veered from the narrower "ego values" of morality, differences, power, competition, pure intellect, reason, and a win–lose mentality, to the societally compassionate "being values" of reality, differentiation, influence, cooperation, intuition, feeling, and a win–win mind-set. This fundamental value shift among America's boomers signals a refocusing of priorities, aspirations, dreams, and the search for ego-identity. Baby boomers in their 40s, 50s, and early 60s are predicted to tailor their lifestyles and life choices in a manner that often matches the best interests of their communities and organizations, and the entire land.

America can certainly benefit from the cumulative effects of a growth in voluntarism, a commitment to the youngest generation, a return to spirituality. Society gains, too, from the historical continuity brought on by nostalgia, the affirmation of entrepreneurship in later life, political activism, adult education, and self-discovery and personal renewal through tourism. As baby boomers turn to these ways of expressing their values, they will serve their nation in a very real sense, deed by deed turning America into a Benevolent Society.

REFERENCES

Birren, J. E. (1987). The best of all stories. *Psychology Today, 21*(5), 91–92.

"Boomers gloomy over money" (1990). *The Vancouver Province* (June 14), 17.

Butler, R. N. (1975). *Why survive? Being old in America.* New York: Harper & Row.

Crosby, L. A., Gill, J. D., & Lee, R. E. (1984). Life status and age as predictors of value orientation. In R. E. Pitts, Jr. & A. G. Woodside (Eds.), *Personal values and consumer psychology* (pp. 201–218). Lexington, MA: Lexington Books.

Easterlin, R. A. (1987). *Birth and fortune: The impact of numbers on personal welfare* (2nd ed.). Chicago: University of Chicago Press.

Edmondson, B. (1991). Burned-out Boomers flee to families. *American Demographics, 13*(12), 17.

Edmondson, B. (1992). Cause-related reasoning. *American Demographics, 14*(1), 2.

Edmondson, B. (1993). Harvest time. *American Demographics, 15*(1), 2.

Ehrlich, E. (1989). How the next decade will differ. *Business Week*, September 25, 142–143.

Eisert, D. C., & Kahle, L. R. (1983). Well-being. In L. R. Kahle (Ed.), *Social values and social change: Adaptation to life in America* (pp. 207–225). New York: Praeger.

Erikson, E. H. (1963). *Childhood and society* (2nd ed.), New York: W. W. Norton.

Erikson, E. H. (1976). Reflections on Dr. Borg's life cycle. In E. H. Erikson (Ed.), *Adulthood.* New York: W. W. Norton.

Greenwald, M. (1989). Bad news for the Baby Boomers. *American Demographics, 11*(2), 34–37.

Hampden-Turner, C. (1981). *Maps of the mind.* New York: Macmillan.

Kahle, L. R. (Ed.). (1983). *Social values and social change: Adaptation to life in America.* New York: Praeger.

Kahle, L. R., Poulos, B., & Sukhdial, A. (1988). Changes in social values in the United States during the past decade. *Journal of Advertising Research, 28* (February/March), 35–41.

Maslow, A. H. (1954). *Motivation and personality.* New York: Harper.

Muller, T. E. (1989). Canada's ageing population and projected changes in value orientations and the demand for urban services. *Service Industries Journal, 94*, 14–28.

Muller, T. E., & Kahle, L. R. (1991, October). *Analyzing long-term changes in consumer values: The case of North America's aging Baby Boomers.* Paper presented at the European Institute for Advanced Studies in Management Workshop on Value and Lifestyle Research in Marketing. Brussels: European Institute for Advanced Studies in Management.

Muller, T. E., Kahle, L. R., & Chéron, E. J. (1992). Value trends and demand forecasts for Canada's aging Baby Boomers. *Canadian Journal of Administrative Sciences, 94*, 294–304.

Munson, J. M. (1984). Personal values: Considerations on their measurement and application to five areas of research inquiry. In R. E. Pitts, Jr. & A. G. Woodside (Eds.), *Personal values and consumer psychology* (pp. 13–33). Lexington, MA: Lexington Books.

Neugarten, B. L. (1968). The awareness of middle age. In B. L. Neugarten (Ed.), *Middle age and aging* (pp. 93–98). Chicago: University of Chicago Press.

Neugarten, B. L., & Neugarten, D. A. (1986). Changing meanings of age in the aging society. In A. Pifer & L. Bronte (Eds.), *Our aging society: Paradox and promise* (pp. 33–51). New York: W. W. Norton.

Peck, R. C. (1968). Psychological developments in the second half of life. In B. L. Neugarten (Ed.), *Middle age and aging* (pp. 88–92). Chicago: University of Chicago Press.

Rokeach, M. (1979). From individual to institutional values: With special reference to the values of science. In M. Rokeach (Ed.), *Understanding human values: Individual and societal* (pp. 47–70). New York: The Free Press.

Rosenfeld, A., & Stark, E. (1987). The prime of our lives. *Psychology Today, 21*(5), 62–72.

Salk, J. (1973). *Survival of the wisest.* New York: Harper & Row.

Thomas, E. (1986). Growing pains at 40. *Time,* May 19, 26–34.

Thurow, L. (1981). [Quoted in] *Downward mobility* (transcript of U.S. Chronicle, Show #U.S.-36). New York: WNET-TV.

Veroff, J., Douvan, E., & Kulka, R. A. (1981). *The inner American.* New York: Basic Books.

Wolfe, D. B. (1990). *Serving the ageless market.* New York: McGraw-Hill.

Yankelovich, D. (1981). [Quoted in] *Downward mobility* (transcript of U.S. Chronicle, Show #U.S.-36). New York: WNET-TV.

Chapter 17

The Adult Longitudinal Panel: A Research Program to Study the Aging Process and Its Effect on Consumers Across the Life Span

Lawrence R. Lepisto
Central Michigan University

The process of aging is common to all consumers. As a person ages obvious physiological changes and subtle psychological and lifestyle changes occur. While the aging process is universal to every person, very little is understood about the role of aging in consumer behavior. With the large cohort of baby boomers approaching middle age and the elderly consumer market continuing to grow, there is an obvious need to examine the aging process and its effect on consumer behavior.

This unique longitudinal research program, designed to measure the effect of aging on consumer behavior, is based on an integrated framework utilizing research from numerous disciplines. This chapter describes the research methodology, theoretical foundation, variables related to aging and consumer behavior, and implications from such a research program.

THE LONGITUDINAL RESEARCH METHODOLOGY

A longitudinal research paradigm is the only approach that can measure the aging process by studying the same adults over a prolonged period of time. This enables the measurement of changes experienced by an adult as he or she grows older. By following consumers with periodic longitudinal measurements, changes (or the lack of changes) in the person and in consumer behavior can be identified (Lepisto, 1985). More importantly, the timing of changes and the factors that may cause those changes can also be identified. In this way the aging process and its relationship with consumer behavior can begin to be understood.

The Adult Longitudinal Panel was first developed in 1987 based on a limited questionnaire sent to respondents. A substantially expanded questionnaire was sent to the same adults in 1991, which became the baseline year for the longitudinal study. The same respondents will again be measured in 1996 and every following 5 years. The sample, stratified by age, was generated from a mailing list of licensed drivers across the United States.

The sampling methodology followed the total response method suggested by Dilman (1978). A first-class mailing was sent several months prior to the administration of the questionnaire to correct for address changes and prepare panel members for the upcoming questionnaire. The first wave of questionnaires were sent in the fall of 1991 followed a week later by a reminder card. A second wave of questionnaires to nonrespondents followed 6 weeks later. The response rate of 65% was considered acceptable given the length (12 pages) of the questionnaire. An incentive, which was a drawing from completed questionnaires with winnings from $100 to $1,000, helped to boost the response rate.

The resulting panel is a sample of 2,450 respondents ranging in age from 20 to over 80 years of age. Table 17.1 presents the demographic

TABLE 17.1
Demographic Profile of the Adult Longitudinal Panel

Sex	*Marital Status*
1339 male separated/divorced 1097 female	1846 married 212 182 widowed 189 single

Occupation	
1096 professional/technical	360 manager/administration
311craftsman/skilledtrade/foreman	163 laborer
120 salesperson	93 equipment operator/truck driver
72 student/military	78 unemployed
55 farmer	42 service worker

Ethnic Background	
2263 Anglo/White	33 Hispanic
67 African American	12 Asian
32 Native American/Alaskan Native	23 other

profile of the panel. These data indicate that the panel is somewhat upscale, not unusual for mail surveys. Although financial limitations did not allow for a sample proportional to the entire population, the size of the sample allows for adequate sampling of subpopulations.

THEORETICAL FOUNDATIONS USED TO STUDY ADULT DEVELOPMENT

Until recently developmental researchers have focused their investigations on child development, often neglecting any development that occurred after adolescence. While gerontologists studied issues related to older persons, little attention was paid to developmental issues between adolescence and old age. A developmental life-span perspective has broadened research attention to include not only children but adults of all ages. Now the aging process of adults is being addressed in numerous separate disciplines under the overall umbrella of adult development or life span research.

Theories of Adult Development

A unifying theory of adult development does not yet exist. Alternative approaches to study adult development are best described as a "family of perspectives" (Baltes, 1987). These are the life stage, life span, and life course perspectives. These perspectives differ on the variables that they emphasize and their supporting assumptions.

The Life Stage Perspective. The life stage perspective suggests that there is an underlying order in the human course of life. An individual is expected to go through relatively universal, age-linked, adult developmental periods (Levinson, 1984). These periods are called stages of development by Erikson (1950), a movement of childhood consciousness to adult consciousness by Gould (1972), and "seasons" or "eras" by Levinson, Darrow, Klein, Levinson, and McKee (1979). These perspectives anticipate transitions between stages, proposing that "unless the individual goes through some level of inner turmoil and reassessment at this time, further development will not occur and overall mental health will be affected adversely" (Bush & Simmons 1981, p. 151).

Movement from one life stage to the next is (a) expected to occur at certain ages, (b) required for human development, and (c) can be a period of discontinuity resulting in tourmoil and/or growth. These transitions have been referred to as "life crises," "passages," and "turning points." The "midlife crisis," a popularized transition expected during the late 30s to mid-40s, has not been validated by empirical research (Costa & McCrae, 1980; Farrell & Rosenberg, 1981).

The life stage perspective has received only limited empirical support. Erickson's propositions were based on Freud's theory of personality and his own experience with children. Levinson and Gould have some empirical justification for their propositions, but their research has been criticized for being based on small samples (Neugarten, 1979). Another concern with the life stage perspective is the different phenomena on which each researcher has focused. As a result of a lack of empirical support and questionable assumptions, the life stage perspective is receiving more limited attention in the adult development literature.

The Life Span Perspective. The life span perspective of adult development is based on less stringent assumptions than the life stage perspective. Rather than viewing adult development as "universal, irreversible, unidirectional, or primarily age-determined" (Bush & Simmons 1981, p. 151), the life span perspective attempts to describe and explain age-related behavior through the adult years in a less normative fashion. This orientation seeks to identify change and stability and the patterns of variables that emerge as adults age. For example, life span research has generally shown stability in personality while intellectual performance gradually declines in the latter stages of life.

Recognized in the life span perspective is the role of environmental effect on shaping one's developmental pattern. A person's demographic profile and the era in which a person is socialized is recognized as impacting on adult development. The result is the incorporation of individual differences within the patterns of adult development.

The Life Course Perspective. The life course perspective is a sociological orientation to adult development that emphasizes the impact of the social environment upon psychological development. Elder (1975, 1979), the most recognized life course researcher, has demonstrated the effect of the depression and the post-World War II prosperity on the adult lives of children who were raised in those eras. Riley (1987) notes that the interdependence of aging and social change can differ for each age cohort. For example, during the past 10 to 20 years people are living longer and women have begun childbearing later in life, resulting in middle-aged people more often being responsible for the simultaneous care of their children and parents.

The life course and life span perspectives have replaced life stage perspectives because it is apparent that development is more complex than moving from one discrete stage to subsequent stages. Sociological and environmental differences for cohorts and individuals are recognized as important in adult development.

Directions for Future Adult Development Research

The theory of adult development is in it infancy. Levinson (1986) noted, "we still know very little about the complexities and contradictions of the human life course" (p. 10). To advance the theoretical understanding of adult development, there are several guidelines for future research: (a) identify the attitudes, behaviors, roles, and values (the phenomena that we want to predict) that are part of adult development; (b) identify the different life paths that various segments of adults follow over the life span; (c) use a longitudinal methodology to study adult development; and (d) develop a consumer life structure to give a framework to the variables studying adult consumers over the life span.

Identify the Phenomena of Adult Development. When theorists constructed developmental theory for children, they sought to explain overt changes in behavior. For example, 2-year-old children have temper tantrums so this period is labeled as "the terrible twos." However, with adults, the actual changes in attitudes, behavior, roles, and values are not nearly as obvious nor are the stages so discretely marked by physical maturation. As Costa and McCrae (1989) pointed out, "The major difference between theories of child development and adult development is that the former generally try to account for well-known phenomena; the latter try to point out phenomena to be explained" (p. 47). Further they noted, "Exploratory empirical research is a much-needed supplement to theory testing, provided it is systematic" (Costa & McCrae, 1989, p. 50). Therefore, the first step in developing a theory of adult development is to identify through systematic research those phenomena.

There are two approaches to guide in the identification of these phenomena. One approach is to look at past theorists to identify those phenomena they suggest as part of adult development. The following is a brief summary of the primary theorists and the major phenomena they identify as part of adult development.

Erickson (1963) feels that adults develop a *concern for the larger social structure.*

Jung (1960) suggests an *increase in introversion* in middle and later life and the reorganization of *value systems.*

Buhler (1967) feels there are changes toward *goal seeking and goal restructuring* as adults age.

Levinson (1978) emphasizes the *increasing individuality* of adults as they pull themselves through transitions.

Cumming and Henry (1961) posit *disengagement theory* for older adults while Maddox (1963) challenged with *activity theory.*

> Neugarten (1977) suggests *stability* evident through much of the life span while sociologists "see *careers* wax and wane, historical changes engulf the individual, and *family roles* change." (Costa & McCrae, 1989, p. 48)

Although these theorists indeed have phenomena identified, the variables often are vague and provide little guidance for their operationalization.

A second approach to the identification of adult development phenomena is to examine empirical research that studied specific variables over the life span. Large bodies of research have examined personality and found substantial stability over the life span (e.g., Bengston, Reedy & Gordon, 1985; Neugarten, 1977). It appears that, once personality is formed by early adulthood, little change occurs. Even when there was a self-perceived change reported by subjects, objective tests found no significant personality differences (Woodruff & Birren, 1972).

An area of research that has found consistent change over the life span is cognitive functioning. Generally, cognitive performance increases through early adulthood, plateaus through middle adulthood, and consistently declines from middle adulthood (e.g., Dobbs & Rule, 1987; Shaie, 1983). These results have been reported on a variety of intellectual tests and cognitive tasks. Although there are various hypotheses to explain this decline in performance, the empirical research findings are substantially consistent (Salthouse, 1989).

Identify Life Paths. A potentially powerful application of longitudinal studies is the identification of the life paths taken by different segments of consumers as they age. Levinson (1986) noted there are profound differences in human development among classes, cultures, and gender. In other words, various groups are likely to psychologically develop differently. Studying the life paths that different segments of consumers take through the life span provides the potential for marketers to develop an alternative basis for segmentation. Once specific life path segments can be identified, the potential for forecasting future behavior is enhanced. As Costa and McCrae (1989) point out, "By understanding individual differences, we can predict careers, life outcomes, and adjustment to the threats, losses, and challenges of adult life" (p. 68).

Longitudinal Methodology. The only research paradigm that measures individual change over time is the longitudinal design. By measuring the *same* individuals over time, longitudinal designs provide better descriptions of the dynamics of change associated with the aging process (Boruch & Pearson, 1988). In contrast to the "snap shot" picture provided by cross-sectional research, longitudinal research provides a sequential frame by frame "movie picture" alternative.

A number of cautions have also been identified with longitudinal designs. Boruch and Pearson (1988) summarize such problems as: nonresponse bias; inadequate sample representativeness; potential learning effects; reliability and validity concerns; and unpredictable changes in respondents (changes in family, employment, social class). In addition Levinson (1986) points out that longitudinal research can become outmoded as new and better measures become available whereas the ongoing longitudinal study must stay with measures developed years earlier.

One unique application of longitudinal designs is to build a database that assists in predicting the behavior of younger cohorts by studying the behavior of older cohorts (e.g., Heslop, 1986; Rentz, Reynolds, & Stout, 1983). Cohort analysis, especially over a long period of time measurements, can help anticipate the behavior of cohorts as they approach certain points in the life span such as retirement.

Due to inherent research and practical difficulties, longitudinal studies of consumer behavior have been limited (Moschis, 1984). One likely problem is the cost and difficulty of developing and maintaining a panel over a long period of time (Lewis, 1989). Investing so much time and effort for a future payoff (as measures are made well into the future) may not be viewed as a positive career decision for marketing academicians. Despite these serious considerations, there is no other method to measure aging over time.

Life Structure. Whereas previous theory provides only limited guidance on appropriate variables to include in a consumer-oriented study of aging, the concept of life structure does offer some direction. A person's life structure is "the underlying pattern or design of a person's life at a given time" (Levinson 1986, p. 6). Levinson (1986) describes life structure as "a boundary between personality structure and social structure and governs the transactions between them. . . . The life structure mediates the relationship between the individual and the environment. . . . A theory of life structure must draw equally upon psychology and the social sciences" (p. 7). Therefore, the concept of life structure permits a rich detailed description of a person's interaction with the social environment and lends itself to the measurement of the aging process.

Life structure variables have only been generally described. Costa and McCrae (1989) proposed general factors that comprise an individual's life structure: physical and psychiatric health; style and success of marriage and parenting; vocational history; accommodation to life stresses; creative achievements; leisure-time pursuits; social activities; and attitudes and attitude changes. The life structure that integrates aging and consumer behavior variables in Adult Longitudinal Panel is examined in the following section.

THE CONSUMER LIFE STRUCTURE

This study incorporated variables suggested by empirical findings from a number of disciplines into the broad framework of a consumer life structure. Several criteria were used to select these variables. First, to be selected for use in the study the variable must be empirically quantifiable in a mail questionnaire. Most longitudinal studies of adult development use personal interviews yielding qualitative results, permitting only limited analysis. Second, the variable had to measure some aspect of the adult development process or had to explain relationships among other variables being measured.

Although the notion of consumer life structure has parallels with lifestyle research, few psychographic items were utilized because there are few apriori predictions that can be made using psychographics. More importantly, there is no substantial theoretical foundation for lifestyles, especially in the context of aging. The Adult Longitudinal Panel utilized the approach of using variables suggested by previous theory and research rather than being a data-driven study with no theoretical underpinnings.

Because aging is accompanied by psychological and perceptual changes, this survey measures a variety of variables associated with the aging process. These aging variables were generated from research in gerontology, developmental psychology, family studies, and consumer behavior. The research framework used in this study is presented in Fig. 17.1.

The variables that measured the psychological dimension of consumer behavior were organized to measure several facets of life structure. The dimensions measured were the respondent's approach to life; the resources one has available to cope with stressors; and how one reacts to life experiences.

Approach to Life

Approach to life variables are used to measure how a person approaches life though the life-span. More specifically, these variables develop a profile of how a person positions him or herself to deal with the issues, challenges, and relationships that are encountered in life.

Locus of Control. A person's locus of control affects the manner in which a variety of issues in life are approached. Locus of control has been shown to affect how people deal with stress (Hutner & Locke, 1984), well-being (Morganti, Nehrke, Hulicka, & Cataldo, 1988), and information seeking (Darley & Lim, 1985). Locus of control has been linked with age in that older people appear to be more externally directed (Hale & Cockran, 1986).

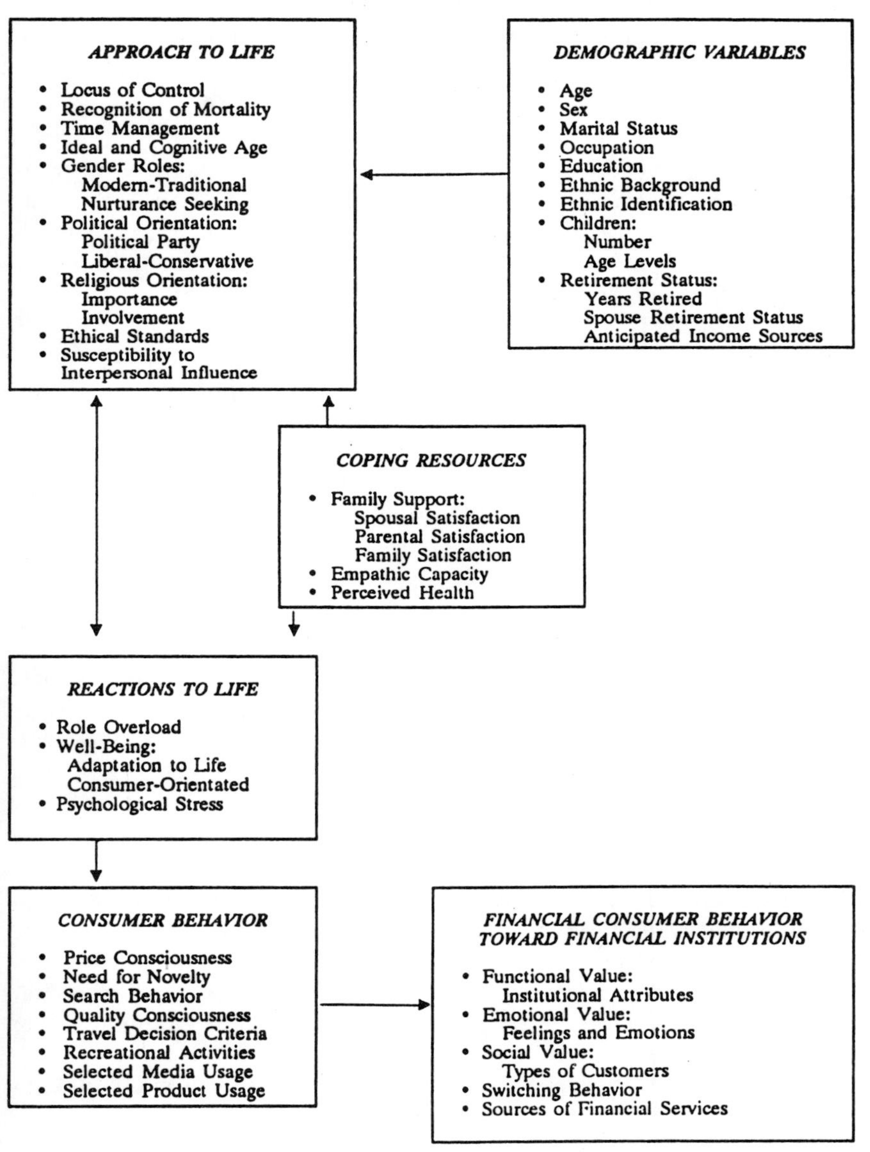

FIG. 17.1. The consumer life structure: The framework for the adult longitudinal panel.

In consumer research, the VALS measure identifies an inner-directed segment of consumers as part of its topology. Schiffman and Kanuk (1991) suggest that inner-directedness is positively related with seeking innovations. Lifestyle research has found that inner-directeds exercise more regularly (Edmondson, 1987).

Recognition of Mortality. The recognition of one's mortality occurs during the aging process leading to changing perceptions of one's time left in life (Neugarten, 1970). From middle-age on, people begin to think more in terms of time left rather than time lived. This perception could affect consumer decisions when planning future purchases.

Time Management. The impact of sufficient time on consumer lifestyles is well-accepted. This phenomenon has been termed "time squeeze" (Robinson, 1989), "time famine" (Robinson, 1990), and "time poverty" (Solomon, 1992). The ability to plan and manage time affects lifestyles and consumer behavior. For example, this ability has also been shown to affect retirement planning (Abel & Hayslip, 1987).

Ideal and Cognitive Age. Cognitive or perceived age assesses how old one feels. Cognitive age has been found to affect life satisfaction (Montepare & Lachman, 1989), psychological functioning (Linn & Hunter, 1979), well-being (Lepisto, 1989), decisions on retirement housing (Wolfe, 1990) and consumer behavior (e.g., Barak & Schiffman, 1981; Cooper & Mialoulis, 1988). Given the age-related orientation of the study, these age measures will provide a multidimensional perspective of age.

Gender Roles. The perception of gender roles is a major component of a consumer life structure. Gender roles can be measured on a modern-traditional continuum or the need for nurturance. When using the modern-traditional continuum, as expected, younger people tend to be more modern while older people tend to retain a more traditional perspective. Modern-traditional gender roles have been shown to have an effect on consumer decision making (e.g., Qualls, 1987: Rosen & Granbois, 1983; Schaninger, Buss, & Grover, 1982).

The second way to assess gender roles is through an examination of nurturance seeking from one's partner. Some women and men experience changes in their need for nurturance in their 40s and 50s. Once children are launched and their major home responsibilities have been lightened, women become more independent. At a similar stage, men begin to realize that their careers will not likely advance much further and they "feel their age." As a result, men as they age are more likely to express a higher need for nurturance while women show a declining need for nurturance (Smith & Moen, 1988).

Political and Religious Orientations. Political and religious orientations can have a significant role on consumer life structures for some consumers. Older people tend to be more conservative in their political orientation and attitude toward religion.

Ethical Perspectives. Ethical standards have been found to differ across age levels with older people being increasingly likely to behave in a more ethical fashion (Boroson, 1987; Ma, 1985). Vitell, Lumpkin and Rawwas (1991) found that elderly consumers scored higher on an ethics measure than did younger consumers.

Susceptibility to Interpersonal Influence. The susceptibility to interpersonal influence measures the degree to which a person is susceptible to influence by others. Eagly and Carli (1981) suggested that, with age and experience a person becomes less susceptible to influence. Bearden, Netemeyer, and Teel (1989) found that consumers who were more susceptible to influence were more likely to follow the lead of other consumers or to seek information from them.

Reactions to Life

Reactions to life assess the ways in which a person reacts to the issues and conditions encountered in life. These focus on the psychological reactions to issues and problems that adults must face.

Role Overload. Role overload measures the load of demands placed on people (more often women) as a result of attempting to balance the roles of parenthood and employment. As result of more demands and limited time, parents can feel significant pressure. Reilly (1982) found that women feeling overloaded reported using more convenience foods and time-saving products.

Well-Being. Well-being is how satisfied a person feels with his or her life (Campbell, Converse, & Johnson, 1977). It is used to describe how comfortably a person adapts to issues and conditions.

Well-being can also be viewed from a consumer behavior perspective. As a person ages, it has been suggested that possessions become less important as experiences and relationships become more important (Cooper & Miloulis, 1988). Well-being can assist in the measurement of the role of products, relationships, and experiences in a consumer's satisfaction and acceptance of life.

Stress. Stress can have a far-reaching impact in a person's life. Stress can cause anxiety and panic (Schafer, 1978), depression (Brown & Siegel, 1988), and guilt and distress (Janis & Mann, 1977). Lepisto, Stuenkel, and Anglin (1991) have shown that stress can affect consumer decision making.

Coping Resources

The ability to deal with stress and other reactions to life issues can be moderated by coping resources. The level of these resources can help to reduce or exacerbate one's level of stress and well-being.

Family Relationships. Family relationships can reduce or increase the amount of stress that the person experiences (Caspi, Bolger & Eckenrode, 1987). Children and spouses can provide a haven from the stresses of life or can contribute yet another layer of stress to an already stressful situation.

Empathy. Empathy is the ability to understand others' needs and issues from the other person's perspective. Empathy can be a coping resource because to understand how others feel adds a feeling of control in relationships. When empathy is felt from others, it is perceived as a validation and acceptance leading to an enhanced sense of well-being.

The role of empathy could also contribute to the assessment of wisdom. While wisdom has been assumed to be associated with advanced age, there has been considerable difficulty in opertionalizing wisdom (Neugarten, 1979). The ability to understand the needs and points of view of others could be a dimension of wisdom and aging.

Physical Health. A person's physical health can influence the ability to cope with stress (Gray & Calsyn, 1989). Obviously as consumers move into the older age brackets, one's health becomes a more important factor. Okun and Stock (1987) found that the well-being of elderly respondents was related to perceived health, regardless of their actual health status.

Consumer Behavior Variables

In addition to life span variables discussed earlier, numerous dimensions of consumer behavior were measured in this study. Items from a number of shopping and psychographic studies were used to construct the following shopping-oriented scales.

Price Consciousness. Price consciousness is the importance of price in the evaluation of products. It is the role that price plays in that evaluation.

Need for Novelty. One's need and interest in trying new or different products reflects the innovative side of a consumer.

Quality Consciousness. Quality consciousness suggests the importance of quality as a criteria in product evaluations.

Search. The degree to which consumers are willing to spend on search activities can vary. It indicates the amount of time and effort consumers take in gathering information on which to base a product choice decision.

Travel Criteria. The criteria used to make decisions on travel destinations outline the attributes and benefits of these destinations.

Product Usage. The usage of a variety of products were measured utilizing the questionnaire items of Mediamark Research, Inc. Categories of products measured were: alcoholic and nonalcoholic beverages; breakfast products; pain relievers; frozen and convenience products; vacation spending; catalog spending; brokerage firms; and automobile ownership. The specific items are presented in Fig. 17.2.

Lifestyle Activities. Items that measured selected physical fitness and other avocations and hobbies were used in the survey. The lifestyle activities measured in the study are also found in Fig. 17.2.

Media Usage. Media usage items includes: readership of selected magazines; daytime and evening television viewing on a weekday and on a Saturday; and newspaper readership.

Financial Consumer Behavior. A detailed measurement of the consumer behavior toward financial institutions was included. The cognitive, emotional, and social dimensions of banks, credit unions, and savings and loans were measured along with usage and switching behavior. The financial instruments used in financial planning for retirement were also identified.

OBJECTIVES FOR THE ADULT LONGITUDINAL PANEL

There are several objectives for the Adult Longitudinal Panel. The immediate task is to report the cross-sectional findings from the 1991 survey.

The long-term objectives of this study are to replicate the study in 1996 and every following five years. This longitudinal database will contribute

How many drinks, cups, or glasses of the following beverages have you had in the **last 7 days.** If you have not used a product, leave blank.

Drinks/glasses/cups

7-Up ______
Cola:
Coca Cola ______
Diet Coke ______
Pepsi Cola ______
Diet Pepsi ______
Beer:
Michelob ______
Budweiser ______
Old Milwaukee ______
Miller Lite ______
Pabst Beer ______
Malt liquor ______
Wine ______
Wine coolers ______
Cognac ______
Tequila ______
Milk ______
Orange juice ______
Regular coffee:
Folgers ______
Maxwell House ______
Decaffinated coffee:
Sanka ______
Maxim ______
Taster's Choice ______

Bottled water ______
Total beer ______
Total mixed drinks ______

During the **past 30 days,** how many times have you had the following breakfast items?

Hot breakfast cereal ____ times
Cold breakfast cereal ____ times
Frozen waffles ____ times
Frozen breakfast meals ____ times
Pancakes ____ times
Eggs ____ times
Bacon ____ times
Sausage ____ times
Coffee ____ times
Soft drink ____ times
Fruit ____ times
Yogurt ____ times
Orange juice ____ times
Sweet rolls ____ times
Restaurant meals:
Waitress-served meal ____ **times**
Fast food restaurant ____ **times**

How many times (or how much), **in the past 30 days,** have you used the following products or participated in the following activities? If you have not used the product or participated in an activity, leave blank.

Products:
Shampoo ____ times
Headache remedies/ Pain Relievers:
Aspirin ____ times
Excedrin ____ times
Tylenol ____ times
Electric shaver ____ times
Disposable shaver ____ times
Sleeping tablets ____ times
Vitamins ____ tablets
Stomach remedies ____ times
Shake 'n Bake mix ____ times
Chewing gum ____ sticks
Frozen yogurt ____ servings
Ice cream ____ servings
Hamburgers ____ times
Steak ____ times
Chicken ____ times
Fish ____ times
Potato chips ____ servings
Corn chips ____ servings
Pretzels ____ servings
Unpopped corn ____ servings
Popped corn ____ servings
Tortilla chips ____ servings
Peanuts, cashews ____ servings
Frozen dinners:
TV dinners, meat pies ____ dinners, pies
Diet gourmet dinners ____ dinners
Reg. gourmet dinners ____ dinners
Artificial sweetners ____ times
Salads from delicatessans ____ servings
Meals from delicatessans ____ meals
Broccoli ____ times
Salads (lettuce based) ____ times
Frozen dinners ____ times
Mouthwash ____ times

Activities:
Jogging ____ times
Walking for exercise ____ times
Swimming ____ times
Weight lifting ____ times
Baking ____ times
Aerobic exercise ____ times
Dancing ____ times
Go to bars/nightclubs ____ times
Cooking for fun ____ times
Dining out ____ times
Photography ____ times
Outdoor gardening ____ times
Woodworking ____ times

How much did you spend on vacations in the past 12 months?

(1) ____ I took no vacation
(2) ____ Less than $1,000
(3) ____ $1,000 - $2,999
(4) ____ $3,000 - $4,999
(5) ____ $5,000 or more

How many plane trips did you take in the past 12 months for vacation or personal reasons?
____ trips

How much did you personally spend on catalog or phone order items in the last 12 months?

(1) ____ Nothing
(2) ____ $1 - $49
(3) ____ $50 - $99
(4) ____ $100 - $199
(5) ____ $200 - $399
(6) ____ $400 - $499
(7) ____ $500 - $999
(8) ____ $1,000 or more

Check if you have used any of these brokerage firms in the past year.

(1) ____ Charles Schwab
(2) ____ Dean Witter
(3) ____ Merrill Lynch
(4) ____ Paine Webber
(5) ____ Prudential-Bache
(6) ____ Shearson/American Express
(7) ____ Edward D. Jones

FIG. 17.2. Questionnaire items measuring product usage and lifestyle activities.

to the understanding of adult development and consumer behavior in several ways. One, the study will contribute to the understanding of aging versus age differences. By following cohorts over the years, the changes that occur in these cohorts can be measured. This will assist in the development of a better assessment of the useful variables in a consumer life structure.

A second contribution of this study will be a better understanding of the generational differences in our population. This information can then be used to better anticipate the future behavior of younger cohorts. With a longitudinal study, differences among generations can be measured over time and compared.

A third contribution is the identification of life paths that different segments take through life. It has been suggested that consumers can be segmented by their life structures and the relatively homogenous manner in which they age. An examination of their life structures would also assist in understanding the issues and motivations present at different stages of life. This would contribute to both the academic literature and marketing practitioners.

The fourth potential use of this study is determine if a forecast of future cohorts can be made by the examination of the behavior of older cohorts. For example, by understanding how present 50- or 60-year-old consumers face and plan for financial retirement decision, it is anticipated that the behavior of younger consumers beginning to face the same situation can be better understood and forecasted.

ACKNOWLEDGMENT

This study was supported by a research grant from the Filene Research Institute.

REFERENCES

Abel, B. J., & Hayslip, B., Jr. (1987). Locus of control and retirement preparation. *Journal of Gerontology, 42,* 165–167.

Baltes, P. (1987). Theoretical propositions of life-span developmental psychology: On the dynamics between growth and decline. *Developmental Psychology, 23,* 611–626.

Bearden, W., Netemeyer, R., & Teel, J. (1989). Measurement of consumer susceptibility to interpersonal influence. *Journal of Consumer Research, 15,* 473–482.

Bengtson, V., Reedy, R., & Gordon, C. (1985). Aging and self-conceptions: Personality processes and social contexts. In J. Birren & K. Schaie (Eds.), *Handbook of the psychology of aging* (pp. 544–593). New York: Van Nostrand Reinhold.

Boronson, W. (1987, November). Money and ethics. *Sylvia Porter's personal finance,* pp. 66–80.

Boruch, R., & Pearson, R. (1988). Assessing the quality of longitudinal surveys. *Evaluation Review, 12,* 3–58.

Brown, J., & Siegel, J. (1988). Attributions for negative life events and depression: The role of perceived control. *Journal of Personality and Social Psychology, 54,* 316–322.

Bush, D., & Simmons, R. (1981). Socialization processes over the life course. In M. Rosenberg & R. Turner (Eds.), *Sociological perspectives.* New York: Basic Books.

Campbell, A., Converse, P., & Rodgers, W. (1976). *The quality of American life.* New York: Russell Sage Foundation.

Caspi, A., Bolger, N., & Eckenrode, J. (1987). Linking person and context in the daily stress process. *Journal of Personality and Social Psychology, 52,* 184–195.

Cooper, P., & Miloulis, G. (1988). Altering corporate strategic criteria to reflect the aging: The role of life satisfaction in the growing senior market. *California Management Review, 31,* 34–42.

Costa, P., & McCrae, R. (1980). Still stable after all these years: Personality as a key to some issues in adulthood and old age. In P. Baltes & O. Brim (Eds.), *Lifespan development and behavior* (pp. 65–105). New York: Academic Press.

Costa, P., & McCrae, R. (1989). Personality continuity and the changes of adult life. In M. Storandt & G. VandeBos (Eds.), *The adult years: Continuity and change* (pp. 45–77). Washington, DC: American Psychological Association.

Cumming, E., & Henry, W. (1961). *Growing old.* New York: Basic Books.

Darley, W., & Lim, J. (1985). Family decision making in leisure-time activities: An exploratory investigation of the impact of locus of control. In R. Lutz (Ed.), *Advances in consumer research* (pp. 370–374). Ann Arbor, MI: Association for Consumer Research.

Dillman, D. (1978). *Mail and telephone surveys: The total design method.* New York: Wiley.

Dobbs, A., & Rule, R. (1987). Prospective memory and self-reports of memory abilities in older adults. *Canadian Journal of Psychology, 41,* 209–222.

Edmondson, B. (1987, April). The inner-directed work out. *American Demographics,* 24–25.

Elder, G. (1975). *Children of the Great Depression.* Chicago: University of Chicago Press.

Elder, G. (1979). Age differentiation and life course. *Annual Review of Sociology,* 165–190.

Erikson, E. (1950). *Childhood and society.* New York: Norton.

Gould, R. (1972). The phase of adult life: A study in develop mental psychology. *American Journal of Sociology, 129,* 521–531.

Gray, D., & Calsyn, R. (1989). The relationship of stress and social support to life satisfaction: Age effects. *Journal of Community Psychology, 17,* 214–219.

Hale, W., & Cochran, C. (1986). Locus of control across the adult lifespan. *Psychological Reports, 59,* 311–313.

Heron, A., & Chown, S. (1967). *Age and function.* Boston: Little Brown.

Heslop, L. (1986). Cohort analysis of the expenditure patterns of the elderly. In M. Wallendorf & P. Anderson (Eds.), *Advances in consumer research* (pp. 553–557). Provo, UT: Association for Consumer Research.

Hutner, N., & Locke, S. (1984). Health locus of control: A potential moderator variable for the relationship between life stress and psychopathology. *Journal of Psychosomatic Medicine, 41,* 186–194.

Janis, I., & Mann, L. (1977). *Decision making: A psychological analysis of conflict, choice and commitment.* New York: Free Press.

Lepisto, L. (1985). A lifespan perspective of consumer behavior. In E. Hirschman & M. Holbrook (Eds.), *Advances in consumer research* (pp. 47–52). Provo, UT: Association for Consumer Research.

Lepisto, L. (1989). *The effect of cognitive age and sex on consumer well-being.* Paper presented at the Conference on the Elderly Consumer, Gainesville, FL.

Lepisto, L., Stuenkel, K., & Anglin, L. (1991). Stress: An ignored situational variable. In R. Holman & M. Solomon (Eds.), *Advances in consumer research* (pp. 296–302). Provo, UT: Association for Consumer Research.

Levinson, D. (1984). The career is in the life structure, the life structure is in the career: An adult development perspective. In M. Arthur, L. Bailyn, D. Levinson, & R. Zucker (Eds.), *Further explorations in personality* (pp. 44–79). New York: Wiley.

Levinson, D. (1986). A conception of adult development. *American Psychologist, 41,* 3–13.

Lewis, J. (1989). *The birth of the family: An empirical inquiry.* New York: Brunner/Mazel.

Linn, M., & Hunter, K. (1979). Perception of age in the elderly. *Journal of Gerontology, 34,* 46–52.

Ma, Hing-Keung (1985). Cross-cultural study of the development of law-abiding orientation. *Psychological Reports, 57,* 967–975.

Montepare, J., & Lachman, M. (1989). You're only as old as you feel: Self-perceptions of age, fears of aging, and life satisfaction from adolescence to old age. *Psychology and Aging, 34,* 1–25.

Morganti, J., Nehrkek, M., Hulicka, I., & Cataldo, J. (1988). Life-span differences in life satisfaction, self-concept and locus of control. *International Journal of Aging and Human Development, 26,* 45–56.

Moschis, G. (1984). A longitudinal study of consumer socialization. *Proceedings of the Winter Conference of the American Association.*

Neugarten, B. (1970). Dynamics of transition of middle to old age. *Journal of Geriatric Psychiatry, 4,* 71–87.

Neugarten, B. (1977). *Personality in middle and late life.* New York: Atherton Press.

Neugarten, B. (1979). Time, age, and the life cycle. *The American Journal of Psychiatry,* 887–894.

Okun, M., & Stock, W. (1987). Correlates and components of subjective well-being in the elderly. *Journal of Applied Gerontology, 6,* 95–112.

Qualls, W. (1987). Household decision behavior: The impact of husbands' and wives' sex role orientation. *Journal of Consumer Research, 14,* 264–279.

Reilly, M. (1982). Working wives and convenience consumption. *Journal of Consumer Research, 8,* 407–418.

Rentz, J., Reynolds, R., & Stout, R. (1983). Analyzing changing consumption patterns with cohort analysis. *Journal of Marketing Research, 20,* 12–20.

Riley, M. (1987). On the significance of age in sociology. *American Sociological Review, 52,* 1–14.

Robinson, J. (1990, February). Time squeeze. *American Demographics,* 30–33.

Rosen, D., & Grandbois, D. (1983), Determinants of role structure in family financial management. *Journal of Consumer Research, 10,* 253–258.

Salthouse, T. (1989). Age-related changes in basic cognitive processes. In M. Storandt & G. VandenBos (Eds.), *The adult years: Continuity and change* (pp. 9–40). Washington, DC: American Psychological Association.

Schafer, W. (1978). *Stress, distress and growth.* Davis, CA: Responsible Action.

Schaie, K. (1983). The Seattle Longitudinal Study: A 21-year exploration of psychometric intelligence. In P. Baltes & O. Brim (Eds.), *Life-span development and behavior* (pp. 67–115). New York: Academic Press.

Schaninger, C., Buss, W., & Grover, R. (1982). The effect of sex roles on family financial handling and decision influence. In B. Walker (Ed.), *1982 Educators' Conference Proceedings* (pp. 43–47). Chicago: American Marketing Association.

Schiffman, L., & Kanuk, L. (1991). *Consumer behavior.* Englewood Cliffs, NJ: Prentice-Hall.

Smith, K., & Moen, P. (1988). Passage through mid-life: Women's changing family roles and economic well-being. *The Sociological Quarterly, 4,* 503–524.

Solomon, M. (1992). *Consumer behavior.* Needham Heights, MA: Allyn & Bacon.

Vitel, S., Lumpkin, J., & Rawwas, M. (1991). Consumer ethics: An investigation of the ethical beliefs of elderly consumers. *Journal of Business Ethics, 10,* 365–375.

Wolfe, D. (1990). *Serving the ageless market: Strategies for selling to the fifty-plus market.* New York: McGraw-Hill.

Woodruff, D., & Birren, J. (1972). Age changes and cohort differences in personality. *Developmental Psychology, 6,* 252–259.

Part IV

INTERNATIONAL APPLICATIONS

Chapter 18

Food-Related Lifestyle: Development of a Cross-Culturally Valid Instrument for Market Surveillance

Klaus G. Grunert
Karen Brunsø
Søren Bisp
The Aarhus School of Business, Denmark

CRITICISM OF PREVIOUS LIFESTYLE RESEARCH

The lifestyle research instruments developed and used by most of the larger market research firms have been criticized by academic marketing scholars mostly on five grounds (e.g., Anderson & Golden, 1984; Askegaard, 1993; Banning, 1987; Lastovicka, 1982; Roos, 1986).

1. *There is no agreement on what lifestyle actually means.* The term seems to defy definitional consensus. Anderson and Golden (1984), after perusing a large number of published lifestyle studies, conclude that in most cases the term is not defined at all, and when it is defined, the definitions range from the contradictory to the trivial.

2. *The methods used are purely inductive and not guided by theory.* Lifestyle types come about based on dimensions derived by exploratory data analysis techniques like factor analysis or correspondence analysis. These techniques are applied to sets of items, the generation of which is not theoretically guided either, but is very much based on common sense reasoning and implicit experience in carrying out market research. Although such a research procedure may be appropriate in the early phase of the life cycle of a research technique, one should hope that, based on such exploratory analysis, theory should develop, which could then guide the analysis of new and better measurement instruments. Also, many feel that

consumer behavior is such a well-researched area that it should be possible to obtain some theoretical input from there that could enrich lifestyle research.

3. *The derivation of the underlying dimensions is unclear and unsatisfactory.* Because commercially marketed instruments, like VALS, RISC, or CCA, are usually proprietary, information necessary to evaluate the statistical soundness of the derived dimensional solutions is often missing. A priori, many social science researchers tend to be suspicious when several hundred variables are reduced to just two dimensions (which is the case in many instruments). On the other hand, *if* a large part of the variance in the data can be explained by just two dimensions, it should be possible to capture these dimensions with a much simpler instrument, which would considerably reduce the cost involved in data collection.

4. *The explanatory value of lifestyle types or dimensions with regard to consumer choice behavior is low and not well documented.* Evidence supplied has been mostly in the form of cross-tabulations of lifestyle items or types with self-reported use of or attitude towards certain products (see Wells, 1975). Also, users of a certain brand or product can be placed on the lifestyle maps based on their mean factor scores. When it has been attempted to relate purchase data and lifestyle data in such a way that the amount of variance in the former explained by the latter can be ascertained, the amount of variance explained has been very modest, sometimes even below the variance explained by demographic variables alone (Bruno & Pessemier, 1971; Wells & Tigert, 1971). As Wells put it in a review article in 1973: "Stated as correlation coefficients these relationships appear shockingly small—frequently in the .1 or .2 range, seldom higher than .3 or .4" (Wells, 1973). Newer studies do not show improvements in this respect (Aurifeille & Valette-Florence, 1992; Valette-Florence, 1989, 1991). It seems that lifestyle items are especially poor when it comes to explaining consumer behavior at brand level, while explanatory power at product category level may be a little higher (Hustad & Pessemier, 1974).

5. *The cross-cultural validity of the international lifestyle instruments remains to be demonstrated.* The larger pan-European lifestyle studies like RISC and CCA provide data that aim at identifying similar lifestyle segments across borders, and numerous other lifestyle studies have tried to identify cultural differences in lifestyle (e.g., Douglas & Urban, 1977; Hui, Joy, & Laroche, 1990; Laroche, McTavish, Johnson, Joy, Kim, & Rankine, 1990; Linton & Broadbent, 1975). Collecting data in different cultures with the aim of obtaining comparative results requires that the measurement instrument has cross-cultural validity, that is, that *translation* and *measurement equivalence* are ensured or at least tested (cf. Chandran & Wiley, 1987; Green & White, 1976; Sekaran, 1983).

Whether *translation equivalence* can be achieved depends on the *conceptual, functional, and experiential equivalence* of the concepts to be translated. Conceptual equivalence presupposes that the lifestyle aspects to be measured can be meaningfully expressed in each culture/language that is part of the study—like, for example, the concept of *fashion*. Functional equivalence refers to the similarities of goals of behavior covered by the concept. Are, for example, the societal functions of fashion the same in the cultures investigated? Experiential equivalence finally refers to the existence of equivalent referents or symbols in different cultures, like, for example, the main symbols indicating that somebody is fashion conscious. Only when these aspects of equivalence are met, does it become meaningful to investigate to which extent respondents across cultures differ with regard to the extent to which they endorse the concept in question, that is, various degrees of fashion consciousness. There is every reason to believe that such equivalence cannot be taken for granted in many studies, and this would apply all the more in such a culture-dependent area as food intake.

Measurement equivalence refers to construct operationalization, item, and scalar equivalence. Equivalence of operationalization presupposes that the psychological processes occurring in the respondent while answering are the same or at least to some degree comparable in the various cultures investigated, while item and scalar equivalence refer to the equivalence of response categories and metric. That the use of scales may be culture bound has been demonstrated (Yu, Keown, Jacobs, & Glynn, 1990).

For the kind of data involved in lifestyle studies, *factor invariance* is a good criterion for investigating the degree of translation and measurement equivalence actually achieved. Various degrees of factor invariance can be distinguished, corresponding to various degrees of cultural comparability (Grunert, Grunert, & Kristensen, 1992). However, such investigations have not yet been reported for lifestyle data.

The remainder of this chapter is devoted to discussing some ways towards improvement of lifestyle research in marketing, and especially in the food sector.

ALTERNATIVE APPROACHES TO LIFESTYLE RESEARCH

The predominating approach in lifestyle research in marketing can be called a *cognitive, inductive approach*. As already mentioned, the approach is inductive, because a collection of items, which has come about with very little theoretical guidance, is subjected to exploratory data analysis techniques, resulting in lifestyle dimensions and types. It is cognitive, because what is measured are mental constructs, and the measurement as such is made by asking respondents to complete a questionnaire. Attitudes, interests, and opinions are clearly mental constructs, but it should be noted also that with regard to activities not the activities themselves are measured (although they are observable in principle). Instead, one measures self-reported activities.

A *cognitive, deductive approach* would retain the questionnaire as the basic form of operationalization, but the dimensions to be measured would be formulated in advance, based on theory, and the suitability of questionnaire items for measuring these dimensions would be investigated by confirmatory techniques.

In a *manifest approach,* the way lifestyle manifests itself in consumer choices, budget allocations, time use, and so on would be measured. Once again we can distinguish between an inductive and a deductive mode (Fig. 18.1). Strictly manifest approaches have to be based on observation instead of questioning. In practice, a number of studies in the academic sphere have adopted a semimanifest approach, in which the data are obtained by questioning, but the questions refer to observable variables only. Uusitalo (1979), for example, used consumption data obtained from official statistics, from a questionnaire, and from a diary technique, and time use data, also obtained by a diary technique, and submitted these data to factor analysis, resulting in three lifestyle dimensions. The study could be characterized as (mostly) manifest inductive. Jelsøe, Land, and Lassen (1991) are underway with a study using Højrup's (1983) *life form* typology, which is based on the notion that lifestyle, including consumption behavior, is determined by the form of work life (conventional wage earner, career-oriented wage earner, self-employed). The approach could be characterized as semimanifest—being self-employed or a wage earner is quite manifest, but the career orientation is measured by a few questionnaire items—and deductive, because the life form types are determined in advance on theoretical grounds.

Manifest studies have, however, been few in consumer research, compared to the dominating cognitive approach.

	inductive	deductive
cognitive approach	most commercially marketed instruments like VALS, CCA, RISC	the approach proposed here
manifest approach	analyses based on use of time and money, e.g., Uusitalo (1979)	e.g., Højrup's life form analysis

FIG. 18.1. A taxonomy of lifestyle studies.

RECENT IMPROVEMENTS IN THE COGNITIVE APPROACH

The criticism of the dominating cognitive inductive approach has led to a number of proposals for improvement, which can be regarded as building on each other. The first relates to sharpening the distinction between values and lifestyles. The second is concerned with placing the lifestyle concept in a hierarchy of cognitive categories.

Values and lifestyles have originally not been distinguished in marketing research, neither at the conceptual nor the operational level. The most popular U.S. lifestyle instrument is actually called *Values and Lifestyles* (*VALS*), and makes no attempt to distinguish between the two concepts. However, value research has gained considerable momentum of its own in recent years, also in marketing. Establishing value measurement as a distinct research tradition in consumer research could make lifestyle research superfluous, but this has not happened, partly because attempts to relate value data directly to consumption data have not been more successful than attempts to relate lifestyle directly to consumption data (Silberer, 1991). Instead, value research helped to bring about the idea of a hierarchy of cognitive categories. Values are commonly regarded as the most abstract types of cognitive categories, whereas product attitudes or product attribute perceptions are usually regarded as the most concrete cognitive categories related to buying behavior. Between these two extremes, there should also be categories at an intermediate level.

This basic idea has appeared in several guises. Several authors (Homer & Kahle, 1988; Schürmann, 1988; Vinson, Scott, & Lamont, 1977) have argued for a value–attitude–behavior hierarchy, in which values, as measured by LOV, would impact on product attitudes, which then influence behavior. In the most complete statement of such causal chains, Olson (e.g., Olson & Reynolds, 1983; Peter & Olson 1990), in his *means–end chain theory*, argues that consumer choice behavior is triggered by how products are linked to self-relevant higher order cognitive categories in consumers' cognitive structures. As the highest order and most self-relevant type of cognitive category, he again mentions values, but in between he distinguishes between psychosocial and functional consequences, and abstract and concrete product attributes. The idea of a hierarchy of cognitive categories determining consumer behavior can be taken as a starting point for a new cognitive view of the lifestyle concept.

TOWARDS A NEW CONCEPT OF LIFESTYLE

In the following, an attempt will be made to provide a fresh approach to the lifestyle concept in analyzing consumer behavior. The approach is cognitive, that is, lifestyle is regarded as a mental construct which explains, but is not identical with, actual behavior. Thus, we adopt Anderson and Golden's criticism that it is questionable to include mental states and overt behavior in one construct, but we draw the opposite conclusion of theirs with regard to defining lifestyle, which has the advantage that our approach is more in accordance with the way the term is actually used in practice. We start from the idea of a hierarchy of cognitive categories and try, based on modern cognitive psychology, to develop a cognitive model that relates lifestyle to other cognitive categories, and also how they are related to behavior. Thus, the approach can be said to be in the Kelly tradition of defining lifestyle as a set of mental constructs, which interrelate perceptions of the environment with goals and behavior.

The approach proposed is based on the following general assumptions, which summarize major results from current cognitive psychology (see Anderson, 1983; Grunert, 1990; Peter & Olson, 1990).

1. *Human behavior can be explained by a cognitive paradigm, that is, by the interaction of comprehension processes, integration processes, and cognitive structure.* Cognitive structure is the organization of knowledge in human memory. Comprehension processes refer to how information in the environment is perceived, comprehended by retrieving information from cognitive structure, and stored, thus changing developing cognitive structure. Integration processes refer to the use of stored knowledge in determining behavior and includes processes like the formation of evaluations, attitudes, and behavioral intentions.

2. *Cognitive structures consist of declarative and procedural knowledge.* Declarative knowledge refers to semantic or episodic information that can be verbalized—like, for example, information about products, about expected consequences of behavior, about personal goals and values. Procedural knowledge refers to stored skills, motoric or perceptual, which cannot easily be verbalized.

3. *Declarative knowledge can be conceived as a system of cognitive categories and their associations. Cognitive categories vary in level of abstraction; associations vary in strength.* Associative networks are the most parsimonious way of modeling declarative knowledge. A cognitive category can be described as a classification of a class of objects which, for some purpose, are regarded as equivalent. Cognitive categories and their associations can be regarded as the result of life-long learning.

4. *Procedural knowledge can be conceived as a system of scripts.* A script is the cognitive representation of a sequence of acts, or motions, or behaviors, which is typical for a given task.

5. *Behavior is motivated by linking cognitive categories referring to concrete acts or objects to abstract cognitive categories referring to values.* Other ways of saying

this are that objects in the environment become relevant to a person only to the degree to which they are related to that person's self-concept, as mirrored in its system of goals and values.

6. *This linkage can be stored as a system of associations in cognitive structure, and can then influence behavior without becoming conscious, or can be formed by conscious thought in a problem-solving situation.* Hence, while behavior in some way will be goal-oriented or self-relevant, the way such goals direct behavior will not necessarily be conscious to the actor. The more common a certain link between value and behavior is to a culture, the more likely is it that such behavior occurs without deliberate conscious reflection.

7. *The linkage can involve both procedural and declarative knowledge.* That is, the way in which some object in the environment is related to self-relevant consequences may depend on motoric and perceptual skills, or both.

This set of assumptions, which is in good accordance with most modern cognitive theories of consumer behavior (e.g., Grunert, 1990; Peter & Olson, 1990), can now be used as a basis to define consumption-related lifestyle in a new way. It is proposed to define *consumpion-related lifestyles as the system of cognitive categories, scripts, and their associations, which relate a set of products to a set of values.*

This proposed definition warrants a number of comments.

1. It makes lifestyle distinct from values, since values are self-relevant and provide motivation, while lifestyle links products to self-relevant consequences, or values.

2. Lifestyles transcend individual brands or products, but may be specific to a product class. Thus, it makes sense to talk about a food-related lifestyle, or a housing-related lifestyle.

3. Lifestyles are clearly placed in a hierarchy of constructs of different levels of abstraction, where lifestyles have an intermediate place between values and product/brand perceptions or attitudes. In this way a brand may be part of a lifestyle, but can not be a lifestyle in itself.

4. Lifestyles can include both factual and procedural knowledge. They include the subjective perceptions, based on information and experience, about which products contribute to the attainment of life values, but they also include learned procedures concerning how to obtain, use, or dispose of products.

5. Lifestyles refer to enduring dispositions to behave, not to single behavior acts. Lifestyles in the way defined, change slowly and will always frame behavior, but any single act can always be modified at will by constructing ad hoc chains linking that act to the attainment of value(s).

AN APPLICATION TO FOOD PRODUCTS

How are food products related to values in consumers' cognitive structure? Food products are an especially intricate aspect of consumer behavior. The relationship between the product and value attainment can be very indirect. The value attainment finally achieved will depend not only on the product itself, but to a large degree also on the usage situation and on the way food products are transformed into meals (Steenkamp & van Trijp, 1989). This on the one hand makes it difficult for the consumer to have his or her choice of food products directed by expected value attainment, but on the other hand gives consumers many degrees of freedom in just how they try to use food products to attain values. These degrees of freedom, put in another way, open up for the possibility of different food-related lifestyles.

The following areas, depicted in Fig. 18.2, can be regarded as possible *elements* of food-related lifestyles, because they contribute to the link between food products and values.

Ways of shopping. How do people shop for food products? Is their decision making characterized by impulse buying, or by extensive deliberation? Do they read labels and other product information, or do they rely on the advice of experts, like friends or sales personnel? Do they shop themselves, or through other members of the family? In which shops—one-stop shopping versus speciality food shops?

Cooking methods. How are the products purchased transformed into meals? How much time is used for preparation? Is preparation characterized by efficiency, or by indulgence? Is it a social activity, or one characterized by family division of labor? To which extent does it involve technical aids? Human help? To which extent is it planned or spontaneous?

Quality aspects. This refers not to concrete attributes of individual products, but to attributes that may apply to food products in general. Examples may be healthy, nutritious, natural, fancy, exclusive, convenient.

Purchasing motives. What is expected from a meal, and what is the relative importance of these various consequences? How important is nutrition compared to the social event? How important are emotional/feeling consequences and hedonism (cf. Grunert, 1993).

Consumption situations. What are "the" meals? How are they spread over the day? Which products are typical for which meals? In which environment do they take place? Is a meal perceived differently when eaten alone, rather then with the family? With friends, guests?

Differences in lifestyle, according to the proposed definition, are related not only to differences in importance of the various cognitive categories/scripts just mentioned. They are related to the way these cognitive

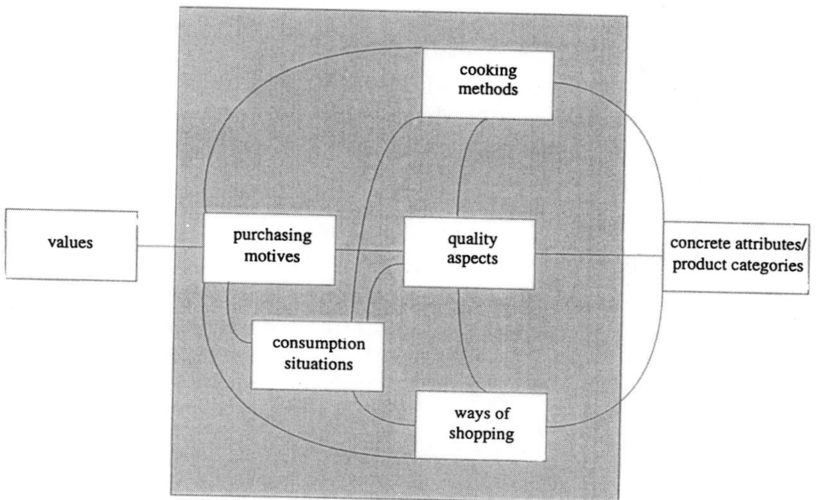

FIG. 18.2. A cognitive structure model for food-related lifestyle.

categories are related to each other, and to the way they are related to products on the one side, values on the other side.

DEVELOPING A SURVEY INSTRUMENT

We have tried to develop a survey instrument that fulfills the following criteria:

1. It covers the five elements of food-related lifestyle defined earlier.
2. It taps these five elements in a cross-culturally valid way.
3. It is easy to administer and allows data collection at a cost that is considerably below that of known lifestyle instruments.

Development of the instrument proceeded in the following steps:

1. Generation of a pool of items covering the five elements of food-related lifestyles based on the theoretical foundation.
2. Collection of data, using the item pool, in three European countries.
3. Exploratory factor analysis, within each of the five elements, and separately for each country.
4. Search for factors that seem to be stable across the three samples.
5. Construction of scales for each of the remaining factors. Analysis of scale reliability across and within samples. Modification of scales with the aim to retain three items per scale.

6. Testing the set of cross-cultural factors by confirmatory factor analysis.
7. Investigation of intercorrelation between the scales.
8. Assessment of construct validity by looking at differences in food-related lifestyle between the three samples.

Generation of Item Pool

Two hundred and two Likert-type items were constructed that were supposed to cover the five elements of food-related lifestyle defined earlier (ways of shopping, quality aspects, cooking methods, consumption situations, and purchasing motives). Inspiration for formulating these items was drawn from the food choice literature, food journals, women's magazines, and earlier lifestyle studies like RISC. Agreement with the items had to be rated on a 5-point scale.

The items were originally formulated in English and checked by both U.S. and U.K. natives. They were subsequently translated into Danish and French. Translation into French was done by two native Frenchmen; translation into Danish was done by one of the authors. Items were arranged by the five constructs in the questionnaire; the sequence in which the five constructs appeared was varied at random in the questionnaire.

Data Collection

Data were collected in Denmark, England, and France. Given the nature of this study, sampling was done not with respect to representativeness, but with respect to obtaining three samples that would be as homogeneous as possible. In each country, the target population was defined as married women with children at school age living in metropolitan areas. In each country, one metropolitan area was selected, namely, Copenhagen, London, and Paris. In each of these areas schools were selected (2 in Copenhagen, 4 in London, 3 in Paris), with the aim of soliciting the cooperation of teachers in asking school children to take a questionnaire home to their mothers. In each country, 300 questionnaires were distributed in this way. Questionnaires were distributed on Monday and had to be returned on Wednesday or Thursday. The response rates were 78% in Denmark, 47% in England, and 32% in France, resulting in sample sizes of 233, 139, and 94.

Exploratory Factor Analysis and Construction of Scales

For each sample and for the five groups of items, separate exploratory factor analyses (principal component analysis, varimax rotation) were carried out. The aim of this procedure was to check whether items would tend to group together in similar factors across the three samples. Factor congruence across cultures is a major indicator of a cross-culturally similar interpretation of the items (Grunert et al., 1992). Twenty-one factors were identified which seem to appear across the three samples. They were:

- ways of shopping: importance of product information, attitude towards advertising, joy of shopping, speciality shops, price criterion, shopping list
- quality aspects: health, price-quality-relation, novelty, organic products
- cooking methods: involvement with cooking, looking after new ways, convenience, whole family, spontaneity, women's task
- consumption situations: snacks versus meals, social event
- purchasing motives: self-fulfilment in food, security, social relationships.

Items with high loadings on these factors in at least two of the three samples were combined into scales. Scale reliabilities (Cronbach's alpha) were computed, and where scales contained more than three items the items, which gave the highest reliability for the pooled data, were retained. Subsequently, the reliabilities were checked also for the three samples separately.

Not all the resulting scales are satisfactory. In a number of cases, only two suitable items were found for a scale. Some items performed not as good in one country as in the others. The analyses reported in the following section will shed more light on these difficulties, as the confirmatory factor analyses allow to detect which items in which sample deviate most from the prespecified structure.

Confirmatory Factor Analysis

Confirmatory factor analysis can be used to find out whether a set of data is compatible with a prespecified factor structure. It can also be applied to multiple samples, and can then be used to check whether the data are compatible with the assumption that the factor structure in the samples is the same.

Factor invariance has often been suggested as a validation instrument in cross-cultural research. Grunert et al. (1992) have recently suggested that several levels of factor congruence may be distinguished, and have related these levels to different degrees of cultural compatibility based on a cognitive view of cultural differences. The basic argument is as follows: If we have a vector of measures which, like in the present study, are taken as indicators of a smaller set of underlying latent variables, then we have, in LISREL notation,

$$X = \Lambda\xi + \delta \quad \text{and}$$
$$\Sigma = \Lambda\Phi\Lambda' + \Theta_\delta$$

with X a vector of measured values, Λ a matrix of factor loadings, ξ a vector of factor scores, δ a vector of error terms, Σ the covariance matrix of the measured values, Φ the covariance matrix of the factor scores, and Θ_δ the covariance matrix of the error terms.

When talking about factor congruence, the common interpretation is that the matrix of loadings in two samples has the same pattern, that is, the same non-zero elements. However, this is obviously only the weakest form of comparability between two sets of data. A stronger form of comparability would exist when the matrix of loadings were in fact identical, as this seems to indicate that the way in which the measurement items relate to underlying constructs was in fact the same across samples. This would still allow, however, differences in how the factors are correlated in the two samples, and differences in error, that is, in the reliabilities of the individual items. Identical correlations between the factors would strengthen our confidence in that the factors do in fact tap the same sets of meanings in different cultures, whereas identical item reliabilities would strengthen our belief in that the individual items in fact were perceived (cognitively processed) in the same way. In cross-cultural research, which usually involves translation and therefore mapping questionnaire items from one set of cognitive categories into another, we would not usually expect item reliabilities to be the same.

Thus, 4 levels of cross-cultural comparability can be distinguished (Grunert et al., 1992):

- Λ_i and Λ_j have the same pattern: *minimal cultural comparability*
- $\Lambda_i = \Lambda_j$: *weak cultural comparability*
- $\Lambda_i = \Lambda_j$, and $\Phi_i = \Phi_j$: *strong cultural comparability*
- $\Lambda_i = \Lambda_j$, $\Phi_i = \Phi_j$, and $\Theta_{\delta_i} = \Theta_{\delta_j}$: *weak cultural identity*

The strongest condition is called *weak cultural identity,* because the only way in which the samples can differ is in the level of endorsement of the various items, while everything else—their complete meaning structure, including item reliabilities—is the same. When also the levels of endorsement are the same, one would talk *about strong cultural identity.*

For each of the five areas of food-related lifestyle, the items retained after steps 3–5 were entered into confirmatory factor analyses corresponding to the 4 levels of cultural comparability described earlier. The results can be seen in Table 18.1. Several measures of fit are given: For each sample, the goodness-of-fit index (GFI) and the root mean square residuals (RMR), and for the set of three samples the χ^2 value and the degrees of freedom. Because the χ^2 value is vulnerable to sample size, a rule of thumb

TABLE 18.1
Confirmatory Factor Analysis

	Copenhagen		*London*		*Paris*		
FRL Area	*GFI*	*RMR*	*GFI*	*RMR*	*GFI*	*RMR*	*x^2/df*
Ways of shopping							
Minimum cultural comparability	.907	.093	.850	.154	.898	.102	1.683
Weak cultural comparability	.901	.096	.832	.144	.887	.107	1.711
Strong cultural comparability	.894	.110	.822	.176	.869	.135	1.657
Weak cultural identity	.877	.118	.799	.178	.854	.134	1.724
Quality aspects							
Minimum cultural comparability	.969	.046	.978	.049	.954	.067	1.467
Weak cultural comparability	.967	.049	.976	.056	.951	.083	1.324
Strong cultural comparability	.959	.071	.958	.087	.924	.119	1.418
Weak cultural identity	.945	.082	.944	.093	.905	.144	1.530
Cooking methods							
Minimum cultural comparability	.945	.071	.888	.130	.864	.111	1.451
Weak cultural comparability	.941	.077	.874	.137	.861	.119	1.430
Strong cultural comparability	.926	.103	.859	.163	.814	.165	1.558
Weal cultural identity	.898	.122	.828	.185	.792	.178	1.813
Consumption							
Minimum cultural comparability	.964	.082	.984	.061	.982	.051	1.584
Weak cultural comparability	.961	.086	.981	.069	.977	.066	1.345
Strong cultural comparability	.955	.101	.972	.101	.978	.067	1.551
Weak cultural identity	.952	.097	.956	.124	.951	.104	1.354
Purchasing motives							
Minimum cultural comparability	.976	.067	.972	.079	.975	.056	1.337
Weak cultural comparability	.972	.070	.972	.076	.964	.073	1.229
Strong cultural comparability	.970	.075	.959	.113	.945	.104	1.109
Weak cultural identity	.954	.101	.943	.145	.933	.118	1.210

is to divide χ^2 by the degrees of freedom. If the resulting value is lower than 5, the model can be assumed to fit the data as long as the GFI is about .90 and the RMR below .10 (cf. Hildebrandt, 1983). The results from the analysis can also be used to detect weak items. This can be done by inspecting the estimated loadings, the item reliabilities, and the modifications indices for loadings forced to be zero.

Ways of Shopping. The tests yield results indicating that the criteria of minimum and weak cultural comparability can be accepted at least for the Copenhagen and Paris samples. The values for the London sample are clearly worse. The problematic items are mainly *I like to know what I am buying, so I often ask questions in stores where I shop for food,* and *I am influenced by what people say about a food product.* Both items have low reliabilities in all three samples. The modification indices show that *I like to know what I am buying, so I often ask questions in stores where I shop for food* would rather load on the factors *Importance of product information* and *price criterion* in Denmark. The item *I am influenced by what people say about a food product* has no clear attachment to another factor. In the London sample, the most problematic items were *I do not see any reason to shop in specialty shops, I always check prices, even on small items* and *I watch for ads in the newspaper for store specials and plan to take advantage of them when I go shopping,* all of which have low reliabilties. The latter item would, in the London sample, rather load on the *attitude towards advertising* factor than on the *price criterion* factor.

Quality Aspects. All four tests show a reasonably good fit, but weak cultural comparability seems again to be the best description across the three samples, considering especially the behavior of the RMR in the Paris sample. The most problematic items were *I compare prices between product variants in order to get the best value food,* which had only moderate loadings on the *price-quality relation* factor, and which also had low reliabilities, and the item *I alwaus buy organically grown food products if I have the opportunity,* which had low reliabilities. As mentioned before, this item stands alone for the factor *organic products,* because no scale could be constructed.

Cooking Methods. The fit is not as good as for the other aspects of FRL, and the fit for the Danish sample is notably better than for the other two. A main problem seems to reside in the *convenience* scale. All three items had low reliabilities in Denmark; differences in item reliability between the three samples were especially pronounced with regard to the item *I use a lot of mixes, for instance baking mixes and powder soups.* Baking mixes are very rarely used in Denmark, leading to a very skewed distribution, but are popular in England, and seem to be a good indicator of convenience in France, even though they are not widely used. The item *To me, the microwave oven is essential for my cooking* had very low reliabilities both in Denmark and France, where very few respondents endorsed that statement. The most stable item in this scale was *I use frozen foods for at least one meal a day,* and that may not even be a convenience item, since the use of frozen foods—and not just frozen ready meals—may express a storage policy more than a tendency toward convenience. There were also problems with the *women's task* scale, where the item *It is the woman's responsibility* *to keep her family healthy by serving a nutritious diet* had low loadings and reliabilities in both Denmark and England—a possible interpretation may be that this item may have been perceived more than a health item than as a gender role item in these samples.

Consumption Situations. The data have generally a high degree of comparability. All datasets fulfill the conditions of weak cultural comparability, and even for the two more stringent criteria the fit indices are still rather acceptable. The *social event* scale was, however, not without problems. Two out of the 3 items had low reliabilities in all three samples. The high reliability item *Going out for dinner is a regular part of our eating habits* may actually just be a going-out item, whereas *We often get together with friends to enjoy an easy-to-cook, casual dinner* may tap other dimensions like convenience, and the item *I do not consider it a luxury to go out with my family having dinner in a restaurant* may trigger price/economy associations as well.

Purchasing Motives. As for *consumption situations*, the data have generally a high degree of comparability. All datasets fulfill the conditions of weak cultural comparability, and even for the two more stringent criteria the fit indices are still rather acceptable. The internal consistency of the scales *security* and *social relationships* could generally be improved, however, and the item *I am an excellent cook* has low reliabilities.

In general, the results of the confirmatory factor analysis show that the scales developed are a promising starting point for the development of a cross-culturally valid instrument to measure food-related lifestyles. For all five elements of food-related lifestyle, at least the level of weak cultural comparability was obtained. However, the analysis also pointed at certain scale items which could be improved in future studies.

CONCLUSIONS

Starting from the need to develop an efficient instrument for the surveillance of consumers on export markets, we have attempted to present a new view of lifestyle, based on a cognitive perspective, which makes lifestyle specific to certain areas of consumption. The specific area of consumption studied here is food, resulting in a concept of *food-related lifestyle.* We have tried to develop an instrument that can measure food-related lifestyle in a cross-culturally valid way. To this end, we have collected a pool of 202 items, collected data in three countries, and have constructed scales based on cross-culturally stable factor patterns. These scales have then been subjected to a number of tests of reliability and validity. Even though some items and scales did show problems, the overall results are very promising:

It seems we have tapped a set of relevant aspects of food-related lifestyle which can be used in cross-cultural studies aimed at market surveillance.

Three types of tasks are required for future research. First, it would be desirable to replicate the present study, either with the same or an improved set of items, with more samples from more cultures. Second, it is important to supplement the FRL items with items on product-specific action tendencies and with measurements of purchase behavior, in order to investigate the predictive ability of the instrument for purchase behavior. Third, a revised version of the instrument should be applied to larger, representative samples in some countries in order to study its properties for clustering and segmentation.

ACKNOWLEDGMENTS

The research presented in this paper was funded by the MAPP Center. MAPP—*Market-based process and product innovation in the food sector*—is a research center dealing with marketing of food products.

REFERENCES

Anderson, J. R. (1983). *The architecture of cognition*. Cambridge, MA: Harvard University Press.

Anderson, W. T., & Golden, L. L. (1984). Life style and psychographics: A critical review and recommendation. In T. C. Kinnear (Ed.), *Advances in consumer research, Vol. 11* (pp. 405–411). Provo, UT: Association for Consumer Research.

Askegaard, S. (1993). Livsstilsbegrebet: Problemer og muligheder [The lifestyle concept: Problems and possibilities]. *Ledelse og Erhvervsøkonomi, 57*, 91–102.

Aurifeille, J.-M., & Valette-Florence, P. (1992). An empirical investigation of the predictive validity of micro versus macro approaches in consumer value research. In K. G. Grunert & D. Fuglede (Eds.), *Marketing for Europe—marketing for the future. Proceedings of the 21st Annual Conference of the European Marketing Academy* (pp. 65–81). Aarhus: The Aarhus School of Business.

Banning, T. E. (1987). *Lebensstilorientierte Marketing-Theorie* [Lifestyle-oriented marketing theory]. Heidelberg: Physica.

Bruno, A. V., & Pessemier, E. A. (1971). An empirical investigation of the validity of selected attitude and activity measures. In M. Venkatesan (Ed.), *Proceedings of the Third Annual Conference of the Association for Consumer Research* (pp. 456–474). Chicago: University of Chicago.

Chandran, R., & Wiley, J. B. (1987). Instrument equivalence in cross-cultural research. In C. F. Keown & A. G. Woodside (Eds.), *Proceedings of the Second Symposium on Cross-cultural Consumer and Business Studies* (pp. 108–112). Honolulu: University of Hawaii.

Douglas, S. P., & Urban, C. D. (1977). Life-style analysis to profile women in international markets. *Journal of Marketing, 41*(3), 46–54.

Green, R. D., & White, P. (1976). Methodological considerations in cross-national consumer research. *Journal of International Business Studies, 7*, 81–87.

Grunert, K. G. (1990). *Kognitive Strukturen in der Konsumforschung* [Cognitive structures in consumer research]. Heidelberg: Physica.

Grunert, S. C. (1993). *Essen und Emotionen* [Eating and emotions]. Weinheim: PVU.

Grunert, S. C., Grunert, K. G., & Kristensen, K. (1992). The cross-cultural validity of the list of values LOV: A comparison of nine samples from five countries. In J. J. G. Schmeets, M. E. P. Odekerken, & F. J. R. van de Pol (Eds.), *Developments and applications in structural equation modelling* (pp. 89–99). Amsterdam: Sociometric Research Foundation.

Hildebrandt, L. (1983). *Konfirmatorische Analysen von Modellen des Konsumentenverhaltens* [Confirmatory analysis of consumer behavior models]. Berlin: Duncker & Humblot.

Homer, P., & Kahle, L. R. (1988). A structural equation test of the value-attitude-behavior hierarchy. *Journal of Personality and Social Psychology, 54*, 638–646.

Hui, M., Joy, C., & Laroche, M. (1990). Differences in lifestyle among four major subscultures in a bi-cultural environment. In N. E. Synodinos, C. F. Keown, T. H. Becker, K. G. Grunert, T. E. Muller, & J. H. Yu (Eds.), *Proceedings of the Third Symposium on Cross-cultural Consumer and Business Studies* (pp. 139–150). Honolulu: University of Hawaii.

Hustad, T. P., & Pessemier, E. A. (1974). The development and application of psychographic life style and associated activity and attitude measures. In W. D. Wells (Ed.), *Life style and psychographics* (pp. 31–70). Chicago: American Marketing Association.

Højrup, T. (1983). *Det glemte folk: Livsformer og centraldirigering* [The forgotten people: Ways of life and central planning]. Copenhagen: Institut for europæisk folkelivsforskning.

Jelsøe, E., Land, B., & Lassen, J. (1991). *Livsformsteorier i relation til forbrugeranalyser* [Ways of life and consumer behavior]. Roskilde: Roskilde University Center, unpublished manuscript.

Laroche, M., McTavish, R., Johnson, L., Joy, A., Kim, C., & Rankine, S. (1990). Consumption patterns and lifestyle differences betweeen English-French Canadian and Australian consumers. In N. E. Synodinos, C. F. Keown, T. H. Becker, K. G. Grunert, T. E. Muller, & J. H. Yu (Eds.), *Proceedings of the Third Symposium on Cross-cultural Consumer and Business Studies* (pp. 151–160). Honolulu: University of Hawaii.

Lastovicka, J. L. (1982). On the validation of life style traits. *Journal of Marketing Research, 19*, 126–138.

Linton, A., & Broadbent, S. (1975). International life style comparisons: An aid to marketers. *Advertising Quarterly* (Summer), 15–18.

Olson, J. C., & Reynolds, T. J. (1983). Understanding consumers cognitive structures: Implications for advertising strategy. In L. Percy & A. G. Woodside (Eds.), *Advertising and consumer psychology* (pp. 77–90). Lexington, MA: Lexington.

Peter, J. P., & Olson, J. C. (1990). *Consumer behavior* (2nd ed.). Homewood, IL: Irwin.

Roos, J. P. (1986). On way of life typologies. In L. Uusitalo (Ed.), *Environmental impact of consumption patterns* (pp. 38–55). Aldershot: Gower.

Schürmann, P. (1988). *Werte und Konsumverhalten* [Values and consumer behavior]. Munich: GBI.

Sekaran, U. (1983). Methodological and theoretical issues and advancements in cross-cultural research. *Journal of International Business Studies, 14*(3), 61–73.

Silberer, G. (1991). *Werteforschung und Werteorientierung im Unternehmen* [Values research and value orientation in companies]. Stuttgart: Poeschel.

Steenkamp, J.-B., & van Trijp, H. C. M. (in press). Quality guidance: A consumer-based approach to food quality improvement using partial least squares. *European Review of Agricultural Economics.*

Uusitalo, L. (1979). *Consumption style and way of life.* Helsinki: Helsinki School of Economics.

Valette-Florence, P. (1989). Les styles de vie en question: Mythes et réalitées [Life style: Myths and reality]. *Revue Française du Marketing,* (125), 17–26.

Valette-Florence, P. (1991). *A causal analysis of the predictive power of selected life-style indicators.* Brussels: Paper presented at the 1st Workshop on Value and Life Style Research in Marketing of the European Institute for Advanced Studies in Management.

Vinson, D. E., Scott, J. E., & Lamont, L. M. (1977). The role of personal values in marketing and consumer behavior. *Journal of Marketing, 41*(2), 44–50.

Wells, W. D. (1973). Seven questions about lifestyle and psychographics. In B. W. & H. Becker (Eds.), *American Marketing Association Combined Proceedings* (pp. 462–465). Chicago: American Marketing Association.

Wells, W. D. (1975). Psychographics: A critical review. *Journal of Marketing, 12*(2), 196–213.

Wells, W. D., & Tigert, D. J. (1971). Activities, interests, and opinions. *Journal of Advertising Research, 11*(4), 27–35.

Yu, J. et al. (1990). Cross-cultural considerations in attitude scale methodology. In N. E. Synodinos, C. F. Keown, T. H. Becker, K. G. Grunert, T. E. Muller, & J. H. Yu (Eds.), *Third Symposium on Cross-cultural Consumer and Business Studies* (pp. 293–301). Honolulu: University of Hawaii.

Chapter 19

The Edge of Dream: Managing Brand Equity in the European Luxury Market

Daniel Weber
Research Institute on Social Change

Bernard Dubois
Groupe HEC, France

A major challenge to the increasingly global luxury industry is to identify and reach common consumer targets across a diverse range of cultures and markets. Not too long ago several marketing analysts claimed that, under the dominant influence of technology as well as increased and improved communication networks all over the world, consumers' values and expectations are becoming more and more alike, justifying a new "globalization" approach based on people's similarities rather than differences (Levitt, 1983).

Applied to the luxury industry, such a development would imply that consumer tastes and preferences for luxury brands are moving towards greater uniformity. Such a scenario would certainly make the luxury brand manager's life easier and allow for economies of scale and scope in product development, distribution, pricing, and advertising. Recent evidence, however, does not confirm such a tendency.

Today's luxury market is in a situation of constant and at times radical change. The rapid and continuing evolution of consumer attitude and behavior patterns is paralleled by an ongoing restructuring and concentration among producers (McKinsey, 1991). In fact, if there is any common denominator in the luxury markets across countries, it is the growing internal diversity of consumer tastes and habits. This leads to market fragmentation, a loss of economies of scale, and a splintering of brand identity within any particular country. Such market conditions make it imperative to identify transnational targets that share enough common traits to allow for a similar positioning in different countries (Douglas & Wind, 1972).

Demographic and product consumption data are necessary but insufficient means to reveal the complexity of cross-cultural markets. This is because the underlying motivations and inhibitions relating to specific product consumption are likely to differ across segments and countries (Douglas & Dubois, 1990). The proper way to identify such targets is through an understanding of how changing cultural values shape and reshape perceptions and images of luxury brands.

LUXURY: THE EDGE OF DREAM

Even though, for many decades, consumer researchers have emphasized the cognitive information-processing aspects of buying decisions, most of them now recognize that all markets are driven, at least to some degree, by consumer fantasies and dreams in addition to utilitarian needs and attribute preferences (Holbrook & Hirschman, 1982).

Luxury goods certainly tower above most other product categories in the importance of the "dream factor." The desire to wear an exquisitely designed piece of jewelry from Bulgari, treat oneself to an original designer ensemble from the venerable house of Dior, or perhaps heighten one's sensuality with a soft yet recognizable fragrance from Chanel or Guerlain, are but a few of the fairy tales that can come true in the world of luxury. The dream of owning a luxury brand item, whether it be a car, jewelry, fashion, perfume, or high-tech sound system, is at the core of consumer fantasies.

Why is the dream so important to the luxury business? And where did it come from? Traditionally, economists have stressed the role of income as a determinant of consumption behavior. According to their view, consumer solvency and purchasing power are essential elements in defining the demand for any item offered for exchange. Given the premium prices charged by luxury goods companies, it would seem natural to expect income to be a rather powerful segmentation variable.

As early as 1899, Thorstein Veblen developed a theory according to which consumers use product prices as a means of ostentatiously displaying their wealth (Veblen, 1899). Because income is a major contributor to wealth, and because the price differential has often been used to identify and even define what constitutes a luxury product, one would expect Veblen effects to be particularly "conspicuous" in the realm of luxury goods.

At the same time, it seems equally clear that the purchase of luxury goods does not obey economic factors only. As already visible in Veblen's approach, the symbolic and social value attached to the consumption of such goods reveals a significant impact of culture.

Early work in anthropology had already stressed the key role of rituals surrounding ownership, distribution, and consumption of goods for understanding the value system of "primitive" societies (Malinowski, 1922; Mauss, 1954). In subsequent years many social scientists started to explore the various facets of sociocultural influence on consumption behavior.

Liebenstein (1950), for example, when studying "external" effects on demand, introduced the dialectic of "snob" versus "bandwagon" effects, so essential for understanding the dynamics of the status goods market (Masson, 1981). While snobs buy exclusive items as an attempt to differentiate themselves from others, followers purchase them to be identified with a reference group serving as a role model (see also Bourdieu, 1984).

More recently, a group of consumer researchers have developed a "hedonic" perspective, according to which purchasing luxury goods would primarily satisfy buyers' appetite for symbolic meanings (Hirschman & Holbrook, 1982; McCracken, 1988), while other writers have emphasized the desire of consumers to extend their own personality through their possessions (Belk, 1988).

For all these reasons, it would seem that consumer dreams are essential to explore if one wants to understand attitudes toward luxury goods. Obviously, the aura of exclusiveness surrounding luxury brands has contributed significantly to the birth and growth of the dream for luxury. Over the last 20 years, however, the luxury business has expanded into $60 billion worldwide industry, which was accomplished largely through a process of democratization. Even at Tiffany's, one can now find an item of jewelry for less than $100.

Indeed, according to luxury marketing experts, today's luxury sector is characterized by a paradox: A brand needs a certain level of penetration to be successful, yet if its penetration is too high, it loses its aura of luxury. Managers in the luxury business must learn the difficult art of increasing awareness and purchase while remaining elitist. The key question is *how to manage the dream?* (Dubois, Duquesne, & Finskud, 1991).

OPERATIONALIZING THE KEY CONCEPTS: AWARENESS, DREAM, AND PURCHASE

Awareness is clearly the first condition of the dream. One cannot wish for a brand if one does not know it exists. The luxury market's history has shown that it is crowded with names that have remained in a closed circle and have faded away because they were never able to attain the status of a "Brand."

Professionals in the luxury field are especially concerned with a brand's long-term value. In order to assess a brand's potential in this very distinct market, one needs to know what it will be worth tomorrow. The difference between a luxury product and another is not based on functional attributes but rather on immaterial values embodied in the luxury product for which the brand name constitutes a powerful symbol. It is because the brand induces one to dream that it acquires more value. But the "dream capital" of a brand is a very difficult concept to measure. One can, however, evaluate it through a question in which respondents are asked to identify the brands that would bring them the most pleasure, should they receive one of those brands as a beautiful gift.

Finally, the present value of a luxury product is measured through the penetration of the brand in its market. One can operationalize this concept through turnover, profits, or the number of consumers who have chosen it, those who have, for instance, purchased at least one of the brand's products in the last 2 years.

Awareness, dream, and purchase are thus the three key concepts for understanding the inner workings of the luxury market. What is most important is to empirically evaluate their functional interrelationships to answer the following questions. Is there a simple "hierarchy of effects" whereby awareness builds dream which generates purchase? A brand loyalty process at work whereby purchase reinforces the dream? Or a "scarcity" effect whereby purchase would destroy the dream?

The results presented in this paper have been obtained from the Research Institute on Social Change (RISC) annual sociocultural survey of the five major European countries (France, Italy, Germany, Spain, and the United Kingdom) and the United States. The survey consists of a nationally representative sample of 12,500 respondents in Europe, 3,000 in Japan, and 3,000 in the United States. In this paper, we focus on the European results.

The RISC annual survey contains a module devoted to the luxury market that includes measures of awareness, dream, and purchase with respect to a list of 30 luxury brands (see Fig. 19.1). The list was initially developed from the responses of a pan-European unaided awareness test and represents a wide range of product categories and prices. The heterogeneity

ARMANI	*DUNHILL*	*REMY MARTIN*
LAURA ASHLEY	*GIVENCHY*	*MONT BLANC*
BANG & OLUFSEN	*GUERLAIN*	*OMEGA*
BULGARI	*GUCCI*	*REVLON*
CARTIER	*HERMES*	*ROLEX*
PIERRE CARDIN	*LACOSTE*	*YVES SAINT LAURENT*
CHANEL	*LANCOME*	*SHISEIDO*
CHIVAS REGAL	*LANVIN*	*LOUIS VUITTON*
CHRISTOFLE	*ESTEE LAUDER*	*WATERMAN*
DAUM	*RALPH LAUREN*	*CHRISTIAN DIOR*

FIG. 19.1. I.M.A.G.E. database. List of luxury brands.

reflects the simple fact that the definition of a luxury brand can change across countries or even subgroups of the population.

Respondents were asked in a face-to-face interview the following three questions for the list of brands presented on a show card.

Q1. Here is a list of brands. Please tell me which ones you have heard of before.

Q2. And which of these brands, if any, have you bought during the past 2 years?

Q3. Imagine that you win a contest and the possibility of choosing a beautiful present. Among all the brands listed that you know, which are the *five* you would like best?

RESULTS AND DISCUSSION

The Dream Equation

The dream or the desire to own an upscale luxury brand is essential to the brand's long-term value. Some brands such as Cartier, Rolex, and Christian Dior enjoy a dream penetration in over 30% of the European population. Other brands such as Bulgari and Guerlain inspire a dream in less than 10% of the population. What accounts for such variation? Is it merely that the first group is better known than the second? If this is so, then why does a brand like Rolex create more dream than Omega for a similar level of awareness? And why do brands with very different levels of purchase such as Cartier and Dior produce about the same level of dream (see Fig. 19.2)? Finally, and of direct managerial relevance, is there an optimal balance to achieve between dream, awareness, and purchase?

A multiple regression model was built to evaluate dream as a function of awareness and purchase. The advantage of using such a model instead of correlation analysis is that the multiple regression shows the contribution of each independent variable while holding the other constant. It can illuminate relationships that might otherwise be obscured by Pearson correlations. Although some multicollinearity is present to the extent that awareness and purchase are related to each other, both of the estimated regression coefficients are highly significant (99% confidence in rejecting the null hypothesis of slopes equal to zero). The regression includes all 30 brands for the entire European sample of 12,500. The adjusted R-square is .77 (the amount of variance explained in the dependent variable-dream) indicating a close fit with the empirical data. The linear model has the equation:

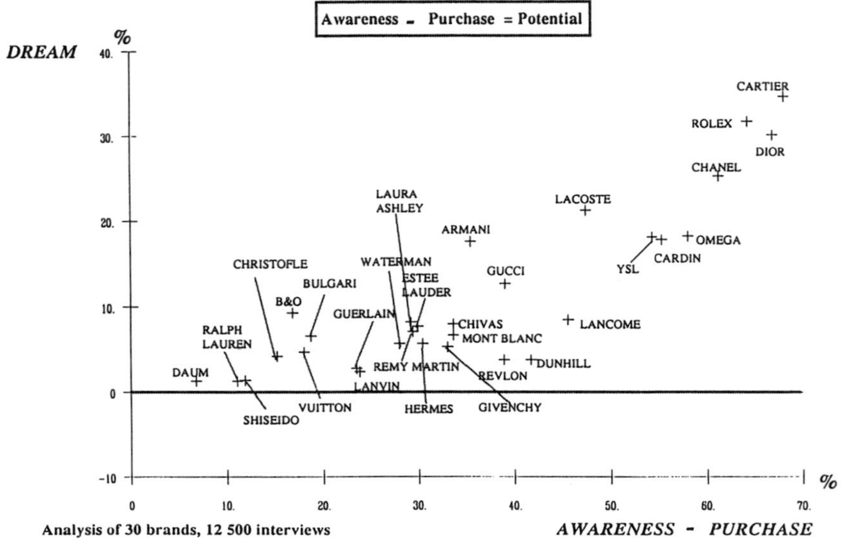

FIG. 19.2. Luxury brands' positions relative to value parameters.

$$\text{Expected Dream} = .51(\text{Awareness}) - .66(\text{Purchase}) - 5.7$$

The positive sign of the awareness regression coefficient is expected and implies that a 10% increase in awareness will contribute to about a 5% increase in the expected dream. Therefore building awareness through marketing effort will enhance the long-term value of a luxury brand. On the other hand, the significant negative coefficient associated with purchase is surprising. It implies that a 10% expansion in sales will *decrease* the dream capital of the brand by about 6½%. In simple words, overdiffusion can kill the dream. Finally, the negative intercept term reflects the fact that a brand needs to surpass a given level of awareness to achieve even a small dream capital.

The regression line (Fig. 19.3) shows the expected level of dream for each level of dream potential (awareness minus purchase) within this representative set of luxury brands. Brands falling above the line enjoy a better-than-expected level of dream (a "dream premium") compared to those falling below the line (a "dream deficit"). For example, Armani has a dream premium of 6.8% (actual 17.6% minus expected 10.8%) while Givenchy has a dream deficit of −4.5% (expected 10% minus actual 5.5%; see Fig. 19.4).

These results imply that consumers hold Armani in *relatively* high esteem within the world of luxury. In particular, Armani has a reserve of potential customers and is probably doing a good job in balancing an image of

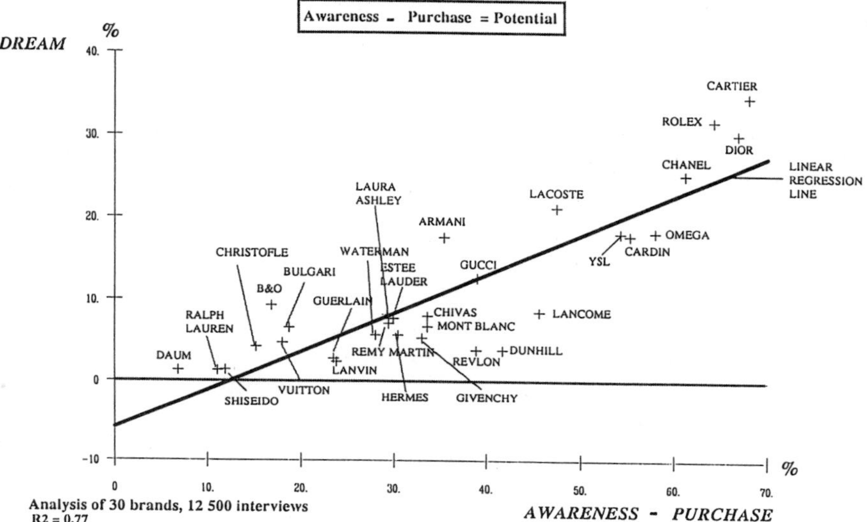

FIG. 19.3. Luxury brands' positions relative to value parameters.

elitism with diffusion through a concerted marketing effort. On the other hand, consumers hold Givenchy in *relatively* low esteem. One might ask if expectations are not fulfilled or if priority is given to distribution rather than communication. Obviously, the situation of the two brands can significantly differ across the various European countries (Givenchy enjoys a better position in France than Armani while the reverse is true in Italy).

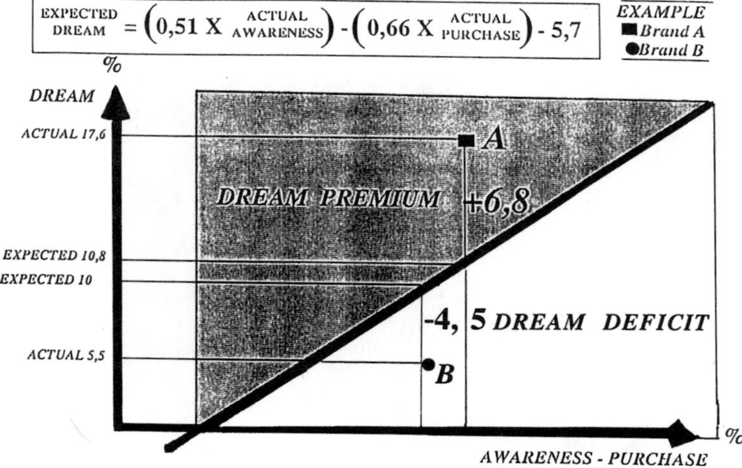

FIG. 19.4. Dream equation.

THE BRAND POWER MATRIX

The Dream Equation highlights the core functional relationship among awareness, dream, and purchase for each brand within the context of a representative set of luxury brands. These are the key brand parameters operating in the sector. Continuing the example of Armani and Givenchy we can show that: The levels of awareness are relatively close, whereas the purchase and dream factors vary greatly from one brand to another (see Fig. 19.5).

In order to have a deeper understanding of the interaction of awareness, dream, and purchase, another analytical tool, the Brand Power Matrix, has been developed. The matrix divides the population of those who know the brand into four categories, by combining those that dream and do not dream with those who bought or did not buy the brand. It enables us to further partition the interactive effects with a specific focus on dream and purchase (see Fig. 19.6).

(%)	Awareness	Purchase	Dream
ARMANI	46.1	10.7	17.6
GIVENCHY	41.0	7.9	5.5

FIG. 19.5. The brands' parameters.

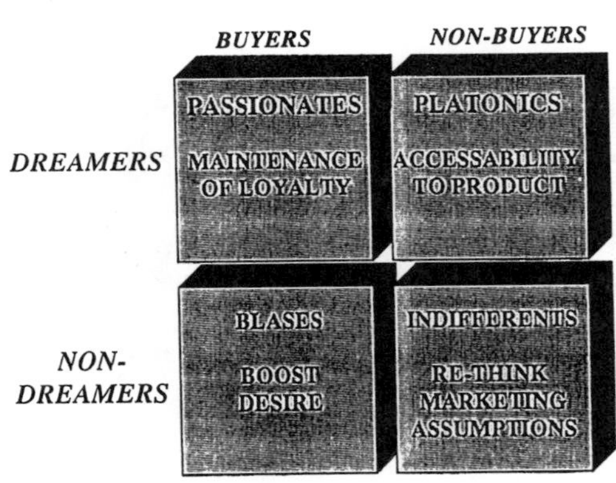

FIG. 19.6. The brand power matrix. Key issues in each area.

In the first quadrant, one finds the Passionates, who not only buy the product but continue to dream about it. Passionates represent a valuable capital for luxury brands. They are simultaneously their essential assets and their ambassadors.

Platonics, for whom the dream has not yet materialized, form the reservoir of Passionates. The Platonic category contents itself, for the time being, with an imaginary consumption, requiring the brand to take upon itself to surmount all the obstacles that could intervene with the final step of purchase.

On the opposite side, one finds the Blasés. They have bought, but no longer dream of the brand. In this case the brand must evaluate and understand why it was incapable of keeping the dream alive, and must at all costs try to reduce the drain of customers into the Blasés.

Finally the Indifferents: Even though they know the brand name, they neither buy the brand's product nor dream about it. The objective here is to transform them into Platonics, and if possible Passionates.

The Brand Power Matrix illustrates two very different problems for the two cases of Armani and Givenchy (see Fig. 19.7).

Percentages have been calculated relative to the awareness level of each brand to standardize comparability. The allocation of consumers in the four categories varies considerably. Armani has almost three times as many Passionates as Givenchy. Where does this substantial difference come from? The matrices hold some of the answers. To begin with, Armani has fewer Indifferents than Givenchy. The capacity to induce the act of dreaming is thus very different. This is clearly illustrated in the percentage of Platonics for both brands and reconfirms the findings from the Dream Equation.

On the other hand, Givenchy's "rate of conversion" from Platonics to Passionates is much more productive than that of Armani: 63% for

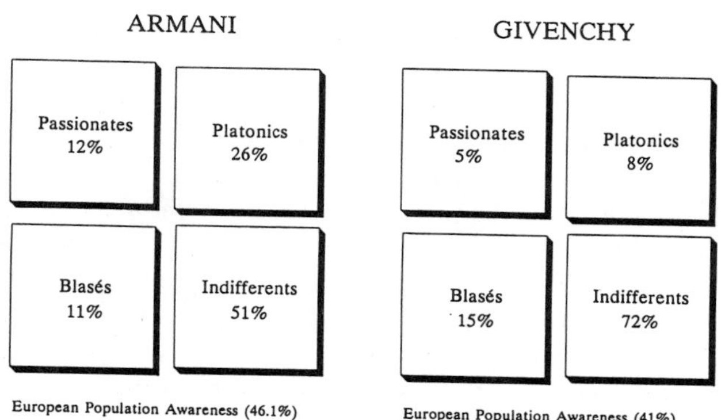

FIG. 19.7. Brand power matrices.

Givenchy and 46% for Armani. Thus Givenchy does a better job of materializing the act of buying from the dream it incites.

Finally, Armani has fewer Blasés than Givenchy. Of those who purchase, Armani is more effective at retaining the dream factor.

In sum, the problems of the two brands are opposite from one another. One can consider each cell in the matrix as one phase in the relationship between the consumer and a luxury brand: The normal evolution going from Indifferents to Platonics, then to Passionates, and then finally to Blasés. In this perspective, Givenchy has fewer "recruits" and maintains less in both intermediate phases (Platonics and Passionates), which are central and vital to the global penetration of the brand. On the other hand, Armani converts more Indifferents and keeps better its Passionates than Givenchy. Givenchy's problem lies in showing and spreading the dream it embodies, whereas Armani's problem lies in transforming the dream into buying.

THE EUROSCAN: A SOCIOCULTURAL SEGMENTATION OF THE LUXURY MARKET

It is possible to further refine the analysis of these results which until now have been construed on European averages, through RISC's specific sociocultural segmentation technique: the Euroscan.

In order to monitor social change over 27 countries, RISC uses 120 items designed to measure consumers' underlying value system. These items serve as multiple indicators to construct 35 sociocultural trends. The multiple indicator approach used to tap sociocultural sensitivities has two essential advantages over other value segmentation techniques that rely on single items with either a rank or scale measurement. The first one is of a theoretical nature: Sociocultural trends are akin to constructs or latent variables which are reflected by empirical indicators (i.e., the statements used to measure the trend). There is no one-to-one correspondence between a latent variable and its empirical indicators; rather it is preferable to use multiple indicators which can cover the many facets of a particular trend. Each statement serves to measure a specific dimension of the sociocultural trend. The second advantage is methodological: Multiple indicators increase reliability and reduce the attenuating effects of measurement error. The correlations among trends are more robust than correlations among individual items because a portion of measurement error is controlled. Furthermore, this approach allows for an annual check of convergent and discriminant validity, assuring that the trends are significantly different from one another. Finally, since the measuring instrument is designed to monitor sociocultural change over time and across countries, the scale construction using multiple indicators provides greater stability and comparability.

RISC applies the Benzecri method of Correspondence Analysis (Lebart, Morineau, & Warwick, 1984). The technique calculates distances and proximities among respondents based on their responses to the 120 sociocultural items and their positioning on the top tertile of each of the 35 sociocultural trends. Correspondence Analysis has a major advantage over classical factor analysis and principle components analysis in that it can evaluate simultaneously respondents and variables (i.e., trends, dreamers of Armani, buyers of Givenchy, etc.) in the *same multidimensional space.*

The technique calculates the distances between all 12,500 European respondents and constructs a multidimensional cloud of dots. RISC works primarily with the first two axes which together account for about 70% of the variance in the responses to the sociocultural questions (see Fig. 19.8).

The cloud of dots can be divided into 10 equal segments of 10% of the population thus producing the Euroscan. In the south there are those individuals who are impermeable to or fearful of change; they are attached to conventions and a need for basic security. In the north, one finds personal expression, openness toward change and others. In the east, the search for pleasure, breaking from social norms, flexibility, and intense sensations. In the west, one finds an orientation toward the community, family, religion, and a sense of social responsibility.

Figure 19.9 reveals the Euroscan obtained for Armani and Givenchy. Both brands occupy a clearly identifiable sociocultural territory across all five European markets which implies the possibility of developing a transnational strategy that focuses on each of its particular targets. It is evident that Givenchy's and Armani's dreamers are *not* found in the same territo-

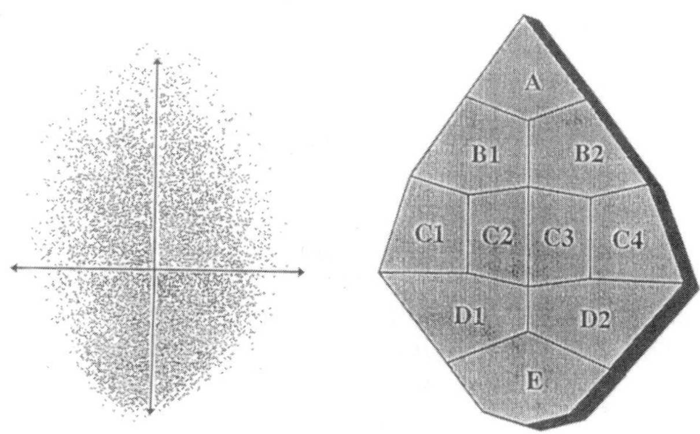

FIG. 19.8. Euroscan showing cloud of dots divided into 10 equal segments of 10% of the population.

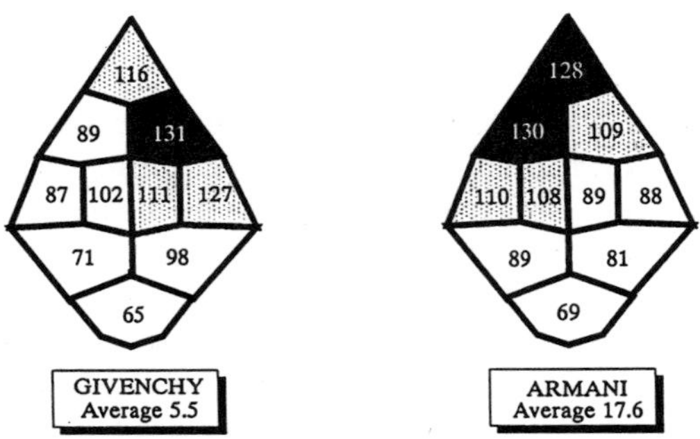

FIG. 19.9. Dream penetration across sociocultural territories.

ries. The "dream capital" for Givenchy is mainly situated in the east (in the universe of hedonism and the driving trends of the 1980s) and in the west for Armani (in a universe which is open to change yet attached to certain social norms and institutions—an emerging set of sensitivities for the 1990s). Several strategies are thus possible.

A first strategy is to reinforce the link between the values brought forth by the brand and its loyal customers. For example, in Givenchy's case one could aim at focusing the communication on the dominant values of these groups: emotional experience, risk taking, search for pleasure. On the other hand, one could try to extend the brand's influence by widening the field of values that mark its territory. This must be done with great care so as to achieve credibility in the new territories and not lose the core customer franchise. Both Armani and Givenchy could concentrate on the northern territories which are characterized by persons with strong social leadership qualities. These people, however, are not attracted to luxury communication codes that emphasize status. For them, luxury is more part of personal expression and their desire for authenticity. Communication codes should emphasize culture and heritage as opposed to fashion and novelty.

CONCLUSION

Today's changing luxury market is indeed complex but far less enigmatic than it was first thought to be. It is now a $60 billion global industry which has extended its access to a wider range of the population. Luxury brand managers must, however, maintain an aura of elitism while expanding awareness and sales. This delicate balancing act requires a careful analysis of the interrelationship among awareness, dream, and purchase. This chapter has demonstrated how three analytical tools can provide the information and direction to optimize the marketing effort.

First, the Dream Equation shows the variance in dream (the long-term value of a brand) attributed to awareness and purchase. It was discovered that while building awareness enhances the dream capital of a brand, too wide a diffusion can kill the dream and therefore weaken the long-term potential of a luxury brand. Furthermore, the Dream Equation offers a framework for assessing a possible "dream premium" or "dream deficit." We saw that Armani is in a favorable position which is attributed to the strong symbolic value of the brand and its ability to balance elitism and diffusion. On the other hand, Givenchy occupies a less favorable position in that its level of dream is less than the expected level given the parameters of the luxury market. It is likely that this is due to a possible mismatch between communication and distribution as well as to inflated expectations.

Second, the Brand Power Matrix provides a further refinement to the analysis of the interaction between dream and purchase at the individual level, for a given level of awareness. Following through with the examples of Armani and Givenchy, we found that the two brands are confronted with two very different problems: Givenchy is better at transforming the dream into purchase but is weak in establishing a broad base for the dream. On the other hand, Armani does an excellent job in consolidating its dream capital but is relatively poorer at transforming that dream into purchase.

Finally, the Euroscan sheds light on the sociocultural determinants of purchase and consumption behavior of luxury brands. It has been illustrated over and over again that the dream factor is a key to both understanding and acting in the luxury market. But *who* dreams of your brand? Part of the answer lies in demographics. Another part lies in specific attitudes and habits with respect to luxury. And finally, another part lies in sociocultural values. For the sake of brevity, this chapter has only looked at the latter for now. By applying a pan-European value segmentation technique called the Euroscan it was possible to demonstrate that those who dream of Armani are not the same as those who dream of Givenchy. In particular, we observed that the Armani dreamers are more in tune with the changing values of the 1990s; namely, the rise of ethics, belongings, and sense of responsibility toward society and the environment. By contrast, the Givenchy dreamers are closer to the values of the 1980s; that is, self-gratification, materialism, and the pursuit of an active and intense lifestyle.

These three basic techniques—the Dream Equation, the Brand Power Matrix, and the Euroscan—provide a simple yet actionable approach to cross-cultural segmentation, targeting, and positioning in today's rapidly changing luxury market.

REFERENCES

Belk, R. (1988). Possessions and the extended self. *Journal of Consumer Research, 15*, 139–168.

Bourdieu, P. (1984). *Distinction: A social critique of the judgement of taste.* London: Routledge and Kegan Paul.

Douglas, S., & Dubois, B. (1990). Looking at the cultural environment for international marketing opportunities. In B. Enis & K. C. Cox (Eds.), *Marketing classics: A selection of influential articles* (7th ed., pp. 542–549). Boston: Allyn & Bacon.

Dubois, B., Duquesne, P., & Finskud, L. (1991). *Value management in the luxury industry.* Unpublished manuscript. Paris, September 18.

Hirschman, E. C., & Holbrook, M. (1982). Hedonic consumption: Emerging concepts, methods and propositions. *Journal of Marketing, 46*, 92–101.

Holbrook, M. B., & Hirschman, E. C. (1982). The experimental aspects of consumption: Consumer fantasies, feelings and fun. *Journal of Consumer Research, 9*, 132–140.

Lebard, L., Morineau, A., & Warwick, K. M. (1984). *Multivariate descriptive statistical analysis: Correspondence analysis and related techniques.* New York: Wiley.

Levitt, T. (1983). The globalization of markets. *Harvard Business Review, 61*, 92–102.

Liebenstein, H. (1950). Bandwagon, snob and veblen effects in the theory of consumer's demand. *Quarterly Journal of Economics, 64*(2), 183–207.

McCracken, G. (1988). Culture and consumption: A theoretical account of the structure and movement of the cultural meanings of consumer goods. *Journal of Consumer Research, 13*, 71–84.

McKinsey & Co. (1991). *The luxury industry: An asset for France, Paris,* June 7. See also *L'Industrie Mondiale du Luxe,* Paris: Eurostaf, 1991.

Malinowski, B. (1922). *Argonauts of the Western Pacific.* London: G. Routledge & Sons, Ltd.

Mason, R. (1981). *Conspicuous consumption.* New York: St. Martin's Press.

Mauss, M. (1954). *The gift.* London: Cohen & West.

Veblen, T. (1899). *The theory of the leisure class.* New York: Macmillan.

Chapter **20**

Transferability of the Concept of Environmental Awareness Within the EUROSTYLES System Into Tourism Marketing

Andreas H. Zins
University of Economics and Business Administration, Vienna

THE NEED FOR EARLY ADOPTERS OF ENVIRONMENTALLY CONSCIOUS PRODUCTS

Environmental concern is one of the most powerful and fastest growing cultural trends throughout the industrialized world. The reinforced public discussion of environmental protection against water, soil, and air pollution, acid rain, oil spill at sea, the greenhouse effect, and the thinning of the ozone layer supports the development of the ecological movement. Longitudinal studies in Europe confirm the constantly growing sensibility of the population toward environmental issues. Whereas unemployment remained the top concern of the German nation during the 1980s the importance of environment climbed from 9% to 57%, weighing equally with unemployment, by the end of that decade (Voller & Winkler, 1991).

As a reflection as well as a self-enforcing process of this trend we can observe at the public level the emergence of green parties, separate administrative institutions dealing with environmental problems, a more restrictive legislation, and a growing number of environmental conferences. What is happening at the individual level? Companies have incorporated ecological issues into their business strategies. Some companies are translating the challenges of the "green movement" toward efficient design of instrumental programs to a more or less successful extent.

Market research has focused on defining and profiling the ecologically concerned consumer. At the beginning, it was elementary to operationalize constructs like "ecological concern" (Antil & Bennett, 1979; Cotgrove & Duff, 1980; Cowles & Crosby, 1986; Kley & Fietkau, 1979; Maloney & Ward, 1973; Maloney, Ward, & Braucht, 1975; Urban, 1986). The commonalties of these studies defined in the cognitive construct "environmental consciousness" can be seen three dimensionally covering ecologically relevant values, ecology-related attitudes, and ecology-oriented behavioral intentions. Especially the affective dimensions of the relevant attitudes revealed the increasing individual evaluation of ecological problems (Basis Research, 1985). The next step in the screening process of the ecologically concerned consumer was the investigation of the relationship between "green" values and attitudes and actual commitment. Several studies and results from panel surveys corroborated the positive association between the environmental awareness and green purchase habits (Adlwarth & Wimmer, 1986; Kristensen & Grunert, 1991; Voller & Winkler, 1991).

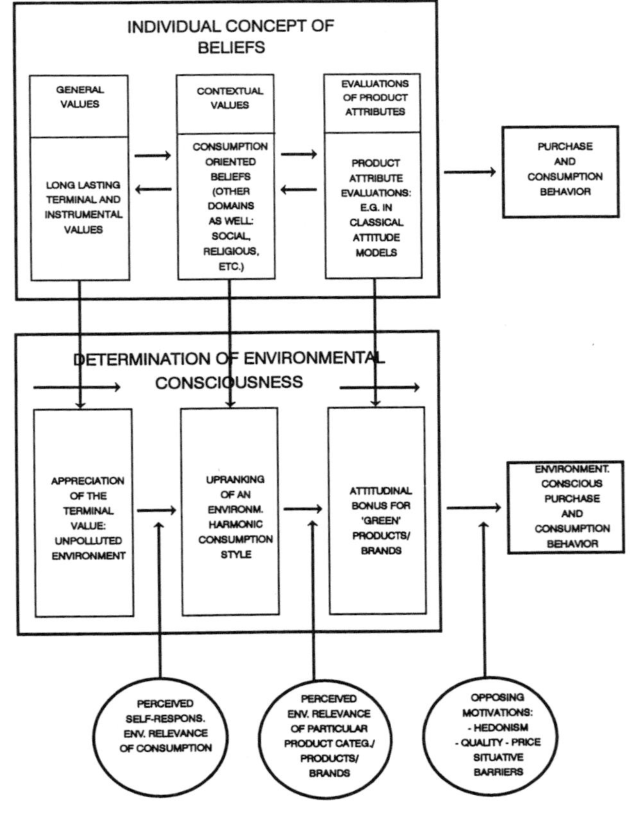

FIG. 20.1. Concept of determination of environmental consciousness. Adapted and translated from Dahlhoff (1980).

Nevertheless, the question arises for which products and to what extent these findings pertain. For this purpose it may be useful to differentiate the structural relations according to the degree of determination of the environmental beliefs and attitudes, as Dahlhoff (1980) put it (see Fig. 20.1). The global value "unpolluted environment" stimulates at the level of contextual values the individual's higher ranking of an environmentally conscious consumption style. It is hypothesized that this may be true for other domains such as leisure and tourism as well. This up-ranking is influenced by the perceived self-responsibility for ecological behavior and the perceived environmental relevance of one's consumption. This effect differentiates at the more determined stage of evaluation: that is, at the level of certain product categories, products, and brands. Before a need transforms into environmental conscious demand opposing motivations and attitudes (e.g. hedonistic, quality, or price orientation) as well as situative barriers may intervene and inhibit the green purchase decision.

From this perspective we can deduce that scales of environmental consciousness will result in a stronger association with purchase decisions stemming from the same or at least related area of life as the scale orientation itself. Furthermore, we may argue, that the fewer dissonant motivations and attitudes occur within this particular process the more stable are forecasts for green purchase decisions.

The basic relationships among the cognitive levels of ecological values, ecological attitudes, and ecological actions, which had been suggested by the model of Dahlhoff, can be found in the LISREL model of environmental consciousness developed by Urban (1986). Additionally, another construct called *predispositions to ecological actions* was introduced between ecological attitudes and ecological actions, which, in fact, had a very strong impact on ecological actions. Apart from the well-known and well-tested influencing variables such as age and education, some additional relationships had been hypothesized and observed within this model.

Take, for example, the business sector in which an individual works, whether employed or self-employed. This work variable has no direct effect on values and attitudes but determines the development of attitudes toward the problem-solving capacity of science and technology. These attitudes influence both ecological values and attitudes. In addition to this set of sociodemographic variables, two socioecological factors can be observed in this model. First, is the perceived ecological impacts at the place where the individual lives, which is interrelated with ecological attitudes. Second, is a variable covering the knowledge of individual opportunities for protecting and conserving the environment, which are offered by the society and community. This factor has a positive influence on ecological values and predispositions for ecological actions.

Another methodological issue refers to the concept of environmental concern. Many different multiitem scales have been introduced to define constructs as valid equivalents for the concept of environmental concern. Some studies concentrate on one issue, others use several constructs or mix different issues such as concern about the population, natural resources, pollution, or energy resources in one construct. In addition, every substantive issue may be operationalized within a different theoretical framework: attitudes, support for government regulations, government spending priorities, or individual behavior. Van Liere and Dunlap (1978) pointed out that it makes a substantial difference how environmental concern is measured and the convergent validity does not hold for every variation in the measurement process. So what's the case in tourism?

Almost all travel destinations, whether big cities or recreation areas, are greatly dependent on the attractiveness of their natural and social environment. Both tourism and leisure activities are phenomena of travel; both make intensive use of natural and cultural resources causing tourism to act as its own ecological enemy—a situation quite different from other industries. World-wide, tourism can be regarded as the largest and fastest growing industry. So, it is no surprise that the new trends of important tourism studies are "representing a shift from former more orthodox concerns (such as natural resource management and planning, environmental features, and recreational opportunities) to newer areas (such as ecotourism and especially tourism as an element of sustainable development)" (Farrell & Runyan, 1991). Whereas international declarations and strategies (WCED, 1987) have committed to sustainable development as focusing on the simultaneous "integration of major elements, closely charted development, conservation, cultural compatibility, and local input" (Farrell & Runyan, 1991), the individual tourist's insight into and awareness of those interrelationships are just at beginning to develop.

Under this assumption, we can re-examine the theoretical model presented in Fig. 20.1 in order to differentiate the decision process for products and services. The penetration of scientific results concerning the negative effects of different materials (e.g., plumbed gas, carbon monoxide, nitrates, nonrecyclable fabrics) is quite advanced. The industry has, in turn, responded to this trend by labeling and even standardizing ecological friendly products. Gradually, the individual consumer is able to decide in front of the shelves whether or not to be environmentally conscious.

But how to communicate such attributes for intangibles like tourism products? In absence of reliable, worldwide, and high quality scientific findings of the complex interlacement of the tourism system with the whole ecosystem it is impossible to perceive the individual tourist's negative or positive contribution to the ecosystem. Nevertheless, there is a vital discussion and development for classification and labeling of environmentally healthy recreational sites throughout Europe (e.g., Blue Flag for coastal zones, spa standards). What can be ascertained is the fact that tourism is essentially a mass phenomenon and even alternative forms of tourism are destined to move in this direction (Butler, 1990).

Considering again the main influential factors of the previous model we admit that perceived self-responsibility as well as perceived environmental relevance of particular tourism products are less developed and objectively more difficult to evaluate. As to the third factor of opposing motivations to the final consumption behavior, an extensive discussion of travel and leisure motives would be necessary. In short, growing welfare—at least of a considerable part of the world's population—maturing travel experiences, improvement of transportation and communication facilities, and worsening of environmental and sociopsychological living conditions are obvious tourism promoters. Escape, change, relaxation, entertainment, and new experiences are up to now predominant travel motives. So, tourism will not be curbed soon by its proper evolution. Another trend may support alternative forms of (soft, green, or eco-) tourism. Inglehart (1977) states that the change in personal values may be characterized by a shift from materialism to postmaterialism which is determined by the growing importance of values such as self-fulfillment, achievement, experience-based orientation, and harmony with oneself and with the environment.

Hence, tourism management, if incorporating strategic issues towards an ecological tourism, must first address those people representing the leaders in an emerging health and ecology conscious society. Several marketing oriented studies have identified this segment of innovators and early adopters as younger, socially and economically established people who tend to be less conservative, self-controlled, well-organized, and goal oriented (Adlwarth & Wimmer, 1986; Anderson & Cunningham, 1972; Belch, 1979; Kinnear, Taylor, & Ahmed, 1974; Pettus & Giles, 1987). What answers to this particular market segmentation task can we expect from one of the largest pan-European market research projects: The Europanel Database, which is connected to the lifestyle typology EUROSTYLES?

CONTRIBUTION OF LIFESTYLE TYPOLOGIES

The Concept of EUROSTYLES

The EUROSTYLES system represents a multinational lifestyle typology that has been developed since 1972 by the French enterprise Centre de Communication Avancé (CCA) of the Havas-Eurocom group. This research concept was established in 1989 in 15 European countries by a two-step procedure by the market research companies and panels affiliated to the EUROPANEL network.

In the first step, a sample representation of the entire national population was formed that had to administer a relative lengthy questionnaire comprising 3500 variables in 160 questions. This instrument covers 5 principal dimensions of lifestyle: objective personal criteria; concrete behavior; attitudes; motivations and aspirations; and sensitivities and emotions. This database supports the global monitoring of "Socio-Waves" and a typology called Sociostyles (Cathelat, 1985) which is invariably defined for Europe.

During the second step a reduced-set questionnaire was sent out to a five-fold larger sample (i.e., 20,000 in Europe) and served as a link between the founding survey and future studies. This procedure aimed at covering each region, each age-group, each social class, and each ethnic subgroup in order to measure the weight and distribution of each Sociostyle.

For marketing purposes the EUROSTYLES offer different instruments:

1. A topography of socioclimatic zones: that combines Sociostyles with mentalities and serves as an instrument of sociocultural segmentation of the population.
2. A sociocultural compass rose: that reveals the main cultural trends. Which of them are coming up, are mobilizing, which of them are declining?
3. A social geographical map: which represents the mathematical position of the Sociostyles on a sociocultural map and helps in developing new positioning strategies.
4. A cultural compass: that indicates the principal axis of the socio-structure of the mapping and acts as an instrument for image-based strategies.
5. Scenarios: describing hypotheses about the medium-term future and serves therefore as an instrument of innovation.

Understanding the EUROSTYLES Typology

The EUROSTYLES system consists of 16 different lifestyle portraits resulting from a series of multivariate analyses (factor-, correspondence-, cluster analysis). The 16 EUROSTYLES are congruently defined in each European country and in all sectors of activity (e.g., politics, advertising, media, buying or consumption of goods and services). Figure 20.2 locates the 16 EUROSTYLES on a two-dimensional map. The horizontal axis bridges two opposing poles that can be described as *settlement* on the right and *movement* on the left. The vertical axis describes the bipolar dimension of *valuables* (pleasure) in the North and *values* in the South.

The settlement pole or region combines several values, behavioral models, and schemes of ideas that are illustrated by key words such as: priority to the individual's defense and survival at the current social status, con-

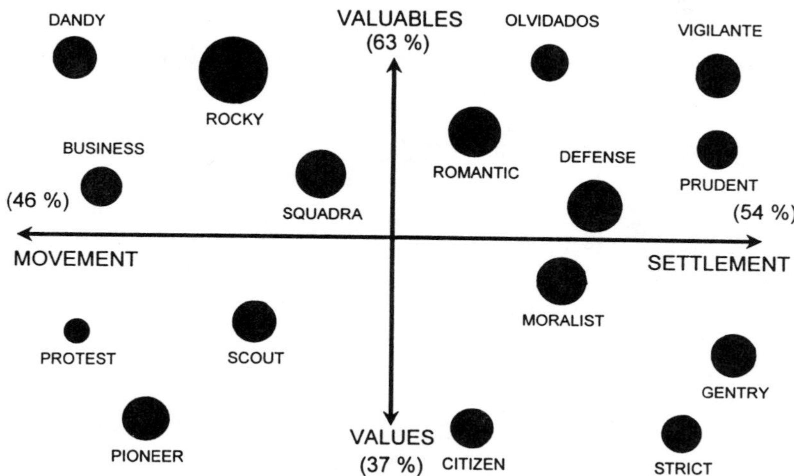

FIG. 20.2. Sociocultural map of 16 EUROSTYLES. Redrawn from CCA/EUROPANEL and GfK Vienna.

vergence on habits and traditions, group protection, obedience to the culture's rules of life without reluctance, critical sense or revolution. In contrast, movement means dynamism, liberty of criticism, priority to the individual, distance to norms, law and authorities. The vertical axis combines two opposing positions as well. The Northern region can be characterized by values of pleasure, sensuality, and hedonism, which all together are strongly associated with values of money and substantial equipment in a system of expenditure and even waste. The label attached to each type may be misleading in its interpretation. A complete list of the 16 EUROSTYLES combined with a short description can be found in the Appendix.

Distribution Over Europe

In order to determine the potential of different social mentalities or consumption patterns it is necessary to know the share of each of the 16 EUROSTYLES. As a mean value of the 15 investigated European countries the diameter of the circles in Fig. 20.2 reveals the share of the 16 styles. The major types in Europe are ROCKY (13.5%), DEFENSE (8.5%) and ROMANTIC (7.8%). Obviously, the rank order of each style is not the same for each country. The type ROCKY, for example, dominates the socio-cultural grid especially in the Netherlands, Great Britain, France, and Switzerland. The share of the MORALIST and the ROMANTIC is very high in Germany, Austria, Belgium, and Switzerland. On the other hand, in Denmark and Sweden the type PIONEER is much above average.

The practical use for marketing purposes does not end here. Much more sophisticated correlations can be analyzed from the huge database covering a sample of around 100,000 households. According to the particular request, the analyst may conclude from existing consumption patterns of certain product category, on the one hand, and the aggregated attitude towards several sociocultural trends on the other hand, the market potential for a new product line. The marketing practitioner may receive spending propensities for different EUROSTYLES on the regional, national, and international level. Once a target segment has been defined, the market researcher is able to obtain detailed information about media habits, communication styles and themes, as well as image preferences. Combining the results from all available sectors the design of a new product and the creative development of the corresponding advertising campaign are well supported.

It is not necessary to design and implement different marketing programs for each individual EUROSTYLE. According to attitudinal and behavioral aspects several types uniformly share two or more EUROSTYLES and can be grouped together into so-called SOCIO-TARGETS. The lifestyle research center of the EUROPANEL group developed and refined a multi-item list (see complete list of statements in the Appendix) to construct a standardized environmental awareness index. Along this index the 16 EUROSTYLES were rearranged into five groups of environmentally conscious styles (ECO-STYLES). In the Southwest of the sociographic map (cf. Fig. 20.3) the types PROTEST, PIONEER, CITIZEN, and SCOUT represent the group of *Environmentalists* that show the highest scores of environmental awareness. The group of *Uninterested* (VIGILANTE, PRUDENT, and OLVIDADOS) is located in the Northeast of the map. A brief outline of the characteristics of the Environmentalists coincides with former findings: young people between the age of 25 and 40, single or young married couples. According to Winkler (1991):

> In general they have a high level of education and, a job corresponding to their education: senior employees or professionals with an above average income. They are intellectual opinion leaders claiming to be liberal, tolerant and humanistic. Of course they try to improve their quality of life in line with the idealistic ideas and principles they hold. Their consumer spending concentrates on leisure, travel and culture. . . . Above all, they prefer to form their own opinion of products—it is necessary to convince or disarm them in order to sway their views. (p. 10)

Is this portrayal in conjunction with above average purchase rates of environmentally friendly products sufficient to address to this target segment as the innovators and early adopters for ecological tourism products and services? A detailed answer is given in the next section where steps of empirical validation using the EUROSTYLES typology on a national guest sample are undertaken.

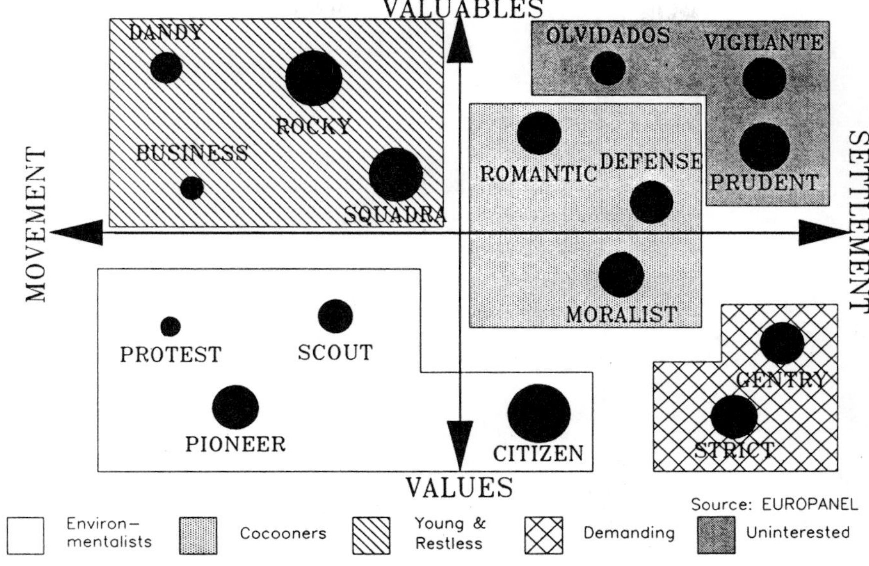

FIG. 20.3. ECO-STYLES as SOCIO-TARGETS.

EMPIRICAL VALIDATION THROUGH THE EUROSTYLES SYSTEM

Research Design

The EUROSTYLES approach is a commercial lifestyle typology that can be contracted to any other market research project conducted by one of the research institutes affiliated to the EUROPANEL group. By adding 15 standardized questions to the questionnaire comprising approximately 70 variables acting as lifestyle indicators within a secret key procedure the research institute is able to identify every respondent as belonging to a particular EUROSTYLE. The partners of the Austrian National Guest Survey (GBÖ) decided to integrate the EUROSTYLES typology into the periodically repeated international visitor survey for the tourism year 1991–1992. The GBÖ comprises 10,000 personal interviews distributed over the summer and winter season covering 15 (primarily European) guest nations.

Comparing the findings of both samples (household samples with 14,000 respondents in 9 European countries on the one side, guest sample of 14 European nations in Austria on the other side; cf. Fig. 20.4) shall help to explain whether environmental awareness is robust to different life settings. There are two methodological constraints to be considered making a direct comparison impossible:

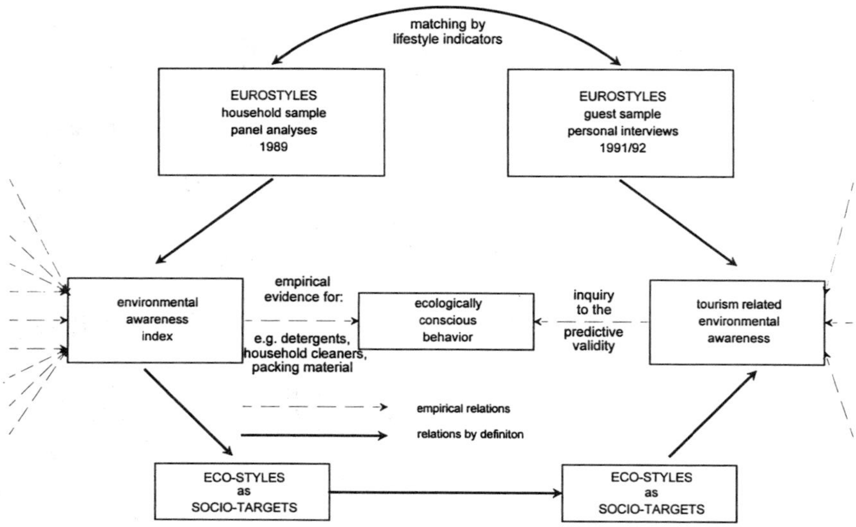

FIG. 20.4. Structure of the research design.

1. The construction of the environmental awareness index was based on a multi-item-statement-list representing comprehensive environmental values and attitudes as well as behavioral intentions embedded in a typical household surrounding. The use of these statements (see Appendix for details) would not had been adequate in a tourism setting. Moreover, the duration of the personal guest interviews would not had allowed additional questions.

2. As no standardized and transparent classification of environmentally friendly tourism resorts exists up to now we cannot deduct any ecologically conscious behavior from the traveler's destination decision. This was possible for some physical products by means of several panel data.

In turn, it is contingent to examine some other indicators for environmental awareness that can be found in the guest questionnaire. Transferring the ECO-STYLES defined by the index applied in the panel analyses to the Austrian guest sample, the discriminant effect of the tourism-related environmental aspects can be analyzed. As the three ECO-STYLES in between did not reveal a distinct profile the subsequent investigation focuses particularly on the two opposing extreme ECO-STYLES the *Environmentalist* and the *Uninterested.*

It was hypothesized that the variables presented in Table 20.1 may contribute to some extent to the tourism related environmental awareness.

TABLE 20.1
List of Environmental Variables in the GBO Questionnaire

Number of Variables	*Type of Variables*	*Content of Variables*
1	attitudinal	Importance of environment and countryside for the present stay here.
1		Importance of a well cared-for countryside for the destination decision.
1	evaluative	Overall satisfaction with the environment and countryside at the vacation area.
1		Impression of environmental conditions in the vacation town or village: adverse effects noticeable.
4		Rating of environmental criteria: quality of air, purity of water, variety of countryside, and diversity of plants and animals, condition of countryside (harmony of paths and streams, etc.).
1	behavioral intentions	Willingness to pay individually for caring for the maintenance of the countryside.
8		Traffic limitations that would be accepted by the guest in the holiday area.
1		Consequences of negative environment influences on the holiday planning and activities.

Findings

With the exception of the last variable of Table 20.1 (less than 0.3% of the sample responded to this open-ended question; therefore it was eliminated) all variables entered a discriminant analysis on a dichotomous level in order to explain the discriminant power between the Environmentalists (58%) and the Uninteresteds (42%). After processing 2,527 cases (summer sample) out of the 17 input variables only 11 significant variables remained in the canonical discriminant function that is characterized by a very small eigenvalue of .03867 and a canonical correlation of .193. The discriminant function coefficients and the within-groups correlations between the discriminating variables and the canonical discriminant function are presented in Table 20.2. The group centroid for the Uninteresteds is located at –.2263 whereas that of the Environmentalists at .1707 on the function. The discriminant function improves the predictive accuracy from 50% to 55.7% which is a rather poor result. With 60.6% correctly classified the group of the Uninteresteds seem to be better predictable than the Environmentalists by this set of variables.

Before exploring the overall weak discrimination between the two opposing ECO-STYLES it is important to examine the contribution of each

TABLE 20.2
Standardized Discriminant Function and Correlation Coefficients

Variable	*Discriminant Coefficient*	*Correlation Coefficient*
Willingness to pay for maintenance of countryside	.5985	.6062
Introduction of traffic free areas in particular areas of town	.5855	.3966
Stricter speed limits in thetown	.3201	.2773
Overall satisfaction with environment and countryside	-.3193	-.2683
Areas with little traffic and without public parking	-.2980	.0007
Purity of water	.2635	.3105
Condition of countryside	.2509	.3475
Areas with little traffic and traffic ban during night hours	-.2413	-.0536
Overall importance of environment and countryside	-.1650	-.2697
Ban on cars in whole town (transport service into town)	-.1355	.0474
Noticeable adverse environmental impacts	.1254	.1292
Diversity of countryside	n.s.	.2118
More general ban on private transport while prioring public transport	n.s.	.2004
Quality of the air	n.s.	.1998
Ban on private transport to outing destinations and attractions	n.s.	.0910
More general ban on private transport keeping public transport the same	n.s.	.0241
Importance of a well cared-for countryside on decision	n.s.	-.0037

Note. n.s. = not significant.

of the used variables. It is striking that the agreement to planned actions that would reduce some facets of the guest's sovereignty counts for the highest distinction. In comparison, evaluative variables have less impact. As for this set of variables, it was expected that environmentally conscious guests would be more sensible to all aspects of environment. Nevertheless, the signs of the coefficients do not reflect this homogenous image. The stated perception of environmental impacts are consistent with a worse rating of explicit factors such as *purity of water*, *condition of countryside*, *the diversity of countryside*, and *the quality of the air*. Surprisingly, the overall satisfaction with the environment and the countryside goes in the opposite direction. The attitudinal variable describing the importance of the factors *environment* and *countryside* for the destination seem to be higher for the group of Uninteresteds. Univariate statistics confirm these findings (cf. Table 20.3). The positive relationship between behavioral intentions and the group of Environmentalists can be seen as confirmative as well. What troubles the concise interpretation is the observation that this group of guests do not care about an intact environment at their holiday destination.

Though some of the environmental questions have been dropped and some similar ones have been added a partial cross-validation was performed by analyzing the winter sample in the same way. The discriminant function (eigenvalue: .0537, can.corr: .2258) accounted for 54.2% correctly classified cases (n = 1,356). Again, some of the intended steps toward traffic limitations differentiated very strongly between the two ECO-STYLES. Whereas

TABLE 20.3

Univariate Statistics for Describing Two Opposing ECO-STYLES

Variable	*Uninterested in %*	*Environmentalist in %*	*CHI^2 Value*	*Significance Level*
Willingness to pay for maintenance of countryside	31.4	39.5	17.252	>0.001
Introduction of traffic free areas in particular areas of town	52.0	60.3	17.017	>0.001
Stricter speed limits in thetown	55.8	60.8	6.248	-.012
Overall satisfaction with environment and countryside	31.0	25.4	9.621	0.002
Areas with little traffic and without public parking	49.7	49.1	0.068	n.s.
Purity of water	18.7	21.8	3.638	0.056
Condition of countryside	33.1	36.8	3.603	0.058
Areas with little traffic and traffic ban during night hours	54.1	52.9	0.372	n.s.
Overall importance of environment and countryside	92.8	92.0	0.626	n.s.
Ban on cars in whole town (transport service into town)	21.5	23.1	0.856	n.s.
Noticeable adverse environmental impacts	11.8	14.2	3.074	n.s.
Diversity of countryside	35.9	36.5	0.116	n.s.
More general ban on private transport while prioring public transport	25.5	30.2	6.794	>0.010
Quality of the air	42.6	42.1	0.072	n.s.
Ban on private transport to outing destinations and attractions	27.9	28.9	0.289	n.s.
More general ban on private transport keeping public transport the same	12.1	13.0	0.415	n.s.
Importance of a well cared-for countryside on decision	100.0	100.0	--	--

Note. n.s. = not significant.

TABLE 20.4
Rank Comparison of National Differences in Environmental Awareness

Country	*EAI Rank*	*Willingness-to-Pay for Countryside-Maintenance*		*Overall Rating of Environment*
		Share	*Amount*	
Germany	1	2	5	1
Switzerland	2	1	1	2
Denmark	3	5	5	3
Sweden	4	4	2	5
Great Britain	5	3	3	6
Italy	6	7	6	7
France	7	6	7	4

Note. From Voller and Winkler (1991, p. 27).
EAI = environmental awareness index (household sample in 9 European countries).

perceived environmental impacts are responsible for a location nearer to the Environmentalists, a worse overall rating of the environment and countryside moves toward the Uninteresteds. The attitudinal aspect of this factor differs insignificantly.

Another step of external validation was exercised by comparing national differences of the environmental awareness index constructed by the EUROPANEL group and selected tourism related environmental variables found in the Austrian National Guest Survey (cf. Table 20.4). Taking the share of guests willing to contribute financially for the maintenance of the countryside in Austria the rank order of the tourism generating countries is almost the same. A larger deviation, though not a completely reverse order, can be observed when considering the proposed amount per night and person. Examining another variable (the overall rating of environment on a 4-point scale) that presented the group of Uninteresteds to be more sensible to environmental aspects, this analysis reproduces almost the identical rank order of the original environmental awareness index.

CONCLUSION

On the examination of the environmental awareness of European consumers and its implication for ecologically conscious behavior two data samples were compared: a household sample covering 9 European countries representatively and a sample of the Austrian National Guest Survey comprising 13 European tourism generating countries. Both samples used the EUROSTYLES typology in order to identify the share of each of the

16 standardized EUROSTYLES in the sample. Within the household sample a special environmental awareness index was constructed that reduced the 16 lifestyle types into five homogenous groups of ECO-STYLES. By means of panel analyses empirical evidence was shown on the relationship between environmental conscious consumers and higher purchase rates of environmentally friendly products. Therefore, it was investigated whether this particular definition of environmental awareness can be held responsible for other domains of life such as leisure and tourism as well.

For methodological reasons a direct comparison of the measurement instrument in both samples was not feasible. Instead, a list of 17 different indicators for tourism related environmental awareness was examined at an univariate and a multivariate level in order to discriminate between the two extreme ECO-STYLES: Environmentalists and Uninteresteds. Some convincing findings concerning ecologically conscious behavioral intentions supported the usefulness of the ECO-STYLES as an appropriate tourism market segmentation approach. Nevertheless, the poor degree of determination of the discriminant function, the stability of the results at the test-retest occasion (summer vs. winter sample), and the confirming outcome of the external validation of the tourism related indicators remind us to be cautious. There are several sources of variability in this research design that cannot be explained definitively.

1. The construction of the environmental awareness index centers around the household and the regular life settings (at home, in the home country). Therefore, it may not be surprising that products bought and consumed within this area have a positive association with environmental values and attitudes. As the theoretical model presented by Dahlhoff suggests other values may be predominant in other domains and life settings. The empirical results of this study would support this assumption.

2. The effect of the lack of objective and transparent environmental labels for tourism products and services on the perceived self-responsibility and environmental relevance of someone's consumption was discussed in the introductory section. The influence of other travel-inherent motivations and benefits sought was reviewed as well. A trade-off analysis between these factors and tourism-related environmental considerations within the tourist's decision-making process should elucidate the impact on individual behavior.

3. A conceptual source of instability of these results is found in the matching process for identifying the 16 EUROSTYLES. As this procedure is a black-box step for the end-user of the EUROSTYLES we have to accept the reported overall degree of correctly classified respondents amounting to 70% to 80%.

4. A smoothing effect throughout the 16 EUROSTYLES by choosing the same destination country may have biased the representative coverage

of each of the lifestyle types. This could be examined only with cross-reference to the whole EUROPANEL database.

This study aimed at making an inquiry to the usefulness of the EUROSTYLES concept in the field of tourism. In this case an add-on tool to the EUROSTYLES system has not proven to be efficient in solving tourism marketing problems. Results of other analyses (Mazanec & Zins, 1993) showed that the 16 original EUROSTYLES cannot be considered to be ready-made segments for tourism marketing. At any rate, the "environmentalist movement has the potential to significantly change marketing in the 90's" (Voller & Winkler, 1991), and will change tourism marketing with a particular timelag as well.

REFERENCES

Adlwarth, W., & Wimmer, F. (1986). Umweltbewußtsein und Kaufverhalten—Ergebnisse einer Verbraucherpanel-Studie [Environmental consciousness and buying behavior—results from a household panel study]. *Jahrbuch der Absatz- und Verbrauchsforschung, 2*, 166–192.

Anderson, T. W., Jr., & Cunningham, W. H. (1972). The socially conscious consumer. *Journal of Marketing, 36*(3), 23–31.

Antil, J. H., & Bennet, P. D. (1979). Construction and validation of a scale to measure socially responsible consumption behavior. In K. E. Henion & T. C. Kinnear (Eds.), *The conserver society* (pp. 51–68). Chicago, IL: American Marketing Association.

Basis Research (Ed.). (1985). *Trend-Monitor*. Frankfurt. Unpublished results.

Belch, M. A. (1979). Identifying the socially and ecologically concerned segment through life-style research: Initial findings. In K. E. Henion & T. C. Kinnear (Eds.), *The conserver society* (pp. 69–81). Chicago, IL: American Marketing Association.

Butler, R. W. (1990). Alternative tourism: Pious hope or trojan horse? *Journal of Travel Research, 28*(3), 40–45.

Cathelat, B. (1985). *Styles de vie* (Vols. 1 & 2). Paris: Editions d'industrie.

Cotgrove, S., & Duff, A. (1980). Environmentalism, middle-class radicalism and politics. *Sociological Review, 28*, 333–351.

Cowles, D., & Crosby, L. A. (1986). Measure validation in consumer research: A confirmatory factor analysis of the voluntary simplicity lifestyle scale. In P. J. Lutz (Ed.), *Advances in consumer research, Vol. 13* (pp. 392–397). Provo, UT: Advances in Consumer Research.

Dahlhoff, H. D. (1980). *Individuelle Wertorientierungen. Analyse und Aussagewert personenspezifischer Werthierarchien im Marketing* [Individual values. Analysis and meaning of personal value hierarchies for the marketing]. *Arbeitspapier Nr. 23*. Münster: Institut für Marketing der Universität Münster.

Farrell, B. H., & Runyan, D. (1991). Ecology and tourism. *Annals of Tourism Research, 18*, 26–40.

Inglehart, R. (1977). *The silent revolution—changing values and political styles among western publics*. Princeton, NJ: Princeton University Press.

Kinnear, T. C., Taylor, J. R., & Ahmed, S. A. (1974). Ecologically concerned consumers: Who are they? *Journal of Marketing, 38*, 20–24.

Kley, J., & Fietkau, H.-J. (1979). Verhaltenswirksame Variablen des Umweltbewußtseins [Behavior-related variables of environmental consciousness]. *Psychologie und Praxis, 1,* 13–22.

Kristensen, K., & Grunert, S. C. (1991). The effect of ecological consciousness on the demand for organically produced food. In *Marketing thought around the world, Proceedings of the 20th Annual Conference of the European Marketing Academy, Vol. 2* (pp. 299–318). Dublin: University College.

Maloney, M. P., & Ward, M. P. (1973). Ecology: Let's hear from the people. *American Psychologist, 28,* 583–586.

Maloney, M. P., Ward, M. P., & Braucht, G. N. (1975). A revised scale for the measurement of ecological attitudes and knowledge. *American Psychologist, 30,* 787–789.

Mazanec, J. A., & Zins, A. H. (1994). Tourism behavior and the new European lifestyle typology. In W. Theobald (Ed.), *Global tourism. The next decade* (pp. 199–216). Oxford: Butterworth.

Pettus, A. M., & Giles, M. B. (1987). Personality characteristics and environmental attitudes. *Population and Environment, 9*(3), 127–137.

Urban, D. (1986). Was ist Umweltbewußtsein? [What is environmental consciousness?]. *Zeitschrift für Soziologie, 15*(5), 363–377.

Van Liere, K. D., & Dunlap, R. E. (1978). Environmental concern. Does it make a difference how it's measured. *Environment and Behavior, 13*(6), 651–676.

Voller, B., & Winkler, A. R. (1991). European consumers and environmental behaviour. *The growing individualisation of consumer lifestyles and demand* (pp. 25–32). Amsterdam: European Society for Opinion and Marketing Research.

World Commission on Environment and Development. (1987). *Our common future ('Bruntland Report').* New York: WCED.

Winkler, A. (1991). EURO-STYLES in panel analyses. *EUROPANEL Marketing Bulletin,* 8–11.

APPENDIX

The 16 EUROSTYLES in Brief

These profiles are taken from the *Europanel Marketing Bulletin,* 1991 (Andreas R. Winkler, Euro-Styles in Panel Analysis, p. 8):

1	PRUDENT	Retirees resigned to their fate, seeking security
2	DEFENSIVE	Younger inhabitants of small town seeking protection and support in their traditional family structures
3	VIGILANTE	Frustrated blue-collar workers trying to preserve their identities
4	OLVIDADOS	Retirees and housewives threatened and left out by society's growing complexity; seek protection
5	ROMANTIC	Sentimental, romantic young next builders seeking modern progress and a secure life for their families
6	SQUADRA	Tolerant suburban young couples seeking a secure life of sports and leisure; smaller group gives feeling of security
7	ROCKIES	Working class youth, excluded in their own eyes, seeking integration via money-making/consumption; frustrated by low education
8	DANDY	Hedonistic young "show-offs" with modest income and concern for outward appearances
9	BUSINESS	Spendthrift, well-educated, ambitious young "wolves," seeking leadership in a competitive society
10	PROTEST	Intellectual young critics seeking to revolutionize society
11	PIONEER	Young well-off, ultra-tolerant intellectuals seeking social justice
12	SCOUT	Tolerant middle-aged conservatives seeking orderly social progress
13	CITIZEN	Community organizers seeking leadership in social activities
14	MORALIST	Quiet, religious citizens seeking a peaceful future for their children
15	GENTRY	"Law and order" conservatives belonging to "old money" established elite
16	STRICT	Repressive puritans

List of Statements for Constructing the Environmental Awareness Index

1 This country does not need more industries.
*2 The car has nothing to do with the problems.
3 Safeguarding nature is more important to me than continued economic growth.
*4 In my position, I don't have the possibility to contribute very much personally to the protection of the environment.
5 In the home, we use a lot fewer products harmful to the environment today than we used to.
6 I would be prepared to give up total cleanliness of my home if it would mean causing less damage to the environment.
7 I am prepared to pay higher prices for products whose packaging does not pollute the environment.
*8 Far too much importance is attached to the protection of the environment.
*9 Basically, I am not particularly worried about he danger that certain products present to the environment.
*10 What is presently being done for the protection of nature is perfectly sufficient.

Source: GfK-scale for measuring the environmental awareness; 5-point scale; scale of items labeled with * was inverted; the additively constructed index is unidimensional.

Chapter 21

Cross-Cultural Values Research: Implications for International Advertising

Gregory M. Rose
University of Mississippi

Levitt (1983) predicts that emerging global markets will create an international homogenization of preference. The rise in international advertising attests to the globalization of the world economy. Yet, the standardization of advertising has declined. Less than 1 in 3 international advertisers currently use a standardized approach (James & Hill, 1991) and advertising has clearly not become culturally homogenous (Mueller, 1992; Ramaprasad & Hasegawa, 1992).

Although local tastes remain an important influence on advertising, the underlying argument of standardization is still valid. Intermarket similarities permit economies of scale and standardization can reduce overhead costs and produce a consistent worldwide image. Furthermore, identifying international market segments can increase the size and profitability of existing target markets and may allow a company to appeal to a market niche that would be unprofitable in any single nation. In short, while local tastes remain important, commonalties in international consumers must be found. The central argument of this chapter is that values can provide a cross-cultural means of grouping consumers. The current problem, however, is in identifying the salient cross-cultural dimensions of values.

This chapter examines current practices in international advertising and summarizes cross-cultural values research. It attempts to identify consistent and important value dimensions, and to assess the implications of these dimensions for international advertising. Initially, current trends in advertising are examined. Then the distinction between an individualist and a collectivist culture is described, and the cross-cultural research of both social psychologists and consumer behaviorists is summarized. Finally, suggestions for future research are advanced.

CURRENT TRENDS IN INTERNATIONAL ADVERTISING

Advertising is in a state of transition. The decline of advertising expenditures in the United States has made international advertising an essential source of future growth for U.S. agencies. In 1991 U.S. advertising expenditures were 3.9% below 1990 expenditures (Advertising Age, 1993). In contrast, 1991 expenditures by the top 50 international advertisers increased 11.3% (Hill, 1992), with the top 50 advertisers spending a total of 17.8 billion dollars on advertising outside the United States.

Increasingly clients are demanding full-service international agencies. The consolidation of Europe into a single economic market with its promise of a united policy on currency, advertising regulations, and transportation, has become a symbol of the globalization of advertising. The emergence of pan-European media, such as Sky Channel, and the record pace of mergers and acquisitions has facilitated the placement and creation of advertising across Europe (Cook, 1992). In Asia, newly affluent consumers are purchasing an increasing variety of goods and services. Strong economic growth and currency appreciation have increased the wealth of consumers, while market openings are allowing foreign investments in service industries (including advertising), and government policies are beginning to promote domestic consumption (Goldstein, 1989). Both the rise of Asia and the economic consolidation of Europe are creating global opportunities for success. This success, however, will depend on the ability of advertisers to understand a growing number of diverse cultures.

One of the most fundamental questions in international advertising is whether to standardize, customize, or adapt advertising across markets. Advocates of standardization focus on the similarity of global consumers (Mueller, 1992). They argue that standardization provides a consistent worldwide image and reduces advertising costs through economies of scale (Hite & Fraser, 1988). Levitt (1983) argues that economic development and technology will homogenize world taste and lead to a convergence of international preference. Proponents of customization, on the other hand, emphasize differences in international tastes. They argue that differences in culture, economic development, available media, and legal requirements necessitate the customization of messages across nations (Mueller, 1992).

Although proponents of each approach can cite numerous examples of the success or failure of standardization, the standardization of advertisements has declined substantially since the 1970s (Hite & Fraser, 1988). Most firms currently adapt standardized themes to local tastes (Kanso, 1992).

Cross-cultural studies of advertising also underscore differences across nations. Japanese advertising generally employs an image-oriented soft-sell approach, while American advertising tends to emphasize product benefits (Benedetto, Tamate, & Chandran, 1992; Mueller, 1992). In a comparison of Japanese print advertising from 1978 to 1988, Mueller (1992) found little support for the belief that Japanese commercials were becoming more westernized. Use of the western product-benefit approach had declined, while the frequency of soft-sell appeals had increased. Far from becoming westernized, Japanese advertising may be becoming more distinctly Japanese (Mueller, 1992).

Crucial differences also exist between American and Japanese television commercials. Even when Japanese commercials use an informational strategy, such as hyperbole or a unique selling proposition, their executions are emotional in appeal (Ramaprasad & Hasegawa, 1992). In short, there appears to be little support for the westernization of Japanese advertising. Although English words are frequently borrowed, they are imbedded and interpreted in a uniquely Japanese context (Mueller, 1992).

European tastes also appear to be far from homogenous. In a comparison of French, British, and American print advertisements Cutler and Javalgi (1992) found substantial differences between all three countries. For example, French advertisements featured larger visual presentations and utilized more symbolic and aesthetic appeals than American or British advertisements. In general, American and French advertising tended to be the most divergent, while British advertising incorporated elements of each. This suggests that while Britain's status as a European country has some impact, its Anglo-Saxon roots provide some similarity to American advertising as well.

Finally, a comparison of French, Taiwanese, and American television commercials revealed clearly distinct patterns of advertising between the three countries (Zandpour, Chang, & Catalano, 1992). Generally, U.S. commercials directly address the consumer. They lecture on the benefits of the product and often feature celebrities or other credible sources providing testimonials or making arguments in favor of the product. French and Taiwanese commercial are generally more dramatic and feature less brand visibility and copy than American commercials. They focus on entertainment and frequently use symbolic and dramatic presentations (Zandpour et al., 1992).

The comparison of French, Taiwanese, and U.S. advertising provides an especially good illustration of the complexity of cultural norms and values. On the surface, one might expect advertising from the two western countries to be more similar. Yet, in many respects, French and Taiwanese advertising is more similar than French and American advertising. Despite these similarities, there are clear and important differences between each country.

In short, studies of international advertising do not reflect a homogenization of preference across nations. Culture remains an important consideration in formulating an advertising strategy. Both studies which compare advertising content and surveys of practitioners demonstrate the influence of culture on advertising. The customization or adaptation of advertising messages is likely to remain the dominant mode of advertising in the foreseeable future.

Yet, clearly, there are similarities as well as differences in international preference. Zandpour et al. (1992) discuss the importance of a "systematic assessment of what's culturally acceptable and aesthetically palatable" (Zandpour et al., 1992, p. 36). Yet, without a framework to evaluate the nuances and subtleties between cultures, one is left with a series of idiosyncratic cultural differences. To cross-culturally group consumers requires a basic understanding of human needs and aspirations. For this grouping to be meaningful it must occur at a level beyond the idiosyncratic level of tastes. That is, it must occur at a higher level of abstraction. Values offer a higher-order method of grouping consumers. They emphasize the similarity of basic human needs while allowing for cross-cultural differences. This chapter now evaluates some major explanations of cultural values, beginning with the individualist and collectivist distinction. The objective of this discussion is to evaluate to what extent the individualist and collectivist distinction provides a meaningful framework for explaining differences in consumer behavior.

COLLECTIVISM VERSUS INDIVIDUALISM

The distinction between a collectivist and an individualist culture is probably the most important concept in cross-cultural psychology (Triandis, 1989). In an individualist culture personal aspirations and goals are the primary concern. It is socially acceptable to place self-interests ahead of group interests. In a collectivist culture, group interests are primary and personal goals are secondary. The interests of the family, the tribe, or other group take precedence over the interests of the self (Triandis, 1989).

An individualist culture defines individuals as ends in themselves. As such, individuals must attempt to realize their full potential. The emphasis is on individual development and self-actualization. Individuals are taught to resist group pressure; and conformity carries a negative connotation (Triandis, 1989). Collectivism places a greater emphasis on the views and needs of in-groups. Social norms and duty shape actions to a greater extent than individual interests. In a purely collectivist culture individual interests do not exist, the interests of the group are the interests of the individual.

Collectivist cultures are marked by a strong association with a few in-groups. The self is largely defined by association with these in-groups. In contrast, individualists have weak affiliations with many groups. The "self is defined almost entirely in individual terms" (Triandis, 1989, p. 59), and in-groups are often defined as those who agree with me on important issues and values (Rokeach, 1960).

Generally, eastern cultures tend toward collectivism and western cultures focus on individualism. As eastern societies have become affluent they have become increasingly individualistic (Hsu, 1983); however, eastern societies are still generally more collectivist than western societies.

Schwartz (1992a) argues that people's value structures are more complex than the individualist and collectivist distinction. Although the collectivist and individualist distinction provides a great deal of insight into understanding and classifying a culture, important refinements need to be made. Because the collectivist and individualist distinction is based on goals (either the goals of the individual or the collective), and values represent desirable end-states or goals, the cross-cultural study of values can provide important additional insights.

CROSS-CULTURAL VALUES RESEARCH

Several studies have assessed the structure (Schwartz, 1992b) or underlying dimensions of human values (e.g., Hofstede & Bond, 1984; Kahle, 1983). Hofstede (1980) studied the values of the employees of a multinational corporation in 53 countries. He found 4 basic dimensions: (a) power distance—the acceptance or rejection of an unequal distribution of power; (b) uncertainty avoidance—"the extent to which people feel threatened by ambiguous situations, and have created beliefs and institutions that try to avoid these"; (c) individualism versus collectivism—where "individualism is defined as a situation in which people are supposed to look after themselves" and "collectivism is defined as a situation in which people belong to in-groups or collectivities which are supposed to look after them in exchange for loyalty"; and (d) masculinity versus femininity—where "masculinity is defined as a situation in which the dominant values in society are success, money, and things" and "femininity is defined as a situation in which the dominant values in society are caring for others and the quality of life" (Hofstede & Bond, 1984, pp. 419–420).

The Chinese Cultural Connection (CCC; 1987) also found a four factor solution. Three of these factors (integration, human-heartedness, and moral discipline) were found to be correlated with one or more of Hofstede's (1980) dimensions. The fourth, labeled Confucian work dynamism, appeared to be empirically based and did not correlate with any of Hofstede's factors. In further interpreting their factor structure the CCC noted that all four of their factors could be represented by a single second-order dimension. They propose that this dimension represents the degree of collectivism and individualism in a society and note an east to west ordering on this continuum.

Schwartz (1992b) conducted an extensive multicountry analysis of human value structures. Fifty-six values were selected from various sources (e.g., Chinese Culture Connection, 1987; Hofstede, 1980; Rokeach, 1973) and administered to samples in 20 countries. Through smallest space analysis, these values were placed into 10 motivational domains: self-direction, universalism, benevolence, conformity, tradition, security, power, achievement, hedonism, and stimulation. Each of these domains was empirically demonstrated to have compatible (adjacent) and conflicting dimensions.

In reviewing these compatibilities and conflicts, Schwartz categorized his 10 basic motivational domains into four second-order dimensions: self-transcendence, conservation, openness to change, and self-enhancement. Self-transcendence is basically a concern for others; it includes universalism and benevolence. Conservation includes conformity, tradition, and security; it stems from a desire for stability. Self-enhancement includes achievement and power, both of which imply a self orientation. Finally, openness to change encompasses self-direction and stimulation.

Schwartz provides a valuable framework for interpreting cross-cultural values. His first- and second-order dimensions provide an integrated and comprehensive value structure. Moreover, if this structure is generally universal, as his work indicates, and his list is comprehensive and complete, then values research can move on to the priority placed on value dimensions within this framework.

Although Schwartz's research demonstrates a great deal of promise, it still needs to be validated by other instruments. Further study of the structure of values is still necessary before researchers focus completely on value importances. Although the research of Schwartz represents an important substantive step toward understanding values, the question of a universal value structure still requires further research. A study empirically comparing his value structure to the findings of others would be a logical way to proceed. In addition, his findings of universal and conflicting values begs for a paired comparison approach to values research. If values can be classified into a universal set of conflicting priorities, then a paired comparison approach should allow a researcher to determine the differential importance of each value.

Cross-Cultural Applications of the List of Values

Recent cross-cultural applications of the List of Values (LOV) have examined the intergenerational correlation of values between parents and children (Beatty, Yoon, Kahle, & Grunert, 1992), and the difference between ratings and rankings (Beatty, Yoon, Grunert, & Kahle, 1992). Both of these studies examined the values of parents and students from the United States, Japan, New Zealand, France, West Germany, and Denmark. In general, the values of students and parents within a culture were relatively similar, with the greatest similarity between Japanese students and parents. Although culture had a strong influence on the values of both parents and students, some intergenerational differences were found. Parents placed a greater emphasis on security and accomplishment, while students were more hedonistic (Beatty, Yoon, Kahle, & Grunert, 1992).

Grunert and Scherhorn (1990) explicitly examined the dimensions of the List of Values. They found two dimensions: pleasure/change versus comfort/constancy and love versus achievement. The latter dimension is consistent with an individualist and collectivist distinction in that self and other oriented values are separated, while the former could also be labeled variety seeking or stimulation-oriented (Lee & Beatty, 1992).

Beatty, Yoon, Kahle, and Grunert (1992) also found two dimensions: security versus hedonism, and self-respect/sense of belonging versus warm relationships/self-fulfillment. The first is consistent with a variety seeking or pleasure/change-comfort/consistency dimension. The second (sense of belonging/self-respect versus warm relationships/self-fulfillment) is more complex and may reflect differences in the meaning of specific values across nations. Japanese respondents, for example, were high in self-fulfillment and low in sense of belonging and being well-respected. They explained that in the status conscious Japanese culture an overt reference to being well respected and sense of belonging would not be appropriate. "To belong to others or to obtain respect from others they must first do their best (i.e., self-fulfillment)" (Beatty, Yoon, Kahle, & Grunert, 1992, pp. 15–16).

These findings illustrate two important points. First, there are cross-generational as well as cross-cultural differences in values and birth cohort is an important consideration in a cross-cultural study. Second, the interpretation of a specific item may vary across culture. It may be necessary to supplement the LOV with additional items when applying it to eastern samples.

A Synthesis of Values Research

Studies of cross-cultural values consistently find four factors that comprise two second-order dimensions. Hofstede (1980) found four basic dimensions (power distance, uncertainty avoidance, individualism and collectivism, and masculinity and femininity). Schwartz (1992b) found two pairs of second-order dimensions (self-transcendence versus self-enhancement and conservation versus openness to change), and the Chinese Cultural Connection found four dimensions (integration, confucian work dynamism, human heartedness, and moral discipline) which could be represented by two second-order factors (individualism versus collectivism). Research on the List of Values has also found two basic dimensions: pleasure change versus comfort constancy (Grunert & Scherhorn, 1990) and internal versus external (Kahle, 1983).

Looking at these findings as a whole, two basic dimensions consistently appear: stimulation/change versus traditional/constant and self versus other. Although the specific items included in these dimensions differ, the similarity of dimensions across studies is striking, given the different methods, purposes, and instruments.

The first dimension that consistently emerges involves the relative importance placed on stability versus change. The desire for stability is often tied to traditionalism (Schwartz, 1992b) and a need for security (Beatty, Yoon, Kahle, & Grunert, 1992; Grunert & Scherhorn, 1990). Thus, a basic stimulation/change versus traditional/constant dimension appears to emerge across several studies. This dimension has been labeled conservation versus openness to change (Schwartz, 1992b), pleasure/change versus comfort/constancy (Grunert & Scherhorn, 1990), dynamism (MacEvoy, 1991), and uncertainty avoidance (Hofstede, 1980).

The second dimension is more complex. It consists of the emphasis placed on the self versus others. This dimension has been labeled self-transcendence versus conservation by Schwartz (1992b), and appears to underlie the findings of several other studies. Hofstede's (1980) individualism and collectivism and masculinity and femininity dimensions both involve the degree to which an individual emphasizes the self versus others, as do the internal-external and individual-interpersonal dimensions of the List of Values (Kahle, 1983), and the human heartedness and integration dimensions of the Chinese Cultural Connection (1987).

Although there are differences in the specific dimensions found across studies, all involve the degree of concern one has with the self versus others. Furthermore, caring, conformity, status, and fulfillment appear to be important components of this basic dimension and the relative emphasis placed on each appears to be linked to the degree of collectivism and individualism present in a society. Collectivist societies emphasize conformity and obligation, and caring is generally confined to the in-group (Triandis, 1989). Individualist cultures emphasize status and fulfillment. Caring is an extension of the sanctity of the individual and is defined as benevolent feelings toward others.

In short, the emphasis placed on the self versus others appears to be a basic cross-cultural dimension, but conceptions of the self and others (in-groups, humankind) vary across cultures. Future research should examine the cultural specificity of self-conceptions and the role of others in relation to the self. Presently, a self versus other distinction appears promising, but refinements are necessary.

In sum, two basic dimensions (stimulation/change versus traditional/constant and self versus other) consistently emerge in studies of cross-cultural values. These dimensions may offer a useful basis for cross-culturally classifying consumers. Future research, however, is necessary to validate and refine these dimensions.

SUMMARY AND IMPLICATIONS FOR FUTURE RESEARCH

A globalization of preference has not occurred. Local tastes, customs, and preferences are still an important consideration in advertising strategy. Both surveys of practitioners and studies of cross-cultural advertising indicate substantial differences across nations. Practitioners generally adapt messages to conform to local tastes. Yet, the economic arguments for standardization are still valid. If similar segments of consumers can be identified, economies of scales in advertising production can be realized. Furthermore, important demographic and psychographic variables need to be identified across cultures. Currently, advertising research is generally directed at the national level and does not include an overall theory of the specific dimensions on which cultures differ. This leads to a series of idiosyncratic descriptions of national tastes.

There are several theoretic and pragmatic problems with this approach. First, most advertisers standardize some portion of their message and need some method of determining which elements of a commercial need to be customized. Second, unless an advertiser is willing to prepare a separate message for each country, some standardization is required. Research, however, indicates that national tastes defy simplistic groupings. British advertising is in some respects similar to American advertising, and in other respects similar to French advertising (Cutler & Javalgi, 1992). French television commercials are in many respects more similar to Taiwanese commercials than to American commercials (Zandpour et al., 1992). Thus, neither an East and West nor European and non-European distinction captures the subtle nuances of cultural differences. Without some method of grouping individuals across cultures an advertiser is forced to prepare a separate message for each market.

Third, many nations have distinct subcultures within a nation. Belgium, Singapore, and the United States all contain substantial subcultures within their borders. Must an advertiser prepare a separate message for each group? Obviously there must be some method of grouping individuals. Although demographic variables are important, they only capture some of the necessary information. Clearly what is needed is an integrated approach to analyzing consumer behavior. This approach should incorporate both the demographic and psychographic characteristics of consumers.

Currently cross-cultural values research needs to be synthesized across disciplines. The social psychologist, Schwartz, may offer the most promising approach. His instrument, however, was developed to measure all human values and is currently too long to be applied in a marketing context. Future research should attempt to identify the items that are relevant to consumer behavior. A more domain specific questionnaire could significantly reduce the number of items and increase the practical significance of Schwartz's instrument for marketing.

Other studies could empirically compare the value dimensions obtained by the LOVs and Schwartz's items. Two important questions emerge: (a) How similar are the dimensions obtained by Schwartz to those obtained by the LOV? and (b) Do one or both of these approaches capture all of the relevant cross-cultural dimensions that influence consumer behavior?

Research also needs to examine the relationship between attitudes, behaviors, and values. Presently, little is known about the relationship of values to attitudes and behaviors cross-culturally. Two important research questions in this area are: (a) What dimensions are most important in explaining consumer behavior? and (b) Do specific values correlate with the same attitudes and behaviors across cultures?

Other research questions include the link between a cultures' values and its media (Grunert, Grunert, & Beatty, 1989) and the impact of cultural values on the diffusion of information (Liu & Kahle, 1990). Research also needs to compare the variation of values within nations to the modal characteristics of values across nations. Are values more similar within two or more specific cultures or within cross-cultural demographic groups? Are there demographic and psychographic characteristics that predict preferences across cultures? Finally, research needs to address the cultural context and meaning of specific values. For example, How does self-respect differ in eastern versus western cultures?

In general, advertising research needs to focus on identifying the important cultural dimensions of behavior. Values may offer an abstract method for grouping consumers across cultures, but more research is needed to identify the specific dimensions underlying behavior. The collectivist and individualist distinction appears to be one important cross-cultural means of classifying consumers. Numerous studies have substantiated this distinction and cross-cultural values appear to center around self versus other directed behavior. Further exploration of the impact of this distinction on consumer behavior is in order; others need to be identified. A distinction between stimulation/change and traditional/constant appears promising. Several past studies have found a basic difference in the degree of change or stability people desire in their environment (e.g., Grunert & Scherhorn, 1990) and a differential desire for stimulation appears to be an important means of classifying both individuals and societies.

Future research is needed to identify both the basic dimensions of values and the higher-order groupings of these dimensions. Only through a substantial amount of empirical research will we be able to understand the subtleties and differences in values across cultures and the influence of these differences on consumer behavior. Only then will we be able to apply this knowledge to cross-cultural advertising campaigns.

ACKNOWLEDGMENTS

The author would like to thank David Boush, Aviv Shoham, and the editors for their helpful comments on earlier versions of this chapter.

REFERENCES

Advertising Age (1993). Advertising fact book: National ad spending by Media. *Advertising Age, 64*(1), 20.

Beatty, S. E., Yoon, M. H., Grunert, K. G., & Kahle, L. R. (1992). *Alternative measurement approaches to values: Ratings versus rankings in a cross-cultural context.* Tuscaloosa: University of Alabama. Unpublished paper.

Beatty, S. E., Yoon, M. H., Kahle, L. R., & Grunert, S. C. (1992). *Values across generations in six countries.* Tuscaloosa: University of Alabama. Unpublished paper.

Benedetto, C. H., Tamate, M., & Chandran, R. (1992). Developing creative strategy for the Japanese marketplace. *Journal of Advertising Research, 32*(1), 39–48.

The Chinese Cultural Connection (1987). Chinese values and the search for culture-free dimensions of culture. *Journal of Cross-Cultural Psychology, 18*(2), 143–164.

Cook, W. (1992). Here's to Europe 1992 and global glue. *Journal of Advertising Research, 32*(1), 7–8.

Cutler, B. D., & Javalgi, R. G. (1992). A cross-cultural analysis of the visual components of print advertising: The united states and the european community. *Journal of Advertising Research, 32*(1), 71–79.

Goldstein, C. (1989). The selling of Asia. *Far Eastern Economic Review, 144*, 60–65.

Grunert, K. G., Grunert, S. C., & Beatty S. E. (1989). Cross-cultural research on consumer values. *Marketing and Research Today, 17*, 30–39.

Grunert, S. C., & Scherhorn, G. (1990). Consumer values in west Germany: Underlying dimensions and cross-cultural comparison with North America. *Journal of Business Research, 20*, 97–107.

Hill, J. S. (1992). Global media & marketing. *Advertising Age, 63*(51), s-1.

Hite, R. E., & Fraser, C. (1988). International advertising strategies of multinational corporations. *Journal of Advertising Research, 28*(3), 9–17.

Hofstede, G. (1980). *Cultures consequences: International differences in work-related values.* Beverly Hills, CA: Sage.

Hofstede, G., & Bond M. (1984). Hofstede's culture dimensions: An independent validation using Rokeach's value survey. *Journal of Cross-Cultural Psychology, 15*(4), 417–433.

Hsu, F. L. K. (1983). *Rugged individualism reconsidered.* Knoxville: University of Tennessee Press.

James, W. L., & Hill, J. S. (1991). International advertising messages: To adapt or not to adapt (That is the question). *Journal of Advertising Research, 31*(2), 65–71.

Kahle, L. R. (1983). *Social values and social change: Adaptation to life in America.* New York: Praeger.

Kanso, A. (1992). International advertising strategies: Global commitment to local vision. *Journal of Advertising Research, 32*(1), 10–14.

Lee, J., & Beatty, S. E. (1992, Winter). A review and new view of personal values. *AMA Educators' Conference Proceedings,* 251–257.

Levitt, T. (1983). The globalization of markets. *Harvard Business Review, 61,* 92–102.

Liu, R., & Kahle, L. R. (1990). Consumer social values in the People's Republic of China. In Gardner (Ed.), *Proceedings of the Society for Consumer Psychology* (pp. 52–54).

MacEvoy, B. H. (1991, August). Cross-national comparisons of consumers and markets. *Contemporary Approaches in Applied Psychographics at the American Psychological Association.*

Mueller, B. (1992). Standardization vs. specialization: An examination of westernization in Japanese advertising. *Journal of Advertising Research, 32*(1), 15–24.

Ramaprasad, J., & Hasegawa, K. (1992). Creative strategies in American and Japanese TV commercials: A comparison. *Journal of Advertising Research, 32*(1), 59–67.

Rokeach, M. (1960). *The open and closed mind.* New York: Basic Books.

Rokeach, M. (1973). *The nature of human values.* New York: The Free Press.

Schwartz, S. H. (1992a). Individualism-collectivism: Critique and proposed refinements. *Journal of Cross-Cultural Psychology, 21*(3), 139–157.

Schwartz, S. H. (1992b). Universals in the content and structure of values: Theoretical advances and empirical tests in 20 countries. In M. P. Zanna (Ed.), *Advances in Experimental Social Psychology* (Vol. 25, pp. 1–65). San Diego: Academic Press.

Triandis, H. C. (1989). Cross-cultural studies of individualism and collectivism, In J. Berman (Ed.), *Nebraska Symposium on Motivation: Vol. 37. Cross-Cultural Perspectives* (pp. 41–134). Lincoln: University of Nebraska Press.

Zandpour, F., Chang, C., & Catalano, J. (1992). Stories, symbols, and straight talk: A comparative analysis of French, Taiwanese, and U.S. TV commercials. *Journal of Advertising Research, 32*(1), 25–38.

Author Index

Subject Index

L

M